The College at
BROCKPORT
STATE UNIVERSITY OF NEW YORK

The Psychotherapy of Hope

The Psychotherapy of Hope

The Legacy of *Persuasion and Healing*

EDITED BY

Renato D. Alarcón, M.D., M.P.H.
Emeritus Professor
Department of Psychiatry and Psychology
Mayo Clinic College of Medicine
Rochester, Minnesota

AND

Julia B. Frank, M.D.
Associate Professor
Department of Psychiatry and Behavioral Sciences
George Washington University School of Medicine
Washington, D.C.

The Johns Hopkins University Press

BALTIMORE

© 2012 The Johns Hopkins University Press
All rights reserved. Published 2012
Printed in the United States of America on acid-free paper
9 8 7 6 5 4 3 2 1

The Johns Hopkins University Press
2715 North Charles Street
Baltimore, Maryland 21218-4363
www.press.jhu.edu

Library of Congress Cataloging-in-Publication Data

The psychotherapy of hope : the legacy of Persuasion and healing / edited
by Renato D. Alarcón and Julia B. Frank.
    p. ; cm.
    Includes bibliographical references and index.
    ISBN-13: 978-1-4214-0304-5 (hardcover : alk. paper)
    ISBN-10: 1-4214-0304-8 (hardcover : alk. paper)
    1. Psychotherapy. 2. Psychiatry. 3. Neuroscience 4. Persuasion
(Psychology) I. Alarcón, Renato D. II. Frank, Julia (Julia B.)
III. Frank, Jerome D. (Jerome David), 1909–2005. Persuasion and healing.
    [DNLM: 1. Psychotherapy. 2. Psychiatry. WM 420]
    RC480.P827 2011
    616.89′14—dc22   2011010035

A catalog record for this book is available from the British Library.

Special discounts are available for bulk purchases of this book. For more
information, please contact Special Sales at 410-516-6936 or specialsales@
press.jhu.edu.

The Johns Hopkins University Press uses environmentally friendly book
materials, including recycled text paper that is composed of at least 30
percent post-consumer waste, whenever possible.

To Jerome D. Frank (1909–2005)
Professor Emeritus of Psychiatry
The Johns Hopkins University School of Medicine
father, mentor, colleague, friend

. . . more territory remains to be explored. And so my
intellectual journey ends, not with conclusions, but with
questions, as all such journeys should.

—*PERSUASION AND HEALING*, 1991, P. 301

Contents

Foreword

Jerry Frank was a great human being, a man I was privileged to know. Just how splendid he was will become evident to readers of these essays on facets of his life and career. As a medical scientist, he legitimized research on the effectiveness of psychotherapy, a field many thought it impossible to undertake. His creativity and methodological elegance set psychiatry out on a multidecade endeavor that culminated in the development of reliable and valid psychological treatments, treatments that have been shown to be equal and sometimes superior to drug- and device-based interventions. As a political activist, he was a leader in the international effort to create a sane nuclear policy in a world a button-press away from the extinction of all life. As a caring and nurturing human being, he mentored and fostered the careers of countless young men and women. He was unstinting in making himself available to others whenever a problem, large or small, arose.

Michael Gelder, professor of psychiatry emeritus at Oxford University, attested to Jerry's stature as an intellectual leader in psychiatry. He was asked by the *British Journal of Psychiatry* to "select ten books that had a significant impact on his professional life." Gelder (2003) included Frank's *Persuasion and Healing* (Frank and Frank 1991) in his list, along with such other classic authors as Kraepelin, Jaspers, Beck, Brown and Harris, and Goffman. Gelder singled out Jerry's demonstration that "the shared features of the various methods of psychological therapy are more important than those by which they differ. At the time, this was a controversial message, although it is widely accepted today" (pp. 270–71).

I came to Johns Hopkins as a fellow in child psychiatry not long after Jerry's return from the Pacific Theater in World War II. Sheer good luck enabled me to meet Jerry and his research coworkers, Stan Imber and Earl Nash (psychologists), Otto Kernberg (psychiatrist), and Tony Stone (social worker). They were not only good friends but also a continuing source of intellectual stimulation and academic instruction during my fifteen years at Hopkins.

In the decades when Frank "et al." were in full flower, their research was by all odds the most outstanding scholarly contribution from Johns Hopkins psychiatry.

The State of American Psychiatry in the 1940s and 1950s

When Jerry Frank completed his residency, American academic psychiatry could well have been characterized as "monotheistic," with Sigmund Freud as the Mosaic lawgiver. The dominant sect, psychoanalysis, subscribed to an orthodox belief in the biblical inerrancy of Freud's *Collected Works*. Within this frame, Jerry was a "doubting Thomas." But, like Thomas, he was not an atheist; he was an agnostic. He wanted to believe in psychotherapy but needed proof. His search for the evidence opened the path to evidence-based psychiatry before the term *evidence-based medicine* was coined.

Jerry was not alone in raising questions about psychoanalysis; many of his contemporaries, I among them, had serious reservations about its hegemony. I wrote about my dismay that "in some centers . . . almost all the residents enter personal analysis . . . [and] in my observation, it has been the bright and not the incompetent, the curious and not the unimaginative, residents who have been attracted to psychoanalysis and thus lost to research, university teaching and public service" (Eisenberg 1962, pp. 787–88). Why were they "lost"?

Psychoanalytic training restricted the resident's geographic mobility for the duration of his didactic analysis (often five years or more). Many residents engaged in after-hours private practice to pay for the analysis. They acquired, at great cost (and great effort), a therapeutic technique altogether inappropriate for public service. Worst of all, such training ate away at any intellectual curiosity: analytic trainees were given answers instead of being encouraged to raise questions.

Although Johns Hopkins under John Whitehorn was eclectic in its theoretical orientation, many psychiatric residents signed on as candidates at the local psychoanalytic institute. Few read Jerry's work, so intent were they on their assigned readings at the institute (and so sleep deprived were they by their after-hours practice). It may be hard for those who were not in Baltimore during that period to believe how many Hopkins psychiatric residents of the 1950s and 1960s dismissed Jerry as a therapeutic nihilist, when the opposite was true. Jerry had seen most psychiatric outpatients improve with psychosocial care. It was the apparent successes of the psychotherapies, not their failures, that attracted his interest. The questions that engaged him were: What was it in the psychotherapeutic process that truly made the difference? For which patients did it work? Did one variety work better than another?

The Evaluation of the Psychotherapies

Through the 1950s and 1960s, psychotherapy was what psychiatrists did (except for those in state hospitals). Lack of evidence was more or less irrelevant because no other treatment could offer proof of efficacy. The flavor of the times can best be conveyed by comments from cynics. At the 1952 American Psychological Association Conference on Graduate Education in Clinical Psychology, Morris Parloff, a leading psychologist at the National Institute of Mental Health, commented: "Therapy is an undefined technique which is applied to unspecified problems with non-predictable outcome. For this technique, we recommend rigorous training."

Paul Meehl (1965), professor at the University of Minnesota, offered a rationale for the difficulty in demonstrating the effectiveness of psychotherapy. Three out of four patients, he estimated, would either recover on their own or remain ill, regardless of whether or not they received treatment. Meehl's own assessment of practitioners led him to conclude that only one in four therapists had the skill to make a difference for the one in four patients who were potentially responsive to treatment: "Let us suppose that 1/4 represents an upper bound on the proportion of patients . . . who are appropriate; and let 1/4 also represent an upper bound on therapists who are much good at their job . . . [then] the joint probability of a suitable patient getting to a suitable therapist is about .06, a very small tail to wag the statistical dog in an outcome study" (p. 157). No wonder treatment outcome studies fared so poorly!

The Effectiveness of Psychotherapy

Attempts to measure the effects of psychotherapy and to contrast schools of treatment with one another were beset by difficult methodological problems. At the fundamental level, there was no way to be sure that therapists professing adherence to a given theory and its derivative technique provided treatments sufficiently similar to each other to distinguish them from treatments by subscribers to another theory and its technique. More than a generation had to pass before the first manualized psychotherapies (cognitive behavioral therapy and interpersonal psychotherapy) were introduced and showed that trained therapists demonstrated sufficient conformity to a technique to justify comparing outcomes across treatments. Other critics contended that the very introduction of research goals into the sanctum of psychotherapy was unethical; it violated the primary norm: commitment solely to the patient's welfare. Introducing a recorder or, worse, an observer (or even asking the therapist to take on a dual role as researcher) would make it impossible for patients to associate freely.

Psychoanalysis dismissed comparisons of symptom counts and symptom severities before and after treatment as meaningless. Patients would attempt a "flight into health" rather than face uncomfortable truths about themselves. Symptoms thus abandoned would appear in a different guise at a later time. Evidence that symptoms did not pop up as often as expected was simply ignored. What mattered was fundamental change in underlying psychic structure. How was that to be measured? Analysts, of course, "knew" when enough change had occurred to terminate treatment, but they were indifferent to the need for reproducible ways to measure change. Given the receding goalposts, Jerry compared research in psychotherapy to "the nightmarish game of croquet in *Alice in Wonderland* in which the mallets were flamingos, the balls, hedgehogs, and the wickets, soldiers. Since the flamingo would not keep its head down, the hedgehogs kept unrolling themselves and the soldiers were always wandering to other parts of the field . . . It was a very difficult game indeed" (Frank 1973, p. 332).

Jerry persisted with rigorous research to measure therapy outcomes. What did it reveal? Therapy outcomes were better than waiting-list outcomes. Equally noteworthy was that the outcomes from different schools of psychotherapy were remarkably similar, despite professed differences in the theories and techniques. Jerry looked for common denominators: nonspecific psychological and social processes that underpinned successful psychotherapy. Because patients come to treatment at a time when they have despaired of their ability to control their mental distress, the first and essential task of the therapist is to arouse hope. All psychotherapies offer a confiding relationship with a therapist, a set of "explanations" for the patient's distress, alternative ways of dealing with identified problems, and engagement in a joint enterprise—an enterprise that restores morale (remoralization).

In the 1960s, Jerry's conclusions offended proponents of each of the separate schools of psychotherapy. Nonetheless, his conclusions were affirmed by study after study. Finally, when Smith, Glass, and Miller reported in 1980 that meta-analyses of extant studies of psychotherapy demonstrated significant effect sizes, they were hailed by beleaguered practitioners as having established the effectiveness of psychotherapy. What all found it convenient to overlook was the inability to detect significant differences in outcomes between competing schools of psychotherapy or even between the outcomes "produced" by experienced therapists and by novices within the same school! Were all equally good (or bad)? Jerry had answered that question a decade earlier with the epigraph to the first chapter of *Persuasion and Healing*, a passage from Lewis Carroll's *Alice's Adventures in Wonderland*:

> They all crowded round it, panting, and asking, "But who has won?"
> This question the Dodo could not answer without a great deal of thought . . .
> At last the Dodo said, "*Everybody* has won, and all must have prizes."

The Dodo bird no longer presides. As part II of this book, on current practices in psychotherapy, makes amply clear, psychotherapies have been devised that are reliably and validly different from each other, psychotherapies whose effects are robust enough to survive the test of randomized trials. Does that mean *Persuasion and Healing* is no longer relevant? To the contrary, remoralization remains an enduring characteristic of effective treatment processes. More to the point, it was the very contributions of the Johns Hopkins team in identifying key aspects of psychotherapy, in developing appropriate investigational methods, and in calling attention to the variability in the way techniques were employed that made scientific progress toward effective psychotherapies possible. Put simply, Jerry Frank and his colleagues enabled psychiatry to move beyond "*Everybody* has won, and all must have prizes."

Leon Eisenberg, M.D. (1922–2009)
Professor of Social Medicine
and Psychiatry, Emeritus
Harvard Medical School

REFERENCES

Eisenberg, L. 1962. If not now, when? *American Journal of Orthopsychiatry* 32:781–93.
Frank, J. D. 1973. *Persuasion and Healing: A Comparative Study of Psychotherapy*, rev. ed. Baltimore: Johns Hopkins University Press.

Frank, J. D., and Frank, J. B. 1991. *Persuasion and Healing: A Comparative Study of Psychotherapy*, 3rd ed. Baltimore: Johns Hopkins University Press.

Gelder, M. 2003. Ten books: chosen by Michael Gelder. *British Journal of Psychiatry* 182:269–72.

Meehl, P. E. 1965. Discussion of Eysenck's "The effects of psychotherapy." *International Journal of Psychiatry* 1:156–57.

Smith, M. L., Glass, G. V., and Miller, T. I. 1980. *The Benefits of Psychotherapy*. Baltimore: Johns Hopkins University Press.

Of course the first thing to
do was to make a grand
survey of the country she
was going to travel through.
—*Through the Looking Glass*

The history of psychotherapy encompasses periods of solid and universal acceptance as well as times of discredit and obscurity. The fortunes of the field rise and fall in relation to developments in science and medicine, social organization, politics, and other approaches aimed at regulating and moderating human experience. In our tumultuous era, psychotherapy necessarily must reexamine its creeds, goals, and technical approaches to find its proper place in the theoretical, didactic, and clinical landscape.

The work of Jerome D. Frank, for fifty years a professor of psychiatry at the Johns Hopkins University School of Medicine, first catalyzed and now shapes much of the continual reassessment that characterizes psychotherapy as a research and clinical discipline. Frank's ideas, developed and promulgated through three editions of his classic book *Persuasion and Healing: A Comparative Study of Psychotherapy*, engendered a quiet revolution in twentieth-century psychotherapy. His incisive critique of the principles and practice of psychoanalysis in the American psychiatry of the 1950s helped dislodge Freud's disciples from their position of dominance. Applying the methods of academic psychology to the real-world problems of psychiatry and medicine, Frank refused to accept the impossibility of doing research on feelings and emotions, entities once considered "unmeasurable" and therefore beyond the reach of objective evaluation. His research replaced unprovable suppositions about unconscious determinants of behavior with empirical data, and his exquisite scholarly common sense forged a coherent link with wise clinical intuition. In the process, Frank identified features common to all forms of psychotherapy, as well as qualities common to those who respond to it.

For some critics, Frank's theses, in particular his deconstruction of the extravagant claims of various brands of psychotherapy, contributed to the decline of psychotherapy as both a useful social activity and a valid medical treatment. We believe that the opposite is true: Frank's integrity, empiricism, and open-mindedness helped sustain psychotherapy as an acceptable treatment for recognized forms of distress. In an age that demands scientific proof of the validity of professional endeavor, rigorous scrutiny of psychotherapy serves both to foster improvements in technique and outcome and, at a broader level, to confirm its legitimacy.

Given the many controversies that characterize the field, assigning an appropriate role for psychotherapy among the contemporary healing arts is a never-ending process. This volume, *The Psychotherapy of Hope: The Legacy of "Persuasion and Healing,"* is a collection of original, stand-alone essays about psychotherapy that are intended to contribute to this effort by updating Frank's ideas (1961, 1973; Frank and Frank 1991) for a new generation of researchers and practitioners.

From *Persuasion and Healing* to *The Psychotherapy of Hope*

The first edition of *Persuasion and Healing* addressed issues thrown into prominence by seismic shifts in then-prevailing academic, medical, and general American culture. It appeared at a time when psychoanalysis enjoyed great popularity as treatment for both defined mental illness and unspecified distress. Behind a confident facade, definitions of what constituted a psychiatric disorder, classifications of psychopathology, and the development of several professions dedicated to its treatment were in profound flux. Even as the superstructure of psychoanalysis grew grander and more expansive, the supporting pillars—underlying theories of "neurosis" and the social support offered by training institutes—were crumbling under the weight of new information, new forms of training, and new sociocultural realities. Frank, assigned to teach psychotherapy and psychopathology to medical students, psychology graduate students, and psychiatrists in training, sought to solve basic problems: What is (and is not) psychotherapy? Does it "work"? How does it work? Whom does it help or harm?

Frank did not consider these merely rhetorical questions, and his answers to them still command respect. Psychotherapy, he concluded, is a form of relationship between healers of culturally assigned status and sufferers with culturally acknowledged forms of distress, conducted in a defined context. It indubitably "works," a statement that could be proved by scientific research, identification of forms of psychotherapy in a wide variety of cultures, and persistence of psychotherapeutic activities throughout history. The mechanisms of therapy, the subject of Frank's own research, include the mobilization of expectant faith, or hope, the encouragement of mastery, and the reinterpretation of personal experience facilitated by emotional arousal. In general, psychotherapy most benefits people, however distressed, who are demoralized, people who may or may not be diagnosed as psychiatrically ill in contemporary terms. This line of argument eventually led Frank to propose that efforts to study psychotherapy as applied behavioral science should be supplemented, if not replaced, by applying methods from the philosophical disciplines of rhetoric and hermeneutics, the study of meaning.

Subsequent developments in society, and particularly in Euro-Western medicine and psychiatry, have not disproved Frank's original assertions. His insights do, however, require reevaluation and extension in the face of developments in diagnosis within medicine and psychology, neuroscientific investigation of ideation and emotion at the molecular and tissue levels, and changes in the social environment in which psychotherapy occurs.

Frank himself conducted two thorough reevaluations, bringing forth the second and third editions of *Persuasion and Healing* in 1973 and 1991. In 1973, psychotherapeutic activities of many kinds were proliferating, especially in the United States; in 1991, new generations of medical students, graduate students, and mental health professionals were grappling with the ascendancy of descriptive, categorical diagnoses of psychiatric disorders, regulation of psychotherapy under changing models of reimbursement, and the early results of revolutions in neuroimaging, genetics, behavioral research, and psychopharmacology. The third and final edition of the book reasserted those elements of the original that had weathered the storms of earlier decades, but could only begin the process of aligning a general, empirically and culturally grounded theory of psychotherapy with the changing environment of practice and scientific investigation. This book attempts to take that step.

The chapters of *Persuasion and Healing* provided the framework for the essays we assigned to ourselves and the contributing authors of *The Psychotherapy of Hope*. Each chapter picks up on a thread of Frank's work and weaves it into the fabric of the writers' area of interest. In consequence, like *Persuasion and Healing*, this volume ranges across topics not usually grouped together. We include discussions of the current status of research into the common elements of psychotherapy, further elaboration of the concept of demoralization as the target of psychotherapy, and implications of these unifying concepts for training. We also review the neurobiological underpinnings of psychotherapy, bringing together biological science with the study of meaning. Specific chapters explore the theory and practice of cultural psychotherapies, the sociocultural dynamics of the therapeutic encounter, and research into different elements, modalities, and targets of psychotherapy (including therapy offered to children). Our contributors describe the place of psychotherapy in the care of medically and psychiatrically ill populations, critically assess the status of psychodynamic and behaviorally derived approaches, and review group psychotherapy as currently practiced. In keeping with the spirit of *Persuasion and Healing*, these essays bridge gaps that currently divide students, teachers, practitioners, and researchers from diverse intellectual traditions.

Within these general domains, different authors pick up on particular aspects of Frank's work, using methods that range from meta-analysis to heuristic synthesis and personal experience or clinical anecdotes. Some of the original concepts of *Persuasion and Healing*, particularly the central role of Frank's "common factors" or ingredients in accounting for the effectiveness of psychotherapy, have become so widely accepted that they do not require extensive discussion. These ideas form the background for nearly all the chapters in this volume but receive the greatest attention in the first chapter, by Wampold and Weinberger, which discusses the status of psychotherapy research. The idea that demoralization is the common feature of conditions that respond to psychotherapy, introduced in the second edition of *Persuasion and Healing* and developed in the third, has taken on a life of its own, especially in the care of people who have medical illness. Herein it receives extended attention in the essays by de Figueiredo (chapter 6), Griffith and DSouza (chapter 8), Griffith (chapter 15), Clarke (chapter 7), and Freeman (chapter 9). In chapter 2, Treisman and McHugh describe the relation between the Johns Hopkins Perspectives of Psychiatry and the role of demoralization in distress and disorder, noting how demoralization is one of several concepts that cut across disciplines and organize clinical practice for heuristic purposes.

Frank's suggestion that psychotherapy, as a cultural enterprise, may be less a form of applied behavioral science and more akin to rhetoric (Frank and Frank 1991, chap. 3) also requires further exposition. Frank developed the argument that psychotherapy fundamentally *transforms the meaning* that sufferers give to their experience. This concept remains robust in contemporary culture and in medicine (Charon 2001), particularly in what are sometimes called "narrative therapies" (Romanoff and Thompson 2006).

The neuroscientific revolution of the past three decades has opened up and now explores the terrain of meaning well beyond the psychological and sociocultural bounds of the concepts that Frank discussed. Techniques for studying the living brain have illuminated the mechanisms by which humans and animals construct meaning, refining our understanding of how many forms of treatment might influence meaning for therapeutic ends. In the current volume, Viamontes and Beitman (chapter 3) and Frank (chapter 4) go beyond Jerome Frank's discussion of placebos to explore the interface between meaning and neurobiology. These essays seek to assign an appropriate role for psychotherapy, as a meaningful enterprise, in the treatment of disorders we are coming to understand in neurobiological and evolutionary terms.

The neuroscientific connotations of meaning supplement but do not replace older ones, as the translation of research findings into clinical action remains an elusive goal for the field. Most psychotherapy continues to modify meaning by helping patients make sense of their current experience in light of their personal past, their ongoing capacities and vulnerabilities, and the actions and expectations of those around them. These concepts are particularly relevant in psychodynamic psychotherapy, as discussed by Wells and Frank (chapter 10), and in group psychotherapy, discussed by Rutan and Shay (chapter 13). Explicit meaning and the ways in which patients may construct it, the focus of cognitive therapies, are also essential elements of contemporary psychotherapy. The implications of construing meaning in this way are discussed particularly by Forsyth and Nash (chapter 11), who review research into the outcomes of cognitive behavioral therapy. Raishevich Cunningham, Ollendick, and Jensen (chapter 12) also analyze evidence for the outcomes of psychotherapy, especially cognitive behavioral therapy, for children and adolescents.

Persuasion and Healing examined faith healing and indigenous healing specifically to find evidence to support the common factors accounting for the effectiveness of psychotherapy, factors that Frank's scientific studies assessed from a different angle. The study of culture in general and religion in particular has enormous relevance in this era of globalization, mass migration, and religion as a force in social and political movements around the world. In consequence, Alarcón and Williams (chapter 5) expand on the precise cultural connotations of several concepts used by Frank, including the cultural dynamics between patient and therapist and the status of cultural psychotherapies. Griffith and DSouza (chapter 8), Alarcón, Frank, and Williams (chapter 14), and Griffith (chapter 15) then review more specific aspects of the relation between religion, culture, forms of distress, and corresponding healing activities.

Unsolved Problems: Researching Claims to Specificity and Superior Effectiveness

Jerome Frank and his colleagues at Johns Hopkins were modern pioneers of research in psychotherapy. They combined methods of academic psychology, experimentally manipulating elements of therapeutic process, with the goals of medical research, measuring outcomes, defined as the effects of treatment on recognized disorders or syndromes. This work contributed to the development of rigorous standards for evaluating the claims of various research groups or schools that their form of psychotherapy was specific, or superior, for one form of distress or another. Such assessment proved extremely challenging at the time, and remains so. Wampold and Weinberger (chapter 1), Forsyth and Nash (chapter 11), and Raishevich Cunningham, Ollendick, and Jensen (chapter 12) focus most clearly on the continuing challenges of developing valid methods of studying psychotherapy and it effects.

In his research, Frank weighed the claims of what he called "evocative" and "directive" therapies (terms borrowed from John Whitehorn) and concluded that exposure, a directive element derived from behaviorism, might be best for anxiety, but that all other assertions of relative superiority were unproven. In the current environment, the issue of specificity, or nonspecificity, of therapeutic effects demands further attention and critical discussion. Cognitive behavioral approaches, which abjure any inferences about patients' unconscious experience, align well with the empiricism and positivism of contemporary American culture. Their emphasis on particular techniques and reliable observation is, metaphorically at least, compatible with Americans' fondness for things that "work" and are efficient. Because behavioral techniques can be applied to animals, neuroscientific research into behaviorally based interventions far outstrips research into methods of therapy that rely more on human symbolic capacities. Moreover, to the extent that psychotherapy is supported by health insurance, the current paradigm for reimbursement requires that treatment be tied to diagnosis, well focused, and as brief (or cheap) as possible. For all these reasons, like psychoanalysis in decades past, cognitive behavioral therapies now dominate the field of psychotherapy, at least in academic settings.

Just as Frank took on the prevailing paradigm of his era, the essays that follow express a principled skepticism about the comparative superiority of cognitive behavioral therapies or any other particular approaches. Beyond Wampold and Weinberger's discussion of research into common factors, three other chapters in this volume return to the issue of evaluating evocative (psychodynamic) and directive (cognitive behavioral) therapies in general and for specific disorders. Wells and Frank (chapter 10) reassess psychodynamic therapy through historical review, current research, and Wells's own experience. Raishevich Cunningham, Ollendick, and Jensen (chapter 12) reaffirm the difficulty of providing adequate placebo or comparison conditions for randomized, controlled trials of psychotherapy. The common features of psychotherapy that Frank proposed include an organized approach supported by a plausible rationale. Research that compares an active treatment with a waiting-list control or with "treatment as usual," which lacks a strong rationale, does not control for the impact of the common factors.

The difficulty of creating appropriate placebo conditions is but one of many factors that complicate studies of the effectiveness of psychotherapy. Group psychotherapy, guided by many different principles, is paradoxically recognized as highly effective yet difficult to study in a controlled fashion. Rutan and Shay (chapter 13) describe the challenges of developing and maintaining this valuable treatment approach in the current environment of practice and research.

Ongoing controversies about the value of different psychotherapeutic approaches have implications for readers outside the academic research community: those who are training the next generation of practitioners, trainees trying to decide what type of psychotherapy they need to learn, and those who seek to influence the social policies that support or undermine psychotherapy as a professional enterprise. Creating a research foundation to support clinical practice and inform social policy has proved a daunting task.

The three essays that evaluate empirical research (chapters 1, 11, and 12) were written independently, but their conclusions are remarkably consistent. All the authors find evidence for the effectiveness of cognitive behavioral approaches in general, and all suggest that some versions may be differentially effective for a small number of defined conditions. Such narrow conclusions paradoxically demonstrate that the competing claims of psychotherapies representing different schools of thought remain unsettled. Controlled research does not discredit or disprove the efficacy of therapeutic approaches that rely on inference, language, and the manipulation of symbols and telling of stories. As Griffith (chapter 15), Griffith and DSouza (chapter 8), Clarke (chapter 7), Wells and Frank (chapter 10), and Alarcón, Frank, and Williams (chapter 14) suggest, nonbehavioral or culture-based methods are still more widely practiced, and more generally available, than approaches promoted as scientifically developed for specific disorders. Taken together, the chapters in this volume offer continued support for Frank's controversial position that the power of a given approach lies more in its plausibility than in the truth of its assumptions, and that the similarities between all forms of psychotherapy outweigh their apparent differences.

In sum, after roughly dividing the chapters into theoretical discussion and application, we grouped the chapters around major themes of *Persuasion and Healing*. Part I covers common features of all therapies, the role of life stories, biological determinants of thought and behavior in relation to psychotherapy, meaning as an organizing principle of psychotherapeutic action, culture, and demoralization. Part II describes applications, especially psychotherapy, in the care of the medically ill, the current status of psychodynamic psychotherapy and group psychotherapy, and recent research findings in specific psychother-apies and psychotherapy with children. We close part II with essays about ap-plication of cultural principles in psychotherapy and about the role of religion as a form of healing.

Beyond the genuine devotion of a disciple (RDA) and the tender love of a daughter (JBF), the editors have tried to make the essential and transcending messages of Jerome D. Frank accessible to diverse audiences: trainees, practi-tioners, and researchers in psychology, psychiatry, and other counseling pro-fessions, medical students, and nonpsychiatric physicians. Interested laypeople and scholars, particularly those working at the interface of psychology and anthropology or medicine and the humanities, may also derive insights and inspiration for their work from the pages that follow.

REFERENCES

Charon, R. 2001. Narrative medicine: a model for empathy, reflection, profession, and trust. *JAMA: Journal of the American Medical Association* 286:1897–1902.
Frank, J. D. 1961. *Persuasion and Healing: A Comparative Study of Psychotherapy*. Balti-more: Johns Hopkins University Press.
———. 1973. *Persuasion and Healing: A Comparative Study of Psychotherapy*, rev. ed. Baltimore: Johns Hopkins University Press.
Frank, J. D., and Frank, J. B. 1991. *Persuasion and Healing: A Comparative Study of Psy-chotherapy*, 3rd ed. Baltimore: Johns Hopkins University Press.
Romanoff, B. D., and Thompson, R. 2006. Meaning construction in palliative care: the use of narrative, ritual, and the expressive arts. *American Journal of Hospice and Palliative Medicine* 23:309–16.

Acknowledgments

We wish to express our warmest appreciation, first, to one another, and then to our contributors, who have taught us so much. We are especially grateful to Dr. Leon Eisenberg, a towering figure in the field, who died before the manuscript was complete. Wendy Harris, who shepherded the publication of the third edition of *Persuasion and Healing*, was the first editor at the Johns Hopkins University Press to work with us on *The Psychotherapy of Hope*. Her enthusiasm for the project, her nurturing of our collaboration, and her careful and well-informed review of the manuscript have shaped the final text in ways too numerous to count and for which we are both deeply grateful. We also thank the Press's current editor, Jacqueline Wehmueller, who has guided us through the stages of production with grace and professional sophistication. We are indebted also to Linda Strange, Sara Cleary, and other members of the production team. No source was too elusive for Laura Abate, friend and reference librarian of the Himmelfarb Library at George Washington University School of Medicine and Health Sciences. We are also grateful to James C. Harris, MD, for finding a beautiful cover to symbolize our theme.

Last but not least, each of us owes boundless thanks to members of our families. Renato D. Alarcón's wife, Graciela, and his children, Patricia, Sylvia, and Daniel, provided endless support, understanding, and encouragement, assisting in decisive moments of the manuscript's development. Elizabeth Kleeman Frank made unique contributions to this volume, both in her role as professional good listener and as a coauthor of Julia Frank. Mark Graber, Julia Frank's husband, and her daughters, Naomi, Abigail, and Rebecca, graciously shared their scholarly and editorial skills, and fished many lost files out of various computers, over the five years of this book's gestation. Without the unwavering support of our families, this work, at times daunting and demanding, would never have been finished.

RDA and JBF

A Note about Citations

Persuasion and Healing underwent two substantial revisions after initial publication in 1961. Different contributors to the current volume cite different editions in their essays. In addition, Jerome Frank included his daughter, Julia (an editor of this volume), as coauthor on the 1991 edition. While some of the ideas in that edition are indeed hers, most of the text still reflects Jerome Frank's own synthesis of the data he collected and mulled over for fifty years. When authors in this text cite an idea that both Franks take credit for, they are referred to together, but when a particular idea was Jerome Frank's alone, he is cited singularly, even if the associated bibliographic reference is to the third, 1991, edition of *Persuasion and Healing*.

PART I / PSYCHOTHERAPY

Basic Principles

CHAPTER 1

Critical Thinking in the Design of Psychotherapy Research

Bruce E. Wampold, Ph.D., and
Joel Weinberger, Ph.D.

Psychotherapeutic success depends in part on a congruence between the expectations that a patient brings to treatment and what actually occurs.

—*PERSUASION AND HEALING*, 1991, P. 153

G reat scientists observe the same phenomena as do other scientists investigating the same area. What differentiates Isaac Newton, Charles Darwin, Louis Pasteur, and Albert Einstein, say, from their fellow scientists? The biographies of these men reveal that, in comparison to their colleagues, they possessed no greater knowledge, had no more training (and possibly less), did not have prestigious academic chairs that afforded them the time to devote to their work, and did not have greater resources. But Newton, Darwin, Pasteur, and Einstein stubbornly refused to accept received wisdom, attended closely to anomalies in data, and were open to alternative explanations. In a word, they *thought* deeply about what they observed and generated theories that deviated from those around them. The generation of theories outside the canon is far from unusual, but the thinking of these scientists created theories that not only accounted for the extant evidence but also made bold new predictions about evidence that would be collected in the future. Their predictions were later verified by their own and others' observations and experiments. Thus, their theories persisted, while others withered under the onslaught of evidence. The theories of classical mechanics, natural selection, germs, and relativity are the products of stunning scientific thinking.

Psychotherapy comprises phenomena as complex as any in the physical and biological sciences. The field does not lack for theories—Alan Kazdin (2000) counted more than five hundred. As in any area in which multiple research studies require meta-analysis to resolve inconsistent findings, so multiple views create the need for a meta-theory of psychotherapy (Wampold 2001).

In the mid twentieth century, scholars of psychotherapy debated endlessly about which psychotherapeutic theory or modality was correct and, by implication, most effective. At about that time, the randomized control group design, which was well on its way to being *the* experimental method of medicine, came to psychotherapy research. Trained as both a physician and a psychologist, Jerome D. Frank was primed to think of psychotherapy as medical activity that could be tested empirically. This prompted him initially to search for the specific ingredients responsible for the benefits of psychotherapy, at that time mostly of the psychoanalytic type (Frank 1961; Wampold and Weinberger 2010). Instead, examination of the available research, much of it emanating from his research group at Johns Hopkins, led Frank to develop a meta-model of psychotherapy that postulated that certain *common factors* were responsible for the effectiveness of psychotherapy. His was a meta-model because it spanned the array of theories of psychotherapy at a level superordinate to their specific claims. In many ways, Frank's model was a meta-theory of change in any and all healing settings, as it explained traditional and indigenous healing practices as well as psychotherapy (Frank and Frank 1991; Wampold 2007). The various editions of *Persuasion and Healing* (Frank 1961, 1973; Frank and Frank 1991) presented this model, representing for many the zenith of Frank's contributions to understanding psychotherapy. Indeed, the three editions have been cited more than sixteen hundred times in the literature, a prodigious accomplishment. The model so eloquently presented and so meticulously justified involved an iterative process of experiment, theory-building, and further efforts to test the theory. In this chapter, we review research emanating from the Johns Hopkins Psychotherapy Research Project as a model for thinking in psychotherapy research.

In Pursuit of the Common Factors

Frank and the Johns Hopkins group began investigating psychotherapy just as medicine was beginning to use placebo comparisons to control for various psychological factors, such as hope, expectancy, and the relationship with the physician. Trying to shed centuries of unproven therapeutic claims, medical scientists focused on demonstrating that the benefits of medical interventions were due to their specific ingredients. Frank drew parallels with the study of psychotherapy, but soon realized the difficulties in proving that the specific ingredients in psychotherapy were responsible for patients' improvement. In 1956, he and David Rosenthal discussed the problems in making inferences from psychotherapy research:

> It is concluded that improvement under a special form of psychotherapy cannot be taken as evidence for: (a) correctness of the theory on which it is based; or (b) efficacy of the specific technique used, unless improvement can be shown to be greater than or qualitatively different from that produced by the patients' faith in the efficacy of the therapist and his technique—"the placebo effect." This effect may be thought of as a nonspecific form of psychotherapy and it may be quite powerful in that it may produce end-organ changes and relief from distress of considerable duration. (Rosenthal and Frank 1956, p. 300)

Considering that randomized placebo control group designs were just emerging in the United Kingdom and the United States and would not be required for the approval of drugs until the early 1980s (Shapiro and Shapiro 1997), Rosenthal and Frank's understanding of the inferential issues in psychotherapy research was prescient. Their analysis remains central to the debate about the benefits of psychotherapy. They understood that certain factors, such as the patient's faith in the treatment, could be potent in themselves. Frank was open to the possibility that the common factors were therapeutic. He rejected a conclusion generally accepted by medicine that placebo effects were uninteresting and unimportant (Walach 2003; Wampold, Imel, and Minami 2007) (see also chapter 12 in this volume).

Rosenthal and Frank (1956) went further and observed that comparing a treatment intended to be therapeutic with no-treatment controls would necessarily produce ambiguous results. They noted that all therapies that were delivered faithfully by believing therapists benefited most patients. The superiority of a treatment vis-à-vis no treatment was not particularly informative, as the effects of the treatment could be attributed neither to theory-specific ingredients nor to nonspecific effects such as expectancy of change. Rosenthal and Frank concluded that "the only adequate control would be another form of therapy in which patients had equal faith, so that the placebo effect operated equally in both, but which would not be expected by the theory of therapy being studied to produce the same effects" (p. 300).

Heeding their own advice, Frank and colleagues set out to compare various approaches that were roughly equal in terms of the expectations they generated. At the time, treatment manuals did not exist, outcome measures were crude and unreliable, and one learned psychotherapy from one's supervisor. Frank's group embarked on standardizing the treatments to be tested and developing objective outcome measures (e.g., the Hopkins Symptom Checklist). They then compared group therapy, individual therapy, and minimal therapy. As noted by Frank (1992, p. 393), "To our astonishment and chagrin, despite obvious differences in therapies" there were few differences among the treatments, and the research team was "forced to conclude that features shared by all three must have been responsible for much of patients' improvement." The observation that the treatments produced similar outcomes was not the stunning aspect here—it was Frank's willingness (despite his astonishment) to embrace an alternative explanation. Many remain unwilling to recognize that most brand-name treatments, when offered with conviction, are equally effective. In contrast, Frank had a reverence for evidence and unflinchingly sought its meaning. His interpretation of these data gave rise to his common factor model, now one of several in the literature (Marmor 1962; Torrey 1972; Kleinman and Sung 1979; Orlinsky and Howard 1986; Garfield 1992; Wampold 2001, 2007). The three editions of *Persuasion and Healing* have kept the full justification provided by Frank available to subsequent researchers.

Examining the contributions of Louis Pasteur reveals the brilliance of Frank and the extent of his influence. In 1864, Louis Pasteur "discovered" that microorganisms were the cause of fermentation. He is generally given credit as the father (or at least one of the fathers) of the germ theory of illness, which led to vaccines, pasteurization, sterilization, and antibiotics as medical and public health interventions. Though he was not the first scientist to propose a biological explanation (Latour 1999), Pasteur was one of the few who rejected the view, commonly held in 1864, that fermentation was a purely chemical process. Moreover, Pasteur never observed the microorganisms he posited; he inferred their existence by way of beautifully constructed experiments. In a way, the organisms and Pasteur conspired to make their presence known to the scientific community. Similarly, the common factors in psychotherapy conspired to make themselves known; they existed before Frank's "discovering" them (Rosenzweig 1936). Like Pasteur, Frank based his theorizing on beautifully designed experiments, formulated ideas resonant with the evidence, and disseminated his interpretations cogently and convincingly. Moreover, just as Pasteur went on to find bacterial etiologies for multiple conditions, Frank continued to test his theory experimentally. Well into the 1980s, the Johns Hopkins group conducted ingenious experiments to investigate various aspects of the common factor model. Our review of some of those experiments illustrates the critical role of thinking in psychotherapy research.

Mastery

Frank identified *mastery* as one of the key effective elements of all psychotherapy. This variable is defined as "control over one's internal reactions and relevant external events" (Liberman 1978). The Johns Hopkins research team viewed mastery as a human aspiration and psychotherapy as a means of attaining a healthy sense of control, particularly over aspects of life troubling to the patient. From the existing literature of psychological theory and research, they further identified five aspects of mastery that they deemed necessary to change in psychotherapy: (1) the patient's background and current context, (2) the relevance of the therapeutic activity, (3) the difficulty of the activity, (4) the attitudes of significant others, and (5) attributions of the patient about performance. Here we focus on the last aspect of mastery: patients' attributions about their performance.

The Johns Hopkins group hypothesized that the successful performance of a therapeutic task that could be attributed to one's own efforts would be more beneficial than the same performance attributed to an external source (Frank 1974; Liberman 1978). For example, if a socially anxious person engages in a conversation with a stranger and attributes the action to his or her own efforts to overcome anxiety, this will be of more benefit than if the person attributes the action to an external cause, such as a medication or the efforts of the other person. Moreover, the research team hypothesized that individual differences would interact with the internal/external attributions. Specifically, they tested the idea that patients who had high mastery orientation would benefit most when success was attributed to the self, whereas those with low mastery orientation would benefit most when they attributed success to external sources.

Designing an experimental test of this hypothesis proved complex, because ruling out alternative explanations for improvement during therapy is difficult. The Johns Hopkins group overcame these difficulties by assigning patients referred for outpatient treatment to either of two groups: a self-attributed success condition or an external-attributed success condition. The researchers came up with an ingenious way to ensure the two groups differed only on the locus of the attributions—internal versus external. The patients in both conditions participated in three tasks and received feedback about their performance. Performance was measured as (1) reaction times for discriminating between different colored stimuli, (2) content and mood induced by tachistoscopically presented TAT (thematic apperception test) cards, and (3) modification of physiological responses to stressful and nonstressful visual and auditory stimuli based on purported biofeedback. Before the tasks were administered, the patients were informed that success on the tasks was an indication of improvement in their lives. This manipulation was made salient by individualizing the explanation; that is, the rationale for the tasks was tailored to each patient's particular difficulties. Feedback to the patients was independent of their actual performance on the tasks but was designed to indicate that the patient was making steady progress over the course of the sessions.

The research group then manipulated the locus of attribution by means of a placebo medication. In the self-attributed condition, patients were led to believe that improvement on these tasks was due to their own efforts (labeled "mastery condition"), whereas in the external attribution condition, patients were led to believe that improvement was the result of an administered medication. In actuality, the medication was an inert substance (labeled "placebo condition"). In the mastery condition, the patient's apparent improvement was explained as follows: "work on the tasks would enable the patient to gain greater control over important physical and mental abilities and . . . this increased control would enable him to better handle his problems" (Liberman 1978). In the placebo condition, the patients were told that the "medication" would improve their physical and mental abilities and would help them feel better generally. They were led to believe that the experimental tasks were a test of the medication's effectiveness.

To control for extraneous factors, the therapy offered to the patients (i.e., the three tasks) contained no ingredients of any known psychotherapy. Clearly, a psychotherapy involving these three tasks would not constitute a bona fide treatment, then or now. Yet the patients were led to believe that working on these three tasks constituted a viable and legitimate means to improve their lives. They did not reject this, in part because "the presentation by senior staff therapists at the Johns Hopkins Medical Institution provided an element of status and prestige which facilitated acceptance of these explanations" (Liberman 1978). Moreover, staff members provided feedback to patients during the course of therapy by way of supportive notes in response to an audiotape the patient made before each session. This element minimized personal contact and the possibility that the relationship between therapist and patient would be responsible for patients' improvement. Under these conditions, any real gains that patients made during "treatment" could be linked to their attributions of why they apparently improved in performance on the three tasks, and not to the therapy relationship or other aspects of the treatment.

The researchers assessed individual differences in mastery before treatment, using several scales designed to measure the degree to which patients attributed their well-being to internal or external sources. Improvement was assessed primarily by the Hopkins Symptom Checklist immediately after therapy and again at the three-month follow-up.

The results generally corroborated the hypothesis. At the end of treatment, patients in both groups improved significantly, indicating the therapeutic efficacy of sham feedback that performance was improving on tasks purported to be related to improved psychological functioning. The critical question was whether the improvement would be maintained after the therapy ended and patients were no longer participating in tasks supposedly related to their general well-being. Patients in the mastery condition (internal attribution) maintained their improvement, whereas those in the placebo condition (external attribution) deteriorated, confirming that mastery (i.e., attributing one's success to one's own efforts) is an important aspect of treatment. The predicted interaction effect was also present: patients who indicated an orientation toward controlling their worlds had better long-term outcomes in the mastery condition, whereas those who indicated an orientation toward external causes had better long-term outcomes in the placebo condition.

The implications of this research are many. What is particularly impressive is that the results from this ingenious design foreshadowed developments in several different areas related to psychotherapy and behavioral change. The ideas of mastery and of attributional processes are key concepts in Albert Bandura's self-efficacy theory (Bandura 1977, 1997). Self-efficacy is the belief that one can accomplish a given task, a belief similar to the Johns Hopkins group's notion of mastery. The Hopkins group used the term *self-esteem*, but a close reading of their work shows that their use of this term is closer to Bandura's *self-efficacy* than it is to current literature on self-esteem. (See Weinberger and Eig 1999 for a review of the effects of expectancy/attribution on the maintenance of psychotherapeutic gains; see also Weinberger and Rasco 2007; Weinberger, Siefert, and Haggerty 2010.)

The notion that behavioral change attributed to one's own efforts is more enduring than behavioral change attributed to an external source, such as a medication, has resurfaced recently. Powers et al. (2008), in a study reminiscent of the Johns Hopkins attribution study, manipulated attributions by use of a placebo in the treatment of claustrophobia. Phobic patients were randomly assigned to a waiting-list condition, a psychological placebo condition, a one-session exposure-based treatment, or the one-session exposure-based treatment with a pill placebo. For the exposure plus pill placebo, the patients were further randomly assigned to one of three instruction conditions, designed to manipulate attributions. Immediately after the treatment and posttreatment assessments, the patients were told that (1) the pill was a sedating herb designed to make the exposure easier, or (2) the pill was an arousing herb designed to make the exposure more difficult, or (3) the pill was a placebo that had no effect on the treatment.

The results showed that, at the end of the study, the exposure treatment with pill placebo was as effective as exposure without the pill (the placebo had no effect on posttreatment scores) and was more effective than either the waiting-list condition (i.e., no treatment) or the psychological placebo. Overall, the one-session exposure treatment was effective in this experiment, and taking a pill placebo without any explanation did not affect the outcome. Not surprisingly, given the Hopkins group's findings, those who were told the placebo was sedating had greater rates of posttreatment deterioration, as they probably attributed their success in controlling their fear during the exposure to the purported sedating effects of the placebo. However, the results did not support the study authors' hypothesis that those getting the "arousing herb" instruction would have greater maintenance of effects vis-à-vis the neutral instruction. Thus, it was not the amount of effort needed to control fear that was important, but whether the subject attributed improvement to an internal (neutral condition and "arousing herb" condition) or external ("sedating herb" condition) factor. This observation was consistent with the conjectures of the Hopkins group. Powers and colleagues also found that self-efficacy mediated the deterioration effects: the placebo instruction affected self-efficacy, which in turn affected maintenance of effect, an observation also made by the Hopkins group. It seems that several decades later, Powers and coworkers rediscovered the effects of attributions hypothesized and verified by Frank and his colleagues!

The Hopkins group's results on mastery complement Powers et al.'s results (2008) in suggesting that the benefits of psychotherapy should last longer than those of medications for various mental disorders. Hollon, Stewart, and Strunk (2006) found this to be true for cognitive and behavioral treatments for anxiety and depression. They offered two primary explanations for these results. First, the cognitive and behavioral treatments remediate some underlying cause of the disorder, and medications are palliative only. Second, patients in psychotherapy acquire coping skills to manage their distress. Neither explanation recognizes that mastery and self-efficacy may explain these results more parsimoniously. Patients taking medications for mental disorders will have a natural tendency to attribute improvement to an external cause (i.e., the medication) and so will relapse when the medication is discontinued. Overlooking the significance of inducing mastery attributions in psychotherapy, Powers et al. (2008) limited their discussion of the clinical implications of their research to how drug therapies might be designed to make their effects more enduring.

The work of the Johns Hopkins group on mastery also foreshadowed Irving Kirsch's (1997, 1999, 2005) on response expectancies. Response expectancies are individuals' anticipation of their own automatic responses to various stimuli. In many disorders, response expectancies are self-confirming, because they produce the anticipated experiences. For example, anxiety disorders are often debilitating, not because of patients' actual experiences, but because of their fear that these experiences will occur (anticipatory anxiety); that is, the patients' belief in their inability to control the symptoms is more distressing than the symptoms themselves. Frank and his colleagues described mastery, in part, as "control over one's internal reactions" (Liberman 1978), a characterization similar to Kirsch's theory of response expectancies. Moreover, Kirsch's views (2005) on psychotherapy as an elaborate system to change expectations differ little from Frank's.

The Johns Hopkins attribution study also foreshadowed technical eclecticism, which emphasizes the match of patient to treatment based on empirical results (Arkowitz 1992). In the Hopkins study, those with a mastery orientation maintained benefits better in the condition that fostered mastery, providing evidence that therapists should foster internal attributions, particularly for patients who value mastery. This may be the first empirical prescriptive result ever found in the psychotherapy treatment literature. Liberman (1978, p. 49) speculated about other matching hypotheses: "Perhaps some patients would benefit more from a directive style while others would respond best to a nondirective approach." Beutler, Moleiro, and Talebi (2002) pursued this suggestion and found that patients who are characterologically resistant do better with unstructured treatments, whereas less resistant patients do better with more structured treatments. Blatt, Shahar, and Zuroff (2002) found that patients more oriented to relationships do better when therapy is relationship focused; patients more oriented to success and failure are better served by a therapy that is task focused.

It is at first puzzling that the intervention in the Hopkins attribution study was apparently effective, even though it contained no ingredients of any known psychotherapy. Moreover, the treatment did not involve a therapeutic relationship. These conditions were needed for the integrity of the design, but if the treatment had not been effective, the results would have been meaningless. The team must have had great confidence that this bogus treatment was going to be effective to have undertaken the study! Clearly, Frank and colleagues were certain that presenting a convincing rationale to the patient is a critical ingredient of effective psychotherapy. That is, the "truth" of any particular explanation of why a therapy works is suspect; any explanation, however bogus, "works" if it is cogent to the patient and leads to positive and adaptive responses. Wampold (2007) defended this implication of Frank's work.

The prevailing treatment of posttraumatic stress disorder (PTSD) illustrates the efficacy of plausible treatments without scientifically validated components, offered in the right context. Edna Foa and colleagues (1991) sought to design a control group for cognitive behavioral therapy (CBT) for patients with PTSD that did not contain the two specific aspects of CBT that they intended to validate scientifically: exposure and cognitive restructuring. The control condition was treatment by an empathic therapist who listened to the patient's concerns. The authors described the control condition, labeled "supportive counseling," as follows: "Patients were taught a general problem-solving technique. Therapists played an indirect and unconditionally supportive role. Homework consisted of the patient's keeping a diary of daily problems and her attempts at problem solving. Patients were immediately redirected to focus on current daily problems if discussions of the assault occurred" (p. 718).

In Foa and colleagues' first study comparing prolonged exposure, stress inoculation training, and supportive counseling, the investigators provided no cogent rationale for the supportive counseling condition. Certainly the therapists knew the supportive counseling was a sham comparison, and most likely the patients did as well. Not surprisingly, the two active conditions proved superior. However, when the researchers upgraded the supportive counseling by creating a manual and giving it a label that suggested it was a legitimate treatment (present-centered therapy, or PCT), having experts train the therapists, and so forth, PCT was found to be highly effective. Indeed, PCT was nearly as effective as CBT, the current gold standard for PTSD, even though PCT does not contain the specific ingredients postulated to be necessary for success (McDonagh et al. 2005).

Another meta-analysis of psychological placebos found that when they were structurally equivalent to the treatment in terms of dose, training of therapists, format of therapy, and absence of proscription of commonly used therapeutic techniques, the psychological placebos were as effective as the active treatments (Baskin et al. 2003). All of this was foreshadowed by Rosenthal and Frank's article (1956) on placebos in psychotherapy and by their recognition in the attribution study that an effective treatment might not involve any scientifically accepted psychological ingredients!

Beyond being ingenious and informative, the Johns Hopkins group's study of the role of mastery and the importance of attributions in psychotherapy stimulated several important developments in psychotherapy research. In designing the study, Frank and colleagues recognized that patients were susceptible to the suggestion of the experimental setting—namely, that performance on experimental tasks would be therapeutic. Clearly, the team understood that the expectations created by the therapeutic process are critical determinants of the success of psychotherapy (Frank 1974, 1978). Frank also realized that well-educated people have a reasonably accurate notion of what happens in psychotherapy and so are primed to expect that it will be effective. Less-educated persons may lack such sophisticated understanding and hence may not anticipate benefiting from psychotherapy. Moreover, Frank thought that those referred to psychotherapy by their physicians might think the physician was tired of listening to their complaints or was unable to do anything for them (Frank 1978). This analysis led the Hopkins group to study the effect of preparing patients for psychotherapy, the second area we examine here.

Preparation for Psychotherapy

In providing a basis for his work on preparation for psychotherapy, Frank (1978) cited research noting that, in contrast to more privileged patients, patients of lower socioeconomic status expected a therapist to be like a physician: active, directive, and supportive. He concluded that "the expectations of many clinic patients may be highly discrepant from what actually occurs. [There is an] impression that a major reason why patients drop out of treatment is that they do not know what is supposed be going on or how it can be of help to them" (Frank 1978).

This thinking led the Johns Hopkins group to hypothesize that a "role induction" interview, informing patients about the process of psychotherapy and how it could benefit them, would facilitate the process of psychotherapy and increase its benefits. They then designed an experiment to test this hypothesis.

The sample for this study comprised forty psychiatric outpatients assigned to one of two conditions: a role induction interview condition and a control condition. To make the role induction manipulation more salient, the patients had no prior experience with psychotherapy.

Extraordinary care was taken to keep the therapists and patients blind to the experimental purpose and to the assignment to conditions. The therapists, who were psychiatric residents, knew that the patients in the study would differ from ordinary outpatients only in having had a preliminary contact with one of the researchers. One of two senior psychiatrists conducted the role induction session. After the standard clinical evaluation interview, the researcher asked the patient to step outside the room while he dictated a brief note to the treating resident. Only then did the evaluator learn whether or not the patient would receive the induction interview. This kept the psychiatrist's interview and evaluation uncontaminated by the experimental manipulation. Patients were matched on the basis of their anticipated responsiveness to psychotherapy and then randomly assigned.

The induction interview was informal, and the patient was encouraged to ask questions. Psychotherapy was "explained as a way of learning to deal more effectively with problems of personal life, but it was made clear that this would require time and practice" (Frank 1978). The interviewer explained that progress in therapy is uneven and that, at termination, the patient would still have problems but would be able to cope better with them. The patient was informed that the therapist might not talk much, would listen carefully in order to understand the patient better, and would clarify the patient's feelings. The interviewer urged the patient to talk openly and honestly with the therapist, particularly about his or her relationship with the therapist, emphasizing that the patient would find his or her own way to cope with problems and would be responsible for making his or her own decisions. Because the therapy was psychodynamic, the senior psychiatrist also "explained the meaning of the unconscious and the importance of childhood experiences and their consequences for current behavior patterns . . . [The] concept of resistance was explained in everyday terms and interpreted as evidence that the therapy was approaching or actually dealing with the issues the patient was reluctant to face, probably because they were closely related to his complaint" (Frank 1978). The interviewer emphasized that it was important that the patient keep all appointments, even when he or she did not feel like going to therapy.

After the evaluation note was dictated, patients in the induction condition participated in the short interview explained above and received an appointment with the treating resident; those in the control group were given an appointment only. Patients' self-reports and ratings by the treating resident assessed patients' functioning at the end of treatment. Researchers blind as to whether or not patients had had an induction interview rated tapes randomly selected from tapes made of all therapy sessions to assess the therapy process.

Generally, the results supported a modestly positive effect of role induction interviews. On three of the eight outcome measures, the role induction group showed significantly greater improvement than did the control group. Oddly, process differences were found in the third session only, leading the researchers to state: "Why the differences did not appear at any other session, however, remains a mystery" (Frank 1978, p. 25).

Despite offering only modest support for psychotherapy preparation, this study has had a robust legacy. Many therapies, especially cognitive behavioral ones, include a phase of role induction. For example, in the manual for CBT for depression, the first sessions are psychoeducational, with the therapist explaining how cognitions cause depression and how the therapy will progress to change the cognitions (Beck et al. 1979). It is a short leap to conjecture that effective therapists communicate clearly about the process of therapy and offer explanations of how the therapy will be effective for a particular patient. Frank's group provided a theoretical reason for doing so. Expectancy and a therapeutic rationale are important factors in psychotherapeutic success. Most therapies that advocate early education in therapy see this step as helping the patient understand the techniques to be introduced later in the course of therapy. A review by Ilardi and Craighead (1994) suggests that Frank's explanation is more likely. These investigators reviewed eight CBT studies and found that most of the change in CBT for depression occurred before introduction of the cognitive techniques supposedly accounting for that change. Early psychoeducational sessions, in their own right, ameliorated symptoms, exactly as Frank would have predicted.

A comprehensive review of preparatory, role induction techniques found evidence for their effectiveness (Walitzer, Dermen, and Conners 1999, p. 139): "Taken together, the 19 studies on role induction procedures . . . suggest that role induction produces significant benefits relevant to general psychotherapy endeavors. This benefit has been most evident when measures of treatment attendance are evaluated . . . Benefits pertaining to treatment process and outcome, although not as pronounced, have also been found."

It is counterintuitive that simply describing the treatment could have these effects. The process of psychotherapy is quite complex, and a short preparation should have, at most, a moderate effect on the eventual outcome. We cannot think of an explanation other than Frank's that accounts for the findings of Walitzer and coauthors' review. The patient must be convinced that the rationale is cogent and that participating in the process will be beneficial. And, as Frank stated over and over again, the scientific truth of the rationale is subservient to the patient's belief in the myth and ritual (Frank and Frank 1991; Wampold 2007). It is not simply those aligned with a common factor approach who see the wisdom in this perspective. Donald Meichenbaum, a noted cognitive behaviorist, clearly understood Frank's point:

> As part of the therapy rationale, the therapist conceptualized each client's anxiety
> in terms of Schacter's model of emotional arousal . . . After laying this ground-
> work, the therapist noted that the client's fear seemed to fit Schacter's theory that
> an emotional state such as fear is in large part determined by the thoughts in
> which the client engages when physically aroused . . . Although the theory and
> research upon which it is based have been criticized . . . the theory has an aura
> of plausibility that the clients tend to accept. The logic of the treatment plan is
> clear to clients in light of this conceptualization. (Meichenbaum 1986, p. 370)

A review of effective treatments for anxiety disorders led to the following conclusion: "Psychotherapy for anxiety is less likely to be effective if the client does not think it will help" (Newman and Stiles 2006, p. 655).

Role induction was, for Frank, simply one way to study patients' expectations about treatment of various kinds. His thinking about placebos represents another approach to the same problem. When Frank began his research, medicine acknowledged the power of placebos to relieve only subjective symptoms, particularly pain. Since that time, research on placebos has expanded, and we now know that placebos affect physiology as well as subjective judgments. For example, studies show that placebo-engendered expectancy for analgesia results in the release of endogenous opioids (Levine, Gordon, and Fields 1978; Amanzio et al. 2001; Price, Finniss, and Benedetti 2008). Another study showed that the expectation that one will receive a less noxious taste than previously experienced influenced activation in the primary taste cortex, even though the taste stimulus remained the same—that is, expectation of taste influenced the actual experience of taste (Nitschke et al. 2006). Placebos administered to patients who have Parkinson disease produce demonstrable changes in dopamine levels (Price, Finniss, and Benedetti 2008). Price and colleagues (2008) proposed a desire expectation model of placebo action that contains many of the components discussed by Frank and colleagues. These include motivation, emotional regulation, and expectations created by the context in which the placebos are administered. Again, Frank anticipated later developments. It would have been fascinating to see how he might have adjusted his model to account for the current research on placebos.

Implications of Frank's Work for Current Research in Psychotherapy

For more than a decade, the field of psychotherapy has been caught up in an effort to identify therapies and therapeutic methods that "work." This has been termed the "empirically supported treatment" approach (e.g., Chambless and Hollon 1998). Many are searching for methods and techniques that are effective for specific disorders. The task of the psychotherapy researcher has become to identify these methods and techniques, making it the obligation of the practitioner to implement the findings. Efficacy research occupies pride of place in this endeavor. The most valued and supported studies involve random assignment of patients sharing a diagnosis to competing treatments administered according to a detailed treatment manual (Nathan and Gorman 2002). This approach is not without its critics (e.g., Wampold 2001; Westen, Novotny, and Thompson-Brenner 2004; Weinberger and Rasco 2007), but it has become almost impossible to obtain funding for research that does not follow this model (Westen 2007), as Frank (1992) predicted years ago.

Few recognize that the underlying assumptions of a clinical trials approach may be part of a closed system based on an untested belief that treatments for different disorders can be specified in technical detail and that the relevant ingredients of effective therapy are laid out in the accompanying treatment manuals. This belief leads to the sometimes unwarranted conclusion that when a treatment is found to be efficacious, the techniques spelled out in the treatment manual are responsible—a specificity model of psychotherapy effect (cf. Weinberger and Rasco 2007).

In contrast, the work of Frank and colleagues supports a global or meta-approach, the view that the effectiveness of psychotherapy derives from general principles rather than specific techniques (cf. Pachankis and Goldfried 2007). This perspective accounts for the finding of outcome equivalence so often reported in the literature. Even the purported superiority of CBT for anxiety disorders may reflect the power of its general rather than its technical elements—the plausibility of a scientifically tested rationale, for example, or the sense of mastery that comes when the emotional arousal of an exposure exercise is less overwhelming than the patient expected. Comparative efficacy research, currently promoted for medicine in general, may have limited usefulness in studies of competing psychotherapies, given the difficulty of isolating the elements that differentiate them.

Conclusion

We have reviewed the particular principles of mastery/attribution and the reinforcement of positive expectations through therapy role induction as examples of a meta-approach to understanding the effectiveness of psychotherapy. The therapeutic relationship itself is another robust general contributor to effectiveness across all therapies, a point made by Frank and supported by subsequent research (Norcross and Lambert 2006). Overall, the research literature provides as much support for these elements as it does for the efficacy of specific techniques. It is time to go back to the future and continue the systematic study of global principles or common factors begun by Frank and his colleagues. This approach, as an alternative to the empirically supported treatment movement, could only enrich our field, which should thrive in the competing marketplace of ideas. The work of great scientists and thinkers who, like Frank, thought deeply about the issues deserves no less.

REFERENCES

Amanzio, M., Pollo, A., Maggi, G., and Benedetti, F. 2001. Response variability to analgesics: a role for non-specific activation of endogenous opioids. *Pain* 90:205–11.
Arkowitz, H. 1992. Integrative theories of therapy. In D. K. Freedheim (ed.), *History of*

Psychotherapy: A Century of Change (pp. 261–303). Washington, DC: American Psychological Association.

Bandura, A. 1977. Self-efficacy: toward a unifying theory of behavioral change. *Psychological Review* 84:191–215.

———. 1997. *Self-efficacy: The Exercise of Control*. New York: W. H. Freeman.

Baskin, T. W., Tierney, S. C., Minami, T., and Wampold, B. E. 2003. Establishing specificity in psychotherapy: a meta-analysis of structural equivalence of placebo controls. *Journal of Consulting and Clinical Psychology* 71:973–79.

Beck, A. T., Rush, A. J., Shaw, B. F., and Emery, G. 1979. *Cognitive Therapy of Depression*. New York: Guilford Press.

Beutler, L. E., Moleiro, C. M., and Talebi, H. 2002. Resistance. In J. C. Norcross (ed.), *Psychotherapy Relationships That Work: Therapist Contributions and Responsiveness to Patients* (pp. 129–43). New York: Oxford University Press.

Blatt, S. J., Shahar, G., and Zuroff, D. C. 2002. Anaclitic/sociotropic and introjective/autonomous dimensions. In J. C. Norcross (ed.), *Psychotherapy Relationships That Work: Therapist Contributions and Responsiveness to Patients* (pp. 315–33). New York: Oxford University Press.

Chambless, D. L., and Hollon, S. D. 1998. Defining empirically supported therapies. *Journal of Consulting and Clinical Psychology* 66:7–18.

Foa, E. B., Rothbaum, B. O., Riggs, D. S., and Murdock, T. B. 1991. Treatment of posttraumatic stress disorder in rape victims: a comparison between cognitive-behavioral procedures and counseling. *Journal of Consulting and Clinical Psychology* 59:715–23.

Frank, J. D. 1961. *Persuasion and Healing: A Comparative Study of Psychotherapy*. Baltimore: Johns Hopkins University Press.

———. 1973. *Persuasion and Healing: A Comparative Study of Psychotherapy*, rev. ed. Baltimore: Johns Hopkins University Press.

———. 1974. Therapeutic components of psychotherapy. *Journal of Nervous and Mental Disorders* 5:325–42.

———. 1978. Expectation and therapeutic outcome: the placebo effect and the role of induction interview. In J. D. Frank, R. Hoehn-Saric, S. D. Imber, B. L. Liberman, and A. R. Stone (eds.), *Effective Ingredients of Successful Psychotherapy* (pp. 1–34). Baltimore: Johns Hopkins University Press.

———. 1992. The Johns Hopkins Psychotherapy Research Project. In D. K. Freedheim (ed.), *A History of Psychotherapy: A Century of Change* (pp. 392–96). Washington, DC: American Psychological Association.

Frank, J. D., and Frank, J. B. 1991. *Persuasion and Healing: A Comparative Study of Psychotherapy*, 3rd ed. Baltimore: Johns Hopkins University Press.

Garfield, S. L. 1992. Eclectic psychotherapy: a common factors approach. In J. C. Norcross and M. R. Goldfried (eds.), *Handbook of Psychotherapy Integration* (pp. 169–201). New York: Basic Books.

Hollon, S. D., Stewart, M. O., and Strunk, D. 2006. Enduring effects for cognitive behavior therapy in the treatment of depression and anxiety. *Annual Review of Psychology* 57:285–315.

Ilardi, S. S., and Craighead, W. E. 1994. The role of nonspecific factors in cognitive-behavior therapy for depression. *Clinical Psychology: Science and Practice* 1:138–56.

Kazdin, A. E. 2000. *Psychotherapy for Children and Adolescents: Directions for Research and Practice*. New York: Oxford University Press.

Kirsch, I. 1997. Specifying nonspecifics: psychological mechanisms of placebo effects. In A. Harrington (ed.), *The Placebo Effect: An Interdisciplinary Exploration* (pp. 166–86). Cambridge, MA: Harvard University Press.

———. 1999. *How Expectancies Shape Experience.* Washington, DC: American Psychological Association.

———. 2005. Placebo psychotherapy: synonym or oxymoron? *Journal of Clinical Psychology* 61:791–803.

Kleinman, A., and Sung, L. H. 1979. Why do indigenous practitioners successfully heal? *Social Science and Medicine* 13B:7–26.

Latour, B. 1999. *Pandora's Hope: Essays on the Reality of Science Studies.* Cambridge, MA: Harvard University Press.

Levine, J. D., Gordon, N. C., and Fields, H. L. 1978. The mechanism of placebo analgesia. *Lancet* 2:654–57.

Liberman, B. L. 1978. The role of mastery in psychotherapy: maintenance of improvement and prescriptive change. In J. D. Frank, R. Hoehn-Saric, S. D. Imber, B. L. Liberman, and A. R. Stone (eds.), *Effective Ingredients of Successful Psychotherapy* (pp. 35–72). Baltimore: Johns Hopkins University Press.

Marmor, J. 1962. Psychoanalytic therapy as an educational process. In J. H. Masserman (ed.), *Science and Psychoanalysis,* vol. 5 (pp. 286–99). New York: Grune and Stratton.

McDonagh, A., Friedman, M., McHugo, G., Ford, J., Sengupta, A., Mueser, K., et al. 2005. Randomized trial of cognitive-behavioral therapy for chronic posttraumatic stress disorder in adult female survivors of childhood sexual abuse. *Journal of Consulting and Clinical Psychology* 73:515–24.

Meichenbaum, D. 1986. Cognitive-behavior modification. In F. H. Kanfer and A. P. Goldstein (eds.), *Helping People Change: A Textbook of Methods,* 3rd ed. (pp. 346–80). New York: Pergamon Press.

Nathan, P. E., and Gorman, J. M. 2002. *A Guide to Treatments That Work,* 2nd ed. New York: Oxford University Press.

Newman, M. G., and Stiles, W. B. 2006. Therapeutic factors in treating anxiety disorders. *Journal of Clinical Psychology* 62:649–59.

Nitschke, J. B., Dixon, G. E., Sarinopoulos, I., Short, S. J., Cohen, J. D., Smith, E. E., et al. 2006. Altering expectancy dampens neural response to aversive taste in primary taste cortex. *Nature Neuroscience* 9:435–42.

Norcross, J. C., and Lambert, M. J. 2006. The therapy relationship. In J. C. Norcross, L. E. Beutler, and R. F. Levant (eds.), *Evidence-Based Practices in Mental Health* (pp. 308–17). Washington, DC: American Psychological Association.

Orlinsky, D. E., and Howard, K. I. 1986. Process and outcome in psychotherapy. In S. L. Garfield and A. E. Bergin (eds.), *Handbook of Psychotherapy and Behavior Change,* 3rd ed. (pp. 311–81). New York: John Wiley.

Pachankis, J. E., and Goldfried, M. R. 2007. An integrative, principle-based approach to psychotherapy. In S. G. Hofmann and J. Weinberger (eds.), *The Art and Science of Psychotherapy* (pp. 49–68). New York: Routledge.

Powers, M. B., Smits, J. A. J., Whitley, D., Bystritsky, A., and Telch, M. J. 2008. The effect of attributional processes concerning medication taking on return of fear. *Journal of Consulting and Clinical Psychology* 76:478–90.

Price, D. P., Finniss, D. G., and Benedetti, F. 2008. A comprehensive review of the placebo effect: recent advances and current thought. *Annual Review of Psychology* 59:565–90.

Rosenthal, D., and Frank, J. D. 1956. Psychotherapy and the placebo effect. *Psychological Bulletin* 53:294–302.

Rosenzweig, S. 1936. Some implicit common factors in diverse methods of psychotherapy: "At last the Dodo said, 'Everybody has won and all must have prizes.'" *American Journal of Orthopsychiatry* 6:412–15.

Shapiro, A. K., and Shapiro, E. S. 1997. *The Powerful Placebo: From Ancient Priest to Modern Medicine*. Baltimore: Johns Hopkins University Press.

Torrey, E. F. 1972. What Western psychotherapists can learn from witchdoctors. *American Journal of Orthopsychiatry* 42:69–76.

Walach, H. 2003. Placebo and placebo effects: a concise review. *Focus on Alternative and Complementary Therapies* 8:178–87.

Walitzer, K. S., Dermen, K. H., and Conners, G. J. 1999. Strategies for preparing clients for treatment: a review. *Behavior Modification* 23:129–51.

Wampold, B. E. 2001. *The Great Psychotherapy Debate: Model, Methods, and Findings*. Mahwah, NJ: Lawrence Erlbaum Associates.

———. 2007. Psychotherapy: the humanistic (and effective) treatment. *American Psychologist* 62:857–73.

Wampold, B. E., Imel, Z. E., and Minami, T. 2007. The story of placebo effects in medicine: evidence in context. *Journal of Clinical Psychology* 63:379–90.

Wampold, B. E., and Weinberger, J. 2010. Jerome D. Frank: psychotherapy researcher and humanitarian. In L. G. Castonguay, J. C. Muran, L. Angus, J. A. Hayes, N. Ladany, and T. Anderson (eds.), *Bringing Psychotherapy Research to Life: Understanding Change through the Work of Leading Clinical Researchers—Legacies from the Society for Psychotherapy Research* (pp. 29–38). Washington, DC: American Psychological Association.

Weinberger, J., and Eig, A. 1999. Expectancies: the ignored common factor in psychotherapy. In I. Kirsch (ed.), *How Expectancies Shape Experience* (pp. 357–82). Washington, DC: American Psychological Association.

Weinberger, J., and Rasco, C. 2007. Empirically supported common factors. In S. G. Hofmann and J. Weinberger (eds.), *The Art and Science of Psychotherapy* (pp. 103–30). New York: Routledge.

Weinberger, J., Siefert, C., and Haggerty, G. 2010. Implicit processes in social and clinical psychology. In J. E. Maddux and J. Tangney (eds.), *Social Psychological Foundations of Clinical Psychology* (pp. 461–76). New York: Guilford Press.

Westen, D. 2007. Discovering what works in the community: toward a genuine partnership of clinicians and researchers. In S. G. Hofmann and J. Weinberger (eds.), *The Art and Science of Psychotherapy* (pp. 3–30). New York: Routledge.

Westen, D., Novotny, C. M., and Thompson-Brenner, H. 2004. The empirical status of empirically supported psychotherapies: assumptions, findings, and reporting in controlled clinical trials. *Psychological Bulletin* 130:631–63.

CHAPTER 2

Life Story as the Focus of Psychotherapy

The Johns Hopkins Conceptual and
Didactic Perspectives

"We had the best of
educations—in fact, we
went to school every day—"
"I'VE been to a day-school,
too," said Alice; "you needn't
be so proud as all that."
—*Alice's Adventures in
Wonderland*

Glenn J. Treisman, M.D., Ph.D., and
Paul R. McHugh, M.D.

The best way to try to discover the causes of any phenomenon
is to try to change it.
—*PERSUASION AND HEALING*, 1991, P. 296

Throughout his long career, Jerome Frank devoted himself to teaching as well as research. In chapter 8 of *Persuasion and Healing* (Frank and Frank 1991), he spelled out some implications of his ideas for the training of psychotherapists of many disciplines. This opened up new vistas for the psychiatrists, psychologists, and other therapists who followed him, suggesting new strategies for assessing candidates for treatment and for teaching the skills of effective psychotherapy to the next generation of providers. In this essay we describe how the Department of Psychiatry and Behavioral Sciences of the Johns Hopkins University School of Medicine integrated Frank's insights into the approach known as the Hopkins Perspectives of Psychiatry (McHugh and Slavney 1998).

As he promulgated his empirical findings, Frank was justly honored for his diplomatic skill in sustaining a friendly discourse with clinicians of many different schools of thought, adroitly side-stepping the ideological conflicts embedded in the teaching and comprehension of psychotherapy. Willing to consider any idea or critical response, his open-minded posture disguised the revolutionary nature of the alternatives he offered, alternatives that helped transform psychotherapy from a mystery-laden enterprise to a relatively transparent and straightforward means of aiding people in distress.

Assessing the Need for Psychotherapy: From Unconscious Conflict to Demoralization

The paradigm of psychotherapy dominant within medicine when Frank began his research was Freudian psychoanalysis (Frank and Frank 1991, p. 186). Classical analytic treatment involved an extended program of regular sessions devoted to the exploration of a patient's "unconscious" through "free association." Differences reflecting the diverse presumptions of Freudian schismatics (Alfred Adler, Carl Jung, Melanie Klein, etc.) about the nature of pathogenic unconscious conflict could be found in any large clinic, but every analytic school taught its practitioners to discover in patients' life stories proof of its particular theory. In actual practice, much psychotherapy was briefer and more focused on patients' daily struggles (Greben 1984), but such treatment was devalued as falling below the "gold standard" of psychoanalysis (see chapter 10). Nonanalytic therapies were described as "superficial," requiring limited expertise and failing to address the "deep-seated roots" of neurosis in the unconscious (Brown 1961).

From the 1930s through the 1950s, psychoanalysts in academic departments developed and promoted theories that explained mental difficulties as the products of unrecognized, mostly unconscious conflicts between the developing individual's intrinsic, self-oriented motivations and his or her encounters with constraints and refusals from powerful parental figures on whom the child depended. The course of mental development and the nature of the symptoms might have some individual distinctions, but analytically trained psychotherapists found that the structure of the analysand's pathogenic story was inevitably the same. Within this theoretical framework, the purpose of psychotherapy was either bringing this story to consciousness or alleviating its injurious consequences through some temporizing "supportive therapy."

Psychotherapeutic thought and practice were built on the fundamental propositions of Freud's "depth psychology," that all mental life is "determined" and is driven by the dynamic unconscious, built on the repression of conflict memories. Therapists sought to reveal these "truths" in patient after patient (Fish 1986). As Robert Rosenheck (1978) casually characterized the process, the purpose of analytic training was to induce first novice therapists and then their patients to "free associate the party line."

With previous training in psychology, Frank approached psychotherapy empirically, taking the radical step of studying patients, process, and outcome rather than explicating individual narratives (case studies) to further develop theory. Initially, he expected to find the common threads of the prevailing narrative in both the genesis of the mental disorders and their successful treatment.

As has been recounted many times, what Frank discovered confounded the dominant theoretical conception of mental disorders and their treatment. Patients coming for psychotherapy did not inevitably provide a common generative life story. In the treatment of individual and group patients and in the assessment and observation of research subjects, Frank and his colleagues noted wide variation in patients' biographical and emotional lives. Though patients typically experienced discrepancy between their desires and the world around them, such tensions had roots beyond unconscious conflict. Some seemed overly expressive in their demands for support; others presented themselves as victims of various kinds of exploitation. The underlying reasons for these postures might be found in patients' biographies, in their current circumstances (including cultural ones) (see chapter 5), in their biological endowment, or, most commonly, in some combination of these factors.

Like prior theoreticians, and somewhat to his surprise, late in his career Frank did identify a common thread in patients seeking or offered psychotherapy (Frank and Frank 1991, p. 299). Rather than unconscious conflict, they largely shared the sense that in one way or another they had lost their ability to manage their life circumstances. Their *conscious* appreciation of that difficulty produced a variety of cognitive and emotional reactions, most of which took the form of depression, discouragement, or an anxious sense of hopelessness about the future. Patients referred for or responsive to psychotherapy typically felt they were "overmastered" by circumstances and challenges. They were, according to Frank, "demoralized" by the implications and prospects of their situation (see chapters 6, 7, and 8 in this volume). Patients came to this state through multiple life pathways and fell into their difficulties for a variety of reasons.

Frank could tie demoralization sometimes to patients' temperament, sometimes to a concurrent illness, sometimes to a particular life encounter, but often to the person's present habits of response or enduring misguided assumptions, regardless of their roots. People became patients because of a common state of mind rather than some common narrative of psychological development. They came to psychotherapy, not for insight, but for help both in discerning what was handicapping them and in discovering ways of correcting their situation or regaining their morale.

Positive Expectations, Conscious Difficulties, and the Demystification of Psychotherapy

Frank's observations and concepts sparked three crucial changes in the culture of psychotherapy. Of particular importance was his finding that demoralized patients are, by definition, ready and open to accept help (the power of patients' expectation of benefit). He also stressed the central role of conscious rather than unconscious experience as the focus of therapy. Perhaps the most revolutionary impact of his argument was the demystification of psychotherapy in both theory and practice. These changes, disseminated from the platform of Johns Hopkins as a leading academic institution, worked their way into the mainstream of psychiatry, revolutionizing how psychotherapy is practiced and taught, within and outside the establishments of medicine, psychiatry, and academic psychology.

The readiness of the demoralized patient to accept help has had the most obvious implications for the practice of psychotherapy. Positive expectation facilitates the placebo response, which, as Frank pointed out, explains much of psychotherapy's effectiveness. Understanding this influences the initial approach that therapists should adopt. Rather than creating an ambiguous task, telling patients simply to say what is on their minds, therapists do well to openly communicate their assessment and expectations. If a person's problem is a crippling loss of mastery, then the best help the therapist can offer is to *persuade* the individual to see that certain ways of thinking and responding to challenges are defective and lead to self-defeat. To help in this way, the therapist must come to know the patient for his or her assets and vulnerabilities, paying particular attention to the history of how the patient's habits of response have produced previous examples of similar kinds of distress. What the therapist needs to bring forth for the patient's benefit is those handicaps and deviations of thought and behavior previously associated with unfortunate outcomes but now open to change. As a general consequence, psychotherapy after Frank has become more "deficit" than "conflict" focused.

Frank further facilitated the transformation of practice and research by implying that psychotherapists should attend to matters of conscious thought rather than unconscious conflicts and repressed frustrations. Although no one can gainsay the possibility that some hidden generative issue may shape human mental development, the distressing problems that bring people to the clinics are ones that they can describe clearly and are often accessible to mutual assessment with therapists. Therapists need particular skills to persuade patients to see how their psychological habits and assumptions contribute to their distress, but everything about the process of persuasion can be openly discussed and clarified during the course of treatment. Patients' problems are not disguised by repression, nor do symptoms need to be decoded as disguised symbolic expressions of unconscious conflicts and fears. What the patient needs and what the therapist can deliver are matters revealed by the patient's history and approached directly in the succession of treatment sessions.

The last and perhaps most subversive impact of Frank's work was to transform the image of psychotherapy and psychotherapists. The therapeutic process lost most of its mystery and all of its magic. Psychotherapy focused on "demoralization" and providing the benefit of restoring "mastery" has increasingly taken on the form of exercises in coaching and advising—persuading persons to see how they might better manage themselves. Frank noted that even in the psychoanalytic era, many experienced practitioners took this approach, regardless of their theoretical orientation. Compared with psychoanalysis, Frank's writings provided a less distorting mirror to the therapy professions, facilitating the widespread acceptance of his views. In the process, psychotherapy as a discipline lost those characteristics of radical enlightenment and psychological rebirth that held so many people enthralled by Freudian claims.

The Freudian Gnostic stance—we psychotherapists know the secret of human mental life with its fundamental deterministic character and the prime role of unconscious conflicts in directing it—simply could not survive this simplifying conception of the nature of patients' problems. Freud's views were not disprovable (Grunbaum 1984), and they live on in other settings where their dramatic and cultic sense of mystery revealed appeals, especially in university literature and drama departments. Nevertheless, most practicing therapists have set them aside as unnecessary for treatment and probably distracting to the purposes at hand. Certain psychoanalytic skills remain central to education, particularly close listening and a focus on the emotional quality of the therapist-patient relationship, but forced acceptance of a particular theory no longer forms the core of therapeutic training.

The Department of Psychiatry and Behavioral Sciences at Johns Hopkins has been particularly systematic and influential in working out and building on the implications of Frank's findings for psychiatrists, psychologists, social workers, and, to some extent, medical generalists. This process has led to new ways of assessing patients' difficulties and of training practitioners to address them, both in structured psychotherapy and while conducting other forms of treatment.

As Frank acknowledged, all therapy must be guided by some theory of cause and cure. Such theory inevitably guides initial assessment. Training at Johns Hopkins, after Frank, begins with the recognition that therapists should "start where the patient is" and acquire a full knowledge of the individual's history and mental state. This puts them in the best position to help patients find better ways to cope and so recover their capacity for mastering life's inevitable challenges. What counts most is the individual rather than the common elements in patients' life stories. Much of recovery depends on patients' capacity to take responsibility for their actions, cultivate the assets they have, and, with coaching, recover from or replace the habits that have engendered emotional distress and provoked the grim experiences of demoralization and hopelessness. By giving full legitimacy to therapeutic transparency and the importance of the conscious rather than the unconscious mind in creating patients' difficulties, Frank also facilitated the development of manual-driven psychotherapy protocols, in particular the cognitive behavioral therapies first proposed by Aaron Beck (Beck et al. 1979), interpersonal psychotherapy developed by Gerald Klerman and Myrna Weissman (Weissman and Markowitz 2000), and an ever-widening array of methods for addressing psychological trauma (Foa, Hembree, and Rothbaum 2007), grief (Shear et al. 2005), behavioral disorders such as maladaptive eating (Agras and Apple 2007), and so on. Research using these manualized protocols has confirmed the validity of Frank's discoveries and conceptions. As a secondary consequence, many who have anxiety, depression, or disordered behavior treat themselves using manuals adapted into self-help resources (books, support organizations, and, most recently, online materials). The outcome of such treatment is difficult to measure, but the profitability and growth of the self-help sector suggest the benefits are substantial.

Johns Hopkins was particularly open to Frank's ideas, for many reasons. Adolf Meyer, who taught Frank in his first year of residency, began the Hopkins tradition of psychiatry when he described the critical role of a comprehensive life history in the care of psychiatric patients. Meyer advocated passionately for seeing the patient as a whole person, not as merely a list of conditions and symptoms. He spoke, for example, against calling patients "schizophrenics" and taught his students to see them instead as people suffering from schizophrenia. He anticipated the utilitarian murder of mentally ill people in Nazi Germany when he warned that to see people as "schizophrenics" would ultimately lead to their elimination. Frank, who had studied in Germany in 1931–32, was deeply influenced by Meyer's strictures against dehumanizing those who were different or difficult to understand. He further developed this point in his work on the psychology of war and peace (Frank 1967). It was also a central tenet of his psychotherapy research. Frank taught our field to look at the whole patient and to consider the assets patients have to help them overcome their demoralization. Like Meyer, he emphasized the whole patient and saw people as a product of the life they had experienced.

Restoring Assessment in the Era of DSM Diagnosis

Contemporary approaches to understanding psychopathology offer new challenges to the humanistic approach to patients for which Johns Hopkins psychiatry, as the guardian of Meyer's and Frank's legacy, has long been known. The so-called atheoretical scheme of psychiatric classification of the most recent versions of the *Diagnostic and Statistical Manual of Mental Disorders* (DSM-III, -IV, and -IV-R) has imposed a new, forced consensus on our field, achieving a degree of dominance that the most passionate proponents of psychoanalysis never envisioned. The process of developing the third edition of the DSM was an effort to identify agreement among psychiatrists who had been divided into schools of thought—psychodynamic, behaviorist, biological, and so on. The compilers asked all to forgo their theories and accept a descriptive classificatory scheme. In this way, American psychiatry proceeded "ad hoc" and found a kind of internal peace.

The DSM movement developed the empiric and neo-Kraepelinian view that psychiatric disorders can be conceptualized as a series of symptoms recorded on checklists that diagnose "biological" conditions. Its original purpose of bringing reliability to diagnosis has been partly achieved. Demonstrating once again how the problems of today often stem from the solutions of yesterday, the process of extending the DSM approach has led to the multiplication of diagnoses (ontologic incontinence) and the invention of disorders without foundations (fabulism). By failing to differentiate disorders by their underlying nature, the DSM falls far short of classificatory schemes in the rest of medicine. Although regularly espousing a commitment to brain science, psychiatrists now have a classificatory method long on disorders—there appear to be thousands—but short on explanation. It is particularly unhelpful for teaching therapists to assess the likelihood that a patient might benefit from psychotherapy.

Much as Frank contended with the fractious disagreements in the psychoanalytic community, Johns Hopkins has defended psychotherapy from the erosion produced by classification of "disorders" according to the debased research protocols of the DSM. Psychiatrists overly indoctrinated into the DSM method risk becoming prescription-writing machines who use diagnoses generated by checklists of symptoms and algorithms to determine the choice of drugs, leaving professionals from other disciplines to provide "talk therapy" in isolation.

What has this meant to those of us who inherited from Frank an unswerving commitment to the importance of retaining psychotherapy as a crucial skill within medicine and psychiatry and who value his understanding of the commonalities of patients seeking psychotherapeutic help? Our response has been the defense of psychotherapy rooted in case formulations based on diagnostic rubrics that restore the classification of psychiatric disorders by presumed etiology. We teach our students to be systematic in characterizing four interconnected domains from which disorders arise. Each domain stands on a solid foundation of basic research. What is unique about the Hopkins approach is its effort to synthesize information from disparate traditions in their application to individual cases. Historically, each had been championed as explaining all psychiatric conditions, only to be challenged and unseated by research from one of the other domains. In surveying this broad terrain, we recognized that some disorders seemed particularly well understood and researched from each of the perspectives, but each patient's history seemed to require explanation using elements from more than one, and usually all of them. Although no single perspective provides an adequate explanatory framework for all psychiatric disorders, each contributes a way to see how patients may have become overmastered. Recognizing the determinants of patients' demoralized states, in turn, allows for a case formulation that guides the selection of an effective psychotherapeutic approach from the array of available techniques. Such assessment returns psychotherapy to the domain of psychiatric treatment and overcomes the limiting nature of the DSM method.

The Perspectives of Psychiatry

The specific perspectives that guide this type of formulation are neurobiology (the Disease Perspective), goal-directed behaviors (Behavioral Perspective), dimensionally ranked basic dispositions (Dimensional Perspective), and the emergent property of self-reflection (Life Story or Narrative Perspective). Some mental disorders are the direct expression of pathological disruption of the structure or function of the brain—hence the term Disease Perspective. As a bodily organ, the brain is subject to myriad pathologies (vascular, infectious, neoplastic, etc.) along with some processes unique to itself. Psychiatrists note and treat the mental disorders that derive from problems with the mental faculties that the cerebrum sustains. A partial list of these faculties includes consciousness, cognition, memory, language, affect, and executive functions. Delirium, dementia, aphasia, amnestic syndrome, frontal lobe syndrome, bipolar disorder, and schizophrenia constitute a minimum list of the psychiatric disorders best viewed from the Disease Perspective. To the extent that these cause demoralizing handicaps, psychotherapy that fosters building resilience, capitalizing on preserved capacities and sustaining the morale of caregivers (Mace and Rabins 2006), plays an important role in overall treatment.

Emerging as a clear feature of experience and also tied to cerebral mechanisms are the regular and rhythmic alterations of mental life reflecting drive and motivation. Freud first drew attention to this as he identified how various forms of hunger and satiety wax and wane and thus sway the perceptual "attitude" of the subject toward the environment. This "attitude" expresses itself ultimately in such goal-directed behaviors as eating, sleeping, sexual activity, and so on (see chapters 3 and 4).

The interplay of need and fulfillment or frustration over time has been explored within the domain of behavioral psychology, which explains much current thought and activity as resulting from various types of conditioned learning. Drawing on this literature, the Behavioral Perspective, for psychiatrists, identifies disorders of choice and control, including the abuse and dependency syndromes of alcohol and other drugs, the sexual paraphilias, anorexia nervosa, bulimia nervosa, the various sleep disorders, and the so-called impulse-control disorders of kleptomania, pyromania, and pathologic gambling. In all these disorders, interactions among choice, physiological drive, and conditioned learning become aspects of explanation, as well as sites for therapeutic action directed toward reshaping maladaptive behaviors. Psychotherapeutic approaches within this domain include contingency management, group therapies, and direct advice on ways to avoid or interrupt conditioned responses.

Many psychiatric difficulties that generate demoralization depend, not on some disease of the brain or any misdirected drive, but on a patient's affective or cognitive constitution—latent features of vulnerability to distress that come to light under certain provocative circumstances. These constitutional features are graded characteristics universal in humans, including the dimensions of extraversion, neuroticism, and intelligence. As both the emergent characteristics of brain structure and function and the conditioned result of much life experience, these characteristics contribute to psychiatric disorders. Particularly problematic dispositions are suboptimal cognitive capacity (IQ less than 85) (see chapter 6) or an affective constitution that reflects high neuroticism, low conscientiousness, or immaturity. High "neuroticism" is the most frequent substrate for the strong emotional responses that bring patients to psychiatric attention. The Dimensional Perspective grapples with the typologies and categories of Axis II in DSM-III and DSM-IV—more successfully, we would claim, because of its emphasis on gradations along continua rather than invalid categorical distinctions (Oldham, Sokol, and Bender 2005).

The ultimate emergent psychological feature of the human brain is self-reflection, defined both as the sense of the self as the agent of one's life plans and as the reflexive subject experiencing the world, the culture, and the outcome of plans and commitments. How the material brain produces self-reflection that confers a sense of ownership and vitality on persons' choices and beliefs is a fundamental mystery embedded in the brain-mind problem. Though neuroscience cannot explain the self and the personal chronicle, psychotherapists will always be asked to help explain and treat distress emerging from within this domain.

Psychotherapists working with life stories aim to help patients forge a narrative that illuminates a troubled state of mind as the outcome of some disruption within the life history. Guided exploration of this history produces a revised, coherent narrative—setting, sequence, and outcome—that suggests some modifiable role of the self in its course and direction. Therapists turn to the life story to explain grief from losses, homesickness with acculturation, jealousy or hostility resulting from threats to valued relationships, and anxiety due to real or suspected threats to personal integrity.

The method of the "Perspectives" allows the psychotherapist to look at the deficits that generate the demoralization that patients experience, the temperaments and endowments that confound them, the behaviors that disrupt their ability to fulfill their potential, and the life experiences that shape their conceptions and circumstances. This allows the psychotherapy that Jerome Frank described and pioneered to fit seamlessly into psychiatry. Psychotherapy is intrinsic to the practice of psychiatry, and, as such, the teaching of psychotherapy must be integrated into all elements of psychiatric training.

Conclusion

Jerome Frank's diplomatic but tough-minded assault on the citadel of psychoanalysis restored a Meyerian focus on explicit life history as the appropriate target of psychotherapy. The Hopkins Perspectives of Psychiatry provide a systematic framework for the kind of humanistic assessment that both Meyer and Frank championed. As an alternative to the neo-Kraepelinian DSM approach to psychiatric patients, the perspectives bring psychotherapy from the periphery of psychiatric practice back to its historical place as a central element of both psychiatric practice and research.

REFERENCES

Agras, W. S., and Apple, R. 2007. *Overcoming Your Eating Disorder: A Cognitive Behavioral Approach for Bulimia Nervosa and Binge Eating Disorder*. New York: Oxford University Press.

Beck, A., Rush, A. J., Shaw, B. F., and Emery, G. 1979. *Cognitive Therapy of Depression*. New York: Guilford Press.

Brown, J. A. C. 1961. *Freud and the Post Freudians*. New York: Penguin.

Fish, S. 1986. Withholding the missing portion: power, meaning and persuasion in Freud's The Wolf-Man. *Times Literary Supplement*, August 29, pp. 935–38A.

Foa, E., Hembree, E. A., and Rothbaum, B. O. 2007. *Prolonged Exposure Therapy for PTSD: Therapist Guide*. New York: Oxford University Press.

Frank, J. 1967. *Sanity and Survival: Psychological Aspects of War and Peace*. New York: Random House.

Frank, J. D., and Frank, J. B. 1991. *Persuasion and Healing: A Comparative Study of Psychotherapy*, 3rd ed. Baltimore: Johns Hopkins University Press.

Greben, S. E. 1984. *Love's Labor: Twenty-five Years in the Practice of Psychotherapy*. New York: Pantheon, Schocken Books.

Grunbaum, A. 1984. *The Foundations of Psychoanalysis: A Philosophical Critique*. Berkeley: University of California Press.

Mace, N. L., and Rabins, P. V. 2006. *The Thirty-six Hour Day: A Family Guide to Caring for People with Alzheimer Disease, Other Dementias, and Memory Loss in Later Life*, 4th ed. Baltimore: Johns Hopkins University Press.

McHugh, P. R., and Slavney, P. R. 1998. *The Perspectives of Psychiatry*, 2nd ed. Baltimore: Johns Hopkins University Press.

Oldham, J. M., Sokol, A. E., and Bender, D.S. (eds.). 2005. *The American Psychiatric Publishing Textbook of Personality Disorders*. Washington, DC: American Psychiatric Publishing.

Rosenheck, R. 1978. Personal communication to J. B. Frank.

Shear, K., Frank, E., Houck, P. R., and Reynolds, C. F. 2005. Treatment of complicated grief: a randomized controlled trial. *JAMA: Journal of the American Medical Association* 293:2601–8.

Weissman, M. M., and Markowitz, J. C. 2000. *Comprehensive Guide to Interpersonal Psychotherapy*. New York: Basic Books.

CHAPTER 3

Neural Substrates of Psychotherapy

George I. Viamontes, M.D., Ph.D., and Bernard D. Beitman, M.D.

"How *can* you go on talking
so quietly, head downwards?"
Alice asked, as she dragged
him out by the feet, and laid
him in a heap on the bank.
  The Knight looked
surprised at the question.
"What does it matter where
my body happens to be?" he
said. "My mind goes on
working all the same. In fact,
the more head downwards I
am, the more I keep
inventing new things."
—*Through The Looking Glass*

High on the list of medical achievements in the twentieth
century is the increasing knowledge of the uniqueness of the
human animal. This knowledge includes, first of all, an understanding of the special qualities of the brain—not just as the
seat of consciousness, but as the control mechanism for bodily
functions and changes.

—NORMAN COUSINS, FOREWORD TO *PERSUASION AND*
HEALING, 1991, P. XI

A t the time *Persuasion and Healing* first appeared (1961), theories of psychotherapy emphasized the importance of human symbolic capacities—
especially language and the manipulation of cultural symbols—in structuring
or modifying inner experience and governing behavior. Psychiatrists and psychologists assumed that the brain was structurally static (or deteriorating).
Hope for any helpful change required a dualistic approach, postulating fundamental differences between mental and physical activity. As a treatment for
"mental illness," psychotherapy resembled the legendary cure in search of a
disease; conversely, brain disorders such as schizophrenia and melancholia remained diseases in search of a cure.

Jerome and Julia Frank's exploration of psychotherapeutic effectiveness partly
circumvented mind-body dualism (Frank and Frank 1991). *Persuasion and
Healing* linked psychology with neuroscience by emphasizing the importance
of emotional arousal in rendering established beliefs open to change and in
relating psychotherapy to placebos, which have measurable physical effects

(see chapter 1). The Franks also described the impact of psychotherapy on bodily processes, including surgical healing and survival or recovery from various diseases. Jerome Frank's insight that psychotherapy relieves demoralization, a psychobiological state, further supported the mind-body bridge he envisioned. More systematic reconciliation of the physical and psychological determinants of human experience, however, required a level of neuroscientific sophistication not available at the time.

New methods of directly investigating the brain-mind interface have prompted reexamination of how elements of psychotherapy both derive from and may modify brain activity. Since the Decade of the Brain (1990–2000), functional neuroimaging, genetic investigation, and advances in neurobiology have demonstrated that human subjective experience and behavior are more stereotypic and rigid than postulated in many theories of psychotherapy. At the same time, such research has demonstrated that human brains are far more plastic than classic neural science suggested.

As stated in *Persuasion and Healing*, much of the power of the psychotherapist derives from his or her ethos, an ability to inspire trust by acting as a conduit between the individual and some socially reinforced system of interpreting the world. In Western societies, science has long since eclipsed religion as the dominant principle organizing our understanding of phenomena. To retain a place among the healing arts, contemporary approaches to psychotherapy must align themselves with current models of the neural circuitry that constrains and structures behavior. Beyond linking psychotherapy to the most powerful interpretive paradigm of our age, such alignment offers hope for improving psychotherapeutic effectiveness by targeting areas in which experience and symbolic reasoning reshape brain activity. This chapter reviews our current understanding of these issues, offering a potentially new grammar for psychotherapy in the twenty-first century.

Neural Circuits and Behavior: What Psychotherapists Need to Know

The evolution of the human brain has been driven by the adaptive advantages of flexible behavior. The key to behavioral flexibility is the human ability to consider multiple variables before taking action. During human evolution, the neural networks that drive basic behavior in lower animals have not been

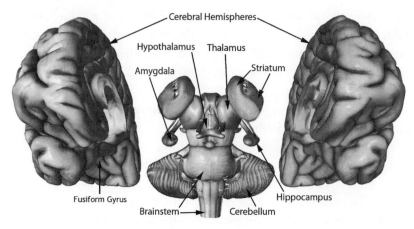

Figure 3.1. Exploded View of the Brain (*front to back*). Note the brain's core, with the thalamus in a central position above the brainstem. The striatum, of which the caudate nucleus (*upper arrow*) and putamen (*lower arrow*) are visible, overlies the thalamus in the intact brain. The nucleus accumbens and the globus pallidus (*not visible here*) are located on the internal surface of the striatum, facing the thalamus. Also visible are the hippocampus, amygdala, hypothalamus, and cerebellum. The fusiform gyrus, which functions in object and face recognition, is labeled on the lower surface of the right hemisphere.

phased out, merely overlaid with more complex and flexible circuits. In consequence, the highest human faculties are built around a basic core of reactive and relatively inflexible neural circuits. At times, the output of these primitive circuits emerges unchanged through the veneer of higher functions. Figure 3.1 shows an exploded view of the brain, including the brain's core and the cerebral hemispheres. The cerebral hemispheres, and in particular the prefrontal cortex (figure 3.2), evolved as an overlay around the brain's core to facilitate complex, flexible behavior.

Certain maladaptive emergences of fundamental behavior patterns encoded in neural circuitry are recognized as disorders, some of which fit loosely within current diagnostic categories. Neuroimaging, for example, has linked the negative symptoms of schizophrenia to diminished frontal lobe activity. The panic attacks seen in various anxiety disorders are the direct expression of stereotypic fear responses that humans share with other mammals. Other types of neurologically mediated maladaptation, such as the loss of motivation and the indecisiveness that characterize demoralization, await precise classification. Whether or not a particular method of psychotherapy aims to relieve a discrete

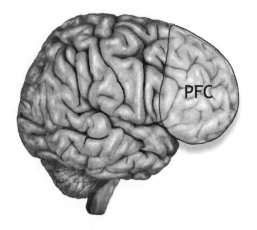

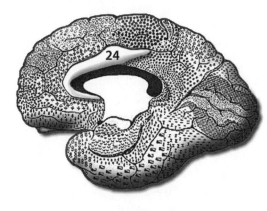

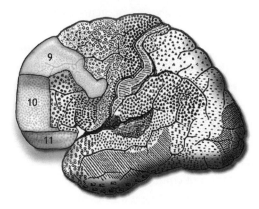

Figure 3.2. Schematic Views of the Brain's External and Medial Surfaces. *Top*, General location of the prefrontal cortex (PFC) on the brain's outer surface.

Middle, Brodmann area (BA) 24 on the brain's medial surface, which represents the anterior cingulate gyrus. This is the region that participates in the thalamocorticostriatal circuit described in the text. The black area below the cingulate is the corpus callosum, which is the main fiber tract that connects the cerebral hemispheres. The cingulate gyrus extends caudally as far as the corpus callosum. The area of the cingulate below the rostral end of the corpus callosum (which is called the genu, or "knee," of the corpus callosum) is referred to as the subgenual cingulate.

Bottom, External view of the brain showing BAs 9, 10, and 11. BA 9, together with the upper portion of BA 10, participates in the dorsolateral prefrontal circuit, and BA 11 and the lower portion of BA 10 participate in the lateral orbitofrontal circuit; both circuits are described in the text.

syndrome or improve unclassified distress, all psychotherapies succeed in part by restoring degrees of flexibility, building on capacities rooted in the most recently evolved parts of our nervous systems.

Developmentally, children often behave in ways that are impulsive, inflexible, and driven by the here and now. As children mature, they develop inhibitory overlays that enable more flexible, future-oriented, and socially acceptable behavior. In adults, persistent or overwhelming stress, intense emotional states, and strong responses to environmental cues may cause core circuits to override normal inhibition. Environmental cues may be physical, psychological, or both. Drugs of abuse, for example, overstimulate fundamental reward systems and trigger rapid learning. Eventually, drug cues acquire the power to preferentially drive the brain's motivational circuits, generating the stereotypic, inflexible behaviors that we recognize as addiction.

The evolutionary history of brain development further suggests that the brain's core of simple, inflexible behavioral circuits has significant adaptive value, given that it has been retained even in the most advanced brains. From a biological perspective, it is not always advantageous to consider large numbers of options before initiating behavior: many real-life situations require rapid action. In this arena, core circuitry, which can trigger fast reactions to perceived threats, excels. Relaxing the normal inhibitions on core circuitry can be adaptive in dangerous situations because it leads to simpler behavior and improved reaction speed. Conversely, neural adaptations that involve increased reliance on core circuits may become maladaptive if they persist beyond the end of the stressful conditions, as in posttraumatic stress disorder (PTSD).

The ability to function flexibly within complex environments, including social settings, requires the action of inhibitory elements that can postpone the intense motivational drives induced by core circuits, thus providing additional time for the evaluation of potential threats and opportunities. Such inhibitory elements permit the pursuit of reward in a manner consistent with contextual considerations, learned rules, and a vision of the future. Often, the motivational elements of appetitive networks and higher circuits lead in opposite directions, generating emotions and bodily sensations that signal the conflict. The manner in which such conflicts are represented is an important determinant of psychopathology. The resolution of conflicts between impulse and its inhibition is essential to many forms of psychotherapy, including psychoanalysis, therapy that focuses on interpersonal distress, and therapy that changes cognitive interpretations of experience.

Basic and Inhibitory Circuitry: A More Detailed View

The higher circuits that determine human behavior depend on the activity of the prefrontal cortex, the region of the brain located, based on external landmarks, roughly behind the forehead and between the temples. Internally, this area is found directly in front of the premotor and motor strips, with its rostral portion overlying the orbits (figure 3.2).* The prefrontal cortex contains 30 percent of the human neocortex, although not all of the prefrontal cortex is neocortex. The neocortex is far more developed and proportionally much larger in humans than in other species. Its activity facilitates transcendence of simple reward-driven behavior, allowing the person to consider internal and external circumstances, memory, applicable rules, and projected consequences.

Functional and anatomical studies demonstrate three distinct circuits that connect areas of the prefrontal cortex with the basal ganglia and thalamus, each with a specific behavioral function. (The oculomotor circuit, a fourth prefrontal network that controls automatic eye movements, is not discussed here.) Each circuit is named for a particular prefrontal area, based on its relative position or shape (figure 3.3). These are: the dorsolateral prefrontal cortex (DLPFC), which lies on the outer surface of the brain; the orbitofrontal cortex (OFC), which comprises the lateral, medial, and ventral surfaces of the brain immediately above the eyes; and the cingulate gyrus, a midline structure that lies inside the brain's central fissure immediately above the corpus callosum. Figure 3.4 shows the relative positions of these and other important areas. All the prefrontal circuits have nodes in older brain structures: the thalamus, cortex, basal ganglia, and globus pallidus–substantia nigra pars reticulata (Burruss et al. 2000; Mega and Cummings 2001). These three circuits are somatotopically mapped, which means that numerous "channels" that carry streams

* In addition to consulting Viamontes, *An Atlas of Neurobiology* (2011), readers who wish to further visualize the structures mentioned in this chapter may find "Salamon's Neuroanatomy and Neurovasculature Web-Atlas Resource" (Bank et al. 2010) particularly useful. To search for a particular structure, it helps to remember that regions of the brain may be named by their shape or relative position, or occasionally by the name of the person who first described them. The anatomical landmarks visible on the brain have also been assigned Brodmann numbers that do not directly correspond to the structures named by earlier researchers or to those recognized as having discrete functions. In consequence, the same brain region or circuit may be referred to by any one of several names or by number(s). To add to this complexity, contemporary research has found that many disparate areas are functionally linked and may serve multiple purposes. Neuroanatomical terminology can be confusing, but knowing the precise location of the nodes of any given network is not necessary for understanding how that network is activated by particular processes or modified by experience, as this chapter describes.

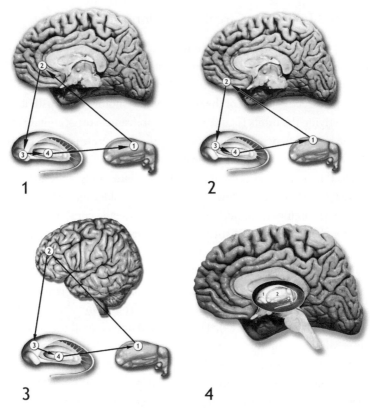

1   2

3   4

Figure 3.3. Circuits Linking Older and More Recently Evolved Areas of the Human Brain **1.** The *anterior cingulate circuit*, with nodes in (1) the dorsomedial nucleus of the thalamus; (2) BA 24 of the anterior cingulate gyrus; (3) the ventromedial caudate, ventral putamen, nucleus accumbens, and olfactory tubercle; and (4) the ventral globus pallidus, or ventral pallidum. **2.** The *medial orbitofrontal circuit*, with nodes in (1) the ventral anterior and dorsomedial nuclei of the thalamus; (2) BA 11 of the medial orbitofrontal cortex; (3) the ventromedial caudate; and (4) the internal globus pallidus and substantia nigra pars reticulata. *Note:* The *lateral orbitofrontal circuit* is as above, except that node 2 would be BA 11 and inferomedial BA 10 of the lateral orbitofrontal cortex. **3.** The *dorsolateral prefrontal circuit*, with nodes in (1) the ventral anterior and dorsomedial nuclei of the thalamus; (2) BA 9 and dorsolateral BA 10; (3) the dorsolateral caudate; and (4) the internal globus pallidus and substantia nigra pars reticulata. **4.** Medial view of the brain with cutout, showing the location of the basal ganglia (1) and thalamus (2).

of information related to specific body regions can be identified within each circuit component. These information streams are segregated from one another and can be modulated independently (Mega and Cummings 2001).

All three prefrontal circuits are able to modulate the flow of information from thalamus to cortex. The thalamus (figures 3.1, 3.4) relays all afferent sensory information to the cortex except for olfactory signals. In addition, some of the thalamic nuclei (such as the pulvinar, which relays visual signals) serve to move partially processed signals from one part of the cortex to another. Thalamic circuitry is tonically inhibited by the globus pallidus, which is an output nucleus of the basal ganglia (Mega and Cummings 2001) (figure 3.3). This inhibition limits the amount of incoming information that the cortex

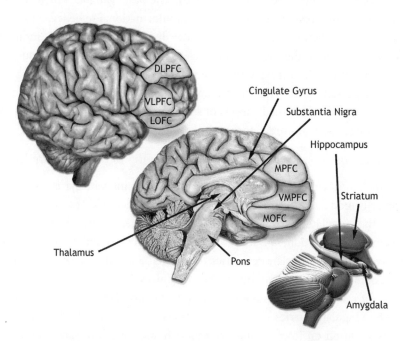

Figure 3.4. Schematic View of a Variety of Important Brain Regions. These regions include (*from left to right*) the dorsolateral prefrontal cortex (DLPFC), the ventrolateral prefrontal cortex (VLPFC), the lateral orbitofrontal cortex (LOFC), the cingulate gyrus, the substantia nigra, and the thalamus. Note that the cingulate gyrus wraps around both ends of the corpus callosum (not labeled or highlighted), and the anterior cingulate is a part of the medial prefrontal cortex (MPFC) and the ventromedial prefrontal cortex (VMPFC). Also note the medial orbitofrontal cortex (MOFC), the hippocampus, striatum, and amygdala.

receives. The inhibition of selected channels can be attenuated through the action of the basal ganglia, which can suppress default pallidal inhibition. Self-excitatory loops that sustain representations of interest in the brain can therefore be activated selectively. Because of their unique components, these circuits are given the general name of thalamocorticostriatal circuits.

We have hypothesized that the presence of both expanded and compressed information within the same neural circuits affords enhanced opportunities for data processing. Since areas that contain compressed information are relatively small and bring individual data channels close together, their physical layout facilitates the linking of information streams to form action or cognitive sequences and simplifies the selective amplification of specific information channels (Viamontes and Beitman 2006b). The basal ganglia, which contain segregated, compressed versions of cortical information, are believed to serve these special functions in the circuits under discussion. Additional "indirect" loops pass through the subthalamic nucleus and external globus pallidus and complement the circuitry described above (Mega and Cummings 2001).

Table 3.1 summarizes the three main behavioral circuits that link the prefrontal cortex with defined subsets of subcortical components (Burruss et al. 2000; Mega and Cummings 2001).

Functions of the Cortical-Subcortical Circuitry of the Cingulate Gyrus

The thalamocorticostriatal circuit that contains the cingulate gyrus (figure 3.3) primarily modulates the motivation of goal-directed actions. At a more detailed level, the cingulate gyrus is heterogeneous, with specific processing modules for emotion, cognition, sensation, and movement. The cingulate influences the motivation of appropriate responses to internal and external stimuli. It promotes emotional-cognitive integration, organizes "attention for action," prepares for motor activity, and monitors conflict (Bush, Luu, and Posner 2000).

The cingulate carries out these functions by triggering body states that focus attention on internal and external demands and motivate appropriate behavior. It generates emotional motivation through its projections to autonomic, visceromotor, and endocrine systems (Critchley et al. 2003). In its reciprocal connections with the nucleus accumbens, the cingulate also participates in reward circuitry. In integrating thought and emotion, the cingulate receives cognitive data from the DLPFC (Barbas et al. 2003) and coordinates the elements of emotional states (Critchley et al. 2003) appropriate to cognitive content. In reciprocal fashion, cingulate circuitry conveys information about

Table 3.1.   Cortical-Subcortical Circuitry and Functions

	Anterior Cingulate Circuit	Orbitofrontal Circuits	Dorsolateral Prefrontal Circuit
Cortical area	Brodmann area 24	Brodmann areas 10 and 11	Brodmann areas 9 and 10
Subcortical nodes	Dorsal medial thalamic nucleus Caudate, putamen, globus pallidus, nucleus accumbens, olfactory tubercle	Thalamus (ventral anterior and dorsomedial nuclei) Caudate, globus pallidus, substantia nigra, pars reticulata	Thalamus (ventral and dorsal medial nuclei) Caudate, globus pallidus, substantia nigra, pars reticulata
Functions	Attention for action, motor preparation, conflict monitoring, reward circuitry	Consideration of risk and consequences of actions	Executive functions: organization, problem solving, working memory, self-direction, processing novelty, use of language to guide behavior

Note: The nodes of the anterior cingulate circuit are the dorsal medial nucleus of the thalamus, Brodmann area 24 and adjacent cortical areas, structures within the basal ganglia (ventromedial caudate, ventral putamen), nucleus accumbens, and olfactory tubercle. The orbitofrontal circuit connects the ventral anterior and dorsomedial nuclei of the thalamus, Brodmann area 10 and inferomedial Brodmann area 10, the ventromedial caudate, the dorsomedial globus pallidus, and substantia nigra pars reticulata. The dorsolateral circuit comprises the ventral anterior and dorsomedial nuclei of the thalamus, Brodmann area 9 and dorsolateral Brodmann area 10, the dorsolateral caudate, the dorsomedial globus pallidus, and substantia nigra.

the body's emotional state to the DLPFC, which processes the information cognitively.

Much of what we know about the functioning of these cortical-subcortical circuits comes from lesion studies and studies of psychopathology. Damage to the cingulate gyrus can result in a state of apathy in which responses to internal and external stimuli are significantly diminished (Mega and Cummings 2001). Cingulate gyrus–nucleus accumbens circuitry figures prominently in addictive states. The cingulate gyrus also generates the autonomic tone necessary to support many types of movement, and it signals behavioral conflicts by increasing arousal and autonomic tone (Critchley et al. 2003). To summarize, the cingulate modulates arousal, motivation, autonomic tone, and attentional focus. Through such modulation, it can drive behavioral responses to salient internal or external stimuli (Bush, Luu, and Posner 2000).

The cingulate's ability to raise autonomic tone to signal conflict and its strong connections to both cognitive (DLPFC) and emotional centers are consistent with the hypothesis that it may be one of the neural targets of psychotherapeutic techniques that arouse emotion. The emotional arousal that occurs in many types of psychotherapy is believed to be crucial to outcome. While *Persuasion and Healing* offered research findings and observational data in support of the importance of emotional arousal, modern neuroscience has tentatively identified some of the neural circuits that might be active when an intense emotional state precipitates a shift in previously held beliefs during psychotherapy.

Functions of the Cortical-Subcortical Circuitry of the Orbitofrontal Cortex

The functions of the prefrontal circuits are generally complementary and combine to generate complete behavioral sequences. The lateral OFC and its associated circuitry modulate the pursuit of reward by adding considerations of risk, context, and potential consequences to the behavioral equation. The medial OFC (figure 3.3) connects reciprocally to the amygdala. The two act in concert to generate emotional states relevant to the pursuit of reward and avoidance of risk. Both OFC and amygdala receive rich inputs from multiple sensory cortices. They organize such input into a comprehensive view of external and internal milieus. Visual, auditory, and somatosensory information each reach a dedicated, unimodal area of the cortex (vision, occipital cortex; hearing, temporal cortex; somatosensory information, parietal cortex). Simultaneously, the OFC-amygdalar circuit receives input from areas that blend information from several different sensory channels. Information that reaches the prefrontal cortex can therefore convey recognition of a whole object or a multidimensional appreciation of the environment. Amygdalar projections to those areas of the OFC that receive direct sensory input are thought to allow the rapid extraction of the emotional significance of sensory events (Barbas et al. 2003). At a football game, for example, if we see a player on our favorite team making a leaping catch in the end zone, we experience instant excitement and pleasurable emotion as we rise automatically to cheer with those around us. We do not simply see a moving ball intersect the path of a moving person, then hear the crowd roar, then feel happy and excited in fragmented or dyssynchronous ways.

Both the amygdala and the OFC ignore neutral sensory inputs that lack implications of risk or reward. They also stop responding to any inputs that lose motivational value. As the work of Barbas et al. (2003) in nonhuman primates shows, the amygdala and OFC together modulate the autonomic nuclei of the hypothalamus, which in turn control the autonomic nervous system. This modulation can be either stimulatory or inhibitory, facilitating either the generation or the suppression of emotional states.

The circuits that include the lateral and medial OFC are functionally distinct. Together they induce anticipatory body states that promote reward seeking, as well as aversive body states that reduce the likelihood of risky actions (Mega and Cummings 2001). The aversive states are believed to be centered primarily in the lateral areas of the OFC. These inhibitory functions most likely evolved to prevent injury in the pursuit of reward, to facilitate behavioral restraint by animals at lower levels of the social hierarchy, to promote the preferential pursuit of low-risk rather than high-risk rewards that are consistent with internal needs, and to inhibit pursuit of contextually inappropriate rewards, such as seeking food when sated. The medial orbitofrontal circuit (figure 3.3) modulates mood and neurovegetative functions. Humans with damage to the OFC usually demonstrate personality changes that include high impulsivity, social inappropriateness, explosive behavior, disregard for rules and consequences, and an inability to inhibit risky behavior in the face of aversive emotions (Mega and Cummings 2001).

Connecting behavioral pathology to disordered brain activity does not preclude the use of psychotherapy to promote adaptive change. A structurally sound but underfunctioning orbitofrontal circuit may be the brain area that responds to psychotherapeutic approaches that attempt to shape behavior through reward and punishment. In a psychotherapeutic context, reward can include the gratification of having a therapist's empathic attention. Punishment can include both the negative reinforcement provided in some behavioral therapies and the deflection of the therapist's attention and endorsement in more "psychodynamic" ones.

Functions of the Cortical-Subcortical Circuitry of the Dorsolateral Prefrontal Cortex

The dorsolateral prefrontal cortex modulates executive functions. These include organization, problem solving, working memory and memory retrieval, self-direction, the ability to process novelty, and the use of language to guide behavior (Mega and Cummings 2001). The DLPFC, like the OFC, receives sensory inputs, primarily from visual, auditory, and somatosensory cortices. Sensory information is less integrated in the DLPFC than in the OFC, possibly enabling more detailed analysis of specific stimuli (Barbas et al. 2003). Verbal psychotherapeutic interventions must exert their influence through the DLPFC, since this area is essential for advanced reasoning and for modulating experience through words. At the end of this chapter, we provide evidence supporting this speculation.

Individuals who have damage to the DLPFC have difficulty organizing behavior to meet internal or external demands. They perseverate in their thought and speech, their decision making is impaired, and they show a strong tendency to be drawn toward objects and situations with high salience, even if the interaction is contextually inappropriate. They have significant difficulty with problem solving and are unable to analyze novel information (Mega and Cummings 2001).

Sigmund Freud (1960) defined the concepts of ego, superego, and id to address three functional modalities whose interplay, in his estimation, was a central driver of human behavior. While Freud's theoretical constructs cannot be mapped precisely onto the topography of the brain as we now understand it, it is not difficult to identify the circuits whose functions inspired his basic conceptualizations. The constant tension between unconscious appetitive urges and executive control, which is central to Freud's vision, has definable neural origins (table 3.2).

The circuitry associated with the DLPFC, as described above, subserves many attributes of the ego. It facilitates problem solving, decision making, and the integration of perceptual information (Burruss et al. 2000; Mega and Cummings 2001). Imaging studies have also implicated the DLPFC, possibly in conjunction with the cingulate gyrus, as a key element in the suppression of unwanted memories (Anderson et al. 2004).

Many manifestations of Freud's id are analogous to the functions of cingulate gyrus–nucleus accumbens circuitry. This circuit amplifies signals that suggest the attainability of reward and generates body states that motivate pursuit of potential pleasure. In the presence of remembered cues, this circuit can generate overwhelming motivational pressure to engage in reward-producing behavior, as in chemical dependence. In advanced chemical dependence, the simple perception of drug-related cues is sufficient to trigger intense desire for the drug and to motivate automatic behaviors through nucleus accumbens circuitry that initiate drug pursuit (LaLumiere and Kalivas 2008). Nucleus ac-

Table 3.2.   Neural Version of Freud's Vision of the Brain

	Ego	Id	Superego
Functions	Executive functions, integration of sensory information, problem solving, decision making, suppression of memory	Motivational pressure to attain reward	Modifying pursuit of pleasure with considerations of reward and danger
Circuit	Dorsolateral prefrontal	Cingulate gyrus–nucleus accumbens	Orbitofrontal–amygdalar (especially lateral)

cumbens circuits therefore drive the pleasure-driven, cognitively dissonant behaviors that Freudian formulations attribute to the id.

Orbitofrontal circuitry embodies many of the functions of the superego. The medial OFC and amygdala detect the presence of both potential reward and danger. In addition, the lateral OFC normally tempers the pursuit of pleasure with considerations of context and risk. Orbitofrontal-amygdalar circuits are directly wired to autonomic centers and can produce body states conducive to disengagement and withdrawal. The actions of orbitofrontal circuitry can set limits on risk taking and normally convey the visceral feelings of potential punishment or embarrassment (Mega and Cummings 2001).

Much of the apparent conflict between emotion and cognition in the determination of behavior results from parallel processing. Cognitive and emotional centers process information both simultaneously and sequentially. Initial emotional processing is usually completed before full cognitive evaluation. An emotionally charged stimulus, therefore, may engender a body state that motivates approach or withdrawal, followed by a cognitive assessment that dictates the opposite. Harmonious integration of cognition and emotion is not always possible, even in common social and occupational situations. The imbalance is even greater when psychopathological processes have altered the relative strength of emotional and cognitive circuits.

The prefrontal circuits described above, which support adaptive behavior by making it possible to consider many variables before responding to a stimulus, are important targets for the psychotherapist. Many psychotherapies enlist dorsolateral prefrontal circuitry, which facilitates the use of words to shape behavior. One of the most common conditions for which people seek psychotherapy is emotional dysregulation, related to the activity of circuits connecting the OFC, the cingulate gyrus, the amygdala, and the autonomic nuclei of the hypothalamus. Imaging studies have shown that orbitofrontal and amygdalar circuits can be modulated through conscious cognitive processes, such as the ones that characterize psychotherapeutic interactions (Ochsner et al. 2002).

Understanding brain circuitry can help to refine the therapist's understanding of the possible scope and potential limitations of psychotherapy for a given person. For example, the thalamocorticostriatal circuit through the OFC, in concert with the amygdala, tempers the unbridled pursuit of reward or of objects with perceived positive salience. Someone in whom this circuit is completely nonfunctional would show impulsivity, social inappropriateness, lack of empathy, disrespect for social conventions, and lack of response to the threat of personal risk, embarrassment, or punishment, qualities notably unresponsive to psychotherapy of any kind.

Alternatives to Ego, Id, Superego: The Neurobiology of the Unconscious as a Target of Psychotherapy

Fear, Rage, Homeostatic Functions, and Impulsive Action: Unconscious Levels 1–4

Many of the most basic adaptive functions do not require conscious deliberation and, in fact, would be hindered by extended processing. Information about these functions flows into the brain and elicits responses, but never directly reaches consciousness. These informational streams and the reactions they trigger form the core of what is known as the unconscious. Neurobiological research has begun to map unconscious processes onto neural circuits. We have proposed a provisional, five-tiered classification for unconscious processes (Viamontes and Beitman 2007). Level 1 processes organize homeostatic functions, automatic actions, and stereotypic behaviors. Level 2 processes modulate the intensity of engagement with the environment and its objects. Level 3 processes govern interactions with primary rewards and punishers, whose parameters are encoded in the genes. Level 4 processes define unconscious reactions to secondary rewards and punishers, which have been learned. Level 5 processes, discussed below, control automatic reactions to the appearance, movement, verbal outputs, and facial expressions of other persons. (See also chapter 4.)

Level 1 unconscious processes take place within the brainstem, basal fore-brain, and hypothalamus (Parvizi and Damasio 2001). Most of the body's ho-meostatic processes are unconscious: homeostasis can thus be accomplished rapidly and accurately, without taxing the resources devoted to conscious en-deavors. The brainstem, basal forebrain, and hypothalamus also trigger several body states that shape psychopathology and may be influenced by treatment. The outputs of these regions have a significant impact on the actions of the well-known hypothalamic-pituitary-adrenal axis. They control such critical functions as heart rate, respiration, arousal, and autonomic tone. The func-tional pathways that coordinate the main outputs of level 1 unconscious pro-cesses are, in turn, modulated by a variety of other circuits potentially modifi-able by psychotherapy: the amygdala, the OFC, the ventromedial prefrontal cortex, and the subgenual cingulate (Barbas et al. 2003). Inappropriate activa-tion of level 1 pathways can cause pathological states of anxiety, anger, and fear.

Level 2 processes control the intensity of environmental interactions. Their functions range from balancing the output of arousal and sleep centers in the brainstem to modulating the state of serotonin, norepinephrine, acetylcholine, and dopamine receptors and their corresponding neurotransmitters through-out the brain. Psychotropic medications act directly on some level 2 processes.

Level 3 unconscious processes organize reactions to primary, or genetically encoded, rewards and punishers. The major nodes in the network that medi-ates these responses are the amygdala and the OFC (Rolls 2005). Both regions receive rich sensory inputs, share numerous reciprocal connections, and jointly modulate autonomic centers in the hypothalamus (Barbas et al. 2003).These areas act as couplers that tie recognition of a primary reinforcer to the somatic state genetically preprogrammed as a response. Primary reinforcers are limited to certain tastes and smells, pleasant touch, and, possibly, selected visual stim-uli such as smiling human faces (Rolls 2005). Human babies, for example, like sweet tastes from birth and do not have to learn this response (Berridge and Winkielman 2003). Primary punishers that are genetically prewired include unpleasant tastes and odors, painful somatosensory stimuli, and possibly loud noises and angry or frightened human faces. The basic states that are induced in encounters with primary rewards and punishers are the foundation of all complex emotions (Rolls 2005).

Understanding neurobiology allows the psychotherapist to refine emotional distinctions and help patients accurately label emotional states. Goldstein (2006), for example, provides data that discriminate between the overlapping body states of fear and anger. He has shown that the trembling from fear results from uncoordinated muscular contractions, whereas the trembling associated with anger reflects purposeful muscle tension. Humans display pallor with fear but redden with anger. Pallor results from contraction of smooth muscle cells in skin blood vessels, mediated by adrenaline. The release of acetylcholine and possibly nitrous oxide presumably triggers flushing from vascular dilation. Loss of bowel and bladder control further differentiates intense fear from rage. These fear-specific symptoms are mediated by parasympathetic activation of the gastrointestinal tract in combination with the effects of adrenaline on the gastrointestinal tract and sphincter muscles. Salivary secretion, another manifestation of parasympathetic activity, is increased in anger and reduced in fear. In sum, the ratio of adrenaline to norepinephrine varies between fear and anger. Individuals in fearful states, such as those with flight phobias who are forced to board a plane, show markedly increased levels of adrenaline, but not of norepinephrine. In contrast, aggressive, emotional displays (measured in professional hockey players) involve increases in norepinephrine, but not in adrenaline (Goldstein 2006).

Anger and fear involve different patterns of cortical as well as neurochemical activity. Damasio and coworkers (2000) studied individuals who generated emotions on command by imagining emotional situations. The researchers found that anger activated the midbrain and pons, as well as the anterior half of the left cingulate gyrus. In contrast, in this experiment, remembered fear activated only the midbrain and right insula, possibly recalling the autonomic body state connected with the experience. Amygdalar activation occurs in fear reactions to specific objects, but is usually not found in remembered fear. Making precise distinctions between related emotional states and recognizing that mixed states are also common may help psychotherapists become more attuned to patients and enhance their ability to help patients recognize and label, and thereby modulate, their emotions. This understanding has already influenced the development of treatment for PTSD. In PTSD, remembered emotion remains tied to bodily arousal, a process implicating amygdalar activation out of context. Repeated verbal recounting of the arousing memory may attenuate this response, as seen in Edna Foa's prolonged exposure therapy (Foa, Hembree, and Rothbaum 2007).

The neural mechanisms for responding to learned reinforcers and punishers, or level 4 processes, have particular clinical importance. Many categories of psychopathology involve the person's learned, inappropriate responses to previously neutral stimuli. In addition to mediating responses to primary reinforcers, the amygdala and OFC can also mediate responses to simple objects that have become associated with intrinsic rewards or punishers. Humans, moreover, react not only to objects but also to verbal and cognitive content, even to imagined events. The hippocampus and associated structures are important in organizing responses to complex stimuli that require remembered information and transcend the simple perception of objects.

Bechara, Noel, and Crone (2006) hypothesize that the brain contains two main systems for responding to reinforcers in the environment: an impulsive system that generates somatic states in reaction to primary reinforcers, and a reflective system that generates similar states from secondary reinforcers. The impulsive system generates somatic states directly through amygdalar activation of autonomic centers in the hypothalamus and brainstem, whereas circuitry of the reflective system passes through the ventromedial prefrontal cortex (including the OFC and subgenual cingulate) to activate the same autonomic centers. The latter pathway is able to engage high-level cognitive circuits before it generates an output.

The ventromedial prefrontal cortex (figure 3.4) is an integrative area that can access memories of previous instances of simultaneous firing in sensory and limbic structures. If a sensory pattern is repeated, its remembered limbic correlate is triggered automatically to recreate the specific somatic state associated experientially with the perceived object (Bechara, Noel, and Crone 2006). Secondary reinforcers, therefore, are created during learning by attaching the somatic state pattern that normally accompanies a primary reinforcer to a previously neutral object.

In normal interactions with the environment, encounters with reinforcers induce parallel processing in rapidly responding, unconscious systems such as the amygdala, as well as in slower, more future-oriented areas such as the prefrontal cortex. The system that is amplified most intensely in any given situation will control behavior. Adaptive functioning in social settings demands attenuation of the impulsive tendencies that arise when perceived reinforcers are coupled with motivational body states and the tempering of these primitive impulses with considerations of the future. Impulse control is a complex process that involves, in part, comparing the somatic state generated by exposure to a reinforcer with a second somatic state generated by neural simulation of the contemplated action with respect to the reinforcer. Damasio (1999) and Bechara et al. (2006) call this internal simulation an "as-if-body-loop." The tempering of initial impulses by the simulation of as-if-body-loops is essential for social organization and also inhibits the pursuit of potential rewards associated with high risk.

Bechara and colleagues (2006) further refine the definition of impulse control by distinguishing between motor impulse control, in which impulsive movements are inhibited, and perceptual impulse control, which permits contextually appropriate shifts in attention. Both these processes may be brought partly under conscious control. Cognitive behavioral therapy capitalizes on this capacity, teaching patients to inhibit behavior by consciously shifting their attention. If unconsciously generated impulses are successfully inhibited, decision making with consideration of many variables, including future consequences, takes place in the anterior regions of the ventromedial prefrontal cortex, within the frontal pole and Brodmann area (BA) 10.

Level 5: Unconscious Circuitry of Social Function: The Neurobiology of Interaction

An understanding of level 5 unconscious processes, which mediate social functioning, is of critical importance for the psychotherapist. Living in social groups has been a highly adaptive strategy for the human species, and millions of years of natural selection have refined the tools necessary for success in the social realm.

Brothers (2002, p. 367) defined social cognition as "the processing of any information which culminates in the accurate perception of the dispositions and intentions of other individuals." Social cognition has several components. Basic human facial expressions and the ability to interpret them are genetically encoded and need not be learned. Babies smile and frown and respond to smiles and frowns long before they learn cognitively what these expressions mean. Building on preprogrammed recognition networks, humans begin to determine meaning by modeling the actions of others in their own brains. As maturation progresses, the ability to reason abstractly allows humans to make "theory of mind" interpretations (mentalization), in which an observer attempts to guess the mental contents of another person.

Adolphs and colleagues (2000) reviewed the basic processing sequence involved in social cognition; the following account is based on that review. The structural processing of faces appears to be accomplished in the fusiform gyrus (see figure 3.1) of the human extrastriate cortex (Kanwisher, McDermott, and Chun 1997). Activation of this area is essential for determining identity from facial features and for subsequently linking known faces with pertinent memories. One can speculate that this area functions abnormally in Capgras delusions, the belief that familiar persons have been replaced by impostors.

The amygdala, described above as a critical node in emotional response networks, seems to contain prewired programs for the recognition of negative facial emotions, especially fear (Davis and Whalen 2001). The OFC, which is richly connected with the amygdala, also plays a role in recognition of facial emotion and reacts to angry faces (Blair et al. 1999). Faces judged to be attractive activate the ventral striatum and OFC (Adolphs et al. 2000). Together, the amygdala, the OFC, and the ventral striatum are involved in the evaluation of facial expression and inference of the observed person's motivation. Such evaluation also generates autonomic responses and prepares the observer to react to the perceived emotions. Several cortical regions in the right hemisphere have also been implicated, through lesion studies, in the recognition of emotions (Adolphs et al. 2000).

Other brain circuits subserve the recognition of gestures, as well as inferences about other individuals' goal-directed behaviors and attributions about others' mental states. Interpreting gestures involves activation of the superior temporal sulcus (Saxe and Kanwisher 2002; Saxe et al. 2004). The ability to infer the meaning of another person's actions entails a fascinating process of modeling elements of the action in the observer's brain, measured as activation of mirror neurons. Such modeling involves mirror neuron areas in the frontal operculum (BA 44) and in the anterior part of the posterior parietal cortex. The cingulate gyrus, hippocampus, and basal forebrain modulate attention and engagement and facilitate the recruitment of associated memories. Finally, the ventromedial prefrontal cortex, including the OFC and anterior cingulate, is essential for making social and moral judgments and for generating appropriate somatic states (Adolphs et al. 2000).

Emotions are a necessary factor in the integration of conscious and unconscious processes. Edmund Rolls (2005) concisely and powerfully defines emotions as the body states that arise in response to perceived rewards and punishers. These states prepare the body to deal with a predicted type of event. Although emotions define a tendency toward an environmental object, they do not dictate specific behavior, other than initial stereotypic movements. Emotions thus improve adaptation by increasing the probability of certain types of response, leaving the specifics to systems that can integrate many elements of the context into the final response.

Over the course of evolution, emotions developed in parallel with consciousness. They serve to facilitate continued modulation of behavior by unconscious factors, even in the presence of advanced conscious processes. Flexible and open-ended behavior contributes to survival, but the paths prompted by emotion confer different evolutionary advantages by priming responses to environmental challenges. For example, if we feel afraid, we are watchful and cautious; if we feel angry, we are more aggressive; and if we feel sick or sad, we are less engaged with the environment.

Because both enhance survival, conscious and unconscious processes coexist, assessing information in parallel. The human social order is based on the preeminence of conscious circuits. In consequence, the emergence of unconsciously determined behaviors and emotional states may disrupt people's ability to work or maintain important relationships. Psychotherapy seeks to engage conscious circuits to modulate the effects of both conscious and unconscious representations on the generation of internal states and behavior. Psychopharmacology changes the molecular environment of the brain to promote the generation of adaptive body states and to optimize responses to environmental cues. This perspective justifies the combination of treatment modalities, in which psychotherapy influences the shape and direction of attitudes, while the scope and intensity of emotional and cognitive processes are optimized by psychopharmacological intervention.

Core Psychotherapeutic Processes and the Brain

Persuasion and Healing emphasizes the importance of the therapist-patient relationship. A long tradition identifies the core elements of a healing relationship as engagement (establishment of the working alliance), self-awareness, pattern search, change, termination, transference, countertransference, and resistance (Beitman and Yue 2004). The processes of engagement, self-awareness, self-observation, pattern search, and change, in particular, may be mapped onto brain circuitry in ways we describe below.

Engagement

The working alliance between therapist and patient correlates positively with psychotherapeutic outcome (Krupnick et al. 1996; Wampold 2001). At every meeting, therapist and patient infer each other's emotional state by observing facial expression, verbal output, and bodily demeanor. Work by Rizzolatti and colleagues in nonhuman primates (for a review, see Rizzolatti, Fogassi, and Gallese 2001) and by Iacoboni and coworkers (1999) in humans shows that transformation of observation to inference requires a critical neural processing step. As mentioned above, observations of another's bodily movements and emotional expressions must be represented in the observer's own brain (Rizzolatti, Fogassi, and Gallese 2001) before they can be understood. An array of mirror neurons in primates, consisting of a series of dedicated frontoparietal circuits, becomes activated when the actions and expressions of others are modeled internally, enabling one individual to attribute meaning to the actions of another. In neurological terms, *meaning* is defined operationally and subjectively. In other words, the meaning of objects and movements is defined by their functional significance to the individual. In the case of mirror neurons, the meaning of observed actions is encoded by the activation of some of the neurons that would normally fire in the observer's brain if he or she were preparing to perform the same action.

Human brains contain mirror neurons in the form of dedicated circuits between two specialized brain regions: the pars opercularis of the inferior frontal gyrus (within Broca's area) in the frontal lobe, and the anterior area of the posterior parietal cortex. Together with the superior temporal sulcus, this circuitry supports certain forms of motor imitation (Dapretto et al. 2006). The superior temporal sulcus provides a detailed visual description of the action to be imitated, the inferior parietal lobe defines its motoric components, and the pars opercularis defines its perceived goal. Beyond mirroring motor activity, these areas comprise a complex system for understanding the intentions and emotional experiences of others. The "meaning" of what is sensed both physically and emotionally when observing others is an amalgam of actual observations and their internal transformation.

Models of psychotherapy training, particularly those that involve trainees' engagement in personal therapy, may serve to strengthen the circuitry of the therapist's brain that models clinical observations of patients' expressions and actions and subsequently extracts their "meaning." The ability to be empathic may depend on the adequacy of the therapist's own limbic and cognitive circuitry, although the actual mechanisms by which mirror neuron systems support empathy remain speculative (Carr et al. 2003).

Consider, for example, the predicament of the therapist and the anxious patient. The patient's outward signs of anxiety—sweaty palms, quivering voice, and motor agitation—are the result of activation of the neural circuits between the amygdala and the OFC that detect risk and prepare the body to take appropriate action. These circuits also process genetically preprogrammed information about natural "punishers": sensory perceptions (e.g., bitter tastes or pain) that throughout human evolution have been connected with unpleasant outcomes. These connections further encode a unique record of the aversive experiences encountered in the patient's lifetime through synaptic linkages between previously neutral stimuli and some prior unpleasant experience. Idiosyncratic experience, in turn, recruits the genetically determined collection of natural "punishers" in each individual's biological repertoire (Rolls 2005).

Returning to the process of therapeutic engagement, the anxious patient instinctively senses that it will be difficult for the therapist to model internally the subjective components of his or her complex and uniquely determined unpleasant mental state. The cognitive uncertainties of the initial meeting with the therapist may further heighten unpleasant autonomic arousal. In working toward engagement, relieving cognitive tension through an exchange of verbal and emotional signals, the therapist demonstrates the ability to "understand," or internally model, the patient's situation, and the patient's initial arousal subsides. If engagement is successfully negotiated, the therapeutic process can proceed.

The process of associating the therapist with symptom reduction and positive emotions then may recruit reward circuits and other areas in the patient's brain that represent gratifying social interactions. For example, imaging studies have shown that internal representations of individuals perceived as "cooperative" in interactive situations activate the nucleus accumbens, which lies at the center of reward circuitry (reviewed in Viamontes and Beitman 2006b). Release of oxytocin also promotes the feeling of trust and enhances the person's ability to interpret the emotional signals of others more accurately (Domes et al. 2007).

Within the relative safety of an appropriately constructed psychotherapeutic relationship, patients can reflect on their problems and address maladaptive emotions and behaviors in new ways. In neurobiological terms, the circuits associated with negative emotions, social judgment, and "mentalizing" (Viamontes and Beitman 2006a) can be activated safely and their consequences explored. Experimental evidence suggests that secure attachment, as extrapolated from imaging studies of romantic love (Bartels and Zeki 2000) and mother-child affection (Bartels and Zeki 2004), is associated with reduction in amygdalar firing (lessening anxiety), increases in nucleus accumbens activity (possibly related to enhanced reward representations), and lessening of orbito-frontal firing (possibly reducing inhibitions). This implies that controlled activation of negative contents within a trusting relationship helps liberate the patient from past constraints, permitting the exploration of new conceptions of interpersonal relationships (Fonagy 2004). The common mechanism for such self-exploration is probably the activation of self-observation (Beitman and Soth 2006).

Self-Awareness and Self-Observation

Self-observation can produce knowledge about one's internal states, including intentions, expectations, feelings, thoughts, behaviors, and one's perceived effect on others. It can also enhance the capacity for introspection and anchor an individual's understanding of his or her relationship with the environment (Stuss and Benson 1983). Psychotherapy, and specifically the psychotherapeutic relationship, offers the opportunity to create and function within a "reflective space" that allows the patient to explore current maps of reality and alter them. The process of self-observation can be differentiated from consciousness, awareness, and self-awareness.

Consciousness, in the strictest neurological sense, refers simply to the waking state. This type of consciousness requires firing of the reticular activating system and the integrity of basic homeostatic processes such as breathing, cardiac function, and autonomic tone. It represents the "general capacity that an individual possesses for particular kinds of mental representations and subjective experiences" that are "not directed at anything" (Wheeler, Stuss, and Tulving 1997). One must be conscious in order to be aware, but consciousness without awareness is possible.

Awareness, the "particular manifestation or expression" that "always has an object," implies consciousness of content, such as a cloud, another person, or a painful experience (Wheeler, Stuss, and Tulving 1997). In *self*-awareness, the object is internal. The act of being self-aware is the review of subjective neural representations of body state, memories, and current perceptions (Beitman, Nair, and Viamontes 2005). Self-observation, in contrast, is an open-ended exploratory *process* that motivates the active scanning of one's inner world (Deikman 1982).

Self-observation implies a sustained focus on the totality of subjective reality, which includes representations of experiences in the past, present, and future (Wheeler, Stuss, and Tulving 1997) and of inferred representations of what others may think about the self. At least in cultures that value individualism, most psychotherapies foster and strengthen self-observation, helping the person marshal the resources of self-awareness to alter prediction errors (Beitman, Nair, and Viamontes 2005; Pally 2005) and modify expectations. This capability provides a sense of agency, an "I" who is observing, planning, deciding, and evolving toward the future.

The ability to observe the content of one's own mind depends on the healthy functioning of many parts of the brain. Activity within regions along the border between the rostral anterior cingulate and the medial prefrontal cortex is associated with representations of mental states of the self (Frith and Frith 1999) and is consistently activated during self-reflective thought (Johnson et al. 2002). The DLPFC apparently sits atop the functional pyramid of self-awareness, potentiating executive function and working memory (Wheeler, Stuss, and Tulving 1997) and integrating the full range of sensory, affective, and memory data.

The ability to generate a coherent, consistent self with temporal continuity depends on the power of the DLPFC to structure past time and expectations of the future (Wheeler, Stuss, and Tulving 1997). People with dorsolateral prefrontal damage typically lose the temporal sense of themselves, being unable to recall episodic representations of past experiences or to project themselves forward in time. The DLPFC and the right parietal lobe further define the person in space and time by placing the body in the three physical dimensions as well as in past, present, and future. Without this sense, the self erodes and merges with its environment. During meditation, right parietal lobe activity may decrease, stimulating voluntary dissolution of the sense of self in space and time (Newberg, d'Aquili, and Rause 2002). Other studies show that disturbances of the temporoparietal region can generate "out of body" experiences, in which an individual has the sensation of floating above the ground and observing his or her body below (Blanke and Arzy 2005). In a clinical context, the dysfunction of prefrontal circuits characteristic of schizophrenia is thought to explain the finding that many individuals with this condition lack awareness of their disorder (Flashman 2005).

In describing the therapeutic impact of emotionally arousing rituals, *Persuasion and Healing* draws therapists' attention to the healing potential of meditation and other induced disruptions of self-awareness and self-observation. As knowledge expands about the circuitry underlying self-observation, current interest in the study of mindful awareness as an element of psychotherapy may find itself on a more scientific footing.

Pattern Search and Change

A well-functioning human brain creates patterns from a huge array of sensory information to make sense of the environment in ways that optimize individual and species survival functions, including homeostasis, reproduction, and energy acquisition and conservation (Mesulam 1998; Viamontes et al. 2005). Most nonhuman animal brains, by contrast, develop inflexible bonds between sensation and action. The more flexible stimulus-response connections of human brains enable a wider range of alternative responses to specific environmental cues (Tanaka 2003). Brains with reduced cortical activity represent the world at a much coarser level of resolution, because they have less cortical capacity to devote to each aspect of represented reality. Chronic stress or illness may simplify human brain activity (Teicher et al. 2002), manifested in less regulated responses to sensory and emotional stimuli. While such simplification conserves energy and facilitates rapid responses, it can theoretically decrease the "richness" of experiences by limiting the amount of complexity that is represented.

The process of habituation involves the development of internal patterns that organize external stimuli, determine their "meaning," and respond to them. Humans are remarkably adept at inductive reasoning, the ability to infer complete patterns from perception of just a small number of their elements. We can recognize a song from a few notes, a person from a few spoken words, and a concept from a single phrase.

The psychotherapeutic process depends on both the inductive capacities of the therapist and the patient's ability to recognize and reshape his or her own patterns of thought. In ongoing assessment, psychotherapists inductively grasp the patterns that shape the patient's world, drawing inferences from nonverbal cues, key reported events, transference behaviors, and countertransference reactions (Beitman and Yue 2004). Therapists also expect to find certain patterns: past-present connections, narcissistic injury, hidden anger, cognitive distortions, role-relationship conflicts, and many others. Some clinicians even have a "favorite" diagnosis and identify a disproportionate number of their patients as fitting its characteristic constellation of symptoms.

Therapeutic change involves helping patients recognize the patterns that govern their thoughts and behaviors, allowing them to modify maladaptive stimulus-response connections. Patterns of thought shape views of the future as well as the present and past. Well-reinforced pathways in our brains create definitive expectations: if this happens, then that will follow. A remarkable corollary of these experiential encodings is that they may generate expectations from neutral circumstances. For example, the expectation of a person who believes that he or she will be rejected is inevitably fulfilled, in part because the expectation creates the circumstances for recognizing or interpreting experience as rejection however it occurs. Neural patterns of expectation may be more susceptible to therapeutic influence than those encoding prior experience. Early benefit in psychotherapy is related to the instillation of hope. Hope implies changes in a patient's expectations and, presumably, in the patterns of neurological activity that underlie them.

Functional Imaging and Psychotherapy

Functional neuroimaging studies providing information on the circuit-based changes in neural information processing that underlie the effects of psychotherapy are accumulating rapidly, although these studies are far from providing comprehensive models of psychotherapy's effects on the brain (Etkin et al. 2005; Roffman et al. 2005). A brief review of selected findings in this area illustrates the broader point that, no less than drug treatment, psychotherapy causes measurable changes in brain activity.

Roffman and coworkers (2005) extensively reviewed neuroimaging studies in psychotherapy. In one of the reviewed studies (Ochsner et al. 2002), subjects attempted to alter their mood through conscious cognitive intervention; these cognitive efforts generally resulted in noticeable mood improvement. The improvement was significantly correlated with increased metabolism in the DLPFC and dorsomedial prefrontal cortex, as well as with decreased activity in the amygdala and OFC.

Neuroimaging studies have examined many different therapeutic modalities. For example, Brody et al. (2001) compared interpersonal therapy with paroxetine treatment and found decreases in dorsal and ventral prefrontal activity in responders to interpersonal therapy. These findings were similar to those reported by Goldapple et al. (2004) with cognitive behavioral therapy (CBT). Brody's group also reported decreased prefrontal metabolism in responders to paroxetine.

Roffman and colleagues (2005) also reviewed functional imaging findings during behavioral therapy for obsessive-compulsive disorder. Patients whose symptoms responded to either psychotherapy or medication showed a reduction in caudate nucleus metabolism (especially on the right side). This independently replicated finding is consistent with the conceptualization of obsessive-compulsive disorder as a disorder of thalamocorticostriatal circuitry.

Neurobiological investigation can in some cases untangle the effects of different treatments. Goldapple et al. (2004), for example, compared the effects of CBT with paroxetine for depressed patients. In this study, responders to CBT showed significant increases in hippocampal and dorsal cingulate (BA 24) metabolism, as determined by positron emission tomography scanning. CBT responders also showed decreases in frontal cortex metabolism in dorsal (BA 9, 46), ventral (BA 47, 11), and medial (BA 9, 10, 11) regions. By contrast, responders to paroxetine showed increases in prefrontal metabolism and decreases in hippocampal and subgenual cingulate metabolism.

Roffman's group also reviewed studies of the treatment of phobia with CBT and medication. In one study (Furmark et al. 2002), individuals who had social phobia were asked to read a speech about a personal experience to a small audience. At baseline, symptomatic subjects exhibited activation of limbic regions, including the amygdala, hippocampus, and adjacent temporal cortex. After eight weeks of treatment with either CBT or citalopram, the baseline pattern of limbic activation was attenuated. CBT, but not citalopram, also resulted in decreased activation of the periaqueductal gray, an area connected to the ventral prefrontal cortex that mediates fear and defensive responses. Citalopram, but not CBT, also reduced metabolic activity in the thalamus and in the ventral prefrontal cortex itself.

Another functional imaging study measured the effects of dialectical behavioral therapy on the brain and behavioral responses of patients with borderline personality disorder (Schnell and Herpetz 2006). Experimental emotional arousal was induced in subjects through the presentation of standardized images. Patients in the dialectical behavioral therapy treatment group, when compared with controls, showed decreased hemodynamic responses to negative stimuli. Decreased metabolism was demonstrated in the right anterior cingulate, the temporal and posterior cingulate cortices, and the left insula. Reduction in the activity of these regions would be expected to diminish the intensity of emotional responses to cognitively represented objects and situations.

Beyond documenting psychotherapy-induced brain changes associated with symptom improvement, neuroimaging may predict responsiveness to psychotherapy. Bryant and coworkers (2008) studied patients with PTSD who were treated with CBT. Responsiveness to treatment was significantly correlated with the volume of the rostral anterior cingulate cortex (rACC), an area thought to react to emotional conflict by recruiting cognitive resources that can resolve the problem (Etkin et al. 2005). Individuals who had higher rACC volumes showed better responses to psychotherapy. Activation of the rACC in people with active depressive symptoms also predicts responses to antidepressants, which generally decrease metabolic activity in this region (Mayberg et al. 1997).

Conclusion

Psychotherapy developed empirically, based on models of distress that were, at best, metaphorically related to the activity of neural circuits. Although psychotherapy is a top-down activity that relies on derivatives of neural functions—verbal and emotional expressions and behaviors—contemporary research suggests that some elements of therapy, like other elements of the interpersonal world, engage and reshape underlying neural circuitry. As the patient's brain processes the targeted communications of the therapist, dysfunctional representations and their emotional connections are modified. In this manner, participation in therapy induces changes in the patient's internal representations and their subjective meaning, leading to more adaptive behavior. This field of research remains fragmented and correlational, but integration and synthesis are likely to occur as research progresses. An iterative strategy of measuring the impact of interventions and refining treatments to achieve targeted neurobiological results should not only enhance therapeutic effectiveness but ultimately restructure the scientific foundation of our understanding of human nature.

ACKNOWLEDGMENTS

Portions of this chapter have been adapted, with permission, from previous publications by the authors. These include: B. D. Beitman and G. I. Viamontes, "Toward a neural circuitry of engagement, self-awareness, and pattern search," *Psychiatric Annals* 36(4):272–80, 2006; G. I. Viamontes and B. D. Beitman, "Neural substrates of psychotherapeutic change. Part I: the default brain," *Psychiatric Annals* 36(4):225–37, 2006; G. I. Viamontes and B. D. Beitman, "Neural substrates of psychotherapeutic change. Part II: beyond default mode," *Psychiatric Annals* 36(4):239–46, 2006; and G. I. Viamontes and B. D. Beitman, "Mapping the unconscious in the brain," *Psychiatric Annals* 37(4):243–56, 2007. Some of the content in the section "Basic and Inhibitory Circuitry: A More Detailed View" is adapted, with permission, from G. I. Viamontes, *An Atlas of Neurobiology: How the Brain Creates the Self* (New York: W. W. Norton, 2011), in press.

REFERENCES

Adolphs, R., Damasio, H., Tranel, D., Cooper, G., and Damasio, A. R. 2000. A role for somatosensory cortices in the visual recognition of emotion as revealed by three-dimensional lesion mapping. *Journal of Neuroscience* 20:2683–90.
Anderson, M. C., Ochsner, K. N., Kuhl, B., Cooper, J., Robertson, E., Gabrielli, S. W., Glover, G. H., and Gabrielli, J. D. 2004. Neural systems underlying the suppression of unwanted memories. *Science* 303:232–35.
Bank, W., Bergvall, U., Byrd, S., Corbaz, J. M., Choux, M., Combalbert, A., and Yagishita, A. 2010. Salamon's neuroanatomy and neurovasculature web-atlas resource. www.radnet.ucla.edu/sections/DINR/index.htm.
Barbas, H., Saha, S., Rempel-Clower, N., and Ghashghaei, T. 2003. Serial pathways from primate prefrontal cortex to autonomic areas may influence emotional expression. *BMC Neuroscience* 4:25–37.
Bartels, A., and Zeki, S. 2000. The neural basis of romantic love. *NeuroReport* 11:3829–34.
———. 2004. The neural correlates of maternal and romantic love. *NeuroImage* 21:1155–66.
Bechara, A., Noel, S., and Crone, E. A. 2006. Loss of willpower: abnormal neural mechanisms of impulse control and decision-making in addiction. In R. W. Wiers and A. W. Stacy (eds.), *Handbook of Implicit Cognition and Addiction* (pp. 215–32). Thousand Oaks, CA: Sage.
Beitman, B. D., Nair, J., and Viamontes, G. I. 2005. What is self-awareness? In B. D. Beitman and J. Nair (eds.), *Self-Awareness Deficits in Psychiatric Patients* (pp. 3–23). New York: W. W. Norton.
Beitman, B. D., and Soth, A. M. 2006. Activation of self-observation: a core process among the psychotherapies. *Journal of Psychotherapy Integration* 16:383–97.
Beitman, B. D., and Yue, D. 2004. *Learning Psychotherapy: A Time-Efficient, Research-Based, Outcome-Measured Psychotherapy Training Program*, 4th ed. New York: W. W. Norton.
Berridge, K. C., and Winkielman, P. 2003. What is an unconscious emotion? (The case for unconscious "liking.") *Cognition and Emotion* 17:181–211.
Blair, R. J., Morris, J. S., Frith, C. D., Perrett, D. I., and Dolan, R. J. 1999. Dissociable neural responses to facial expressions of sadness and anger. *Brain* 122(pt. 5):883–93.
Blanke, O., and Arzy, S. 2005. The out-of-body experience: disturbed self-processing at the temporoparietal junction. *Neuroscientist* 11(1):16–24.
Brody, A. L., Saxena, S., Stoessel, P., Gillies, L. A., Fairbanks, L. A., Alborzian, S., et al. 2001. Regional brain metabolic changes in patients with major depression treated with either paroxetine or interpersonal therapy: preliminary findings. *Archives of General Psychiatry* 58:31–40.
Brothers, L. 2002. The social brain: a project for integrating primate behavior and

neurophysiology in a new domain. In J. T. Cacioppo, G. G. Berntson, R. Adolphs, C. S. Carter, R. J. Davidson, M. K. McClintock, et al. (eds.), *Foundations in Social Neurosciences*. Cambridge, MA: MIT Press.

Bryant, R. A., Felmingham, K., Whitford, T. J., Kemp, A., Hughes, G., Peduto, A., and Williams, L. M. 2008. Rostral anterior cingulate volume predicts treatment response to cognitive-behavioural therapy for posttraumatic stress disorder. *Journal of Psychiatry and Neuroscience* 33:142–46.

Burruss, J. W., Hurley, R. A., Taber, K. H., Rauch, R. A., Norton, R. E., and Hayman, L. A. 2000. Functional neuroanatomy of the frontal lobe circuits. *Radiology* 214:227–30.

Bush, G., Luu, P., and Posner, M. I. 2000. Cognitive and emotional influences in anterior cingulate cortex. *Trends in Cognitive Science* 214:227–30.

Carr, L., Iacoboni, M., Dubeau, M. C., Mazziotta, J. C., and Lenzi, G. L. 2003. Neural mechanisms of empathy in humans: a relay from neural systems for imitation to limbic areas. *Proceedings of the National Academy of Sciences of the United States of America* 100:5497–502.

Critchley, H. D., Mathias, C. J., Josephs, O., O'Doherty, J., Zanini, S., Dewar, B.-K., et al. 2003. Human cingulate cortex and autonomic control: converging neuroimaging and clinical evidence. *Brain* 126:1–14.

Damasio, A. R. 1999. *The Feeling of What Happens: Body and Emotion in the Making of Consciousness*. New York: Harcourt Brace.

Damasio, A. R., Grabowski, T. J., Bechara, A., Damasio, H., Ponto, L. L. B., Parvizi, J., and Hichwaet, R. D. 2000. Subcortical and cortical brain activity during the feeling of self-generated emotions. *Nature Neuroscience* 3:1049–56.

Dapretto, M., Davies, M. S., Pfeifer, J. H., Scott, A. A., Sigman, M., Bookheimer, S. Y., and Iacoboni, M. 2006. Understanding emotions in others: mirror neuron dysfunction in children with autism spectrum disorders. *Nature Neuroscience* 9:28–30.

Davis, M., and Whalen, P. J. 2001. The amygdala: vigilance and emotion. *Molecular Psychiatry* 6:13–34.

Deikman, A. J. 1982. *The Observing Self*. Boston: Beacon.

Domes, G., Heinrich, M., Michel, A., Berger, C., and Herpetz, S. C. 2007. Oxytocin improves "mind-reading" in humans. *Biological Psychiatry* 61:731–33.

Etkin, A., Pittenger, C., Polan, J., and Kandel, E. R. 2005. Toward a neurobiology of psychotherapy: basic science and clinical applications. *Journal of Neuropsychiatry and Clinical Neurosciences* 17:145–58.

Flashman, L. A. 2005. Disorders of insight, self-awareness, and attribution in schizophrenia. In B. D. Beitman and J. Nair (eds.), *Self-Awareness Deficits in Psychiatric Patients* (pp. 129–58). New York: W. W. Norton.

Foa, E., Hembree, E., and Rothbaum, B. 2007. *Prolonged Exposure Therapy for PTSD: Emotional Processing of Traumatic Experiences—Therapist Guide*. New York: Oxford University Press.

Fonagy, P. 2004. Psychotherapy: attachment and the brain. Paper presented at the 35th annual meeting of the Society for Psychotherapy Research, Rome, Italy.

Frank, J. D., and Frank, J. B. 1991. *Persuasion and Healing: A Comparative Study of Psychotherapy*, 3rd ed. Baltimore: Johns Hopkins University Press.

Freud, S. 1960. The ego and the id. In *The Standard Edition of the Complete Psychological Works of Sigmund Freud* (pp. 11–36). New York: W. W. Norton

Frith, C. D., and Frith, U. 1999. Interacting minds: biological basis. *Science* 286:1692–95.

Furmark, T., Tillfors, M., Marteindottir, I., Fischer, H., Pissiota, A., Langstrom, B., and Fredrikson, M. 2002. Common changes in cerebral blood flow in patients with social phobia treated with citalopram or cognitive-behavioral therapy. *Archives of General Psychiatry* 59:425–33.

Goldapple, K., Segal, Z., Garson, C., Lau, M., Bieling, P., Kennedy, S., and Mayberg, H. 2004. Modulation of cortical-limbic pathways in major depression: treatment-specific effects of cognitive behavior therapy. *Archives of General Psychiatry* 61:34–41.

Goldstein, D. S. 2006. *Adrenaline and the Inner World: An Introduction to Scientific Integrative Medicine.* Baltimore: Johns Hopkins University Press.

Iacoboni, M., Woods, R. P., Brass, M., Bekkering, H., Mazziotta, J. C., and Rizzolatti, G. 1999. Cortical mechanisms of human imitation. *Science* 286:2526–28.

Johnson, S. C., Baxter, L. C., Wilder, L. S., Pipe, J. G., Heiserman, J. E., and Prigatano, G. P. 2002. Neural correlates of self-reflection. *Brain* 125:1808–14.

Kanwisher, N., McDermott, J., and Chun, M. M. 1997. The fusiform face area: a module in the human extrastriate cortex specialized for face perception. *Journal of Neuroscience* 17:4302–11.

Krupnick, J. L., Sotsky, S. M., Simmens, S., Moyer, J., Elkin, I., Watkins, J., and Pilkonis, P. A. 1996. The role of the therapeutic alliance in psychotherapy and pharmacotherapy outcome: findings in the National Institute of Mental Health Treatment of Depression Collaborative Research Program. *Journal of Consulting and Clinical Psychology* 64:532–39.

LaLumiere, R. T., and Kalivas, P. W. 2008. Cocaine addiction: mechanisms of action. *Psychiatric Annals* 38:252–58.

Mayberg, H. S., Brannan, S. K., Mahurin, R. K., Jerabek, P. A., Brickman, J. S., Tekell, J. L., et al. 1997. Cingulate function in depression: a potential predictor of treatment response. *NeuroReport* 8:1057–61.

Mega, M. S., and Cummings, J. L. 2001. Frontal subcortical circuits: anatomy and function. In S. P. Salloway, P. F. Mallory, and J. D. Duffy (eds.), *The Frontal Lobes and Neuropsychiatric Illness* (pp. 15–32). Washington, DC: American Psychiatric Publishing.

Mesulam, M. 1998. From sensation to cognition. *Brain* 121:1013–52.

Newberg, A., d'Aquili, E., and Rause, V. 2002. *Brain Machinery: Why God Won't Go Away.* New York: Ballantine Books.

Ochsner, K. N., Bunge, S. A., Gross, J. J., and Gabrieli, J. D. 2002. Rethinking feelings: an FMRI study of the cognitive regulation of emotion. *Journal of Cognitive Neuroscience* 14:1215–22.

Pally, R. 2005. Non-conscious prediction and a role for consciousness in correcting prediction errors. *Cortex* 41:643–62.

Parvizi, J., and Damasio, A. 2001. Consciousness and the brainstem. In S. Dahane (ed.), *The Cognitive Neuroscience of Consciousness* (pp. 135–39). Cambridge, MA: MIT Press.

Rizzolatti, G., Fogassi, L., and Gallese, V. 2001. Neurophysiological mechanisms underlying the understanding and imitation of action. *Nature Reviews Neuroscience* 2:661–70.

Roffman, J. L., Marci, C. D., Glick, D. M., Dougherty, D. D., and Rauch, S. L. 2005. Neuroimaging and the functional anatomy of psychotherapy. *Psychological Medicine* 35:1–15.

Rolls, E. T. 2005. *Emotion Explained*. Oxford: Oxford University Press.

Saxe, R., and Kanwisher, N. 2002. People thinking about thinking people: the role of the temporoparietal junction in "theory of mind." *NeuroImage* 19:1835–42.

Saxe, R., Xiao, D. K., Kovacs, G., Perrett, D. I., and Kanwisher, N. 2004. A region of right posterior superior temporal sulcus responds to observed intentional actions. *Neuropsychologia* 42:1435–46.

Schnell, K., and Herpetz, S. C. 2006. Effects of dialectic-behavioral therapy on the neural correlates of affective hyperarousal in borderline personality disorder. *Journal of Psychiatric Research* 41:837–47.

Stuss, D. T., and Benson, D. F. 1983. Emotional concomitants of psychotherapy. In K. M. Heilman and P. Staz (eds.), *Advances in Neuropsychology and Behavioral Neurology* (pp. 11–40). New York: Guilford Press.

Tanaka, K. 2003. Columns for complex visual object features in the inferotemporal cortex: clustering of cells with similar but slightly different stimulus selectivities. *Cerebral Cortex* 13:90–99.

Teicher, M. H., Andersen, S. L., Polcari, A., Anderson, C. M., and Navalta, C. P. 2002. Developmental neurobiology of childhood stress and trauma. *Psychiatric Clinics of North America* 25:397–426.

Viamontes, G. I. 2011. *An Atlas of Neurobiology: How the Brain Creates the Self*. New York: W. W. Norton. In press.

Viamontes, G. I., and Beitman, B. D. 2006a. Neural substrates of psychotherapeutic change. Part I: the default brain. *Psychiatric Annals* 36:225–37.

———. 2006b. Neural substrates of psychotherapeutic change. Part II: beyond default mode. *Psychiatric Annals* 36:239–46.

———. 2007. Mapping the unconscious in the brain. *Psychiatric Annals* 37:243–56.

Viamontes, G. I., Beitman, B. D., Viamontes, C. T., and Viamontes, J. A. 2005. Neural circuits for self-awareness: evolutionary origins and implementation in the human brain. In B. D. Beitman and J. Nair (eds.), *Self-Awareness Deficits in Psychiatric Patients* (pp. 24–111). New York: W. W. Norton.

Wampold, B. E. 2001. *The Great Psychotherapy Debate: Models, Methods, and Findings*. Mahwah, NJ: Lawrence Erlbaum Associates.

Wheeler, M. A., Stuss, D. T., and Tulving, E. 1997. Toward a theory of episodic memory: the frontal lobes and autonoetic consciousness. *Psychological Bulletin* 121:331–54.

Wolfe, B. E., and Goldfried, M. R. 1988. Research on psychotherapy integration: recommendations and conclusions from an NIMH workshop. *Journal of Consulting and Clinical Psychology* 56:448–51.

CHAPTER 4

Restoring Meaning to Psychiatric Diagnosis and Psychotherapy in the Age of Evolutionary Biology

Julia B. Frank, M.D.

"If there's no meaning in it,"
said the King, "that saves a
world of trouble, you know,
as we needn't try to find any.
And yet I don't know," he
went on, spreading out the
verses on his knee and
looking at them with one
eye; "I seem to see some
meaning in them, after all."
—*Alice's Adventures in
Wonderland*

The assertion that psychotherapy operates in the realm of meanings raises questions as to which intellectual disciplines are best suited to examining its processes.

—*PERSUASION AND HEALING*, 1991, P. 92

In the third edition of *Persuasion and Healing*, Jerome Frank proposed that psychotherapy acts in the domain of meaning (Frank and Frank 1991b). Meaning, in this sense, connotes the ways in which patients interpret, explain, and make predictions from their daily experience. Explanations or predictions that are disempowering, negative, or isolating, he argued, engender demoralization, a state that manifests itself psychologically and physically. Psychotherapy, bringing to bear the therapist's personally and culturally derived powers to engage and persuade, helps patients rework the "apologia" of their distress (or promotes shifts in patients' assumptive worlds) in ways that promote hope, self-efficacy, and well-being. Psychotherapy, Frank proposed, is thus a form of "noble rhetoric." Patients who benefit rewrite their apologia in ways that relieve demoralization.

The terms *apologia* or *assumptive world* describe essentially psychological processes. In common language, *meaning* connotes semantic meaning, an element of conscious thought. Reflecting this focus, early modern theories of psychopathology, especially psychoanalysis, classified patients according to ideational content, that is, the conscious (or potentially conscious) meanings of their experience as described in words.

Meaning is far less salient within the paradigm of descriptive psychiatry. Our nosology, manualized in the *Diagnostic and Statistical Manual of Mental Disorders* (DSM-IV-TR; American Psychiatric Association 2000), classifies people based on the observable aspects of their disorders, in particular, behaviors and bodily signs (inability to fulfill social expectations, disruptions of sleep, weight change, bodily anxiety, etc.). Certain aspects of subjective experience such as hallucinations, delusions, or paranoia are part of our classificatory scheme, but we note only their presence or absence. The content of these experiences—for example, what the psychotic person's voices say or the actual focus of a paranoid delusion—has little diagnostic importance in the world of descriptive psychiatry. Other meaningful criteria, such as "identity disturbance" in borderline personality disorder, are vague and undefined. Problems of meaning expressed in interactions with others are tossed into the wastebasket of the V codes. Cultural variation, which typically alters the meaning and expression of symptoms, merits merely an appendix in our current classification (see chapters 5 and 14).

The exclusion of meaning from the DSM system undermines its validity (Nathan 2002). Its categories correspond poorly to things beyond themselves, with some categories lumping unrelated symptoms together and others failing to include elements that are systematically linked by some underlying process. For example, the DSM classifies depression without reference to the types of events that depressed people are responding to, though research has identified systematic differences in the patterns of human responses to loss, defeat, or persistent stress (see chapters 7 and 9). Acknowledging such differences could provide a meaningful foundation for a range of diagnoses (Keller, Neale, and Kendler 2007) that would disaggregate the overstuffed category of "major depression."

The DSM approach has radically changed psychiatric education and psychiatric treatment, with particular implications for psychotherapy. Relying on description in the absence of meaning widens the gap between the conditions that may be understood and treated by psychotherapists and those "diagnosed" by others, mainly psychiatrists and psychologists, trained in descriptive nosology. As physicians, psychiatrists, in particular, study diseases first, disorders second, and meaningful human behavior a distant third. In their postgraduate education, psychiatrists may graft psychotherapy skills onto the trunk of their medically acquired knowledge, but the fit is as awkward as a branch of dogwood sprouting from the trunk of an oak. The dominance of a relatively meaningless diagnostic system seriously jeopardizes the future of psychotherapy, at least for psychiatrists and others who must think, practice, and bill by its lights.

Fortunately, several alternative approaches to diagnosis are gaining ground in medicine, psychology, and psychiatry (Barron 2002). Methodologically rigorous efforts including Blatt and Levy's focus (2002) on disorders of relatedness and self-concept, George Vaillant's longitudinal investigation (1993) of psychological defenses, and Heim and Westen's work (2005) on personality show that investigations of meaning need not evaporate into the ether of ungrounded theory nor succumb to the overwhelming weight of accrued individual variation. To prove that they are valid, however, these approaches must be reconciled with evolutionary science, the foundation of the ever increasing body of knowledge that encompasses the genetic, anatomical, and neurochemical elements of various psychological and behavioral disorders.

Beyond the issue of validity, the theory guiding any psychotherapy must be credible—to the therapist, as much as to the patient. Medically trained psychotherapists have particular trouble with conditions not linked to any objective measure, because they have spent years learning to doubt anything that they cannot see, diagnose in the laboratory, prove statistically, or manipulate experimentally. While psychotherapists from other disciplines may happily adopt a guiding theory that is supported by coherent argument, anecdote, and personal experience, psychiatrists are generally plagued by ambivalence: "Is this a psychotherapy problem or should I offer medication?" "Where is the proof that this person's instability is the result of the abuse she claims to have suffered?" "Am I missing a case of lupus here?" To be an effective psychotherapist, a psychiatrist or psychologist trained in neuroscience needs a theory of thought and behavior that incorporates meaning without violating the precepts of his or her scientific training.

Evolutionary Concepts and Psychotherapy

The principles of evolutionary biology and evolutionary psychology provide tools for reconciling meaningful diagnosis with a scientific worldview (see chapter 15). Such reconciliation requires viewing human behavior as the result of processes that we share with animals whose brains can be studied and whose behaviors can be manipulated experimentally or explained through interpretation of the history of a species (Calvin 2004). Neuroscientific research into meaning involves creating models in which analogs to meaningful human qualities such as nurturance, curiosity, or grief may be inferred from observing the behavior of animals under controlled conditions. Such models open the way to rigorously test previously nondisprovable hypotheses—for example, the impact of early experience on later behavior (Spinelli et al. 2009). Psychological inferences from animal studies are justified in part by the fact that humans share many brain structures and much of their genome with other mammals, certain primates in particular.

Animal studies are not the only source of new information about the neurobiology of meaning. Contemporary neuroimaging techniques make it possible to study objectively the activity of the functioning human brain. Positron emission tomography (PET) and functional magnetic resonance imaging (fMRI) provide visual representations of both conscious thought and nonconscious reactions to particular situations. In consequence, beliefs, ideas, predictions, interpretations—the targets of psychotherapy—can be understood as expressions of evolutionary processes by which the genetically structured brain is continuously modified by experience and language as it develops and responds to a variety of environmental inputs (see chapter 3). Beyond helping psychotherapeutically minded psychiatrists find the courage of their convictions, the methods of neurobiological investigation may someday permit us to design rather than merely stumble upon effective treatments.

Prior to the current revolutions in genetics and functional neuroscience, many theoreticians contributed to the project of aligning psychology with evolutionary science. Sigmund Freud started the process. George Engel's biopsychosocial model (1977), the Hopkins Perspectives of Psychiatry (McHugh and Slavney 1998), and Nassir Ghaemi's principled pluralism (2003) all represent efforts to capture the interaction between biology, psychology, and context. Each of these models has strengthened the connections between medicine and behavioral science. All strongly influence medical education. While these perspectives do implicitly link psychological experience with biological and social influences, they still draw arbitrary distinctions between biological processes, personal narratives, and social behavior, leading to oversimplified applications.

Evolutionary science forges more robust links among biology, psychology, and social behavior, partly through the concept of information processing. Recent decades have seen a host of new methods for investigating problems of purpose and cause (LeDoux 1996; Dunbar and Barrett 2007, p. 4), providing tantalizing glimpses of viable alternatives to diagnoses untethered to etiology. Evolutionists have developed animal models in which different variables (gene expression, developmental experiences, social and environmental conditions) can be systematically isolated and their impact identified. To the extent that the findings from these studies can be related to meaningful categories of human behavior and disorder, evolutionary science is carving out paths that unite social behavior, psychiatry, psychology, and neuroscience (or social, psychological, and biological functions) in new and useful ways.

This point will be trivial to those psychologists, physicians, and psychotherapists attuned to the recent explosion of information about the ways that evolutionary processes contribute to complex functions, including those previously considered beyond the realm of biology. The evolutionary building blocks of conscious thought, language, relationships, and even morality are the subject of textbooks (McGuire and Troisi 1998; Workman and Reader 2004; Dunbar and Barrett 2007), journal articles, newspaper reports, and stories in other media. They are not, however, routinely included in the training programs of psychotherapists. Even medical schools and psychiatric residencies do not uniformly require trainees to have extensive knowledge in this area.

Highlighting the role of meaning in evolution implies that the historical distinction between psychosocial and neurophysiological models of illness is neither necessary nor inevitable (see chapter 3). The concept of meaning, broadly defined, bridges the divide. This essay explores meaning as a crucial feature of normal brain functioning and in psychopathology. It examines some of the implications for psychotherapy (understood as a particular kind of healing relationship, structured around a specified theory, as Jerome Frank proposed) of the new evolutionary science. Recognizing meaning as an element of humans' evolved capacity for adaptation realigns psychotherapy with science and underscores its continued relevance and utility.

After reviewing one general typology of meaning, this chapter explores meaning in the study of the fear response, an area of normal functioning where biology and psychology intersect. It then describes the evolutionary importance of the human capacity for narrative. The final section presents an example of the evaluation and treatment of a woman with postpartum depression, considered as an evolutionarily meaningful state. The aim is to highlight how evolutionary concepts might shape the biopsychosocial assessment of patients and influence the choice of therapies—pharmacological, psychological, interpersonal, or cultural—in a variety of combinations.

An Evolutionary Typology of Meaning

As the main target of psychotherapy, meaning can be understood as the inter-mittently conscious recognition of connections between sensation, memory, context, and other neurologically encoded information. Such recognition serves an evolutionary purpose: to facilitate survival, adaptation, and eventual repro-ductive success. Meaning occupies a central place within today's evolutionary science: it is both the byproduct and a shaper of how the brain responds func-tionally and even structurally to the environment.*

The brain is organized by experience; genes provide only a template that experience fills in, altering blood flow (Paquette et al. 2003), creating or at-tenuating synaptic connections, and fostering the survival of some neurons and the extinction of others (Gabbard 2000). Meaning, as a central organizer of how individuals behave, alters neuronal activity and even brain structure in discernible ways. Elemental meanings such as threat or isolation generate re-flexive behaviors whose effects on neural organization can be studied in ani-mals. Complex categories of meaning such as will, motivation, purpose, and interpretation, corresponding to older categories of psychology, derive from these more basic ones. Evolutionary thought even touches on meaning as an element of culture. In recent years, evolutionists have explored humans' unique capacity to transmit information crucial to genetic survival from one individ-ual or generation to another through language or other forms of symbolic ex-pression (Plotkin 2007).

The evolutionary definition of meaning, then, is broad enough to encom-pass biological, psychological, and social determinants of patients' assumptive worlds. As Daniel Moerman (2002, p. 149) succinctly states, "meaning is a re-lationship, a correspondence between one thing and another, literal or other-wise." Contemporary research linking cognitive science with genetically deter-mined capacities for neurochemical transmission across complex networks has elucidated how brain function influences processes that have often been seen as primarily psychological. Such processes include associating ideas, de-termining salience, setting priorities, and anticipating likely responses to fu-

---

* This section assumes the reader has a basic grasp of how the nervous system is organized. If not, Pliszka's *Neuroscience for the Mental Health Clinician* (2004) offers an exceptionally clear review of basic brain physiology in relation to anxiety. "Salamon's Neuroanatomy and Neurovasculature Web-Atlas Resource" (Bank et al. 2010) is a free, searchable atlas of brain anatomy that may also be helpful.

ture conditions (see chapter 3). Particularly in functional neuroimaging stud-ies, these processes have been isolated and mapped onto different patterns of brain activity. In a sense, neurobiology provides the grammar and some of the vocabulary with which persons construct the apologia or life narrative that may be rewritten in psychotherapy.

Daniel Moerman goes further, offering a typology of meaning highly rele-vant to psychotherapy. He differentiates three types, based on the degree to which a process is sensitive to external influence and subject to conscious con-trol. Type I, in his view, is the "meaning" of physiological homeostasis: when the body has sufficient warmth, oxygen, nutrients, and so on, neurological and endocrine control systems automatically maintain this equilibrium. When some-thing triggers an internal sensor, there may be an emotional response. A sub-jectively perceived emotional state such as fear or anger can alter these sensing processes. Cognitive or conscious thought may influence the emotions that regulate this type of activity, but the underlying processes are unconscious and will continue even if the person is comatose.

Type II processes are those that form the boundary between the body and the environment: sensory experience, motor activity, and pain, among others. These processes are more conscious than homeostatic ones, but they remain primarily under unconscious control. That is, we note and respond to uncount-able numbers of sensations all the time—our position in space, posture, the colors of the world around us. Certain peremptory stimuli, such as pain, will focus our attention and suppress even minimal awareness of other sensations. This process of awareness and refocusing, though conscious, is typically auto-matic, not self-directed. Most people cannot, using conscious or cognitive strategies, render themselves blind, deaf, or numb. Psychotherapeutic methods generally cannot alter our moment-to-moment environmental awareness, though methods such as hypnosis may temporarily modify the registration of both ordinary and peremptory stimuli.

Finally, Moerman proposes a third level of meaning that is essentially cog-nitive and conscious—the meaning we attach to words (and music and im-ages). This aspect of meaning (type III) is more highly developed in humans than in all other species. It can be transmitted efficiently between individuals.

Together, these types of meaning influence our adaptive behavior—purposive behavior in particular (Moerman 2002, pp. 142–43). All three types of meaning are mutually influential: we respond physiologically to words and consciously to perceived states of disturbed homeostasis. But the strength and direction of influence is quite different in the three types. Conscious meaning weakly affects physiology, but may have a great impact on purposive behavior. Though nonconscious brain activity regulates our ability to walk, we still choose to walk toward one site and away from another, because we have a goal in mind. Moerman's third level of meaning is the one most amenable to the influence of psychotherapy, though the connections between levels explain how psychotherapy may at times modify more fundamental processes.

Moerman's typology directs our attention to those aspects of meaning that are most crucial to the physical survival of individuals, who must maintain homeostasis and interact with the physical and social environments in complex ways. The ways in which we construct meaning are determined, on the one hand, by the physiology of our nervous systems and, on the other, by the linguistic and cultural communities that transmit meaning from one generation to the next. Recognizing that every level of meaning contributes to adaptation places meaning within the domain of evolutionary science, without denying that the human capacity to construct meaning has unique dimensions that other species lack (Laland 2007). Biology and culture intersect in the individual, whose experiences during different stages of development, extending into adult life, customize both his or her nervous system and his or her assumptive world.

The principles of conditioning and selection explain how this process evolves normally. Experiences that are reinforced or extinguished most frequently early in life become permanently encoded in our nervous systems. Single, overwhelming experiences critical to survival also may influence brain organization, even without repetition over time. A child who hears a particular language for all of its waking life will absorb that language permanently. The neurons needed to meet the demands of that language (e.g., those that discriminate tones in an Asian language) will flourish and develop dense connections with other neurons, while unused neurons will atrophy or die. Similarly, an individual who undergoes life-shattering psychological trauma at any age may be permanently changed by high levels of stress-released hormones in brain areas involved in memory (especially the hippocampus) (McEwen 2002). These hormones damage or even kill some cells and obliterate or generate synapses. Abnormally encoded traumatic memories then intrude into waking life and dreams in ways that ordinary memories do not.

Many types of meaning have a clear impact on adaptation and survival. Three highly relevant to conscious experience, and thus to psychotherapy, are the fear response (LeDoux 1996), memory (Schacter 1996), and processes that mediate our interactions with other individuals, especially attachment behaviors (see chapter 15) and other modules of emotional experience (Panksepp 2007). These aspects of adaptation are meaningful in both the nonconscious and conscious senses of the word. We respond automatically to fear cues, but our cognitive processing of these cues can moderate our responses. Memory, clearly dependent on neurological circuits, is populated with conscious and nonconscious elements of experience, some linked to verbal descriptions. Our early attachments are essential to our survival. Later on, the quality of our early social interactions may influence (but not determine) how we interact with others sexually, within social hierarchies, and in many other ways (Belsky 2007), all of which contribute to our reproductive fitness as individuals and as members of groups.

A full exposition of how the brain creates meaning and how meaning shapes the brain in these domains would require an entire textbook—one written two or three hundred years from now (see chapter 3). One well-studied functional brain system, the fear response (LeDoux 1996), will illustrate the intimate connections between brain and mind, in a domain obviously relevant to psychopathology and psychotherapy. This information cannot be extrapolated directly to the understanding of other emotions, memory, or attachment, but it does bolster the main point: psychotherapy, understood as process that transforms meaning, stands on a solid biological foundation of human activities that enhance adaptation and survival.

The Fear Response

Anxiety occupies a prominent place in the history of psychotherapy, beginning with Freud's interest in anxiety about sexual expression and Adler's recognition that a negative or unrealistic appraisal of one's social position generates symptoms and distress. The fear response, which includes bodily symptoms such as sweating, racing heart, tremor, and other signs of adrenergic activity, is obviously a biological as well as psychological state. Reductionist theories that attribute all contextually inappropriate anxiety to a few types of conflict have given way to a broader understanding of what can trigger fear responses, how they are expressed, and what relieves or terminates them. Briefly, the triggers for anxiety include consciously registered perceptions, often linked to memory, as well as nonconscious perturbations in the monitoring of homeostasis—

for example, a sudden fall in blood pressure or a rise in carbon dioxide levels (Rassovsky et al. 2000) (Moerman's type I meaning). These physiological factors may trigger the reaction instantly, through direct pathways between the brainstem and the thalamus (type II meaning). Activation of the medial prefrontal cortex, conscious awareness, and search for the source of the threat quickly follow (type III) (see figures 3.1 and 3.2 for the locations of these structures).

To complicate the picture, the fear response may be cued by external as well as internal perceptions. External or environmental triggers may lead to reflexive fear or follow a multistep pathway in which a perception is compared to memory before it is recognized as either neutral or threatening. In the nonreflexive pathway, meaning (type III) is assigned before the fear response either occurs or is aborted. In all cases, the person's physiological response to threat (symbolic, actual, or remembered) is mediated by activity of the autonomic nervous system, which triggers both neurotransmitter feedback and hormonal (cortisol) responses that terminate the fear response.

Neuroimaging has shown that each element of the fear response has a geographic home within the brain and that chemical messengers transmitted through the filaments of the nervous system coordinate the activity of these areas. Environmental stimuli activate receptors of the eyes, ears, nose, mouth, and skin. Activation of these receptors causes the release of chemical neurotransmitters that augment or suppress electrical impulses that travel along individual nerves to cortical association areas and then to secondary processing areas of the dorsolateral and orbitomedial areas of the prefrontal cortex. Simultaneously, activation occurs in the subcortical hippocampus, where elements of the stimulus may activate complex memories. Direct pathways from the sensory receptors, and indirect pathways from the frontal cortex and the hippocampus, all converge on the amygdala, from which the outflow mediates the different elements of the anxiety response, including what we pay attention to and whether we fight, run, freeze, or stand down from our state of alarm (LeDoux 1996, chap. 4) (see also chapter 3 in this volume).

Perhaps the most interesting aspect of the whole system is the way in which either repeated or intense stimuli alter the function of the amygdala (Bremner et al. 2008), so that some pathways become express lanes for certain stimuli to reach consciousness or trigger behavior more quickly or more directly than other stimuli. In addition to altering our responses, the amygdala influences attention and perception. When we are hungry, for example, the sensation of hunger stimulates the amygdala to preferentially direct our attention to food cues in the environment. When we are not hungry, we ignore food cues and attend to something else.

The amygdala is particularly sensitive to threat. The experience of repeated or severe trauma makes the person vigilant for signs that the danger will recur. Such cues may be meaningful only in terms of the encoded memories of the experience, memories that activate pathways between the hippocampus and the amygdala. For example, a person who has been assaulted by a man in a blue jacket may scan the environment for the color blue or react fearfully to the sight of a blue jacket, a stimulus that would be completely neutral or even appealing to someone who did not associate the color with the fearful memory. The prefrontal cortex (Berkowitz et al. 2007) and other language-processing areas also regulate the functioning of the amygdala, so that words connoting some aspect of a fearful experience may also activate or inhibit threat response networks. The amygdala, then, embodies neurological individuality; it is indirectly responsive to verbal as well as sensory cues. General and shared processes—the inheritance and expression of genes—determine amygdalar structure and how readily it changes, but its actual activity reflects the meaning the individual assigns to an experience in concrete and lasting ways.

In learning theory, these physiological and behavioral responses are conditioned (strengthened or reinforced) by real and symbolic experience (LeDoux 1996, chap. 6). Psychotherapy may extinguish these conditioned responses by exposing the person repeatedly to the fear-inducing cues, typically words, within the safety of a therapeutic relationship. Edna Foa's prolonged exposure therapy for posttraumatic stress is a well-known treatment based on these concepts (Nemeroff et al. 2006). In this therapy, the therapist instructs and encourages the patient to recount and listen to accounts of a traumatic personal experience many times. The person's emotional distress, measured before, during, and after treatment, drops dramatically after multiple retellings of the story. Outcome studies have documented the efficacy of this technique. It is but one example of how psychotherapy attempts to alter meaning, not just in the semantic sense, but by using language to alter meaning as a property of biological systems.

From this perspective, medication and psychotherapy may have similar effects: medications may change meaning by directly modifying the neural networks that create it, while rhetorical methods such as psychotherapy provide experiences that gradually modify these networks, either by reducing their spontaneous and dynamic neurotransmitter activity or by modifying the anatomical connections between cells, creating new ones or routing transmission away from connections established by prior experience. An effective psychotropic drug changes thought, just as an effective psychotherapy modifies neurological activity.

The Evolution of Human Capacity for Narrative

Evolutionary theory is both broad and minutely specific. In addition to explaining elements of psychopathology in relation to particular types of neurological activity, it provides insight into the importance and structure of personal narratives, the target of most psychotherapies. As William Calvin proposes in *A Brief History of the Mind* (2004), the capacity for narrative is built on the unique biological capacities of the human neocortex. Constructing a narrative requires complex planning of sequences, an ability to pay attention to a single thing for relatively long periods and to direct others' attention to the same focus, an advanced talent for mimicry, and language that is flexible and capable of expressing complex relations and sequences. Observations of other animals and of the artifacts and bones of past societies show that each of these qualities emerged at different points in evolution. These emergences served survival purposes—in particular, allowing humans to improve their diets and live in novel environments. The capacity for stories, Calvin suggests, began with the need for our ancestors to tell each other where they hunted, what they found, how they acted, and what they should try to do together the next morning.

In other words, the creation, revision, and transmission of narrative is a core human behavior that provides an evolutionary advantage to our species. Psychotherapy, an organized approach to modifying the narratives of groups and individuals, is equally robust in evolutionary terms. As Jerome Frank pointed out in analyzing shamanism and faith healing along with psychotherapy (Frank and Frank 1991a), nearly every culture has a variety of practices that serve to modify the personal history of individuals and the shared beliefs of the group, and these practices are built from common elements. In particular, they are based on the relation between a figure of higher status (doctor, shaman, priest) and an individual sufferer or group; they arouse emotion and involve symbols (words, clothing, music, masks, drawings, and ritual objects) that are meaningful within the shared experience of the participants. The persistence and ubiquity of psychotherapy suggests such activities have evolutionary purpose, enhancing adaptation, survival, and reproductive success. Just as evolutionary biology pushes us to a create a new theoretical scheme for recognizing and classifying mental illnesses, it provides a new way of looking at psychotherapy as a method for relieving them.

Many types of psychopathology, from dementia to dysthymia, represent selective failures of established brain subsystems, each of which contributes in the normal state to successful adaptation and reproductive fitness (McGuire and Troisi 1998). These systems all involve characteristic patterns of perceiving, thinking, remembering, and assessing one's environment and social position, the elements of a meaningful classification of psychopathology. Recognizing these patterns could lead to a nosology that relates disorders to causes and elements outside their overt manifestations. Instead of diagnosing depression generally, based on a threshold number of symptoms, for example, we would recognize a variety of depressed moods associated with particular conscious thoughts and particular endocrinological disruptions, related to particular experiences—disrupted attachments (loss), fall in social position, exposure to unpredictable threats, or other hazards of living. Much of folkloric or commonsensical diagnosis already recognizes such meaningful distinctions or subtypes, providing common words to describe bereavement, defeat, and demoralization (see chapter 7). Postpartum depression, a commonsensical diagnosis recognized worldwide, though only grudgingly represented as a specific disorder in DSM-IV-TR, provides a good example of how an evolutionarily informed diagnostic approach could facilitate treatment, including the integration of psychotherapy with other interventions.

Postpartum Depression: A Meaningful Psychopathological State

Let us begin with the facts. Roughly 10 percent of women experience depressed mood, disrupted sleep, fatigue, anxiety, tearfulness, hopelessness, decreased worth, and increased helplessness in the first three months after childbirth (Wisner, Parry, and Piontek 2002). This remarkably robust finding has been verified in industrialized and nonindustrialized societies around the world. Depression in mothers adversely affects the development of their offspring (Weinberg and Tronick 1998). When something so common affects reproductive fitness, it raises the question of why it has persisted in the population. Why have the processes of evolution not selected against it? The answer must be that the traits involved serve some evolutionary purpose, even if a particular combination or degree of expression of these traits is maladaptive.

The perinatal period (pregnancy, birth, and postpartum) involves radical biological, psychological, and social adaptations for women. Biologically, the hormonal changes that follow parturition are the most radical of any in a woman's life time. Estrogen and progesterone drop from their highest possible levels to their lowest, while oxytocin and prolactin rise sharply. Psychologically, the mother develops love for her infant and concern for its protection, including sensitivity to threats she previously ignored. Socially, she enjoys much less freedom of action, temporarily loses interest in sex, and occupies a more dependent role than before. Normally, these processes are adaptive: the mother feeds and protects her infant and derives pleasure and satisfaction from doing so. Her fatigue may keep her in proximity to the child. She accepts her new social constraints and opportunities with little distress, and others are able to adjust their expectations and demands accordingly.

CASE EXAMPLE: **Applying Evolutionary Concepts to Postpartum Depression**
The distressed husband of a thirty-three-year-old woman, father of a three-month-old boy, called to make an appointment with a psychiatrist for his wife. During her evaluation, she reported with great shame that she was having trouble feeling love for her infant. Nursing had led to severe sleep deprivation; she was unable to fall back to sleep after night feedings, and she could not nap when the baby napped. She no longer wanted to be touched by her husband. She cried over trivial things but felt numb when she learned that her mother-in-law was injured in a car accident. She was irritable, and her appetite varied from nonexistent to intense hunger. She felt distracted and noted that she could not even read a whole magazine article. Some days she did not get dressed until mid-afternoon. She was particularly worried because she was scheduled to return to part-time work as a legal researcher within three months. Her own mother, abandoned by the patient's father, was distracted, irritable, and unhappy during the patient's early childhood. The mother had come to help out after the birth, but then returned home. Since that time, the patient had had periodic bouts of intense anxiety. While denying any desire to hurt the child—despite occasional frightening, intrusive thoughts of shaking him or finding him dead—the patient described feeling sometimes that she would like to run away. She admitted that at times she longed to

"just never wake up" and wondered whether the baby would be better off without her.

Dissecting this example illustrates how evolutionary purpose—maternal adaptation and survival of the infant—shaped the meaning of symptoms that developed in the postpartum state and informed the treatment that relieved them. Biologically, normal postpartum adaptations enhance attachment and survival. In the patient described, it was assumed that genetic sensitivity to the effect of hormone flux on neurotransmitter activity had led to degrees of sleeplessness, fatigue, anxiety, and tearfulness that drastically impaired rather than facilitated her ability to care for herself and the child. Estrogen, in particular, covaries with serotonin activity in the brain (Ostlund, Keller, and Hurd 2003), and a fall in one may lead to a fall in the other. The association of low serotonin with violence and suicide may explain the observation that suicide is relatively rare during pregnancy (Marzuk et al. 1998), even when women are depressed, but suicidal thoughts and actions are a common, frightening element of postpartum depression. Serotonin depletion may also explain the association of postpartum depression with mothers' fears of hurting their infants, as this patient described.

Possible violence is less important than anxiety in most cases of postpartum depression. Decreased serotonin activity may dysregulate the activity of norepinephrine, making a woman more sensitive to threat and thus more protective of her infant. When excessive, such sensitivity may take the form of obsessive-compulsive symptoms (intrusive thoughts and compulsive checking), panic, or constant worry, as this patient described. Each symptom might require a different DSM diagnosis, but all relate to common biological and environmental conditions: the challenges of caring for a helpless infant while in a hormonally disrupted state.

Psychologically, the demands of adaptation to a new social role—welcomed by many women—in others generate ambivalence toward the infant, self-doubt, self-loathing, undue helplessness, worthlessness, and the like. Socially, a postpartum woman, who herself needs protection and care, may seem clingy, irritable, preoccupied, or detached from others she once cared for. Recognizing the different purposes and mechanisms behind symptoms can help the therapist choose the most effective strategy for intervention, as well as allowing therapists to exercise common sense and give direct advice where appropriate.

Returning to the case example, the first step in treatment was to offer a selective serotonin reuptake inhibitor, to buffer the hormonal adaptations that were contributing to the patient's uncontrolled anxiety. This relieved the intrusive thoughts very quickly. The psychiatrist/therapist also hypothesized that the new mother felt worthless because her partner and family had not been able to provide the support that she was primed to need and accept, which seemed more useful than positing some developmental deficit and confronting her dependency as "pathological." This formulation prompted the involvement of the patient's husband from the outset of treatment.

Beyond the bounds of this case, interpersonal psychotherapy (IPT) (see chapter 11) would also be justified by an evolutionary view of both postpartum depression and depression during pregnancy (together termed perinatal depression). IPT specifically helps patients recover from depression related to losses, role transitions, role disputes, and developmental deficits (Grigoriadis and Ravitz 2007). Evidence supports the efficacy of IPT for perinatal depression (O'Hara, Stuart, and Gorman 2000). An IPT therapist might characterize postpartum depression as distress related to the role transition from autonomous, working adult to parent. The stress of this transition is known to all new parents: jobs have rules and procedures, but babies are anarchists. New parents often suffer a demoralizing sense of loss of control. In the case described here, while not conducting strict IPT, the therapist did highlight the importance of the patient's perceived loss of control to normalize her ambivalence toward work, relieving some of her guilt.

The therapist also recognized that changes in routine lead to neurochemical adaptations modifiable by behavioral techniques. Guided by this understanding, treatment involved advice that the couple needed to figure out how to share the burden of night feedings in a predictable way to facilitate the patient's sleep. The psychodynamic elements of the case included encouraging the woman to sort through her feelings about how she had been mothered, especially the implications for her confidence in her own mothering.

Finally, recognizing the evolutionary value of cultural integration, the therapist encouraged the patient and her husband to celebrate rather than casually allow the ritual of baptism, so as to garner support for them as parents within their cultural community. Much later, the patient was invited to talk to a class of medical students about her experience. This proved to be a remarkably rewarding step, publicly confirming her in her new role as competent mother.

Evolutionary Thinking and Psychotherapy

As the case example illustrates, evolutionary thinking may offer a much more useful way of analyzing problems than the empirical, descriptive nosology of the DSM or the categorical distinctions of various biopsychosocial models. Postpartum depression involves an accumulation of factors that individually serve evolutionary purposes. The links between elements are systematic, not random or arbitrary. In a meaningful diagnostic system, we would perhaps go further and recognize the association between a range of disorders with different clinical features: we would diagnose postpartum maladaptation characterized by anxiety, obsessions, depressed mood, and/or depressive ideas, rather than invoking multiple "comorbidities" and piling up labels of major depression, panic disorder, obsessive-compulsive disorder, and dependent traits onto a single individual.

Psychotherapy relies on assessment beyond diagnosis. Currently, we ask beginners to provide a biopsychosocial formulation, which typically prompts them to target biological variables with medications, psychological factors with psychotherapy, and social stresses with social resources. A formulation based in evolutionary thought would instead separate predisposing and perpetuating factors (both adverse and protective), then divide them into modifiable and unmodifiable categories. For example, for the new mother described above, the fact of recent parturition was an unmodifiable biological and epidemiological predisposing or risk factor. Her early negative experience with her mother and a prior personal history of depression were unmodifiable psychosocial risk factors. However, her hormonal status, her expressed fears, and her current social support were all modifiable perpetuating factors, each suggesting a biological or psychotherapeutic intervention, separately or together.

Beyond the specific example of perinatal disorders, evolutionary psychology supports the value of psychotherapy within medicine, not just in the parallel universe of psychology or behavioral science. As Jerome Frank pointed out, at an abstract level, most psychotherapies apply shared systems of belief to the relief of individual distress. Medicine is currently reorganizing itself in response to the findings of the Human Genome Project, the great evolutionary science enterprise of our age. Evolutionary thought both in medicine and in society generally has become almost a secular cosmology. Psychotherapy needs to find its appropriate place in this new world of scientific understanding.

As a source for theories to guide therapy, evolutionary biology has certain major but not insurmountable limitations. It may lack salience, or be implausible, to patients who do not ascribe to a scientific worldview. Even while keeping evolutionary principles in mind, a therapist might have to use language derived from another therapeutic tradition (e.g., the theories underlying religious counseling or psychodynamic or cognitive behavioral therapy) with the patient (see chapter 15). In other cases, taking time to explain evolutionary principles to a patient directly may be useful, making the rationale for psychotherapy or psychotherapy plus medication more convincing.

More importantly, evolution is far from a hopeful theory, at least for individuals. Yet elements within it may be emphasized to foster hope and empowerment; for example, a therapist might, with integrity, normalize a patient's distress by explaining it as the result of universal adaptive processes gone awry. Though indifferent Nature's plan for human survival may be far less encouraging than God's, patients and therapists can take comfort from believing that painful experience relates to a plan of any kind, rather than occurring for no reason at all or as the result of personal failures. Put another way, patients will feel less isolated, different, or crazy if the therapist can assure them, with conviction, that their condition exemplifies a disruption of normal adaptive capacities and that treatment merely needs to build on what is already there.

Conclusion

Jerome Frank's view of psychotherapy was Olympian in its perspective. He showed that all systems of meaning, from those evoked in faith healing and shamanism to those of Western psychotherapies, share common elements. He further demonstrated that efforts to modify those meanings have common beneficial effects and that psychotherapies depend on the healer and sufferer sharing a common worldview. In the West, science, and especially evolutionary science, offers a secular worldview that promises to provide medically or scientifically trained healers with a theory to guide psychotherapeutic intervention. Evolution includes theories of origins, learning, and development, and ways of understanding behavior and individual subjective experience. As a system of meaning, an understanding of evolution may be useful to psychotherapists, particularly those with medical or scientific training who are likely to treat people who seek help within a medical framework. As shown by the example of perinatal depression, therapists will benefit from an understanding of how meaning is influenced by the structure and development of the individual brain, and from an awareness of the environmental conditions that have the greatest impact in this process. Such understanding may help therapists identify points of leverage, places where a small intervention (even the longest psychotherapy is small relative to the aggregate experiences of the individual) can have a substantial impact.

REFERENCES

American Psychiatric Association. 2000. *Diagnostic and Statistical Manual of Mental Disorders*, 4th ed., text rev. Washington, DC: American Psychiatric Association.

Barron, J. W. (ed.). 2002. *Making Diagnosis Meaningful: Enhancing Evaluation and Treatment of Psychological Disorders*. Washington, DC: American Psychological Association.

Bank, W., Bergvall, U., Byrd, S., Corbaz, J. M., Choux, M., Combalbert, A., and Yagishita, A. 2010. Salamon's neuroanatomy and neurovasculature web-atlas resource. www.radnet.ucla.edu/sections/DINR/index.htm.

Belsky, J. 2007. Childhood experiences and reproductive strategies. In R. I. M. Dunbar and L. Barrett (eds.), *The Oxford Handbook of Evolutionary Psychology* (pp. 237–53). New York: Oxford University Press

Berkowitz, R. L., Coplan, J. D., Reddy, D. P., and Gorman, J. M. 2007. The human dimension: how the prefrontal cortex modulates the subcortical fear response. *Reviews in the Neurosciences* 18:191–207.

Blatt, S. J., and Levy, K. N. 2002. A psychodynamic approach to the diagnosis of psychopathology. In J. W. Barron (ed.), *Making Diagnosis Meaningful: Enhancing Evaluation and Treatment of Psychological Disorders* (pp. 73–110). Washington, DC: American Psychological Association.

Bremner, J. D., Elzinga, B., Schmahl, C., and Vermetten, E. 2008. Structural and functional plasticity of the human brain in posttraumatic stress disorder. *Progress in Brain Research* 167:171–86.

Calvin, W. H. 2004. *A Brief History of the Mind: From Apes to Intellect and Beyond*. New York: Oxford University Press.

Dunbar, R. I. M., and Barrett, L. 2007. Evolutionary psychology in the round. In R. I. M. Dunbar and L. Barrett (eds.), *The Oxford Handbook of Evolutionary Psychology* (pp. 3–9). New York: Oxford University Press.

Engel, G. 1977. The need for a new medical model: a challenge for biomedicine. *Science* 196:129–36.

Frank, J. D., and Frank, J. B. 1991a. *Persuasion and Healing: A Comparative Study of Psychotherapy*, 3rd ed. Baltimore: Johns Hopkins University Press.

———. 1991b. Psychotherapy, the transformation of meaning. In *Persuasion and Healing: A Comparative Study of Psychotherapy*, 3rd ed. (pp. 52–73). Baltimore: Johns Hopkins University Press.

Gabbard, G. O. 2000. A neurobiologically informed perspective on psychotherapy. *British Journal of Psychiatry* 177:117–22.

Ghaemi, N. 2003. *The Concepts of Psychiatry: A Pluralistic Approach to the Mind and Mental Illness.* Baltimore: Johns Hopkins University Press.

Grigoriadis, S., and Ravitz, P. 2007. An approach to interpersonal psychotherapy for postpartum depression: focusing on interpersonal changes. *Canadian Family Physician* 53:1469–75.

Heim, A., and Westen, D. 2005. Theories of personality and personality disorder. In J. Oldham, A. E. Skodol, and D. S. Bender (eds.), *The American Psychiatric Publishing Textbook of Personality Disorders.* Washington, DC: American Psychiatric Publishing.

Keller, M. C., Neale, M. C., and Kendler, K. S. 2007. Association of different adverse life events with distinct patterns of depressive symptoms. *American Journal of Psychiatry* 164:1521–29.

Laland, K. N. 2007. Niche construction, human behavioural ecology and evolutionary psychology. In R. I. M. Dunbar and L. Barrett (eds.), *The Oxford Handbook of Evolutionary Psychology* (pp. 35–48). New York: Oxford University Press.

LeDoux, J. 1996. *The Emotional Brain: The Mysterious Underpinnings of Emotional Life.* New York: Simon and Schuster.

Marzuk, P. M., Tardiff, K., Leon, A. C., Hirsch, C. S., Portera, L., Hartwell, N., and Iqbal, M. 1998. Lower risk of suicide during pregnancy. *American Journal of Psychiatry* 154:1479–80.

McEwen, B. S. 2002. The neurobiology and neuroendocrinology of stress: implications for post-traumatic stress disorder from a basic science perspective. *Psychiatric Clinics of North America* 25:469–94.

McGuire, M., and Troisi, A. 1998. *Darwinian Psychiatry.* New York: Oxford University Press.

McHugh, P. R., and Slavney, P. R. 1998. *The Perspectives of Psychiatry,* 2nd ed. Baltimore: Johns Hopkins University Press.

Moerman, D. 2002. *Meaning, Medicine, and the "Placebo Effect."* Cambridge: Cambridge University Press.

Nathan, P. E. 2002. The DSM IV and its antecedents: enhancing syndromal diagnosis. In J. W. Barron (ed.), *Making Diagnosis Meaningful: Enhancing Evaluation and Treatment of Psychological Disorders* (p. 328). Washington, DC: American Psychological Association.

Nemeroff, C. B., Bremner, J. D., Foa, E. B., Mayberg, H. S., North, C. S., and Stein, M. B. 2006. Posttraumatic stress disorder: a state-of-the-science review. *Journal of Psychiatric Research* 40:1–21.

O'Hara, M. W., Stuart, S., and Gorman, L. L. 2000. Efficacy of interpersonal psychotherapy for postpartum depression. *Archives of General Psychiatry* 57:1039–45.

Ostlund, H., Keller, E., and Hurd, Y. L. 2003. Estrogen receptor gene expression in relation to neuropsychiatric disorders. *Annals of the New York Academy of Sciences* 1007:54–63.

Panksepp, J. 2007. The neuroevolutionary and neuroaffective psychobiology of the prosocial brain. In R. I. M. Dunbar and L. Barrett (eds.), *The Oxford Handbook of Evolutionary Psychology* (pp. 145–62). New York: Oxford University Press.

Paquette, V., Levesque, J., Mensour, B., Leroux, J.-M., Beaudoin, G., Bourgouin, P., and Beauregard, M. 2003. "Change the mind and you change the brain": effects of cognitive behavioral therapy on the neural correlates of spider phobia. *NeuroImage* 18:401–9.

Pliszka, S. R. 2004. *Neuroscience for the Mental Health Clinician.* New York: Guilford Press.

Plotkin, H. 2007. The power of culture. In R. I. M. Dunbar and L. Barrett (eds.), *The Oxford Handbook of Evolutionary Psychology* (pp. 11–20). New York: Oxford University Press.

Rassovsky, Y., Kushner, M. G., Schwarze, N. J., and Wangensteen, O. D. 2000. Psychological and physiological predictors of response to carbon dioxide challenge in individuals with panic disorder. *Journal of Abnormal Psychology* 109:616–23.

Schacter, D. L. 1996. *Searching for Memory: The Brain, the Mind, and the Past.* New York: Basic Books.

Spinelli, S., Chefer, S., Suomi, S. J., Higley, J. D., Barr, C. S., and Stein, E. 2009. Early-life stress induces long-term morphologic changes in primate brain. *Archives of General Psychiatry* 66:658–65.

Vaillant, G. 1993. *The Wisdom of the Ego.* Cambridge, MA: Harvard University Press.

Weinberg, M. K., and Tronick, E. Z. 1998. The impact of maternal psychiatric illness on infant development. *Journal of Clinical Psychiatry* 59(suppl. 2):53–61.

Wisner, K. L., Parry, B. L., and Piontek, C. M. 2002. Postpartum depression. *New England Journal of Medicine* 347:194–99.

Workman, L., and Reader, W. 2004. *Evolutionary Psychology: An Introduction.* Cambridge: Cambridge University Press.

Cultural Concepts in *Persuasion and Healing*

Renato D. Alarcón, M.D., M.P.H., and
Mark Williams, M.D.

> Then she began looking about, and noticed that what could be seen from the old room was quite common and uninteresting, but that all the rest was as different as possible.
> —*Through the Looking Glass*

Healing rituals . . . bring out the parallels between inner disorganization and disturbed relations with one's group, and illustrate the healing power of patterned interactions of patient, healer and group within the framework of an internally consistent assumptive world.

> —PERSUASION AND HEALING, 1991, P. 87

In chapter 5 of *Persuasion and Healing*, Jerome Frank (1961) developed what was then considered a radical argument—that psychotherapy is essentially a culture-bound activity. In Euro-Western societies, the psychotherapy establishment claims, rightly or wrongly, to be applying science to human behavior. Frank's own investigative work emerged from this tradition, but in trying to make sense of his empirical findings, he recognized that many groups promote similar healing activities grounded in values other than empirical science. Faith healing, shamanistic rituals, cult induction, and even the techniques of coercive interrogation, Frank noted, could be as effective as psychotherapy in inducing shifts in people's assumptive worlds and their related feelings and behavior. Factors that give one person the power to induce change in another include the culturally assigned status of the therapist, the meaning of the patient's symptoms or suffering within a particular context, and the power of the healer to manipulate cultural symbols, be these stethoscopes, charts, and the other trappings of science or the sand paintings of the shaman. Culture, expressed in language, also structures the narratives that psychotherapy helps patients revise. Finally, changes induced by persuasion, such as adopting the beliefs of a cult or expressing the slogans implanted by "thought reform," do not persist in the absence of cultural reinforcement—the sanctions or rewards provided by others in the treated person's reference group.

Persuasion and Healing contributed to the development of what has come to be called cultural psychiatry. Although psychotherapy is a legitimate medical treatment in many respects, much of its power derives, not from the biological mechanisms that justify other types of medical care, but from its relation to powerful forces in whichever culture supports it. Cultural psychiatry seeks to maximize the application of these forces, adapting psychotherapy for use in diverse populations. People who find other sources of meaning more compelling and coherent than Western individualism or scientific positivism may respond better to treatments that mobilize different symbols and practices—for example, healing rituals or the involvement of authoritative family members— in their care. In this chapter we intend to demonstrate that even those who adhere to the so-called Western worldview benefit from the insights that cultural psychiatry provides into the implicit cultural processes that daily influence all people's attitudes and behavior.

The term *culture*, what anthropologists define mostly in terms of context and meaning, broadly describes many of the environmental elements that complement the expression of genes and biology invoked by all models of psychopathology (see chapter 4). We define culture as the set of socially transmitted and learned behavioral norms and values or reference points by which members of a particular society construct their unique view of the world and create their own identity. Culture is not static; it changes under the impact of people's actions and historical events and as it is taught by and transmitted from one generation to the next (Favazza and Oman 1984; Haviland 1990). For didactic purposes, in our exploration of cultural psychiatry concepts in Frank's work, we give first priority to the traditional variables of language, religion, gender, social relationships, sexual orientation, moral practices, traditions, beliefs, family structure and functioning, and expressive modes of thought and emotions. In explaining aspects of psychotherapy, culture also encompasses phenomena as varied as technology, financial philosophies, migration, or traumatic memories (Group for the Advancement of Psychiatry 2002). These elements interact and define and redefine individuals, groups, communities, and societies, as they have throughout history. The complex, rich interactions among these variables generate the dynamic, ever changing nature of culture itself.

In psychiatry and mental health (including psychotherapy), culture has always shaped efforts to categorize and help sufferers (Kirmayer et al. 2003). In the late nineteenth century, an organized body of knowledge started to emerge, adopting over the ensuing decades such names as "comparative," "transcultural," "cross-cultural," and, most recently, *cultural psychiatry* (Tseng 2001). This discipline deals with the description, definition, assessment, and management of conditions that involve aberrant thought or behavior in all human groups, exploring how these conditions reflect the patterning influence of cultural factors, within a biopsychosocial context. Cultural psychiatry uses concepts and instruments from both social and biological sciences to advance a comprehensive understanding of psychopathology and its treatment (Canino, Lewis-Fernandez, and Bravo 1997). In this chapter, as proponents of cultural psychiatry, we comment on the many cultural issues presented and discussed in the first and third editions of *Persuasion and Healing* (Frank 1961; Frank and Frank 1991). The book provides a particularly rich vein of cultural concepts, some of them innovative and solid, others open to the discussion that original ideas invariably generate. A cultural perspective is essential, both to extend Frank's contributions to the field and to reassess and build on the accomplishments, challenges, and future perspectives of this area of inquiry.

Culture and Psychotherapy

As an activity that deals with the essential humanness of a given patient, the connections between psychotherapy and culture are, by definition, rich and deep. Biology shapes humans' physiognomy, genetic predispositions, and, perhaps, temperament, but culture powerfully influences "human nature" and behavior by way of parental modeling (or lack of it), family environment (microculture), social traditions, beliefs, and institutions (macroculture), developmental life experiences, and the like. With its focus on both intrapsychic and interpersonal behaviors, psychotherapy addresses culture directly and indirectly within the specific confines of its many techniques and underlying theories.

Moreover, psychotherapy itself is a cultural product. As practiced in Euro-Western societies, psychotherapy uses particular interpretations or explanations of human behavior, responding to the historical evolution of ideas through the formulation of specific "theories of the mind" (i.e., psychoanalytic, cognitive behavioral, or existential), adopting (or adapting) compatible approaches and procedures. In other words, therapists' interpretations or explanations reflect and reinforce features of a particular culture or subculture (Littlewood 2001). Many "symptoms" of demoralization, such as guilt, inability to follow rules, or feelings of failure to meet others' expectations (worthlessness), are themselves the result of changes in, violations of, or departures from cultural norms. In general, psychotherapies attempt to restore normality, that is, to realign the troubled person with some coherent system of cultural precepts, most often one already familiar to the individual. The process restores patients or clients to their best prior acceptable connection with themselves and with their surroundings.

Cultural Topics in *Persuasion and Healing*

The first chapter of *Persuasion and Healing* offers detailed cultural definitions of aspects of mental illness and psychotherapy. Topics such as help-seeking, attitudes, values, meaning and interpretations, social judgment, labeling and moral codes, ethnicity, economic status, and education appear in bold brushstrokes. Our discussion examines these topics, and Frank's approaches, dividing them into two groups: (1) general culturally based concepts, many of them powerful original features of Frank's contribution to psychiatric knowledge, and (2) specific cultural concepts that embrace and broaden some or all of the fundamental cultural variables mentioned earlier. In chapter 14, we explore cultural psychotherapy practices in light of recent investigations in this field, both building on and revising Frank's original descriptions of such culturally specific practices as faith healing and traditional healing rituals.

Every epistemological investigation related to culture begins with the concept of context (Eisenberg 1988). Sociology and anthropology focus specifically on context, providing insights that profoundly influence other social and biological sciences, as well as the interpretive disciplines of the liberal arts. *Persuasion and Healing* cites context many times—and rightly so—as a life script, a surrounding space or a real or virtual scenario. In particular, Frank conspicuously discusses the contextual/cultural influences on the interpretation of emotions, a key feature of every psychotherapy. Context itself does not figure on our list of factors to be examined here, because it is everywhere in Frank's work and in our reflections throughout this chapter.

General Culturally Based Concepts

Beyond context, other cultural elements capture the essentially humanistic basis of psychotherapy, encompassing both the broad areas of environment and development and the more particular ones of assumptive world, rhetoric and hermeneutics, and meaning.

Environment

Frank uses terms such as *cultural settings* to delineate the surroundings of individuals that may contribute to the etiological (or etiopathogenic) events triggering clinical occurrences. These settings also "largely determine how such conditions are diagnosed," the cultural implication being that American society may identify as "symptoms" behaviors that "may be classified in other times or places as appropriate responses to life's stresses, as evidence of spirit possession requiring exorcism, as wrongdoing requiring punishment, or as mere eccentricity" (Frank and Frank 1991, p. 7). Indeed, one of the great weaknesses of the current *Diagnostic and Statistical Manual of Mental Disorders*–based nosology is its explicit exclusion of context in categorizing the dysfunctions labeled "disorders." By contrast, Frank's perspective consistently encompasses cultural relativism. He clearly saw both the pathogenic and the potentially therapeutic role of patients' near environment in the clinical world.

In chapter 12 of the 1991 edition of *Persuasion and Healing*, "Psychotherapy in a Controlled Environment," Jerome and Julia Frank specifically explore the influence of a patient's immediate surroundings, their historical context, and therapeutic nature. "Most treatment sites," they assert, "embody either the psychosocial or the organic view of the causes, and therefore the treatment of social breakdown syndromes . . . Proponents of the psychosocial approach to treatment attribute patients' breakdowns primarily to intrapsychic or environmental stresses." They describe the "moral treatment" era as the response "to the then widely held American belief that the pressures of an increasingly open and chaotic society lay at the root of many mental illnesses." This kind of treatment, they state, "derived legitimacy not from scientific evidence but from the cultural values of a particular class of citizens at a particular period in history" (pp. 276–77).

The strongest point to be made is that what scientists, clinicians, administrators, and even the general public call "environment" includes significant cultural content. Environment *is* culture. Concepts for analyzing culture highlight how interaction with the surrounding environment influences the everyday behavior of both normal and "ill" or "abnormal" persons. Culture further shapes the responses of communities and societies to the results of those environmental forces, as evidenced by societal responses to the phenomena of mental illness. These responses range from rejection and stigmatization to the compassionate conception and practice of psychotherapy (Duckworth et al. 2003). "Mental illness," as Frank presciently observed, "is not an innate property of the individual, but the product of interactions between the person and the social environment" (Frank and Frank 1991, p. 278). Like the outside environment, treatment approaches in general "shape thoughts and behavior." Such processes are particularly evident in "milieu therapies" or "therapeutic communities," but the idea applies with the same conviction to all group and nearly all individual therapies.

Development

Life cycle, a term denoting the process that accounts for maturity, assumption of new roles and responsibilities, reformulation of intrapersonal and interpersonal experiences and attitudes, and acceptance of evolving biological and social/environmental realities (Jensen, Knapp, and Mrazek 2006), has been the subject of active research in recent decades. Such research relates life stages both to general behavior patterns, such as dramatic but not pathological age-related changes in attitude, demeanor, and the style and nature of an individual's interactions, and to their pathoplastic role in the expression of psychopathology (Alarcón et al. 1999). Current efforts to refine the DSM system give significant weight to the concept of life cycles. Debates about the age of onset of clinical entities, type and nature of symptoms, nosological characterizations, and response to different kinds of treatments all now include discussion of developmental variations (Pine 2009).

Not surprisingly, development intertwines itself with culture. Together with biological changes, the self-image and self-recognition of each individual and his or her accompanying psychological, relational, and behavioral dispositions vary with different periods of personal growth. Culture determines the ways in which people acquire new behaviors and roles by learning, imitating, fighting, searching for, reacting to, and responding to external or internalized stimuli. Parental attitudes and approaches, parent-child transactions, family structure and interactions, educational activities, social factors, and conflict and resolution experiences are the developmental elements of microcultural or macro-cultural origins (Pine et al. 2002; Knapp 2006). Frank recognizes this through-out *Persuasion and Healing*, placing particular emphasis on the impact of culture on the early stages of life, which in turn, he believed, strongly influence adult psychopathology.

As Frank emphasized, the effect of culturally influenced developmental fac-tors in the formation of clinically recognized illness is clearest in the area of persons' reactions to stress or trauma, with posttraumatic stress disorder being the most representative entity in Western societies (and, to some extent, around the world). Other symptoms such as free-floating anxiety and behaviors attributable to different types of personality disorder also reflect developmen-tal stages of learning and behaving that are powerfully influenced by culture. In the therapeutic field, Frank cites reevaluation counseling, primal therapy, and even dianetics as examples of almost "fixed" developmentally influenced approaches. The "reexperiencing of the past" that many techniques (including psychoanalysis) advocate is essentially the reenacting of learned styles or psy-chological responses. Such learning is the end result of the accumulation of culturally shaped events throughout an individual's life. Abreaction, whether spontaneous in the form of flashbacks or nightmares or induced in the context of an emotionally intense healing relationship that promotes the reworking of culturally influenced developmental experiences, has a strong therapeutic value that extends to people from many different cultures.

Hermeneutics and Rhetoric

Frank took the bold, provocative, and eminently original step of viewing psy-chotherapy not as applied behavioral science but as "a form of rhetoric best studied hermeneutically." He defined rhetoric as "the use of words to form at-titudes or induce action," and hermeneutics as "the study of understanding, and of the correct interpretation of what has been understood." From the time of ancient Greece, rhetoric, the "science of persuasion," when linked to medi-cine, was an early, solid "functional equivalent of psychotherapy." An Aristote-lian rhetorician "seeks to win the confidence of the listener," engages the "lis-tener's emotions," and "provides a truth, real or apparent, by argument" (Frank and Frank 1991, chap. 3). Frank places psychotherapists and rhetoricians together, equating them in charisma, ethos-based capacities, delineation of targets, and influence by argument, all therapeutic ingredients that contribute to goals of "indoctrination," arousing hope, stirring emotions, and combating alienation.

In turn, hermeneutics (or exegesis), like psychotherapy, "seeks to understand and interpret the meaning of the patient's communications." The thera-pist's exegesis places the patient's experience into a broader context, ensuring that the sufferer's account is not solely a personal interpretation. Echoing Ar-thur Kleinman (1980), Frank maintains that diagnosis and treatment are "forms of mutual interpretation between healer and patient," a "process of ne-gotiation" arriving at a mutually satisfactory story closing what Karl Jaspers (1964) called the "hermeneutic circle." One can venture here that the "agreed upon" version of events brought into and negotiated in the therapeutic en-counter will correspond to culturally determined expectations; the "plausibil-ity" or "fruitfulness" of therapeutic interpretations (or explanations) depends on their "making sense" to a patient with a particular worldview. Frank tells us that "a therapeutic plot must offer the prospect of a happy ending" (Frank and Frank 1991, chap. 3); there is no more "cultural" outcome of the process and achievements of psychotherapy than this universal, tale- or movie-like process of recasting the narrative of the self.

The cultural content of rhetoric and hermeneutics is indisputable. In recog-nizing that rhetoric derives its power from words, and words are the building blocks of language, one uncovers the cultural roots of psychotherapy. Lan-guage is both the vehicle and the tool of therapeutic influence, the conveyor of clear, accessible communication and the instrument of change by means of—once again—learning mechanisms (Beck 1995). In the culture (or "subculture") of therapy, training provides the future therapist with language whose conno-tations are enriched by a particular theoretical perspective. The process of therapy gives the patient opportunities to learn what he or she needs to learn about such new language and the ideas it expresses.

Hermeneutics, as an exercise in interpretation or provision of plausible ex-planations, plays an obvious role in psychotherapy. From the cultural vantage point, Kleinman (1988) elaborated on what he called "explanatory models," usually elicited from or volunteered by the patient, as the first stages of the therapeutic encounter. In this phase of negotiation, the patient provides a personal interpretation of the plight that brought him or her to therapy. Such explanatory models are heavily influenced by the patient's culture of origin: beliefs, traditions, morals, habits, religion. The therapist is supposed to, re-spectfully, ask and listen (initial rhetorical phase), figure out the background (context) of the problems, and then apply alternatives to the hermeneutic struc-ture of the patient's own narrative. The therapist's hermeneutics may agree with the patient's explanations, modify them slightly or extensively, or reject them.

Most schools of therapy avoid outright, emphatic rejection, as that would deny the relative balance of the parties conducting the therapeutic "negotiation." More important, overt rejection would unnecessarily challenge the patient's most strongly held cultural principles, with all the negative implications—especially prejudice or stigmatization of normal beliefs—that such a step implies.

Frank also explored indoctrination into cults (Frank and Frank 1991, chap. 4) or efforts at coercive "thought reform" (Frank 1961, chap. 4) as applications of rhetoric and hermeneutics. These differ from psychotherapy in that their goal is not to reconcile sufferers with the consoling or empowering elements of their personal, preexisting culture. Rather, they aim to induct their targets into some new, internally consistent but unfamiliar culture. Though such efforts may succeed, in the absence of continued reinforcement by the sect or political authority, the converted often default to beliefs and behaviors they learned earlier in life. Despite the features shared with psychotherapy, these activities derive from radically different ethical principles, being meant to serve and enlarge a group rather than heal a particular individual.

Specific Cultural Concepts

Certain culturally rooted concepts are narrower in scope than general environment and pathways of development, yet closer to clinical events. These factors include issues of cultural heritage (myths) and outcome-related features (survival) (see chapter 14). They express the seminal cultural variables of identity, family, and religion and provide bridges between general concepts and the tools or technical aspects of psychotherapy.

Myths

Persuasion and Healing launched a strong scholarly "assault" on the psychotherapy establishment, and its challenges persist as reminders of how much needs to be done in the field. One of Frank's boldest and most original steps was to declare the existing theories of psychotherapy "myths." He was not being ironic: both myths and psychotherapy theories are "imagination-catching formulations" of recurrent and important human experiences that "cannot be proved empirically." A myth (or theory) is a "conceptual scheme that provides a plausible explanation for the patient's symptoms, and prescribes a ritual or procedure for resolving them." Frank reminds us that Freud, whom he called "a truly great myth-maker," characterized instincts as "our mythology." Despite the undeniable advances of science, *faith* in science (and especially today, in evolutionary science) (see chapter 4 in this volume) wears the clothing of myth in the contemporary world.

Nothing is more essentially cultural than a myth. As the expression of complex threads of fact and fiction, history and tradition, materialism and spirituality, myths have defined target audiences and goals (Geoffrey 1979; Impelluso 2007). Myths play important social and cultural roles: explanation, teaching, reaffirmation, a call for convergence of views. Myths generate rituals in the same way that a theory of human functioning generates techniques of psychotherapy. The transformation of a myth's essential message into an accepted truth is a fascinating cultural dynamic, demonstrated many times throughout history. While strengthening the relationship between the myth narrator (therapist) and the listener (patient), the mythical/therapeutic doctrine or "school" inspires and maintains "the patient's expectation of help." Rituals (rules and procedures for therapy) derived from the myth build morale and arouse hope. In both culture and psychotherapy, the power of myths derives from a "shared belief system . . . [that is] essential to the formation and maintenance of groups." In the case of the therapeutic relationship, this concept prompts "the adherence of therapist and patient to the same therapeutic myth," thus creating a "powerful bond" between them (Frank and Frank 1991, chap. 2).

Finally, like many therapies, myths typically include a didactic purpose and have didactic value (Fagan 2004). Listening to the recounting of a myth or participating in a related ritual are learning experiences, at times repetitive; if taught to groups of people, a myth fosters a sense of mastery "through weathering the stresses of group interactions" (Frank and Frank 1991, chap. 2) (see chapter 13 in this volume). Myths strengthen groups' solidarity through sharing the teachings of their implicit stories.

A myth, like theory underlying therapy, structures beliefs and rules in an acceptable way, blending plausibility, reasonableness, and truth. No matter how much valid empirical information has been gathered over decades, theory remains a necessary point of departure for the acquisition or improvement of knowledge, very much as myths have been the point of departure for civilization-building processes throughout history (Geoffrey 1979; Watson 2006).

Survival

Not surprisingly, the Franks developed several ideas of a cultural nature in the parts of *Persuasion and Healing* (1991) devoted to collective therapies, including encounter groups, evocative therapies, family therapy, and group therapy. Neither actual nor emotional survival occurs as an individual event. Humans begin life in a helpless state and require the care of others, to some degree, at every subsequent point. Emotionally, all experiences involve memories, invocations, and reflections of contacts and relationships that make the individual feel accompanied. Some authors call this "transcending" (Denton 1998; James 2007), overcoming the barriers of individuality, solitude, or loneliness to move into redeeming realizations of belonging. These are the products and results of a good therapy.

Frank reminds us of Jules Masserman's assertion (1971) that "all humans struggle against three basic fears—fear of loss of health, fear of alienation from others, and fear that life is meaningless" (Frank and Frank 1991, chap. 4). Therefore, survival becomes the stated purpose and the expected outcome of efforts aimed at liberating the individual from what Frank calls feelings of "cosmic despair and social alienation." Frank situates psychotherapy as a survival mechanism within the modern historical context of "revival" experiences, both religious revivals and the encounter groups of the "turbulent 1960s . . . [when] attempting to cope with the widespread cultural dislocations and proliferating new ideologies . . . hundreds of people flocked to 'personal growth' centers, exemplifying the 'human potential' movement." Survival becomes, somehow, a sublimated goal of psychotherapy, enriching the patient's life through "experiences designed to promote spontaneity, joy, and feelings of intimacy" (Frank and Frank 1991, p. 246).

Jerome Frank lived through World War II, and we, similarly, are immediate survivors of turbulent times. From this perspective, we highlight two particular types of psychotherapy that make survival their explicit goal: existential therapy and the widespread use of group therapy in Argentina during a tragic period of state-sponsored terror. Viktor Frankl (1984), one of the fathers of existential psychotherapy (known also as the creator of the "paradoxical intention" technique), built his therapeutic ideas firmly on the foundation of his experience in a Nazi concentration camp. Deprived of every possible freedom, of the most elemental respect for his humanity, he created his own therapy for survival, a dramatic self-persuasive effort aimed at the preservation of his human dignity. Specifically, he held consciously to the conviction that no matter what his tormentors did, they would never be able to annihilate his inner beliefs, his moral principles, his most intimate feelings and enjoyment of freedom.

Something similar occurred in Argentina during the long years of a bloodthirsty military regime that killed hundreds of thousands of people, the *desaparecidos* or missing children of the legendary "Mothers of May Square" (Las Madres de la Plaza de Mayo) (Cia 2001). During those years (1980s and 1990s), when both politically and not politically involved persons had survival as their only objective, hundreds of "psychotherapy groups" flourished around Buenos Aires and other large cities, providing support to the victims of government-sponsored terror. Therapists of different persuasions organized these groups, which became widely recognized symbols of hope and freedom, the reaffirmation of essential human principles cynically and cruelly denied by the dictatorship.

As Frank, Frankl, and the Argentine group therapy practitioners all learned, survival entails dropping "social masks, . . . [seeking] to engender peak experiences, not unlike those of a religious revival or the psychedelic experiences sometimes produced by consciousness-altering drugs" (Frank and Frank 1991, p. 247). Issues of survival become most salient at times of crisis (at an individual or collective level). As Frank declared in another of his profoundly visionary (and yet also pragmatic) books, *Sanity and Survival*:

> In the last analysis, the main source of hope that mankind will avert the looming disasters is the recognition that while man's survival has always been problematical, the human species has always been able to muster the resources and ingenuity to enable it to come through by the skin of its teeth. Although it is a subject for ironic reflection, it is also hopeful that the main threats now come from man himself instead of nature, because it implies that he can use his new mastery of his environment to enhance his welfare instead of hasten his destruction. (Frank 1967, pp. 290–91)

Family

Thousands, perhaps millions, of books, essays, and articles have been written about the family as the repository of culture in any person's life. The microculture of family structure, hierarchy, authority, traditions and customs, and beliefs and morals provides the initial setting in which decisive "culturogenic" immersions take place from the moment a human being arrives in the world (Levi 2001). Family life (or any structure that plays a similar role) provides the basis of the child's evolving assumptive world (Epston and White 1992; Pine et al. 2002; Knapp 2006). Gradually, perceptions and feelings influenced by those the child sees as "possessing superior power and knowledge" (parents and other elders) contribute powerfully to what mental health professionals and the public at large call personality (Allport 1937). The Franks (1991, p. 242) summarize this reality by saying: "The standards, expectations, and emotional contagion of a group [in this case, the family group] . . . produce striking and permanent shifts in value and behavior." They make two further sociocultural observations in this regard. First, they describe American individualism as infused by "feelings of suspicion, competitiveness and isolation," related to immigrants' struggle "to maintain a sense of community, as they confronted first the openness and isolation of the frontier, and later the hostility of established groups of earlier settlers." Second, they note that when everything is said and done, "individuals terminate therapy, groups disband, but the family remains a force in a person's life, long after treatment has ended" (p. 272). It follows that outcomes differ depending on whether the family disintegrates or persists as a living, organized, and nourishing entity.

The health of the developing individual depends largely on the cohesiveness of the family group: "Strongly cohesive groups invariably possess high morale, and demoralized groups tend to fragment" (Frank and Frank 1991, p. 260). Family life also inculcates the first components of socialization as a source of identity reinforcement, being-in-the-world existential affirmation, and needed support in times of crisis. Under favorable circumstances, the family is a source of warmth and closeness whenever needed. Focusing strictly on psychotherapy, outside the narrow confines of interventions shaped by descriptive psychiatry and, to some extent, by biomedicine, family therapy enjoys well-deserved recognition and widespread acceptance (Griffin and Slovik 2003; Kreuz-Smolinski and Pereira-Tercero 2005).

From a cultural perspective, family therapy succeeds in part by resurrecting cultural ideals that have been eclipsed by the pathologically disturbed life of the patient. The Franks (1991, p. 268) remind us that "the reciprocity between patients' problems and the family responses suggests that modifying family interactions can increase a patient's motivation to improve." Roles played by members of the family, understood as the patient's subculture, must be revised to change their impact in the patient's life. Furthermore, family interactions, observed or described, either validate or challenge patients' feelings and attitudes. In the course of therapy, such interactions either constitute the initial steps of possible reconciliation with the family microculture or, if reality dictates otherwise, place the patient on the road to new personal and cultural destinations diverging from the past.

Religion

Across the world and throughout history, religion powerfully influences the life and activities of any society. The development and presence of religions and their rituals are always a response to the elemental needs (including social needs related to survival) of individuals and groups (see chapter 15). From the beginning, religions emerged from convoluted phases of systematization, organization, revision, and adaptation. These include the need to know or "explain" mysterious, overwhelming natural phenomena, the need to be protected from predators, foes, or conquerors, and the need to overcome fears of death and destruction (Denton 1998, 2008). Anthropologists and historians have concluded that even when subsistence needs are more or less satisfied, religions fulfill a basic *need to believe*, a substantially human yearning. Religions provide a road toward transcendence, mobilizing the force of spirituality. Yet, those needs also reflect the impact of the surrounding world. Sacred books and teachings, anointed guides and masters, and rituals of complex and generally rigid nature are all tools that channel collective aspirations and justify political or military accomplishments, while also providing consolation, relief, and redemption. In all societies, including ours, religion has preceded psychotherapy, both historically and in the lives of many individuals.

For Frank (1961, chap. 5), religio-magical elements form the third root of psychotherapy, complementing both its secular mythological elements (exemplified by psychoanalysis) and the empirical qualities developed by various cognitive behavioral schools. Terms such as "unshakeable convictions" or the description of "religio-magical experiences [that] cannot be verified or disproved by objective criteria" also capture essential elements of all psychotherapies. Frank analyzes the phenomenon of "revivalism"—"zealous cults with messianic goals . . . a consequence of the confusion and anxiety created by the conditions of modern life" (Frank 1973, p. 84)—in contextual terms. As he notes, proselytizing and religious conversions, with the emphasis on the "contrapuntal themes of salvation and damnation," are cultural ingredients that religion shares with psychotherapy. Religion also shapes people's self-image, images of others and patterns of social participation, and the roles and behaviors of leaders (see chapter 15). These, too, are recognizable psychotherapeutic concerns. An examination of the language found in religious and psychotherapeutic texts would find a significant number of synonyms. It can be said that religion (even with its mythological elements; see Geoffrey 1979; Fagan 2004) and psychotherapy represent two sides of a common cultural coin. Small wonder that, even though psychotherapy "works" (as Frank demonstrated through his "common ingredients" strategy) and may be "cost effective," its generalized acceptance remains an elusive goal; the outcome, as that of the religious experience, may be profound, but it is difficult to measure in objectively verifiable terms.

Frank's assessment of varieties of religious healing highlights their similarities with psychotherapy. He does not miss, of course, the role of ethnically based beliefs (myths), but considers them in light of both the culturally determined "scornful skepticism" of biomedical mental health practitioners and the "gullibility" associated with the acceptance of "flagrant frauds." He navigates masterfully between these two extremes. Furthermore, he recognizes that "in all cultures, religious healing is most often applied to illnesses that have important emotional components," reaffirming the close connection between religion and psychotherapy. In his view, these two cultural products from different historical periods address similar needs and have followed similar paths of development. Being helped by psychotherapy may be linked to the "purification" dear to religious believers; explanations about one's emotional ailments are the equivalent of transcendental truths or revelations restated in accessible language. Both religion and psychotherapy play the eminently cultural role of placing sins and symptoms "within a self-consistent conceptual system" (Frank and Frank 1991, chap. 5).

Frank did not shy away from dealing with the element of religion that proves most awkward for scientists, the occurrence of miracles. At various points he analyzed examples of how belief may profoundly influence undeniably biological processes, ranging from surgical healing to inexplicable remissions of cancer. Although Frank never did anthropological fieldwork (beyond his own clinical practice), he endorsed the anthropological insight into the role of intense emotional arousal in the unfolding of miraculous events, describing the sequence from apprehension to hope, the role of confession and trust in the healer, and the profound therapeutic impact of deep religious beliefs (Fox 1986). Frank ends his chapter on these subjects by recognizing the existence of "curative forces . . . that cannot be conceptually incorporated into the secular cosmology that dominates Western scientific thinking" (Frank and Frank 1991, p. 111).

Conclusion

Persuasion and Healing elegantly introduced and deftly applied cultural concepts to the study of important aspects of the human condition. Frank's pioneering work constituted a profound yet pragmatic treatise on cultural psychiatry, demonstrating how culture interacts with and nourishes the philosophy, the actual transactions, and the techniques of psychotherapy. He understood that treating a fellow human requires a therapist to be immersed in the "assumptive world" of that patient, able to understand the cultural template that may have generated, complicated, or at times buffered the patient's emotional tribulations. Frank also examined carefully how cultural factors enrich the body of psychotherapeutic knowledge. In so doing, he suggested ways for practitioners to improve on their natural abilities and professional skills by connecting history, tradition, myths, and beliefs (all precious cultural variables) with modern concepts and schools of thought. Such an approach ensures comprehensiveness in the management of the therapeutic enterprise.

Expectations about what is considered "normal" interpersonal behavior vary considerably among cultural groups. Roles of husbands and wives, attitudes toward authority, and who may or may not be considered a part of a family are pertinent examples of such variance. Culture determines which issues are "taboo," what confidentiality may or may not mean, and how decisions are made. Patterns of help-seeking are demonstrably culturally influenced. Cultural factors influence what problems constitute appropriate grounds for what type of help, and from whom such help is most likely to come. An excellent psychotherapist working with patients from various cultural backgrounds necessarily cultivates the ability to recognize his or her own cultural assumptions and to see patients in the context of the cultural forces shaping their assumptions, roles, and understanding of the surrounding world.

Culture and psychotherapy are, thus, intertwined at a fundamental level. Sophistication about the impact of culture helps to expose the many sources of misunderstanding that may complicate therapy. Two persons engaging in psychotherapy have many opportunities to become entangled in multiple layers of miscommunication, whether the patient and therapist come from the same cultural background (intracultural therapy) or differ in basic ways (intercultural therapy). The language chosen for the interaction may be more familiar to one than to the other participant. Some concepts are easier to express in one language than another and may not translate well. Much has been written about "idioms of distress" and how they might be understood and misunderstood in different cultures and languages (Kleinman 1980, 1988). The differences between literal and connotative meaning also come into play, particularly in the symbolically rich world of dynamic psychotherapy. Help-seeking patterns are also heavily culturally influenced (i.e., what a person decides is troubling enough to justify requests for assistance, whom he or she turns to for help, and when). As an element of culture, historical relationships between groups also exert profound effects. If one member of a therapeutic dyad comes from a group that has had, or still has, a conflict with the group from which the other member originates, complex issues of transference and countertransference may arise and demand thoughtful exploration (Pinderhughes 1989).

In Frank's time and in our own, the introduction and examination of cultural concepts challenges both practitioners and researchers. Even though psychotherapy is by definition a creation of the culture that supports it, the specific weight of each variable in the conceptualization, success, or failure of any psychotherapeutic modality remains to be more precisely determined (Paris 2008). We must refine our grasp of cultural issues, incorporate them into our clinical work to better match technique to patient, and accurately predict therapeutic outcome. In the best of all clinical worlds, therapists would properly weigh the realities and mythic elements of the patient's story, environment, and overall background. The clinical evaluation of the human being who comes to seek understanding, explanations, and, above all, the materialization of hopes (intuited or rational) would always include an exhaustive social history, the objective assessment and enumeration of interaction styles, personality features, strengths and weaknesses, family dynamics, and identity. Psychotherapy would then fulfill its promise as a culturally derived, unique, and powerfully healing form of human encounter.

REFERENCES

Alarcón, R. D., Westermeyer, J., Foulks, E. F., and Ruiz, P. 1999. Clinical relevance of contemporary cultural psychiatry. *Journal of Nervous and Mental Disease* 187:465–71.
Allport, G. W. 1937. *Personality: A Psychological Interpretation*. New York: Holt, Rinehart, and Winston.
Beck, J. S. 1995. *Cognitive Therapy: Basics and Beyond*. New York: Guilford Press.
Canino, G., Lewis-Fernandez, R., and Bravo, M. 1997. Methodological challenges in cross-cultural mental health research. *Transcultural Psychiatry* 34:263–84.

Cia, A. H. 2001. *Trastorno por estrés posttraumatico*. Buenos Aires, Argentina: Imaginador.

Denton, D. D. 1998. *Religious Diagnosis in a Secular Society: A Staff for the Journey*. Lanham, MD: University Press of America.

——. 2008. *Naming the Pain and Guiding the Care: The Central Tasks of Diagnosis*. Lanham, MD: University Press of America.

Duckworth, K., Blumberg, L., Binenfeld, D., Kahn, M., and Capp, M. 2003. Low ethics and psychiatry. In A. Tasman, J. K. Kay, and J. A. Lieberman (eds.), *Psychiatry*, 2nd ed. (pp. 2289–313). Chichester, UK: John Wiley.

Eisenberg, L. 1988. The social construction of mental illness. *Psychological Medicine* 18:1–9.

Epston, D., and White, M. (eds.). 1992. *Experience, Contradiction, Narrative, and Imagination*. Adelaide, South Australia: Dulwich Center Publications.

Fagan, A. 2004. Challenging the bioethical applications of the autonomy principle within multicultural societies. *Journal of Applied Philosophy* 21:15–31.

Favazza, A. R., and Oman, M. 1984. Overview: foundations of cultural psychiatry. In J. E. Mezzich and C. E. Berganza (eds.), *Cultural Psychopathology* (pp. 15–35). New York: Columbia University Press.

Fox, R. L. 1986. *Pagans and Christians*. New York: Viking.

Frank, J. D. 1961. *Persuasion and Healing: A Comparative Study of Psychotherapy*. Baltimore: Johns Hopkins University Press.

——. 1967. *Sanity and Survival: Psychological Aspects of War and Peace*. Toronto: Vintage Books.

——. 1973. *Persuasion and Healing: A Comparative Study of Psychotherapy*, rev. ed. Baltimore: Johns Hopkins University Press.

Frank, J. D., and Frank, J. B. 1991. *Persuasion and Healing: A Comparative Study of Psychotherapy*, 3rd ed. Baltimore: Johns Hopkins University Press.

Frankl, V. E. 1984. *Man's Search for Meaning: An Introduction to Logotherapy*. New York: Simon and Schuster.

Geoffrey, L. 1979. *Magic: Reason and Experience*. Cambridge: Cambridge University Press.

Griffin, J. L., and Slovik, L. 2003. Family therapy. In A. Tasman, J. Kay, and J. A. Lieberman (eds.), *Psychiatry*, 2nd ed., vol. 2 (pp. 1778–91). Chichester, UK: John Wiley.

Group for the Advancement of Psychiatry, Committee on Cultural Psychiatry. 2002. *Cultural Assessment in Clinical Psychiatry*. Washington, DC: American Psychiatric Publishing.

Haviland, W. A. 1990. *Cultural Anthropology*, 6th ed. New York: Holt, Rinehart, and Winston.

Impelluso, L. 2007. *Myths: Tales of the Greek and Roman Gods*. New York: Abrams.

James, C. 2007. *Cultural Amnesia: Necessary Memories from History and the Arts*. New York: W. W. Norton.

Jaspers, K. 1964. *The Nature of Psychotherapy: A Critical Appraisal*. Trans. J. Hoenig and M. W. Hamilton. Chicago: University of Chicago Press.

Jensen, P. S., Knapp, P., and Mrazek, D. A. 2006. *Toward a New Diagnostic System for Child Psychopathology: Moving beyond DSM*. New York: Guilford Press.

Kirmayer, L. J., Rousseau, C., Jarvis, G. E., and Guzder, J. 2003. The cultural context of clinical assessment. In A. Tasman, J. Kay, and J. A. Lieberman (eds.), *Psychiatry*, 2nd ed. (pp. 19–29). Chichester, UK: John Wiley.

Kleinman, A. 1980. *Patients and Healers in the Context of Culture: An Exploration of the Borderland between Anthropology, Medicine, and Psychiatry.* Berkeley: University of California Press.

————. 1988. *Rethinking Psychiatry: From Cultural Category to Personal Experience.* New York: Free Press.

Knapp, P. 2006. Understanding early development and temperament from the vantage point of evolutionary theory. In P. S. Jensen, P. Knapp, and D. A. Mrazek (eds.), *Toward a New Diagnostic System for Child Psychopathology: Moving beyond DSM* (pp. 11–37). New York: Guilford Press.

Kreuz-Smolinski, A., and Pereira-Tercero, R. 2005. Terapia familiar. In J. Vallejo and C. Leal (eds.), *Tratado de psiquiatria* (pp. 2071–87). Barcelona, Spain: Ars Medica.

Levi, P. 2001. *The Search for Roots: A Personal Anthology.* Chicago: Ivan R. Dee.

Littlewood, R. 2001. Psychotherapy in cultural contexts. *Psychiatric Clinics of North America* 24:507–22.

Masserman, J. H. 1971. *A Psychiatric Odyssey.* New York: Science House.

Paris, J. 2008. *Prescriptions for the Mind: A Critical View of Contemporary Psychiatry.* New York: Oxford University Press.

Pinderhughes, C. A. 1989. *Understanding Race, Ethnicity, and Power: The Key to Efficacy in Clinical Practice.* New York: Free Press.

Pine, D. S. 2009. Increasing the developmental focus in DSM-V: broad issues and specific potential. Paper presented at the annual meeting of the American Psychopathological Association on Evolution of the DSM-V Conceptual Framework: Development, Dimensions, Disability, Spectra, and Gender/Culture, New York, March 5–7.

Pine, D. S., Alegria, M., Cook, E. H., and Costello, E. J. 2002. Advances in developmental science and DSM-V. In D. J. Kupfer, M. B. Furst, and B. A. Regier (eds.), *A Research Agenda for DSM-V* (pp. 85–122). Washington, DC: American Psychiatric Association.

Tseng, W. 2001. *Handbook of Clinical Psychiatry.* San Diego: Academic Press.

Watson, P. 2006. *Ideas: A History of Thought and Invention, from Fire to Freud.* New York: Harper Perennial.

CHAPTER 6

Deconstructing Demoralization

Subjective Incompetence and
Distress in Adversity

John M. de Figueiredo, M.D., Sc.D.

.. when Alice had been all
the way down one side and
up the other, trying every
door, she walked sadly down
the middle, wondering how
she was ever to get out
again.
—*Alice's Adventures in
Wonderland*

All of us must face problems we cannot solve and endure
sources of distress that no amount of effort can alleviate.
—*PERSUASION AND HEALING*, 1991, P. 49

D emoralization may be viewed as a psychological state that occurs when the meaningful connections among cognition, emotion, and volition, or between the past and the present, or between the person and the environment are perceived as threatened or disrupted. Jerome Frank elaborated on this concept and formulated a hypothesis that placed demoralization at the center of research work on help-seeking processes in psychiatry and psychotherapy. This chapter describes recent advances in the operational definition and measurement of demoralization, reviews the ongoing debate on the "normality" of the condition (is it "normal" or "abnormal"?), and explores the implications of Frank's demoralization hypothesis for research and clinical practice. The conceptualization of demoralization as a boundary phenomenon and an existential problem is illustrated with examples drawn from neuropsychiatry, psychosomatic medicine, and transcultural psychiatry. Such exposition suggests avenues for future research.

The Demoralization Hypothesis

Jerome Frank was the first to note that the most frequent presenting complaints of many, if not all, persons seeking psychotherapy, irrespective of diagnosis, are expressions of demoralization. In Webster's dictionary, the meaning of *demoralize* includes "to deprive a person of spirit, courage, to dishearten, bewilder, to throw a person into disorder or confusion." Frank (1973, p. 316) argued that demoralization results from a "persistent failure to cope with internally or externally induced stresses that the person and those close to him expect him to handle." He proposed that, despite differences in content, all forms of psychotherapy and healing ritual attempt to combat demoralization (Frank 1961, 1974; de Figueiredo 2007). Demoralization is recognizable not only among individuals seeking outpatient psychotherapy but also as the "giving up–given up" syndrome among patients in general hospitals who have physical illnesses, as an acute state or "crisis" in the emergency room, and as "social breakdown syndrome," a characteristic presentation of schizophrenia in mental hospitals (Caplan 1964; Engel 1967, 1968; Gruenberg 1967; Mangelli et al. 2005).

Further characterization of demoralization led to the proposal that the clinical hallmark of demoralization is *subjective incompetence* (SI), a self-perceived incapacity to perform tasks and express feelings deemed appropriate in a stressful situation, resulting in pervasive uncertainty and doubts about the future. SI occurs when individuals are facing a stressor that disconfirms their assumptions about themselves and others. Such assumptions, the axioms on which a person's life story is based, constitute the person's ambient world, or *Umwelt*. Individuals who have SI have a sense of being puzzled, indecisive, uncertain, faced with a dilemma, unclear as to ways out of the situation, placed in a deadlock, impasse, quandary, or plight. SI is a feeling of being "trapped" or blocked because of a sense of inability to plan and initiate concerted action. A person with SI has no guides, maps, or hints as to where to go next. Furthermore, demoralization typically occurs within the context of a stressful situation, and it involves not only SI but also some type of distress, such as sadness, discouragement, anxiety, anger, or resentment, or combinations thereof. Perceived stress interacts with inadequate social supports to bring about a state of SI, often allied with depression or other forms of distress (de Figueiredo and Frank 1982; de Figueiredo 1983b, 1993).

Though closely linked, distress and SI do not always occur together. The relevance of the stressful situation to the stressed person's self-esteem determines their joint occurrence. For example, Mrs. A. becomes increasingly upset when her husband fails to return from work. She then finds out that he was killed in a car accident on the way home. Although distressed, she is not demoralized, because she does not perceive herself as incompetent. Even though her life is profoundly changed, Mrs. A.'s self-esteem is unaffected by Mr. A.'s accidental death. But Mrs. B., whose husband also fails to return from work, receives a phone call from his mistress, who tells her about their affair. Mrs. B. is both distressed and demoralized; much of her self-esteem is based on her ability to hold her husband's love, and when that assumption is shattered, she perceives herself as incompetent.

Similarly, SI may exist without distress, as long as a person does not assume that he or she should be competent to deal with a particular stressful situation. Examples of such situations are the surprise of an unexpected and premature job promotion or the initial excitement of migration to a land of promise (de Figueiredo 1983a).

The Measurement of Demoralization

Researchers have offered several definitions of demoralization and criteria to measure it. The pioneering studies conducted on U.S. soldiers and their response to stress during World War II had found that a variety of psychiatric screening scales seemed to measure a common underlying dimension, one that had not, however, been clearly named. In a classic article, Dohrenwend and Crandell (1970) interpreted this common dimension as "nonspecific distress" or "something akin to demoralization," if not demoralization itself. In later studies, Dohrenwend and others referred to that dimension as "demoralization" (Dohrenwend et al. 1980; Link and Dohrenwend 1980).

In contemporary research, while all scales that screen broadly for distress (and there are many of them) presumptively measure demoralization, only two have been designed (and designated) to specifically measure the phenomenon. These are the PERI Demoralization Scale, developed by Dohrenwend et al. (1980) and used in general population epidemiological studies, and the scale developed by Kissane et al. (2004), used in clinical settings with patients who have physical illnesses (Clarke and Kissane 2002) (see chapter 7). Tellegen et al. (2003) also adapted the MMPI-2 (Minnesota Multiphasic Personality Inventory-2), proposing the Restructured Clinical Demoralization Scale as another valid measure.

Many psychiatric screening scales used in research as measures of demoralization contain mostly items that assess nonspecific distress, with a limited number of items that appear to reflect SI (e.g., "I cannot get going"). The combined use of both types of items in these scales makes it difficult to differentiate between SI and nonspecific distress in the analyses of results.

"Demoralization" cannot be found in the *Diagnostic and Statistical Manual of Mental Disorders* (DSM-IV; American Psychiatric Association 1994). Because it is a common occurrence among patients who have general medical conditions, in the absence of guidance from DSM-IV or its TR version, an international group of investigators developed their own criteria. These criteria are embedded in the Diagnostic Criteria for Psychosomatic Research (Fava et al. 1995; Porcelli and Sonino 2007). The following three criteria are proposed for demoralization: (1) feeling of failure to meet one's own expectations (or those of others), or a feeling of inability to cope with some pressing problems, leading to a sense of helplessness, hopelessness, or "giving up"; (2) experiencing those feelings for at least one month; (3) experiencing the feelings in close proximity to the manifestation of a general medical condition or leading to the exacerbation of symptoms already present. These researchers developed an interview to elicit the symptoms and behaviors needed for diagnostic formulations based on the proposed criteria. The Diagnostic Criteria for Psychosomatic Research are an important advance in the study of demoralization and have been widely used in groundbreaking studies to detect its presence in patients with general medical conditions (Porcelli, De Carne, and Fava 2000; Porcelli, De Carne, and Todarello 2004; Ottolini, Modena, and Rigatelli 2005; Rafanelli et al. 2005). The criteria, however, do not clearly differentiate symptoms of nonspecific distress from manifestations of SI.

Using a different method to study demoralization, Kissane, Clarke, and Street (2001, p. 13) proposed that a "demoralization syndrome [should] be recognized as a distinct psychiatric disorder in which loss of meaning and hope can potentially spoil any sense of a worthwhile life and future." Subanalyses identified several factors (dimensions) when the researchers used their Demoralization Scale in a group of cancer patients. They interpreted one of the factors, called "helplessness," as reflecting SI, but some of the items in other factors (e.g., "loss of meaning and purpose," "disheartenment," and "sense of failure") seem to reflect a similar construct. In this study, subgroups of patients scored high on the Demoralization Scale but had low total scores in the Beck Depression Inventory and/or low scores on the items indicating major depression in the

Patient Health Questionnaire, or vice versa. The product-moment correlation coefficient between scores in these other two scales and the factors in the Demoralization Scale was lowest (0.4) for the factor called "sense of failure" (Kissane et al. 2004). Again, the lack of an independent measure of SI precluded the testing of the hypothesis that SI is associated with demoralization but not necessarily with depression and other forms of distress.

In summary, scales exist to measure nonspecific distress or combinations of nonspecific distress and SI, but until recently, no instrument was available to independently measure SI. Two other scales specifically designed to measure SI have now been developed and are found to be both valid and reliable. When one of them was applied to a group of cancer patients, together with measures of social support and perceived stress, the findings supported the view that demoralization is a second-order construct involving nonspecific distress and SI (Cockram 2004; Cockram, Doros, and de Figueiredo 2009, 2010). The Dohrenwend, Kissane, and MMPI-2 Restructured Clinical demoralization scales and the two scales for SI have not yet been used in one setting with a single group of subjects.

Demoralization: Normal or Abnormal?

How can depression be distinguished from demoralization? When does demoralization cease to be a reaction and become a process? And what is the difference between an expected (or "normal") state of distress in a stressful situation and a more severe form of distress that warrants treatment? Whether demoralization should be viewed as a normal or homeostatic response to stress or as an abnormal state requiring intervention has been the subject of debate (Slavney 1999, 2000; de Figueiredo 2000; Clarke and Kissane 2002). Mild distress and mild SI may be viewed as normal and could resolve without any intervention. Increasing distress may set the stage for increasing SI, and the onset of SI may convert a normal reaction to stress into an abnormal state requiring intervention. These and other issues could not be settled without a scale to independently measure SI. The possibility of such independent measurement opens up a new perspective for further research on demoralization.

It would be of great interest to examine two competing models of the overlap of SI and distress: the categorical or "threshold" model and the dimensional or "signal detection theory" model. The first model would predict that when SI reaches a threshold, further increases in SI are irrelevant to the increase of distress; in other words, SI is an all-or-none phenomenon, and when it occurs, distress (normal) becomes demoralization (abnormal). By contrast, the second model would represent SI as a graded phenomenon and predict that as SI increases, distress (thus, demoralization) also increases.

Frank (1974; Frank and Frank 1991) noted that demoralization both aggravates and is aggravated by psychiatric symptoms. The possibility that SI (thus, demoralization) may be the common denominator among some, if not all, mental disorders needs further investigation. The relationship between demoralization and anhedonic or major depression is particularly intriguing. Demoralization was identified in about 30 percent of a group of medical outpatients, while major depression was present in about 17 percent (Mangelli et al. 2005). In this study, about 44 percent of patients who had major depression were not demoralized, and 69 percent of demoralized patients did not meet the criteria for major depression.

Subjective incompetence (thus, demoralization) appears to be an independent risk factor that triggers an ensuing episode of major depression. In a study of seventy-two female monozygotic twins discordant for a lifetime history of major depression, one of the three clusters of variables that were significantly different between affected and unaffected twins included more demoralization, "acting out," and alcohol dependence in the twin with major depression. Demoralization was assessed through attributes that may be viewed as surrogate (proxy) indicators of SI: powerlessness, lack of self-efficacy, and a diminished self-perceived sense of mastery (Kendler and Gardner 2001).

As is now well recognized, available diagnostic systems fail to capture and distinguish the range and nature of mood states observed in the medically ill. In studies of patients with a variety of medical illnesses, including cancer and motor neuron disease, Clarke and colleagues were able to distinguish demoralization, anhedonia, grief, autonomic anxiety, and somatic symptoms, and they demonstrated that each is a component of the current conceptualization of depression (Clarke, Mackinnon, et al. 2000; Clarke, Smith, et al. 2003; Clarke, Kissane, et al. 2005; Clarke, McLeod, et al. 2005) (see also chapter 7).

Genetic predisposition and pathoplastic factors might determine the speed of the transition from demoralization to anhedonic depression, or vice versa, with SI as a main driver of the pathological state. This is certainly suggested by the ways in which patients with major depression describe their mood: "lethargy and inability to do things, whether because of tiredness, a specific inability to summon up effort, a feeling of being inhibited, or an inability to envisage the future" and a "sense of detachment from the environment," all highly suggestive of SI (Healy 1993). Demoralization may also affect the prognosis of both physical and mental disorders. Consistent with this line of thinking is the finding that demoralization, as measured by the PERI scale, predicts the course of posttraumatic stress disorder two years after exposure to a highly traumatic life event (Flaherty et al. 1998; Kohn et al. 2005). Future research should determine whether SI is able to predict psychosocial impairment after controlling for distress, and whether SI is a better predictor of psychosocial impairment than is distress.

The Integration of Cognition, Emotion, and Volition

From a neuropsychiatric viewpoint, demoralization is a manifestation of an imbalance or dysregulation in the normal interrelations among cognition, emotion, and volition. Intellectual disability (mental retardation), traumatic brain injury, and dementia are examples of cognitive impairment in which this imbalance or dysregulation is likely to occur. Demoralization seems to contribute significantly to the excess disability noted in patients who have cognitive impairment (see chapter 2).

DSM-IV defines "mental retardation," more appropriately called "intellectual disability" (ID), as significantly subaverage intellectual functioning (IQ of approximately 70 or lower) with concurrent deficits in adaptive functioning, evident before the age of eighteen (American Psychiatric Association 1994). Two recent studies suggest that demoralization is not uncommon among persons who have intellectual disability. One study examined the presentation and risk factors for depression in 151 adults with mild to moderate ID and found that 39.15 percent of participants had symptoms of depression (McGillivray and McCabe 2007). Sadness, self-criticism, loss of energy, crying, and tiredness appeared to be the most frequent indicators of depression or risk for depression. Automatic negative thoughts, low quality and frequency of social support, diminished self-esteem, and disruptive life events significantly predicted depression scores in people with mild to moderate ID, accounting for 58.1 percent of the variance. Such findings suggest that demoralization may be frequent in this population and may occur even when patients' symptoms fall below the threshold specified by standard diagnostic criteria for depression.

Another line of evidence comes from the study of people who have Down syndrome (Collacott and Cooper 1992). Although stereotyped as happy, these individuals are more likely to become depressed than those with ID from other causes. Individuals who have Down syndrome and depression show reduced adaptive behavior in subsequent follow-up evaluations when compared with matched controls without a psychiatric history. The adaptive deficit persists even after the depression is no longer present, suggesting again that SI may continue after depression is treated. When depression starts later in life, the level of Down syndrome patients' adaptive functioning is higher. Commenting on this finding, Cooper and Collacott (1993) state that depression, even when resolved, may damage a person's confidence and produce a sense of failure, particularly when the first episode occurs early in life. This interpretation supports current views about demoralization and calls for additional research on the role of demoralization and psychotherapy in the treatment of persons with ID.

Dementia is a global decline of cognitive functions in an individual who is alert, occurring after the age of eighteen (American Psychiatric Association 1994). Many years ago, Goldstein (1963) noted that brain-damaged soldiers of World War I, when exposed to stimuli or other challenges they could not master, responded with confusion, irritability, and anxiety, often escalating to explosive reactions of anger and aggression. He called these responses "catastrophic reactions." Such reactions also occur in individuals who have dementia ("sundowning" being an example) and in persons who have intellectual disability. Goldstein noted that some symptoms of individuals with traumatic brain injury result directly from the injury, while others (e.g., fatigue and irritability) reflect a struggle to adapt to the induced cognitive deficit. Other symptoms (e.g., social withdrawal and isolation) may signal efforts to avoid this struggle. He emphasized that neurorehabilitation involves more than working with cognitive impairment and illustrated his point with a case description. The patient under clinical observation is asked to get involved in a task which seems very simple:

> We give him a problem in simple arithmetic which before his sickness he would without any doubt have been able to solve. Now he is unable to solve it. But merely noticing and recording the fact that he is unable to perform a simple multiplication would be an exceedingly inadequate account of the patient's reaction. By simply looking at him, we discover a great deal more than his arithmetical failure. He looks dazed, changes color, becomes agitated and anxious, starts to fumble. A moment before, he was amicable; now he is sullen and evasive

or exhibits temper. He presents a picture of a very much distressed, frightened person, a person in a state of anxiety. It takes some time to restore him to a state which will permit the examination to continue. In the presence of a task which he can perform, the same patient behaves in exactly the opposite manner. He looks animated and calm, and appears to be in a good mood; he is well-poised and collected, interested, cooperative; he is "all there." We may call the state of the patient in the situation of success, "ordered behavior"; his state in the situation of failure, "disordered or catastrophic behavior." (Goldstein 1963, pp. 85–86)

Goldstein goes on to note that catastrophic reactions are due not simply to the lack of capacity to perform but also to the "situation of failing." Again, there is a perceived sense of incompetence combined with distress, now manifested as anxiety and anger as well as depression, making this clinical presentation an expression of demoralization. The hallmark of a catastrophic reaction is SI, not the specific form or intensity of the associated feelings or combination of feelings. Calm and self-confidence are restored by empathetic understanding of the person's predicament and by designing a more predictable environment that fosters the reconstruction of a simplified cognitive map. Catastrophic situations, as Goldstein pointed out, are by definition reactive, to be contrasted with more predictable cognitive, affective, or volitional syndromes resulting from insults to specific regions of the brain.

Future research should examine whether SI is associated with deactivation of the frontal and prefrontal cortices and an increased activation of limbic structures. The interconnections of the lateral cortex and the dorsolateral circuit in the frontal lobe are the seat of faculties such as working memory, organization, planning, problem solving, environmental monitoring, self-awareness, attention, mental flexibility, and abstract reasoning. Initiation of a behavioral response, inhibition of automatic responses, delay of gratification (impulse control), sustaining of behavioral and motor responses, and anticipation of future consequences require the integrity of the pathways connecting the basal ganglia to the orbitofrontal cortex. The limbic system connects with the medial cortex via the anterior cingulate gyrus to produce emotional regulation, emotional arousal, expression of mood, and self-soothing strategies. The sorting out of distractions and executive functions requires the integrity of the prefrontal cortex (see chapter 3). When the pathways from the cortex to the centers in the limbic system regulating emotions (amygdala and/or hippocampus) are severed, associative learning, memory, and decision making cannot take place. Brain mapping of demoralized persons, if technically and ethically feasible, would lead to a better understanding of the complicated relationship between the magnitude of motivation and the direction of action, and of individual and contextual differences in the propensity for demoralization as distinguished from depression. SI occurs because the direction of action is either unknown or unclear. SI is characteristic of demoralization, but not of depression, where the magnitude of motivation is reduced even when the direction of action is known. Demoralization appears to be a "top-down" process, whereas depression seems to be a "bottom-up" phenomenon.

The Boundary between the Past and the Future

Dating from George Engel's pioneering observations (1967, 1968) of what he called the "giving up–given up" syndrome, the concept of demoralization has been recognized as particularly useful for patients who have serious medical illnesses and those receiving palliative care (see chapters 8 and 9). Appropriate understanding of each person's life story is essential to promote the rebuilding of the person's *Umwelt* even under such extreme conditions. The use of the idiographic rather than the nomothetic approach to measure demoralization, as it relates to treatment outcome, needs to be further explored.

Demoralization has been recognized in patients who have motor neuron disease and functional gastrointestinal disorders and is shown to be a risk factor for acute coronary syndromes (Porcelli, De Carne, and Todarello 2004; Ottolini, Modena, and Rigatelli 2005). Supporting the view that demoralization is a second-order construct, a study of outpatients who had gastrointestinal and colorectal cancer found that depression and SI are separate components of demoralization (Cockram 2004; Cockram, Doros, and de Figueiredo 2010). The independent measurement of SI may lead to a better understanding of the extent to which SI contributes to the worsening of the prognosis of diseases affected by psychological factors. Appropriate and timely psychotherapeutic interventions could be instituted to reduce or prevent the excessive disability due to demoralization.

As Griffith and Gaby (2005) noted, demoralization fails to show significant improvement when antidepressant medications are administered. By contrast, the demoralized mood responds, at times rather rapidly, to cessation of adversity. When adversity is omnipresent, the key to counteracting demoralization lies in the strengthening of resilience, what Greer, Morris, and Pettingale (1979) called the "fighting spirit," a determination not to give in, optimism, being informed about the illness and active in treatment—in short, living as normal a life as possible in the face of adversity. The mission of the psychiatrist in palliative care is to help the patient make sense of the past, given the certainty of a time-limited future.

The Boundary between the Person and the Environment

Life stories are influenced and shaped by culture, the symbolic forms transmitted from one generation to the next. Both signs and symbols are vehicles of meaning, but signs denote and present, while symbols connote and represent. The animal *Umwelt* is exclusively based on signs, because animals other than humans cannot symbolize, and its disruption is illustrated by Pavlov's well-known demonstration of what he called "experimental neurosis." By contrast, the human *Umwelt* is primarily based on symbols. A transformation of symbols in a society is called "sociocultural change."

Alexander Leighton's (1959) conceptualization of the relationship between personality and culture is highly relevant to the study of demoralization. Sentiments, according to Leighton, are relatively stable composites of attitudes and values. Attitudes are composed of cognitions, including assumptions and beliefs, and emotions. The *Umwelt* of a person is woven into a fabric of sentiments that we call personality. By means of symbols, members of a society share sentiments, some of which are dominant. Leighton referred to the dominant sentiments as "essential striving sentiments" and to the transformation of dominant sentiments as "sociocultural integration or disintegration." The symbols that represent those dominant sentiments may be called "dominant symbols." To the extent that dominant symbols and the sentiments they represent are shared, a society will approach the state of integration; if they are disrupted or cease to be shared, it will move toward disintegration. Several epidemiological studies have documented, with remarkable consistency, an inverse association between the prevalence of demoralization and the degree of sociocultural integration for a given level of sociocultural change (de Figueiredo 1983a). Persons less integrated into their social groups are more demoralized than those more integrated, even when the former have fewer stressful life events than the latter; the former are also more likely to see a doctor or to be hospitalized for physical illness (Myers, Lidenthal, and Pepper 1975). These findings have led to the conclusion that change becomes demoralizing when it affects dominant symbols.

Acculturation has been defined as "those phenomena which result when groups of individuals having different cultures come into continuous first-hand contact, with subsequent changes in the original culture patterns of either or both groups" (Redfield, Linton, and Herskovits 1936). Many studies have shown that acculturation can be stressful and that acculturative stress can be associated with a variety of physical and mental health problems. However, other studies have found no evidence that acculturation is stressful. To reconcile these seemingly contradictory findings, we may note that the sociocultural change (transformation of symbols) involved in acculturation becomes stressful to a group only when the symbols being transformed influence certain dominant sentiments shared by that group. Research shows that the stress of rapid sociocultural change, when affecting certain dominant sentiments of a group, may result in sociocultural disintegration, making the members of that group more vulnerable to demoralization, physical illnesses, or psychopathology (de Figueiredo 1983b). Although the outcomes of acculturation and the associated impacts on physical and mental health have been widely studied, less is known about the specific cognitive and adaptive strategies used by the members of an assimilating culture when exposed to the invading culture for a prolonged period of time. Better understanding of those strategies would enhance our ability to heal the symbolic wounds of our patients.

Conclusion

The concept of demoralization, first formally introduced in psychiatry by Jerome Frank, has a powerful heuristic value. "Demoralization" is not found in DSM-IV. In an editorial article, Fava and Wise (2007) proposed the inclusion of demoralization in DSM-V as a subheading in a new category called "psychological factors affecting either feared or identified medical conditions." However, as the discussion in this chapter demonstrates, demoralization occurs not only in the context of such medical conditions but across the whole range of psychopathology, and therefore deserves a special diagnostic heading by itself. The recognition of demoralization in a variety of clinical settings and in the general population has led to new insights into the diagnosis and treatment of mental disorders. Research will continue to elucidate the role played by demoralization in the onset, course, and outcome of both psychiatric and non-psychiatric disorders and diseases and to enhance the importance of psychotherapy for the strengthening of recovery, hope, resilience, adaptation, and quality of life.

REFERENCES

American Psychiatric Association. 1994. *Diagnostic and Statistical Manual of Mental Disorders*, 4th ed. Washington, DC: American Psychiatric Association.

Caplan, G. 1964. *Principles of Preventive Psychiatry*. New York: Basic Books.

Clarke, D. M., and Kissane, D. W. 2002. Demoralization: its phenomenology and importance. *Australian and New Zealand Journal of Psychiatry* 36:733–42.

Clarke, D. M., Kissane, D. W., Trauer, T., and Smith, G. C. 2005. Demoralization, anhedonia, and grief in patients with severe physical illness. *World Psychiatry* 4:96–105.

Clarke, D. M., Mackinnon, A. J., Smith, G. C., Mckenzie, D. P., and Herrman, H. E. 2000. Dimensions of psychopathology in the medically ill: a latent trait analysis. *Psychosomatics* 41:418–25.

Clarke, D. M., McLeod, J. E., Smith, G. C., Trauer, T., and Kissane, D. W. 2005. A comparison of psychosocial and physical functioning in patients with motor neuron disease and metastatic cancer. *Journal of Palliative Care* 21:173–79.

Clarke, D. M., Smith, G. C., Dowe, D. L., and McKenzie, D. P. 2003. An empirically derived taxonomy of common distress syndromes in the medically ill. *Journal of Psychosomatic Research* 54:323–30.

Cockram, C. A. 2004. Level of demoralization as a predictor of stage of change in patients with gastrointestinal and colorectal cancer. Ph.D. dissertation, College of Nursing, University of South Florida. May 29.

Cockram, C. A., Doros, G., and de Figueiredo, J. M. 2009. Diagnosis and measurement of subjective incompetence, the clinical hallmark of demoralization. *Psychotherapy and Psychosomatics* 80:137–143.

———. 2010. Subjective incompetence as the clinical hallmark of demoralization in cancer patients without mental disorder. *Primary Psychiatry* 17:54–58.

Collacott, R. A., and Cooper, S. A. 1992. Adaptive behavior after depressive illness in Down's syndrome. *Journal of Nervous and Mental Disease* 180:468–70.

Cooper, S. A., and Collacott, R. A. 1993. Prognosis of depression in Down's syndrome. *Journal of Nervous and Mental Disease* 181:204–5.

de Figueiredo, J. M. 1983a. The law of sociocultural demoralization. *Social Psychiatry* 18:73–78.

———. 1983b. Some issues in research on the epidemiology of demoralization. *Comprehensive Psychiatry* 24:154–57.

———. 1993. Depression and demoralization: phenomenologic differences and research perspectives. *Comprehensive Psychiatry* 34:308–11.

———. 2000. Diagnosing demoralization in consultation psychiatry (letter to the editor). *Psychosomatics* 41:449–50.

———. 2007. Demoralization and psychotherapy: a tribute to Jerome D. Frank, MD, PhD (1909–2005) (editorial). *Psychotherapy and Psychosomatics* 76:129–33.

de Figueiredo, J. M., and Frank, J. D. 1982. Subjective incompetence, the clinical hallmark of demoralization. *Comprehensive Psychiatry* 23:353–63.

Dohrenwend, B. P., and Crandell, D. L. 1970. Psychiatric symptoms in community, clinic, and mental hospital groups. *American Journal of Psychiatry* 126:1611–21.

Dohrenwend, B. P., Shrout, P. E., Egri, G., and Mendelsohn, F. S. 1980. Non-specific psychological distress and other measures for use in the general population. *Archives of General Psychiatry* 37:1229–36.

Engel, G. L. 1967. A psychological setting of somatic disease: the "giving up–given up complex." *Proceedings of the Royal Society of Medicine* 60:553–55.

———. 1968. A life setting conducive to illness, the giving up–given up complex. *Bulletin of the Menninger Clinic* 32:355–65.

Fava, G. A., Freyberger, H. J., Bech, P., Christodoulou, G., Sensky, T., Theorell, T., and Wise, T. N. 1995. Diagnostic criteria for use in psychosomatic research. *Psychotherapy and Psychosomatics* 63:1–8.

Fava, G. A., and Wise, T. N. 2007. Issues for DSM-V: psychological factors affecting either identified or feared medical conditions—a solution for somatoform disorders. *American Journal of Psychiatry* 164:1002–3.

Flaherty, J. A., Kohn, R., Levav, I., and Birz, S. 1988. Demoralization in Soviet-Jewish immigrants to the United States and Israel. *Comprehensive Psychiatry* 29:588–97.

Frank, J. D. 1961. *Persuasion and Healing: A Comparative Study of Psychotherapy*. Baltimore: Johns Hopkins University Press.

———. 1973. *Persuasion and Healing: A Comparative Study of Psychotherapy*, rev. ed. Baltimore: Johns Hopkins University Press.

———. 1974. Psychotherapy: the restoration of morale. *American Journal of Psychiatry* 131:271–74.

Frank, J. D., and Frank, J. B. 1991. *Persuasion and Healing: A Comparative Study of Psychotherapy*, 3rd ed. Baltimore: Johns Hopkins University Press.

Goldstein, K. 1963. *Human Nature in the Light of Psychopathology*. New York: Schocken Books.

Greer, S., Morris, T., and Pettingale, F. W. 1979. Psychological response to breast cancer: effect on outcome. *Lancet* 2:785–87.

Griffith, J. L., and Gaby, L. 2005. Brief psychotherapy at the bedside: countering demoralization from medical illness. *Psychosomatics* 46:109–16.

Gruenberg, E. M. 1967. The social breakdown syndrome: some origins. *American Journal of Psychiatry* 123:1481–89.

Healy, D. 1993. Dysphoria. In C. G. Costello (ed.), *Symptoms of Depression* (pp. 24–45). Chichester, UK: John Wiley.

Kendler, K. S., and Gardner, C. O. 2001. Monozygotic twins discordant for major depression: a preliminary exploration of the role of environmental experiences in the etiology and course of illness. *Psychological Medicine* 31:411–14.

Kissane, D. W., Clarke, D. M., and Street, A. F. 2001. Demoralization syndrome: a relevant psychiatric diagnosis for palliative care. *Journal of Palliative Care* 17:12–21.

Kissane, D. W., Wein, S., Love, A., Lee, X. Q., Kee, P. L., and Clarke, D. M. 2004. The Demoralization Scale: a report of its development and preliminary validation. *Journal of Palliative Care* 20:269–76.

Kohn, R., Levav, I., Donaire Garcia, I., Machuca, E., and Tamashiro, R. 2005. Psychological and psychopathological reactions following Hurricane Mitch in Honduras: implications for service planning. *Pan American Journal of Public Health* 18:287–95.

Leighton, A. 1959. *My Name Is Legion: Foundations for a Theory of Man in Relation to Culture*. New York: Basic Books.

Link, B., and Dohrenwend, B. P. 1980. Formulation of hypothesis about the true prevalence of demoralization in the United States. In B. P. Dohrenwend, B. Dohrenwend, M. Gould, B. Link, R. Neugenbauer, and R. Wunsch-Hitzig (eds.), *Mental Illness in the United States: Epidemiological Estimates* (pp. 114–32). New York: Praeger.

Mangelli, L., Fava, G. A., Grandi, S., Grassi, L., Ottolini, F., Percelli, P., et al. 2005. Assessing demoralization and depression in the setting of medical disease. *Journal of Clinical Psychiatry* 66:391–94.

McGillivray, J. A., and McCabe, M. P. 2007. Early detection of depression and associated risk factors in adults with mild/moderate intellectual disability. *Research in Developmental Disabilities* 12:59–70.

Myers, J. K., Lidenthal, J. J., and Pepper, M. P. 1975. Life events, social integration and psychiatric symptomatology. *Journal of Health and Social Behavior* 16:421–29.

Ottolini, F., Modena, M. G., and Rigatelli, M. 2005. Prodromal symptoms in myocardial infarction. *Psychotherapy and Psychosomatics* 74:323–27.

Porcelli, P., De Carne, M., and Fava, G. A. 2000. Assessing somatization in functional gastrointestinal disorders: integration of different criteria. *Psychotherapy and Psychosomatics* 69:198–204.

Porcelli, P., De Carne, M., and Todarello, O. 2004. Prediction of treatment outcome of patients with functional gastrointestinal disorders by the Diagnostic Criteria for Psychosomatic Research. *Psychotherapy and Psychosomatics* 73:166–73.

Porcelli, P., and Sonino, S. (eds.). 2007. Psychological factors affecting medical conditions: a new classification for DSM-V. In *Advances in Psychosomatic Medicine*, vol. 28. Basel, Switzerland: Karger.

Rafanelli, C., Roncuzzi, R., Milaneschi, Y., Tomba, E., Colistro, M. C., Pancaldi, L. G., and Pasquale, G. 2005. Stressful life events, depression and demoralization as risk factors for coronary artery disease. *Psychotherapy and Psychosomatics* 74:179–84.

Redfield, R., Linton, R., and Herskovits, M. 1936. Memorandum on the study of acculturation. *American Anthropologist* 38:149–52.

Slavney, P. R. 1999. Diagnosing demoralization in consultation psychiatry. *Psychosomatics* 40:325–29.

———. 2000. Diagnosing demoralization in consultation psychiatry: reply to Dr. de Figueiredo. *Psychosomatics* 41:449–50.

Tellegen, A., Ben-Porath, Y. S., McNulty, J. L., Arbisi, P. A., Graham, J. R., and Kaemmer, B. 2003. *The MMPI-2 Restructured Clinical (RC) Scales: Development, Validation, and Interpretation*. Minneapolis: University of Minnesota Press.

PART II / PSYCHOTHERAPY

Current Practices

CHAPTER 7

Depression, Demoralization, and Psychotherapy in People Who Are Medically Ill

David M. Clarke, M.D., Ph.D.

Alice said nothing; she had sat down with her face in her hands, wondering if anything would *ever* happen in a natural way again.
—*Alice's Adventures in Wonderland*

Most people do not seek therapy solely because they halluci-nate, fear snakes or enjoy a few drinks too many . . . Most people are in therapy because, whatever their complaints, they or persons around them are also demoralized.

—*PERSUASION AND HEALING*, 1991, P. 36

Jerome Frank's initial interest in the common features underlying different forms of psychotherapy led him to seek a common, measurable element among the many conditions that seemed to respond to such treatment (Frank 1972). Before about 1980, the prevailing typologies of distress—both theory based and empirical—offered no solution to the problem. While preparing the 1973 edition of *Persuasion and Healing*, Frank found a possible alternative in the results of an epidemiological study conducted by Bruce Dohrenwend and Barbara Link. These researchers had found that instruments they were using to record anxiety, hopelessness, and low self-esteem in the general population were so highly correlated that they were effectively measuring one construct, which they termed "nonspecific psychological distress" (Dohrenwend et al. 1980). Frank recognized that their work provided a rigorous definition of demoraliza-tion, a term he had used casually in the first edition of his book (1961) and in an early study of distressed, medically hospitalized soldiers (Frank 1946). The result was like a crystal dropped into a supersaturated solution, allowing a new framework to coalesce quickly around this formerly vague idea.

Complementing ongoing efforts to link particular treatments to discrete diagnostic categories, the concept of demoralization as a common substrate for the beneficial effects of psychotherapy has proven robust in both psychiatric and general medical contexts. As physicians, Jerome Frank and Julia Frank were and are especially interested in the effects of psychological or symbolic processes, ranging from psychotherapy to faith healing, on patients' physical state. Current research into the importance of recognizing, measuring, and relieving demoralization, particularly in people who are medically ill, represents a development and application of ideas elaborated in *Persuasion and Healing* (Frank and Frank 1991, chaps. 5 and 7).

As researchers, Jerome Frank and many contributors to the Johns Hopkins Psychotherapy Research Project championed the use of reliable and valid measures (see chapters 1, 6, and 12 in this volume). The epidemiological instruments used by Dohrenwend and colleagues were not designed for the intensive study of individuals. Further research into this area has required my colleagues and I to develop new measures of demoralization. This chapter reviews how applying such measures to various populations of patients who have serious chronic medical illness differentiates elements of the syndrome and demonstrates ways in which these elements respond to interventions that foster resilience and raise morale—Frank's "common features" of psychotherapy. Our studies of people who are medically ill restore grief and demoralization to their proper place in the universe of recognized disorders and allow us, finally, to look at developments in psychotherapy that may be particularly useful in medical settings. These include ways to reduce helplessness and to assist patients to review their life goals, renewing their hope and motivation to live in the face of disabling or life-limiting conditions (see chapters 8 and 9).

Limitations of Major Depression as Currently Defined

Before describing our work in detail, I must first locate demoralization within the universe of current psychiatric diagnosis, as dictated by successive editions of the *Diagnostic and Statistical Manual of Mental Disorders*: III, IV, and IV-TR (1980, 1994, and 2000). In particular, this discussion re-evaluates the limits of the category of "major depressive disorder," a remarkably unhelpful construct for guiding the choice of psychotherapeutic approaches for particular patients. The DSM provides one main category of depression: major depressive episode. By ignoring the psychosocial context of the depressive symptoms, the diagnosis completely dismisses the patient's experience and thought processes (Blazer

2005). To be diagnosed with a major depressive episode, a patient must endorse five of nine specific symptom criteria, one of which is *either* depressed mood *or* pervasive loss of interest or pleasure. In addition, the symptoms must occur together in a two-week period, must cause significant distress or impairment in functioning, and may not be better accounted for by bereavement, substance use, or a particular medical condition. For those who fail to meet these criteria, the manual offers the label of "adjustment disorder with depressed mood." To confuse matters further, it also allows, but does not define, "substance induced mood disorder, depressive type" and "depression secondary to general medical condition."

This system has marked conceptual and empirical weaknesses (Van Praag, David, and McQueen 1998; Parker 2006). In an analysis of data from 947 outpatients, for example, Zimmerman et al. (2006) showed that application of the inclusion/exclusion criteria had only a modest impact on diagnosis—that is, added very little to the symptom count. Along the same lines, Kendler and Gardner (1998) examined whether three specific DSM criteria (number of symptoms, severity of distress or impairment of functioning, duration of episode) predicted future episodes in patients or their twins. They did not. Conceptually, DSM-defined major depression is an overinclusive construct in which an arbitrary threshold, five of nine symptoms, defines the boundary between illness and non-illness. Although depressed mood or pervasive loss of pleasure and interest occupy a prominent position among the symptoms, neither is necessary or sufficient for the diagnosis. Other symptoms—increased sleep and decreased sleep, loss of weight and weight gain—are nonspecific. As a result, patients who "meet criteria" may differ from one another to an extraordinary degree. Ultimately, the DSM draws no defensible boundary between what might be considered a normal experience and a pathological mental state akin to a "disease" (Horwitz and Wakefield 2007).

Subtypes of Depression: Phenomenology and Psychosocial Determinants

Beginning with the 1980 version of the manual (DSM-III), the DSM approach arbitrarily and prematurely resolved historically important debates about the nature of depression, specifically whether this should be a unitary or binary/multiple category and whether it is important to distinguish spontaneously occurring, endogenous depression from depression experienced as a reaction to some circumstance or event. While adopting a unitary view, the manual does provide the qualifier "with melancholic features." A large number of studies have validated the concept of melancholia, identifying it as a state of pervasive anhedonia, nonreactivity of mood, and psychomotor retardation (Matussek, Soldner, and Nagel 1981; Grove et al. 1987; Maes et al. 1990; Parker, Hadzi-Pavlovic, et al. 1994; Ambrosini et al. 2002; Sullivan, Prescott, and Kendler 2002). Melancholia is the best recognized depressive syndrome (Parker 2000) and is still the best predictor of a good response to antidepressants (Joyce and Paykel 1989). The nonmelancholic forms of depression have been harder to characterize as a homogeneous group (Parker, Roy, et al. 1999).

The qualifier "melancholic features" superseded the previous categorization of "endogenous depression." Donald Klein (1974) casually concocted the term "endogenomorphic depression" to describe the characteristic symptom picture we now call melancholia, while excluding any necessary inference of causality. He thus implied that situational determinants were unimportant. This has proved misleading (Blazer 2005). The evidence for stressful life events as contributing causes of major depression, with or without melancholic features, is very strong (Paykel 1994; Kendler, Karkowski, and Prescott 1999). Most depressions occur in the context of significant psychosocial events. Brown and Harris (1978) estimated that 83 percent of depressive episodes were preceded by one or more severe negative life events. Moreover, the context and meaning of events in relation to prior vulnerabilities has been shown to be important (Harris 2001). For example, losses associated with humiliation or entrapment are particularly likely to induce depression (Brown, Harris, and Hepworth 1995).

From an evolutionary perspective—that is, if we consider that symptoms serve some meaningful function (see chapter 4)—it makes sense that depressive symptoms might differ according to the specific situation in which they arise. Keller and Nesse (2006) found that among 445 subjects recruited from a nonclinical setting, guilt, rumination, fatigue, and pessimism were prominent following failed efforts; crying, sadness, and desire for social support were prominent following social losses. In another sample, drawn from the Virginia Adult Twin Study of Psychiatric and Substance Use Disorders (N = 4,856), Keller, Neale, and Kendler (2007) showed that losses (bereavement or romantic breakup) were associated with high levels of sadness, anhedonia, and appetite loss; chronic stress was associated with fatigue and hypersomnia. And again, in a study of undergraduate students experiencing low mood, social losses were associated with greater crying and arousal; failure to reach a goal and stress were associated with more fatigue and pessimism (Keller and Nesse

2005). Similarly, Aaron Beck's construct (1987) of "sociotropic" depression suggests that social losses among people high in need for approval are associated with lability, feelings of loss, loneliness, and crying. One further bit of evidence for the validity of recognizing reactive depression is that successful recovery may be associated with the end or absence of stressful events and the occurrence of positive ones (Paykel 1994; Harris 2001).

From this discussion we can conclude that the concept of a unitary category of depression is past its use-by date. It impedes both research and rational treatment decisions. We need to recognize the subtypes of depression and understand the different patient experiences behind each.

Our studies of depression in people who are medically ill (detailed below) suggest that melancholia should remain a categorically distinct form of depression characterized by pervasive anhedonia, mood nonreactivity, and psychomotor retardation. While possibly a sequel of some event, it is still best understood as a "biogenic" depression that may have a degree of "autonomy" (Nelson, Charney, and Quinlan 1980).* Other forms of depression are better understood as the result of interaction between a person and his or her situation. The first meaningful subtype that we identified we term "hopelessness depression" or demoralization, characterized in cognitive terms as strong feelings of helplessness and subjective incompetence. This we differentiate from grief, characterized by a sense of loss and sorrow.

To be clear, in our view, demoralization is not distinct from depression or simply a "minor depression." It is, like melancholia, a subtype of depression and only occasionally a stand-alone problem. Most people who are diagnosed with demoralization also meet criteria for depressive disorder (Clarke, Smith, et al. 2003). The features of demoralization—feelings of helplessness, hopelessness, and worthlessness—are included in descriptions of depression and melancholia, and in commonly used scales such as the General Health Questionnaire (Goldberg 1972), Beck Depression Inventory (Beck, Steer, and Brown 1996), and Kessler's K10 scale (Kessler et al. 2002). Although hopelessness and helplessness are not included in the listed specific symptom criteria for DSM-IV major depressive disorder, an analysis by McGlinchey et al. (2006) again showed their importance as symptoms of depression.

This discussion now turns to the data that support the value of subtyping

---

*The term *biogenic* does not imply any disunity between biological and psychological processes; rather, it conveys that something biological has happened that makes the depression less dynamic and less reactive to immediate psychosocial influences, including psychotherapy.

depression to guide the rational selection of different treatment approaches, pharmacological and psychotherapeutic.

Depression in People Who Are Medically Ill

Medical illness is ubiquitous, affecting nearly everyone at some point in life. Depression is extraordinarily common in people who are medically ill, with average estimates of prevalence being 20–30 percent (Clarke, Minas, and Stuart 1991). Even higher rates are found in people who have chronic or life-threatening conditions (Wells, Golding, and Burnam 1988). Depression, when present, increases the mortality of myocardial infarction (Lesperance, Frasure-Smith, and Talajic 1996) and impedes recovery from cardiac and other surgery (Duits et al. 1996). It slows recovery after stroke (Morris, Raphael, and Robinson 1992) and is associated with a poor outcome for people who have asthma (Rimington, Davies, and Lowe 2001), renal disease (Burton et al. 1986), or cancer (Spiegel 1996; Clarke and Currie 2009). Which forms of depression in people who are medically ill merit treatment and what type of treatment may help remain matters of ongoing debate. Uncertainty exists regarding the meaning of physical symptoms, the role of biological and other etiological factors, and the boundary between normal and pathological.

Efforts to address these questions initially reflected the probably erroneous thought that "medical depression" is different or distinct in some way from the depression seen in psychiatric settings or included in psychiatric research studies. Early studies compared depressed medical patients with nondepressed medical patients, or depressed medical patients with physically well patients, or simply depressed patients with medical patients. They identified a whole array of symptoms as possibly characteristic of depression in people who are medically ill. These symptoms included fatigue, indigestion, headache, anorexia, weight loss, tachycardia, loss of libido, and urinary frequency (Schwab, Clemmons, et al. 1965); guilt, crying, loneliness, and anorexia (Schwab, Bialow, et al. 1967); hopelessness, helplessness, anxiety, a distinct quality to the depression, psychomotor retardation, agitation, and self-pity (Moffic and Paykel 1975); affective and cognitive items such as suicidal ideation, sense of failure, sense of punishment, loss of interest, indecision, and dissatisfaction (Clark, Cavanaugh, and Gibbons 1983); psychomotor retardation, loss of interest, and diminished ability to think (Fava and Molnar 1987); and depressed mood, diurnal variation of mood, and hopelessness (Hawton, Mayou, and Feldman 1990). Unfortunately, no coherent picture of medical depression emerges from these lists. Differentiating the experience of depression from the wide array of physical and psychological symptoms remains difficult at best.

My colleagues and I have sought to advance the field by bringing quantitative methods to bear on the exploration of depression in people who are medically ill. We completed two separate studies of medically ill patients in whom we measured large numbers of symptoms and experiences, then subjected our data to factor analysis. In both studies, we found three distinct syndromes: grief, anhedonic depression, and demoralization (Clarke, Mackinnon, et al. 2000; Clarke, Smith, et al. 2003; Clarke, Kissane, et al. 2005). Grief was characterized by the feeling that something had been lost, accompanied by the typical symptoms of repeated thinking about the loss, memories and pictures associated with the loss, pangs of mourning, pining and yearning for the lost object, and crying. This configuration characterized 30 percent of the depressed medical inpatients in our study, patients who stated they felt "as if they had lost something" (Clarke, Mackinnon, et al. 2000). By contrast, those patients we characterized as having anhedonic depression described an inability to experience pleasure and a consequent loss of interest. Their sadness or depression was pervasive and persistent and not dependent on the environment. The third, and most common, subtype of depression in people who are medically ill, demoralization, captured patients' expression of helplessness and hopelessness. Though being unable to look forward with pleasurable anticipation, the demoralized patients were still able to enjoy the present moment (table 7.1).

Demoralization: The Prevailing Form of Depression in People Who Are Medically Ill

To flesh out these quantitatively identified factors, we completed a qualitative study of forty-nine medical inpatients to whom we posed the request "Describe how you have been unwell and in particular how that has made you feel" (Clarke, Cook, et al. 2006). The subsequent half-hour exploratory interview was audiotaped, transcribed, and analyzed. We found that, although certain symptoms were common to all hospitalized patients whether depressed or not, identifiable qualities of these symptoms differentiated the depressed and nondepressed groups. For instance, many patients did not sleep well because of the hospital environment or their physical symptoms. However, depressed patients had more profound sleeplessness, intensified by thinking and worrying about things. While all patients "thought and worried" to some degree, depressed patients felt "compelled" to do so and felt they had nothing to take

Table 7.1. Forms of Distress in the Medically Ill

	Anhedonic Depression	Demoralization ("hopelessness depression")	Posttraumatic Distress	Grief
Prominent mood/affect	Depressed, sad, black, sullen Loss of mood reactivity	Sad (loss of joy) in current circumstance and for the future (hopelessness) Mood reactive	Anxious Anxiety relates to memories, reminders, and implications of the event	Sorrowful (sad) Sorrow, recognized to be about the loss and lost object Anxiety, if present, is separation anxiety
Hedonic tone	Pervasive (in all situations) and persistent anhedonia (loss of joy and pleasure)	Ability to feel pleasure in the present (consummatory pleasure) retained	Ability to feel pleasure in the present (consummatory pleasure) partly retained	Ability to feel pleasure in the present (consummatory pleasure) partly retained
Volition	Profound loss of motivation and drive	Motivation to action compromised by feelings of incompetence and futility	Not systematically studied; specifically inhibited in relation to trauma; globally reduced if hopeless	Not systematically studied; impaired by fatigue; impairment intermittent
Sense of self	Diminished sense of self and self-worth (feels like a loss of "self")	Loss of competence (of knowing what to do)	May feel fundamentally changed from self before trauma	Self intact, but may feel depleted by loss
Thoughts	Thoughts about self, own predicament, and pitiful state	Hopelessness	Memories of the traumatic event	Thoughts and memories of the person (or lost object)
Behavior	Agitated or slowed	Constrained by circumstances, effort blocked	Avoidant and withdrawing	Forward and approaching; grieving person yearns and pines, seeks out others, wants to talk

their mind off their troubles. All patients were frustrated by not being able to do things, but depressed patients spoke with more distress about being a burden and having to rely on others. Overall, the experience of depression in our medically ill respondents was of a demoralization type. Depressed patients felt frustrated and trapped by having to stay in hospital or because of developing complications; they felt uncertain and apprehensive about not getting better or having side effects; they felt helpless, not being able to do things or to look after themselves. They also expressed subjective incompetence, having to burden others and not being able to take care of themselves (see chapter 6). Additionally, they felt guilty and worthless, both from not being able to look after their families and from feeling they had done something wrong. They described brooding and worrying in terms of being compelled to think, with nothing to distract them. Finally, they expressed hopelessness and despair, viewing life as increasingly or essentially pointless (Clarke, Cook, et al. 2006). (Figure 7.1 summarizes the processes leading to demoralization.)

These factors closely mirror Jerome Frank's observation on demoralization:

> [Demoralization] results from persistent failure to cope with internally or externally induced stresses that the person and those close to him expect him to handle. The characteristic features . . . are feelings of impotence, isolation, and despair. The person's self-esteem is damaged and he feels rejected by others because of his failure to meet their expectations. Insofar as the meaning and significance of life derives from an individual's ties with persons whose values he shares, alienation may contribute to a sense of the meaninglessness of life . . . The most frequent symptoms of patients in psychotherapy—anxiety and depression—are direct expressions of demoralization. (Frank 1974, p. 271)

> Typically [such people] are conscious of having failed to meet their own expectations or those of others, or of being unable to cope with some pressing problem. They feel powerless to change the situation for themselves and cannot extricate themselves from their predicament. (Frank and Frank 1991, p. 35)

Other prominent theoreticians have made similar observations. Klein and Davis (1969, p. 175) noted that "one aspect of psychiatric illness that is frequently not clearly understood is demoralization. Demoralization is the belief in one's ineffectiveness, engendered by a severe life defeat. It is a change in self-image (the complex of attitudes and evaluations toward the self) in the direction

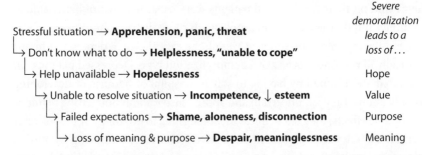

Figure 7.1. The Process of Demoralization. Adapted from D. M. Clarke "Psychological adaptation, demoralisation and depression in people with cancer," in D. W. Kissane et al. (eds.), *Depression and Cancer* (Chichester, UK: John Wiley, 2010).

of helplessness. Any life defeat may produce demoralization." These researchers were clearly aware of the link between depression and demoralization:

> Depression is particularly prone to produce demoralization since a feature of the pathological depressive mood is the profound conviction that one is incapable. This self-denigrating belief seems validated by the person's catastrophic life experience. Even after the pathological mood has remitted so that enjoyment is possible, the ability to anticipate and plan competent activity may be severely diminished because of the persistent change in self-image. Such a state of attitudinal despair does not respond to antidepressant medication because it is not the concurrent manifestation of a pathological mood; rather it is the secondary but now functionally autonomous cognitive residue of a past affective state. (Klein and Davis 1969, pp. 175–76)

Indeed, given Klein's influence, it is puzzling that demoralization never made it into the DSM as either a syndrome or a subtype of depressive disorder, the position we advocate.

Distinguishing Demoralization from Anhedonia

Historically, anhedonia has been considered the hallmark of a clinical or biogenic depression (Snaith 1987). It was a critical component, together with psychomotor retardation, of the clinical description of "endogenous depression" (Parker, Hadzi-Pavlovic, and Boyce 1989)—what Klein later called "endogenomorphic depression." "The endogenomorphic depressions, which may or may not be precipitated, and may or may not require hospitalization, regularly result in a sharp, unreactive, pervasive impairment of the capacity to experience pleasure or to respond affectively to the anticipation of pleasure. This key inhibition of the pleasure mechanism results in a profound lack of interest and investment in the environment" (Klein 1974, p. 449).

In an early textbook, after noting in the introduction that "there are several discrete psychiatric illnesses that share a common core pathological phenomenon—the depressive mood," Klein and Davis (1969, p. 175) go on to describe a person with clinical depression: "A depressed patient states, quite specifically, that he is at present not enjoying himself, and that he cannot, except abstractly and without conviction, conceive that he will ever be able to enjoy himself again."

Anhedonia is the core feature of a DSM-IV-defined depression of the melancholic type (Rush and Weissenburger 1994) and is to be distinguished from demoralization: "The differential diagnosis of demoralization and depression is relatively simple when the central role of pathological depressed mood is recalled. The demoralized person can enjoy himself in a setting in which no demands are made on him. His appetites are not inhibited and his sleep pattern is normal" (Klein and Davis 1969, p. 176). (For a careful analysis of the distinction between anhedonic depression and demoralization, see de Figueiredo 1993.)

Distinguishing Demoralization from Grief and from Posttraumatic Distress

Grief, the third subtype of depression we identified in our studies of people who are medically ill, may be readily distinguished from both anhedonic depression and demoralization (table 7.1). According to Klein and Davis (1969, p. 177), "Bereavement may lead to depression. However, even severe mourning can usually be simply discriminated from retarded depressions. In the mourning state the patient is concerned about his loss and his thinking revolves around the lost object. In depression the patient is concerned about himself and his thinking revolves about his painful depressed state."

Freud also made this distinction, noting in "Mourning and Melancholia" (1917), that in grief the world becomes poor and empty; in melancholia, it is the ego itself that is impoverished. The phenomena of grief include intense sadness and sorrow, crying, and a sense of loss. We have observed grief-like states in the context of physical illness, where the loss is not of a loved person but rather of health or the healthy self (Clarke, Kissane, et al. 2005). This possibility was also noted by Klein and Davis (1969, p. 177): "The term bereavement is commonly limited to the death of a loved one. However, loss of a valued ideal, business or career goal may precipitate analogous states." While significant numbers of grieving people are also demoralized (Clarke, Smith, et al. 2003), the two states are fundamentally distinct.

Grief may also be distinguished from posttraumatic syndromes (table 7.1), though it shares with them distress and anxiety following a serious life event, along with recurrent and often intrusive and distressing thoughts or memories or dreams (Raphael and Martinek 1997; Stroebe, Schut, and Finkenauer 2001). Normal bereavement involves pining and longing; the grieving person usually seeks out others and wants to talk about the experience of loss. The person's overwhelming affect is sorrow. By contrast, after trauma, unpleasant anxiety occurs in response to thoughts about or exposure to reminders of the traumatic event; behavior is consequently avoidant. Estrangement or detachment from others is another recognized element of posttraumatic stress. Simply put, grief is a reaction to the loss of something; posttraumatic syndromes are reactions to terrifying events. Because terrifying events may cause significant losses, patients, including those who are medically ill, sometimes experience elements of both. The phenomena are overlapping but not the same.

In summary, depression in people who are medically ill is a complex construct with multiple overlapping elements. The demoralized, depressed, medically ill population provides a unique opportunity to test Jerome Frank's hypothesis that demoralization is the element of many disorders that is most directly relieved by psychotherapy.

Demoralization and the Outcome of Medical Illness

For people who have psychiatric disorders, recovery is often measured by the relief of mental symptoms. For people who are medically ill, the course of the underlying illness may provide an additional marker of outcome. George Engel (1967) captured this insight in one of the earliest and clearest descriptions of hopelessness and helplessness, describing the "giving up–given up" syndrome that presaged premature death. It was commonly precipitated by a loss and accompanied by a physiological slowing of bodily functions. Greer and Watson (1987) described helplessness and hopelessness as one of five characteristic responses to the development of cancer—the others being the development of a fighting spirit, avoidance or denial, fatalism (or stoic acceptance), and anxious preoccupation. These reactions were determined by the patients' views of illness, their perceived control over it, and their understanding of their prognosis. Helplessness and hopelessness were shown to predict early relapse and death in patients with early-stage breast cancer (Watson et al. 1999).

Jacobsen et al. (2006) assessed the symptoms of 242 patients who had cancer. Factor analysis identified a demoralization/despair factor distinct from major depressive disorder and strongly predictive of the wish to live or die. In this study, demoralization was characterized by feelings of loss of control, loss of hope, anger/bitterness, sense of failure, feeling life was a burden, loss of meaning, and a belief that life's meaning was dependent on health.

The importance of demoralization in predicting the outcome of medical illness has led our research group to try to understand what sustains or rebuilds morale in people who are seriously ill, with the hope of finding ways of reducing their suffering and possibly prolonging their lives. Our interest required us first to adopt a reliable way to measure demoralization in people who are medically ill.

Measuring Demoralization: The Demoralization Scale

For the twin purposes of further exploring the components of demoralization and developing a scale to measure it, Kissane, Wein, et al. (2004) studied a hundred patients in a palliative care setting. From the literature and clinical experience, they developed a set of thirty-four items that included concepts of loss of confidence, subjective incompetence, loss of meaning, hopelessness, helplessness, social disconnectedness, desire to die, and the less-specific symptoms of depression. After factor analysis, they reduced this set to twenty-four items, within which were five factors representing disheartenment and discouragement, general dysphoria, helplessness and hopelessness, sense of failure, and loss of meaning and purpose (table 7.2). The Cronbach's α for the scale as a whole was 0.94 (Kissane, Wein, et al. 2004), which indicates that these concepts comprise a single construct: demoralization. Only a small number of patients in the study sample were identified as demoralized but not depressed (according to DSM-IV criteria) (14%) or depressed but not demoralized (6%).

Sustaining Morale in People Who Are Medically Ill

Hope

Demoralization is not simply a syndrome of symptoms—of mixed depression and anxiety—but a personal experience of not coping and not knowing what to do, a frightening experience that attacks self-efficacy and esteem. As noted in Frank's 1974 description given above, helplessness and hopelessness precede

Table 7.2.   The Demoralization Scale

The questionnaire is introduced as follows: "For each statement below, you are asked to indicate how strongly the statement has applied to you over the last two weeks by circling the corresponding number." Items are rated *Never, Seldom, Sometimes, Often,* and *All the Time,* and scored 0 to 4. Items 1, 6, 12, 17, and 19 are reverse scored.

Over the past two weeks, how often have you felt . . .

Disheartenment
   18. I feel distressed about what is happening to me.
   24. I feel trapped by what is happening to me.
   22. I feel discouraged about life.
   23. I feel quite isolated or alone.
    6. I am in good spirits.
   21. I feel sad and miserable.

Dysphoria
   15. I tend to feel hurt easily.
   16. I am angry about a lot of things.
   10. I feel guilty.
   11. I feel irritable.
   13. I have a lot of regret about my life.

Helplessness
    7. No one can help me.
    8. I feel that I cannot help myself.
    5. I no longer feel emotionally in control.
    9. I feel hopeless.

Sense of failure
   17. I am proud of my accomplishments.
    1. There is a lot of value in what I can offer others.
   12. I cope fairly well with life.
   19. I am a worthwhile person.

Loss of meaning
   14. Life is no longer worth living.
   20. I would rather not be alive.
    2. My life seems to be pointless.
    4. My role in life has been lost.
    3. There is no purpose to the activities in my life.

subjective incompetence, loss of self-esteem, shame, aloneness, and ultimately despair and meaninglessness (figure 7.1). When people describe not coping, losing control, and not knowing what to do, they are beginning to lose critical elements of their sense of self. This process, left unabated, leads to catastrophic loss of self-esteem and despair. While depression and anxiety symptoms certainly make up part of the accompanying clinical picture, as Eric Cassell (1991,

Table 7.3.   Existential Anxieties and the
Phenomena of Demoralization

Fear of . . .	Drive for . . .
Helplessness	Competence and control
Rejection	Acceptance, self-worth
Aloneness	Intimacy
Failure	Achievement
Futility, pointlessness	Meaning
Death	Immortality

p. 43) reminded us, "we often forget that the affect is merely the outward expression of the injury, not the injury itself."

Demoralization is also a dimensional phenomenon; one may be somewhat demoralized or very demoralized. In common parlance, being demoralized identifies a loss of sustaining courage to move forward with confidence in times of adversity (Wein 2007). It is a common observation that humans naturally seek competence, acceptance, intimacy, achievement, and meaning (Cohn 1997). Demoralization, occurring in situations of threat, challenges these aspirations head on, replacing them with feelings of helplessness, rejection, aloneness, failure, and futility (table 7.3). In the clinical setting, demoralization can be severe, leading to despair and the wish not to continue living (Clarke and Kissane 2002; Jacobsen et al. 2006). When people have severe medical illness, demoralization is often associated with existential distress or despair (Kissane 2000).

Not everybody in the same situation becomes demoralized, however. This raises the question of what confers resilience. In particular, we wondered whether certain trait characteristics such as "generalized hope," a sense of lifelong purpose, a strong self-esteem, and "global meaning" might be protective. The Macquarie Dictionary describes hope as the "expectation of something desired, desire accompanied by expectation" (Delbridge et al. 1991). Hope is future oriented and expectant. It can be generalized or particularized (Dufault and Martocchi 1985). Generalized hope preserves the meaning of life when particular hopes are quashed. People who have high optimism, strong global meaning, generalized hope, or a sense of a lifelong purpose may find that these allow them to ride the waves of life's vicissitudes as they arise. As a preliminary examination of this hypothesis, in our study of patients who are receiving palliative care or have motor neuron disease (amyotrophic lateral sclerosis, or

"Lou Gehrig's disease")—the sickest imaginable populations with the most adverse prognoses—we found a significant negative correlation between optimism, as measured by the Life Orientation Test, and demoralization (Clarke, Kissane, et al. 2005).

Sense of Coherence

In examining factors that prevent or reduce demoralization in women with gynecological cancer, Boscaglia and Clarke (2007) explored whether sense of coherence (SOC) might also be protective against demoralization. The concept of SOC was developed by Antonovsky, who defined it as "a global orientation that expresses the extent to which one has a pervasive, enduring though dynamic feeling of confidence that (1) stimuli deriving from one's internal and external environment are structured, predictable and explicable, (2) the resources are available to one to meet the demands posed by the stimuli, and (3) these demands are challenges, worthy of investment and engagement" (Antonovsky 1987, p. 19).

These three components of SOC are summarized as comprehensibility, manageability, and meaningfulness. They capture the idea of generalized hope and confidence in the world and oneself. SOC is a stable trait developed through early life. It is related to general resources and deficits, including family environment, social support, isolation, social class, and spirituality, qualities to which the person is exposed during childhood and adolescence. SOC may deepen further during adult life (Carstens and Spangenberg 1997). It predicts a range of other psychological and physical health variables, including depression in women who have fibromyalgia (Weissbecker et al. 2002), demoralization in refugees (Ying and Akutsu 1997), quality of life in people who have coronary artery disease (Motzer and Stewart 1996), and distress in people who have type II diabetes (Cohen and Kanter 2004).

Our research found a close association between demoralization and sense of coherence (Boscaglia and Clarke 2007). Using SOC as the dependent variable, we found that demoralization accounted for 60 percent of the variance in subjects' SOC, with the dysphoria, disheartenment, and sense of failure components of demoralization making the strongest contributions. Being cross-sectional, this study did not demonstrate causality, but it was consistent with the hypothesis that a strong sense of the meaningfulness, manageability, and comprehensibility of the world might guard against demoralization in the early stages of cancer.

The Cognitive Model of Depression:
The Central Role of Hopelessness

Aaron Beck (1967, 1987) was a leader of the cognitive revolution in understanding depression. His "triad" of negative thoughts of the self (as worthless), the world (as pointless), and the future (as hopeless) remains the foundation of the cognitive model of depression. For Beck, depressive thinking results from negative cognitive schema or dysfunctional attitudes about failure, rejection, or helplessness. Abramson, Metalsky, and Alloy (1989), following on the work of Seligman (1975), emphasized the importance of pervasive expectancies of no control ("learned helplessness") in the development of depression. This cognitive style leads to negative beliefs about personal competence and worth and exaggerated negative assumptions about consequences. Depression marked by prominent hopelessness derives from situations where desired outcomes will not occur and/or aversive outcomes will occur, and where no response seems able to change the outcome (Abramson, Metalsky, and Alloy 1993). Helplessness leads to hopelessness. This is what we and others (as described above) have called demoralization (Clarke and Kissane 2002). Considerable research has explored the distinction between hopelessness and depression. This is particularly clear in studies that show the independent contribution of these two factors to suicidal ideation (Thompson et al. 2005).

Hopelessness is associated with increased risk of suicide across a variety of psychiatric diagnoses (Beck, Brown, and Steer 1989) and with the loss of will to live in serious physical illness. Beck was the first to show that both depression and hopelessness contribute independently to suicidal ideation (Beck, Kovacs, and Weissman 1975). Since then, further studies of physically and mentally ill persons have validated the connection between hopelessness and suicide. For instance, Wetzel et al. (1980) found that suicidal intent in psychiatric inpatients correlated more strongly with hopelessness than with depression. In fact, in this study, when the effect of hopelessness was removed statistically, there was no association between suicidal intent and depression. Other studies, however, suggest that both depression and hopelessness are independently important factors in suicidal ideation (Dori and Overholser 1999). In medically ill populations, hopelessness (Owen et al. 1994; Breitbart, Rosenfeld, and Passik 1996; Chochinov, Wilson, et al. 1998; Breitbart, Rosenfeld, et al. 2000) and demoralization (Jacobsen et al. 2006) have also been shown to be strong predictors of patients' desire to live or die.

The work described above, arising from studies of people who are medically ill, but also drawing on pre-DSM-III descriptions of depression, has highlighted that depression encompasses several different subtypes: anhedonic depression, demoralization, also called hopelessness depression, and grief. While these phenomena are distinct, they do not necessarily occur separately. That is, it is possible, and perhaps usual, to have elements of more than one simultaneously. A cancer patient who has had a long course of chemotherapy that has failed to induce remission and is worn out by the treatment may well be feeling helpless and hopeless as well as grieving the losses associated with the disease and the treatment. Over a period of time, pervasive anhedonia may ensue, signaling the development of a biogenic depression. These distinctions have treatment implications. In considering depression as a unitary phenomenon only subtyped by numbers of symptoms or severity of impairment, the DSM leads clinicians to have unrealistic expectations and to offer the wrong treatment to the wrong patients. Specifically, antidepressant medication helps patients who have melancholia (Joyce and Paykel 1989) but by itself does little to relieve demoralization (Papakostas et al. 2007), while psychotherapy has limited effects for patients who have entrenched anhedonia. The DSM diagnosis of major depression applies equally to both groups. This is misleading in implying that the same treatment should "work" with each.

Applying the Common Features of Psychotherapy for Depressed People Who Are Medically Ill

We now turn to psychotherapy as a class of interventions that have the capacity to restore morale and buffer grief in people who are medically ill, in ways that medications do not.

In the earliest (1961) edition of *Persuasion and Healing*, Jerome Frank identified a number of characteristics that contribute to the effectiveness of all psychotherapies (Frank 1972) (see chapter 1). These so-called common features are listed in the left hand column of figure 7.2. In linking these nonspecific features with the placebo response (Frank 1983), Frank explicitly directed attention to the impact of psychotherapy on patients who have physical symptoms. (Frank 1961, chap. 7). Without disagreeing that these factors are both important and "common," we prefer to join with Klein and Davis (1969, p. 176), who rejected the term nonspecific: "It is demoralization, as an ubiquitous psychiatric phenomenon, that lies behind the misnamed 'nonspecific' effectiveness

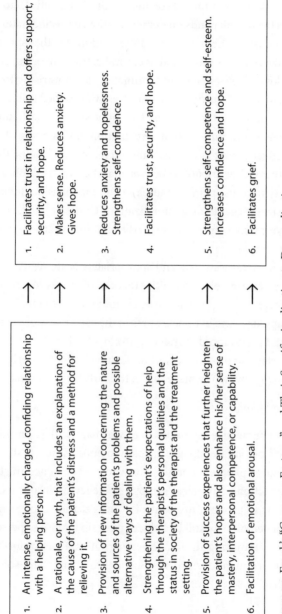

1. An intense, emotionally charged, confiding relationship with a helping person. → 1. Facilitates trust in relationship and offers support, security, and hope.

2. A rationale, or myth, that includes an explanation of the cause of the patient's distress and a method for relieving it. → 2. Makes sense. Reduces anxiety. Gives hope.

3. Provision of new information concerning the nature and sources of the patient's problems and possible alternative ways of dealing with them. → 3. Reduces anxiety and hopelessness. Strengthens self-confidence.

4. Strengthening the patient's expectations of help through the therapist's personal qualities and the status in society of the therapist and the treatment setting. → 4. Facilitates trust, security, and hope.

5. Provision of success experiences that further heighten the patient's hopes and also enhance his/her sense of mastery, interpersonal competence, or capability. → 5. Strengthens self-competence and self-esteem. Increases confidence and hope.

6. Facilitation of emotional arousal. → 6. Facilitates grief.

Figure 7.2. Frank's "Common Features" and Their Specific Application to Demoralization.

of a wide variety of therapeutic interventions, including placebos and supportive psychotherapy. We consider the idea of nonspecific therapeutic factors incorrect, since their effectiveness depends on demoralization, a specific state."

Let us now consider the therapeutic interventions for the "specific state" of demoralization, remembering that demoralization involves helplessness, hopelessness, loss of self-esteem, and ultimately despair arising from a loss of meaning and purpose. Figure 7.3 pairs the already described features of demoralization with relevant interventions. The right side of the figure describes practical interventions: information, explanation, and aspects of therapeutic alliance that reduce a patient's anxiety and increase hope—hope that they can be helped, or that things are not so bad, or that they are not alone. Uncontrollable physical symptoms (pain or nausea) or mental ones (hallucinations, obsessions) are strong agents of demoralization. Concrete medical help, especially good symptom control, is an early and important step when these symptoms are present.

Addressing hopelessness early and appropriately is also essential. Hopelessness, which has a central role in cognitive theories of depression, predicts nonresponse to antidepressants (Papakostas et al. 2007). Kuyken (2004) showed that in psychotherapy, decrease in hopelessness in the early phase of therapy predicts a more rapid and pronounced overall improvement. Giving and sustaining hope is always important, and of the "common features," simply offering help in the form of psychotherapy may achieve this in the early stages of treatment.

Countering Helplessness

Helplessness, or subjective incompetence (see chapter 6), is central to demoralization: once a person is helpless, the path to hopelessness is short. A critical factor in preventing people becoming overwhelmed is to encourage their sense of control. Reduction of physical symptoms (relieving insomnia, nausea, or pain) contributes to this, but full control of the situation is often not possible. Nevertheless, a person may still be helped to regain a sense of personal agency in the face of unremitting disease. Keeping patients well-informed and involved in their treatment decisions is essential to giving them some degree of control (see chapter 8).

Building Hope

As noted earlier, hope is "an expectation of something desired." It involves "thinking about one's goals, along with the motivation to move toward (agency)

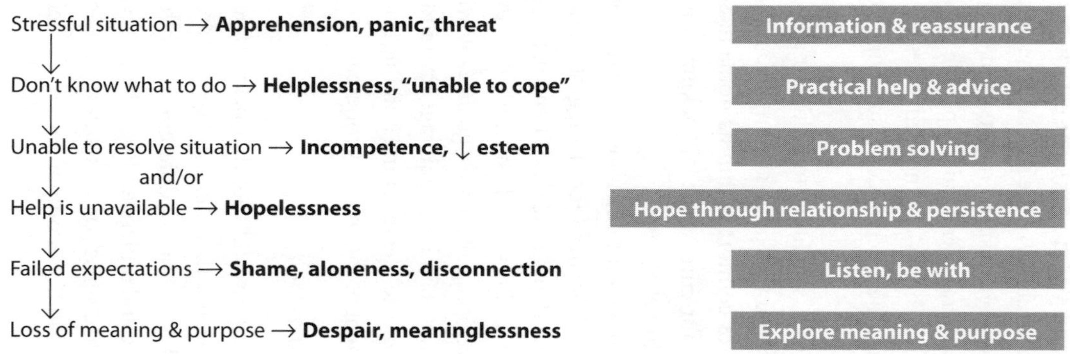

Stressful situation → **Apprehension, panic, threat**

Don't know what to do → **Helplessness, "unable to cope"**

Unable to resolve situation → **Incompetence, ↓ esteem** and/or

Help is unavailable → **Hopelessness**

Failed expectations → **Shame, aloneness, disconnection**

Loss of meaning & purpose → **Despair, meaninglessness**

Information & reassurance

Practical help & advice

Problem solving

Hope through relationship & persistence

Listen, be with

Explore meaning & purpose

Figure 7.3. Interventions Relevant at the Various Stages of Demoralization. Adapted from D. M. Clarke, "Psychological adaptation, demoralisation and depression in people with cancer," in D. W. Kissane et al. (eds.), *Depression and Cancer* (Chichester, UK: John Wiley, 2010).

and the ways to achieve (pathways), those goals" (Snyder 1995, p. 355). Hope has its origins in the infantile balance of trust and mistrust (Erikson, Erikson, and Kivnick 1986). It is expressed differently at different stages in life and in different situations (Bergin and Walsh 2005). For elderly people, hope is tied up with acceptance of the inalterability of the past and the unknowability of the future. It implies a balance between despair (regrets) and ego integrity (valuing one's life experience). Psychotherapy with elderly people must facilitate realistic hope (challenging unrealistic hopes), acknowledge despair (regrets and disappointments), and encourage the acceptance of "surviving not thriving" (Bergin and Walsh 2005).

Balancing hope with honesty is an important skill for all who provide medical care. They must understand that hope is complex and that patients may find many different sources of comfort within its domain. Some patients are able to maintain hope, even for cure, while still acknowledging the terminal nature of their disease (Clayton et al. 2008).

Using Snyder's theory of hope outlined above (considering goals, motivation, and pathways), Gum and Snyder (2002) suggest ways to maintain and even increase hope during the dying process. When goals are blocked and irreversible losses arise, these authors highlight the value and importance of mourning lost goals and developing alternative goals. Following that, assisting patients to identify the pathways and maintain agency (and vigor) is important (see chapter 8). Countering helplessness and building hope will strengthen the "manageability" component of the sense of coherence.

Listening and Being Understood

Empathic listening alone is a powerful tool that helps patients feel that they are understood and not alone and that their experiences are not so far out of the normal. Realizing that they are not so different from other people and are joined to others in experience and understanding relieves their isolation. Talking things over helps to "make sense" of a situation, reduces confusion, and strengthens the "comprehensibility" component of the sense of coherence (Griffith and Gaby 2005).

Facilitating Grief

Grief is always part of therapy for people who have chronic physical illness and have lost things that cannot be regained. Expressing grief and anger, making sense of the circumstances, contemplating the consequences, and challenging denial, all in a safe environment, constitute the core of effective therapy for grief (Worden 2002).

Conserving Dignity

Harvey Chochinov (2002) used the term dignity to provide an overarching framework to define the objectives and therapeutic considerations of end-of-life care. The dignity-conserving model, derived from interviews with patients who had advanced cancer (Chochinov, Hack, McClement, et al. 2002), considers illness-related concerns (physical distress, medical uncertainty, death anxiety, independence), dignity-conserving repertoire (maintenance of role, pride, autonomy, fighting spirit), and social dignity inventory (privacy boundaries, social support, burden to others). This framework suggests ways of caring for the patient that maximize dignity, including simple, practical things such as providing accurate and timely information (reducing medical uncertainty), involving the patient in treatment and care decisions (maximizing autonomy), and asking permission to examine the patient (respecting privacy boundaries). This model highlights how basic professional behavior can affirm patients' dignity. In addition, these interventions will encourage competence and foster patients' self-esteem.

Beyond focusing on the details of how medical care is provided, Chochinov, Hack, Hassard, et al. (2005) introduced a dignity psychotherapy in which patients were invited to review their lives, focusing on those issues that mattered the most or for which they most wanted to be remembered. When people are ill, symptomatic, and facing death, their focus of attention tends to become restricted. Dignity therapy gives people the opportunity to review their lives and relationships, reminding them of what has been important—what has given them meaning and purpose. Reviewing the past and thinking about what they want to be remembered in the future affirms the "continuity of self" across past, present, and future and supports the sense of generativity and worth.

Exploring Meaning

The question of how to counteract the problems of helplessness, aloneness, diminished self-esteem, and hopelessness is considered above. Somewhere between reason and feeling lies meaning (Breitbart, Gibson, et al. 2004). In times of serious life crisis, along with giving up certain goals and hopes and discovering new ones, patients reassess their values. Some things become more important, others less so. Psychotherapy provides the opportunity to do this work. As the third edition of *Persuasion and Healing states*, the fundamental result of psychotherapy is the transformation of meaning: "The aim of psychotherapy is to help people feel and function better by encouraging appropriate modifications in their assumptive worlds, thereby transforming the meanings of experience to more favorable ones" (Frank and Frank 1991, p. 30).

Others have developed this idea more fully in the context of serious medical illness. As Lethborg, Aranda, and Kissane (2008) pointed out, patients who have advanced disease face a number of tasks. One is dealing practically with the disease, a second is coping emotionally with the impact and meaning of the disease, and third comes living life fully in both a personal and social context. Key issues for patients include dealing with the threat of a foreshortened future and the loss of people and goals, the need for connecting with others, the need for a spiritual bridge to a higher being, emotional preparation for death, leaving a legacy, and making the most of time left (Lethborg et al. 2006). By providing space (opportunity) and assistance for patients to do the thinking required, psychotherapy may be a special source of comfort to them.

Greenstein and Breitbart (2000) described a group therapy model based on the ideas of Viktor Frankl (1992). Using a mixture of didactics, discussion, and experiential exercises, they focus on particular themes, such as "meaning derived from the historical context," "meaning derived from creative values and responsibility," and "meaning derived through experiential values." The goal is to enhance coping by strengthening patients' sense of meaning and purpose—the third component of the sense of coherence.

Kissane, Grabsch, Clarke, Smith, et al. (2007) offered supportive-expressive group therapy, modeled on the work of Irvin Yalom (1980) and Spiegel, Bloom, and Yalom (1981), to women who had metastatic breast cancer. Like Spiegel and colleagues (1981) and Goodwin and colleagues (2001), they found significant benefits for patients' psychological adjustment, though not for patient survival. In their analysis of notes and transcripts made during therapy and supervision, they identified several themes that the groups commonly explored (Kissane, Grabsch, Clarke, Christie, et al. 2005). These included discussion of health beliefs, the illness (and confronting avoidance), relationships, and acceptance of death while pursuing life. They also drew attention to the role of humor, celebration, assertiveness, creativity, and altruism. Group members' observations of "courageous dying" confirm that therapy can produce benefit (or growth) even in desperately adverse circumstances (Cordova et al. 2001).

Putting It All Together: Which Psychotherapy Is Best for People Who Are Medically Ill?

So what type of therapy do we recommend for the treatment of depression in both medical and psychiatric populations? Most guidelines give the standard answer that medication and psychotherapy are both effective, alone or in combination, for moderate depression and that medication is necessary for severe depression. We believe that different treatments should be offered based on different types of depression, rather than on severity of symptoms. The specificity of modern antidepressants has not been demonstrated, and their efficacy overall for the broad category of depression is open to serious question (Kirsch et al. 2008). It is likely that a narrower and more specific place will eventually be found for these medications. Regarding psychotherapy, evidence exists for the efficacy of cognitive behavioral therapy (CBT) (Haby et al. 2005), interpersonal psychotherapy (IPT) (de Mello et al. 2005), and dynamic therapy (Leichsenring, Rabung, and Leibing 2004; Lewis, Dennerstein, and Gibbs 2008) for a wide range of conditions. Consistent with our view of the specific effects of Frank's common or nonspecific elements of psychotherapy, we suggest that it may not matter a great deal which therapy is offered. In their review, Churchill et al. (2001) concluded that "patients receiving any variant of psychotherapy were significantly more likely to improve to a degree where they were no longer considered clinically depressed . . . than those receiving treatment as usual." In the NIMH (National Institute of Mental Health) Treatment of Depression Collaborative Research Program, which directly compared CBT and IPT, Ablon and Jones (2002) showed that, in terms of outcome, it was hard to tell the two forms of therapy apart.

It seems reasonable to conclude that the key elements of any psychotherapeutic intervention for people who have depression and demoralization are:

- A strong therapeutic engagement with another human being (the therapist) with a commitment to talking. In this, empathic attunement and reflection provide the vehicle for patients' feeling understood and "not alone." Talking itself leads to reflection and problem solving, making sense of what is going on. The accompanying emotional expression reduces stress and arousal.
- The provision of information (about the illness and what to expect) to reduce anxiety and aid decision making.

- Practical problem solving to strengthen self-efficacy and reduce subjective incompetence.
- A review of life (Chochinov, Hack, Hassard, et al. 2005) that fosters a sense of coherence in a person's relationships, purpose, value, and meaning.
- Goal planning—giving up some hopes, but refreshing commitment to others—to reinvigorate purpose and discover meaning in life. (See chapter 8 for examples of such psychotherapy with the medically ill.)

These elements together, embedded in any empathic and supportive relationship (Meares 1998), encourage activation and engagement in health care decision making. Helping patients negotiate the health system to their benefit, and advocating for them, sometimes become the task of the therapist.

Beyond these general principles, different styles of psychotherapy may usefully address specifics of a patient's problem. Inevitably, existential issues arise that require attention in the treatment of severe demoralization and in the support of healthy adjustment (see chapter 15).

Conclusion

Research on depression in people who are medically ill challenges the current unitary, threshold model of depression promulgated by DSM-IV and instead gives priority to the importance of recognizing the subtypes of anhedonic depression, demoralization, and grief. Understanding the experience of being physically ill, and of depression in people who are medically ill, has informed the development of a range of psychological interventions useful to patients in this circumstance. These interventions range from simple things—good information, good symptom control, involving patients in care, showing respect, and enhancing dignity—to more complex psychotherapy involving exploration of goals and meaning and the acknowledgment of grief.

Providing psychotherapy for people who are desperately or terminally ill is challenging. Such patients' feelings of helplessness and hopelessness are more contagious than influenza. Appropriate supervision and peer support are essential to keep therapists from becoming overwhelmed and losing their effectiveness. In the health care setting, sharing the load in multidisciplinary teams is important. In this context, psychiatrists, psychologists, social workers, chaplains, and other trained counselors can play an important role both in delivering direct patient care and in facilitating psychologically informed care by all staff. The "common features" of psychotherapy, which apply to all caregivers, provide a starting point for a therapy that restores morale. Other specific skills may further enhance patients' self-efficacy and strengthen their courage, allowing them to move forward to confront their challenges in keeping with their preexisting values and identities. Several models, including a brief bedside therapy (Griffith and Gaby 2005) (see chapter 8) and group therapy (Greenstein and Breitbart 2000; Kissane, Wein, et al. 2004) (see chapter 13), offer compelling examples of how this can be done.

REFERENCES

Ablon, J. S., and Jones, E. E. 2002. Validity of controlled clinical trials of psychotherapy: findings from the NIMH Treatment of Depression Collaborative Research Program. *American Journal of Psychiatry* 159:775–83.

Abramson, L. Y., Metalsky, G. I., and Alloy, L. B. 1989. Hopelessness depression: a theory based subtype of depression. *Psychological Review* 96:358–72.

———. 1993. Hopelessness. In C. G. Costello (eds.), *Symptoms of Depression* (pp. 181–205). New York: John Wiley.

Ambrosini, P. J., Bennett, D. S., Cleland, C. M., and Haslam, N. 2002. Taxonicity of adolescent melancholia: a categorical or dimensional construct? *Journal of Psychiatric Research* 36:247–56.

American Psychiatric Association. 1994. *Diagnostic and Statistical Manual of Mental Disorders*, 4th ed., text rev. Washington, DC: American Psychiatric Association.

Antonovsky, A. 1987. *Unraveling the Mystery of Health: How People Manage Stress and Stay Well*. San Francisco: Jossey-Bass.

Beck, A. T. 1967. *Depression: Clinical, Experimental, and Theoretical Aspects*. London: Staples.

———. 1987. Cognitive models of depression. *Journal of Cognitive Psychotherapy* 1:5–37.

Beck, A. T., Brown, G., and Steer, R. A. 1989. Prediction of eventual suicide in psychiatric in-patients by clinical ratings of hopelessness. *Journal of Consulting and Clinical Psychology* 57:309–10.

Beck, A. T., Kovacs, M., and Weissman, A. 1975. Hopelessness and suicidal behaviour: an overview. *JAMA: Journal of the American Medical Association* 234:1146–49.

Beck, A. T., Steer, R. A., and Brown, G. K. 1996. *BDI-II Manual*. San Antonio: Psychological Corporation.

Bergin, L., and Walsh, S. 2005. The role of hope in psychotherapy with older adults. *Aging and Mental Health* 9:7–15.

Blazer, D. G. 2005. *The Age of Melancholy: Major Depression and Its Social Origins*. New York: Routledge, Taylor and Francis.

Boscaglia, N., and Clarke, D. M. 2007. Sense of coherence as a protective factor for demoralisation in women with a recent diagnosis of gynaecological cancer. *Psycho-Oncology* 16:189–95.

Breitbart, W., Gibson, C., Poppito, S. R., and Berg, A. 2004. Psychotherapeutic interventions at the end of life: a focus on meaning and spirituality. *Canadian Journal of Psychiatry* 49:366–72.

Breitbart, W., Rosenfeld, B. D., and Passik, S. D. 1996. Interest in physician assisted suicide among ambulatory HIV-infected patients. *American Journal of Psychiatry* 153:238–42.

Breitbart, W., Rosenfeld, B., Pessin, H., Kaim, M., Funesti-Esch, J., Galietta, M., et al. 2000. Depression, hopelessness and the desire for hastened death in terminally ill patients with cancer. *JAMA: Journal of the American Medical Association* 284:907–11.

Brown, G. W., and Harris, T. O. 1978. *Social Origins of Depression*. New York: Free Press.

Brown, G. W., Harris, T. O., and Hepworth, C. 1995. Loss humiliation and entrapment among women developing depression: a patient and non-patient comparison. *Psychological Medicine* 25:7–21.

Burton, H. J., Kline, S. A., Lindsay, R. M., and Heidenheim, A. P. 1986. The relationship of depression to survival in chronic renal failure. *Psychosomatic Medicine* 48:261–69.

Carstens, J. A., and Spangenberg, J. J. 1997. Major depression: a breakdown in sense of coherence? *Psychological Reports* 80:1211–20.

Cassell, E. J. 1991. *The Nature of Suffering and the Goals of Medicine*. Oxford: Oxford University Press.

Chochinov, H. M. 2002. Dignity-conserving care—a new model for palliative care: helping the patient feel valued. *JAMA: Journal of the American Medical Association* 287:2253–60.

Chochinov, H. M., Hack, T., Hassard, T., Kristjanson, L. J., McClement, S., and Harlos, M. 2005. Dignity therapy: a novel psychotherapeutic intervention for patients near the end of life. *Journal of Clinical Oncology* 23:5520–25.

Chochinov, H. M., Hack, T., McClement, S., Harlos, M., and Kristjanson, L. 2002. Dignity in the terminally ill: a developing empirical model. *Social Science and Medicine* 54:433–43.

Chochinov, H. M., Wilson, K. G., Enns, M., and Lander, S. 1998. Depression, hopelessness and suicidal ideation. *Psychosomatics* 39:366–70.

Churchill, R., Hunot, V., Corney, R., Knapp, M., McGuire, H., Tylee, A., and Wessely, S. 2001. A systematic review of controlled trials of the effectiveness and cost-effectiveness of brief psychological treatments for depression. *Health Technology Assessment* 5(35):1–173.

Clark, D. C., Cavanaugh, S. A., and Gibbons, R. D. 1983. The core symptoms of depression in medical and psychiatric patients. *Journal of Nervous and Mental Disease* 171:705–13.

Clarke, D. M., Cook, K. E., Coleman, K. J., and Smith, G. C. 2006. A qualitative examination of the experience of "depression" in hospitalized medically ill patients. *Psychopathology* 39:303–12.

Clarke, D. M., and Currie, K. C. 2009. Depression, anxiety and their relationship with chronic diseases: a review of the epidemiology, risk and treatment evidence. *Medical Journal of Australia* 190:S54–60.

Clarke, D. M., and Kissane, D. W. 2002. Demoralisation: its phenomenology and importance. *Australian and New Zealand Journal of Psychiatry* 36:733–42.

Clarke, D. M., Kissane, D. W., Trauer, T., and Smith, G. C. 2005. Demoralisation, anhedonia and grief in patients with severe physical illness. *World Psychiatry* 4:96–105.

Clarke, D. M., Mackinnon, A. J., Smith, G. C., McKenzie, D. P., and Herrman, H. E.

2000. Dimensions of psychopathology in the medically ill: a latent trait analysis. *Psychosomatics* 41:418–25.

Clarke, D. M., Minas, I. H., and Stuart, G. W. 1991. The prevalence of psychiatric morbidity in general hospital patients. *Australian and New Zealand Journal of Psychiatry* 25:322–29.

Clarke, D. M., Smith, G. C., Dowe, D. L., and McKenzie, D. P. 2003. An empirically derived taxonomy of common distress syndromes in the medically ill. *Journal of Psychosomatic Research* 54:323–30.

Clayton, J. M., Hancock, K., Parker, S., Butow, P. N., Walder, S., Carrick, S., et al. 2008. Sustaining hope when communicating with terminally ill patients and their families: a systematic review. *Psycho-Oncology* 17:641–59.

Cohen, M., and Kanter, Y. 2004. Relation between sense of coherence and glycemic control in type 1 and type 2 diabetes. *Behavioral Medicine* 29:175–83.

Cohn, H. W. 1997. *Existential Thought and Therapeutic Practice: An Introduction to Existential Psychotherapy.* London: Sage.

Cordova, M. J., Cunningham, L. L., Carlson, C. R., and Andrykowski, M. A. 2001. Post-traumatic growth following breast cancer: a controlled comparison study. *Health Psychology* 20:176–85.

de Figueiredo, J. M. 1993. Depression and demoralisation: phenomenologic differences and research perspectives. *Comprehensive Psychiatry* 34:308–11.

de Mello, M. F., de Jesus Mari, J., Bacaltchuk, J., Verdeli, H., and Neugebauer, R. 2005. A systematic review of research findings on the efficacy of interpersonal therapy for depressive disorders. *European Archives of Psychiatry and Clinical Neuroscience* 255:75–82.

Delbridge, A., Bernard, J. R. L., Blair, D., Peters, P., and Butler, S. (eds.). 1991. *The Macquarie Dictionary*, 2nd ed. Sydney, Australia: Macquarie Library.

Dohrenwend, B. P., Shrout, P. E., Egrie, G., and Mendelsohn, F. S. 1980. Non-specific psychological distress and other measures for use in the general population. *Archives of General Psychiatry* 37:1229–36.

Dori, A., and Overholser, J. C. 1999. Depression, hopelessness and self-esteem: accounting for suicidality in adolescent psychiatric inpatients. *Suicide and Life-Threatening Behavior* 29:309–18.

Dufault, K., and Martocchi, B. C. 1985. Hope: its spheres and dimensions. *Nursing Clinics of North America* 20:379–91.

Duits, A. A., Boeke, S., Duivenvoorden, H. J., and Passchier, J. 1996. Depression in patients undergoing cardiac surgery: a comment. *British Journal of Health Psychology* 1:283–86.

Engel, G. L. 1967. A psychosocial setting of somatic disease: the giving up–given up complex. *Proceedings of the Royal Society of Medicine* 60:553–55.

Erikson, E., Erikson, J., and Kivnick, H. 1986. *Vital Involvement in Old Age.* London: W. W. Norton.

Fava, G. A., and Molnar, G. 1987. Criteria for diagnosing depression in the setting of medical disease. *Psychotherapy and Psychosomatics* 48:21–25.

Frank, J. D. 1946. Emotional reactions of American soldiers to an unfamiliar disease. *American Journal of Psychiatry* 102:631–40.

———. 1961. *Persuasion and Healing: A Comparative Study of Psychotherapy.* Baltimore: Johns Hopkins University Press.

————. 1972. Common features of psychotherapy. *Australian and New Zealand Journal of Psychiatry* 6:34–40.

————. 1974. Psychotherapy: the restoration of morale. *American Journal of Psychiatry* 131:271–74.

————. 1983. The placebo is psychotherapy. *Behavioral and Brain Sciences* 6:291–92.

Frank, J. D., and Frank, J. B 1991. *Persuasion and Healing: A Comparative Study of Psychotherapy*, 3rd ed. Baltimore: Johns Hopkins University Press.

Frankl, V. F. 1992. *Man's Search for Meaning*, 4th ed. Boston: Beacon Press.

Freud, S. 1917. Mourning and melancholia. In *The Standard Edition of the Complete Psychological Works of Sigmund Freud*, vol. 14 (pp. 237–58). London: Hogarth Press.

Goldberg, D. P. 1972. *The Detection of Psychiatric Illness by Questionnaire*. Maudsley Monograph no. 21. London: Oxford University Press.

Goodwin, P. J., Leszcz, M., Ennis, M., Koopmans, J., Vincent, L., Guther, H., et al. 2001. The effect of group psychosocial support on survival in metastatic breast cancer. *New England Journal of Medicine* 345:1719–26.

Greenstein, M., and Breitbart, W. 2000. Cancer and the experience of meaning: a group psychotherapy program for people with cancer. *American Journal of Psychotherapy* 54:486–500.

Greer, S., and Watson, M. 1987. Mental adjustment to cancer: its measurement and prognostic importance. *Cancer Surveys* 6:439–58.

Griffith, J. L., and Gaby, L. 2005. Brief psychotherapy at the bedside: countering demoralization from medical illness. *Psychosomatics* 46:109–16.

Grove, W. M., Andreasen, N. C., Young, M., Endicott, J., Keller, M. B., Hirschfeld, R. M., and Reich, T. 1987. Isolation and characterization of a nuclear depressive syndrome. *Psychological Medicine* 17:471–84.

Gum, A., and Snyder, C. R. 2002. Coping with terminal illness: the role of hopeful thinking. *Journal of Palliative Medicine* 5:883–94.

Haby, M. M., Donnelly, M., Corry, J., and Vos, T. 2005. Cognitive behavioural therapy for depression, panic disorder and generalized anxiety disorder: a meta-regression of factors that may predict outcome. *Australian and New Zealand Journal of Psychiatry* 40:9–19.

Harris, T. 2001. Recent developments in understanding the psychosocial aspects of depression. *British Medical Bulletin* 57:17–32.

Hawton, K., Mayou, R., and Feldman, E. 1990. Significance of psychiatric symptoms in general medical patients with mood disorders. *General Hospital Psychiatry* 12:296–302.

Horwitz, A. V., and Wakefield, J. C. 2007. *The Loss of Sadness: How Psychiatry Transformed Normal Sorrow into Depressive Disorder*. Oxford: Oxford University Press.

Jacobsen, J. C., Vanderwerker, L. C., Block, S. D., Friedlander, R. J., Maciejewski, P. K., and Prigerson, H. G. 2006. Depression and demoralization as distinct syndromes: preliminary data from a cohort of advanced cancer patients. *Indian Journal of Palliative Care* 12:8–15.

Joyce, P. R., and Paykel, E. S. 1989. Predictors of drug response in depression. *Archives of General Psychiatry* 46:89–99.

Keller, M. C., Neale, M. C., and Kendler, K. S. 2007. Association of different adverse life events with distinct patterns of depressive symptoms. *American Journal of Psychiatry* 164:1521–29.

Keller, M. C., and Nesse, R. M. 2005. Is low mood an adaptation? Evidence for subtypes with symptoms that match precipitants. *Journal of Affective Disorders* 86:27–35.

——. 2006. The evolutionary significance of depressive symptoms: different adverse situations lead to different depressive symptom patterns. *Journal of Personality and Social Psychology* 91:316–30.

Kendler, K. S., and Gardner, C. O. 1998. Boundaries of major depression: an evaluation of DSM-IV criteria. *American Journal of Psychiatry* 155:172–77.

Kendler, K. S., Karkowski, L. M., and Prescott, C. A. 1999. Causal relationship between stressful life events and the onset of major depression. *American Journal of Psychiatry* 156:837–41.

Kessler, R. C., Andrews, G., Colpe, L. J., Hiripi, E., Mroczek, D. K., Normand, S. L. T., et al. 2002. Short screening scales to monitor population prevalences and trends in non-specific psychological distress. *Psychological Medicine* 32:959–76.

Kirsch, I., Deacon, B. J., Huedo-Medina, T. B., Scoboria, A., Moore, T. J., and Johnson, B. T. 2008. Initial severity and antidepressant benefits: a meta-analysis of data submitted to the Food and Drug Administration. *PLoS Med* 5(2):e45. doi: 10.1371/journal.pmed.0050045.

Kissane, D. W. 2000. Psychospiritual and existential distress: a challenge for palliative care. *Australian Family Physician* 29:1022–25.

Kissane, D. W., Grabsch, B., Clarke, D. M., Christie, G., Clifton, D., Gold, S., et al. 2005. Supportive-expressive group therapy: the transformation of existential ambivalence into creative living while enhancing adherence to anti-cancer therapies. *Psycho-Oncology* 13:755–68.

Kissane, D. W., Grabsch, B., Clarke, D. M., Smith, G. C., Love, A. W., Bloch, S., et al. 2007. Supportive-expressive group therapy for women with metastatic breast cancer: survival and psychosocial outcome from a randomized controlled trial. *Psycho-Oncology* 16:277–86.

Kissane, D. W., Wein, S., Love, A., Xiu, Q. L., Pei, L. K., and Clarke, D. M. 2004. The Demoralization Scale: a report of its development and preliminary validation. *Journal of Palliative Care* 20:269–76.

Klein, D. F. 1974. Endogenomorphic depression. *Archives of General Psychiatry* 31:447–54.

Klein, D. F., and Davis, J. M. 1969. *Diagnosis and Drug Treatment of Psychiatric Disorders*. Baltimore: Williams and Wilkins.

Kuyken, W. 2004. Cognitive therapy outcome: the effects of hopelessness in a naturalistic outcome study. *Behaviour Research and Therapy* 42:631–46.

Leichsenring, F., Rabung, S., and Leibing, E. 2004. The efficacy of short-term psychodynamic psychotherapy in specific psychiatric disorders. *Archives of General Psychiatry* 61:1208–16.

Lesperance, F., Frasure-Smith, N., and Talajic, M. 1996. Major depression before and after myocardial infarction: its nature and consequences. *Psychosomatic Medicine* 58:99–110.

Lethborg, C., Aranda, S., Bloch, S., and Kissane, D. 2006. The role of meaning in advanced cancer: integrating the constructs of assumptive world, sense of coherence and meaning-based coping. *Journal of Psychosocial Oncology* 24:27–42.

Lethborg, C., Aranda, S., and Kissane, D. W. 2008. Meaning and adjustment to cancer: a model of care. *Palliative and Supportive Care* 6:61–70.

Lewis, A. J., Dennerstein, M., and Gibbs, P. M. 2008. Short-term psychodynamic psychotherapy: a review of recent process and outcome studies. *Australian and New Zealand Journal of Psychiatry* 42:445–55.

Maes, M., Cosyns, P., Maes, L., D'Hondt, P., and Schotte, C. 1990. Clinical subtypes of unipolar depression: part 1. A validation of the vital and non-vital clusters. *Psychiatry Research* 34:29–41.

Matussek, P., Soldner, M., and Nagel, D. 1981. Identification of the endogenous depressive syndrome based on the symptoms and the characteristics of the course. *British Journal of Psychiatry* 138:361–72.

McGlinchey, J. B., Zimmerman, M., Young, D., and Chelminski, I. 2006. Diagnosing major depressive disorder: VIII. Are some symptoms better than others? *Journal of Nervous and Mental Disease* 194:785–90.

Meares, R. 1998. The self in conversation: on narratives, chronicles and scripts. *Psychoanalytic Dialogues* 8:875–91.

Moffic, H. S., and Paykel, E. S. 1975. Depression in medical inpatients. *British Journal of Psychiatry* 126:346–53.

Morris, P. L. P., Raphael, B., and Robinson, R. G. 1992. Clinical depression is associated with impaired recovery from stroke. *Medical Journal of Australia* 157:239–42.

Motzer, S. U., and Stewart, B. J. 1996. Sense of coherence as a predictor of quality of life in persons with coronary heart disease surviving cardiac arrest. *Research in Nursing and Health* 19:287–98.

Nelson, J. C., Charney, D. S., and Quinlan, D. M. 1980. Characteristics of autonomous depression. *Journal of Nervous and Mental Disease* 168:637–43.

Owen, C., Tennant, C., Levi, J., and Jones, M. 1994. Cancer patients' attitudes to final events in life: wish for death, attitudes to cessation of treatment, suicide and euthanasia. *Psycho-Oncology* 3:1–19.

Papakostas, G. I., Petersen, T., Homberger, C. H., Green, C. H., Smith, J., Alpert, J. E., and Fava, M. 2007. Hopelessness as a predictor of non-response to fluoxetine in major depressive disorder. *Annals of Clinical Psychiatry* 19:5–8.

Parker, G. 2000. Classifying depression: should paradigms lost be regained? *American Journal of Psychiatry* 157:1195–1203.

———. 2006. Through a glass darkly: the disutility of the DSM nosology of depressive disorders. *Canadian Journal of Psychiatry* 51:879–86.

Parker, G., Hadzi-Pavlovic, D., and Boyce, P. 1989. Endogenous depression as a construct: a quantitative analysis of the literature and a study of clinician judgements. *Australian and New Zealand Journal of Psychiatry* 23:357–68.

Parker, G., Hadzi-Pavlovic, D., Wilhelm, K., Hickie, I., Brodaty, H., Boyce, P., et al. 1994. Defining melancholia: properties of a refined sign-based measure. *British Journal of Psychiatry* 164:316–26.

Parker, G., Roy, K., Wilhelm, K., Mitchell, P., Austin, M. P., Hadzi-Pavlovic, D., and Little, C. 1999. Sub-grouping non-melancholic depression from manifest clinical features. *Journal of Affective Disorders* 53:1–13.

Paykel, E. S. 1994. Life events, social support and depression. *Acta Psychiatrica Scandinavica* 377(suppl.):50–58.

Raphael, B., and Martinek, N. 1997. Assessing traumatic bereavement and posttraumatic stress disorder. In J. P. Wilson and T. M. Keane (eds.), *Assessing Psychological Trauma and PTSD* (pp. 373–98). New York: Guilford Press.

Rimington, L. D., Davies, D. H., and Lowe, D. 2001. Relationship between anxiety, depression and morbidity in adult asthma patients. *Thorax* 56:266–71.

Rush, A. J., and Weissenburger, J. E. 1994. Melancholic symptom features and DSM-IV. *American Journal of Psychiatry* 151:489–98.

Schwab, J. J., Bialow, M., Brown, J. M., and Holzer, C. E. 1967. Diagnosing depression in medical patients. *Archives of Internal Medicine* 67:695–707.

Schwab, J. J., Clemmons, R. S., Bialow, M., Duggan, V., and Davis, B. 1965. A study of somatic symptomatology of depression in medical patients. *Psychosomatics* 6:273–77.

Seligman, M. E. P. 1975. *Helplessness: On Depression, Development, and Death*. New York: W. H. Freeman.

Snaith, R. P. 1987. The concepts of mild depression. *British Journal of Psychiatry* 150:387–93.

Snyder, C. R. 1995. Conceptualising, measuring, and nurturing hope. *Journal of Counseling and Development* 73:355–60.

Spiegel, D. 1996. Cancer and depression. *British Journal of Psychiatry* 168:109–16.

Spiegel, D., Bloom, J. R., and Yalom, I. 1981. Group support for patients with metastatic cancer: a randomized outcome study. *Archives of General Psychiatry* 38:527–33.

Stroebe, M., Schut, H., and Finkenauer, C. 2001. The traumatisation of grief? A conceptual framework for understanding the trauma-bereavement interface. *Israel Journal of Psychiatry and Related Sciences* 38:185–201.

Sullivan, P. F., Prescott, C. A., and Kendler, K. S. 2002. The subtypes of major depression in a twin registry. *Journal of Affective Disorders* 68:273–84.

Thompson, E. A., Mazza, J. J., Herting, J. R., Randall, B. P., and Eggert, L. L. 2005. The mediating roles of anxiety, depression and hopelessness on adolescent suicidal behaviours. *Suicide and Life-Threatening Behavior* 35:14–34.

Van Praag, H. A., David, W. W., and McQueen, L. E. 1998. The diagnosis of depression in disorder. *Australian and New Zealand Journal of Psychiatry* 32:767–72.

Watson, M., Haviland, J. S., Greer, S., Davidson, J., and Bliss, J. M. 1999. Influence of psychological response on survival in breast cancer: a population-based cohort study. *Lancet* 354:1331–36.

Wein, S. 2007. Is courage the counterpoint of demoralization. *Journal of Palliative Care* 23:40–43.

Weissbecker, I., Salmon, P., Studts, J. L., Floyd, A. R., Dedert, E. A., and Sephton, S. E. 2002. Mindfulness based stress reduction and sense of coherence among women with fibromyalgia. *Journal of Clinical Psychology in the Medical Setting* 9:297–307.

Wells, K. B., Golding, J. M., and Burnam, M. A. 1988. Psychiatric disorder in a sample of the general population with and without chronic medical conditions. *American Journal of Psychiatry* 145:976–81.

Wetzel, R. D., Margulies, T., Davis, R., and Karam, E. 1980. Hopelessness, depression and suicide intent. *Journal of Clinical Psychiatry* 41:159–60.

Worden, J. W. 2002. *Grief Counseling and Grief Therapy: A Handbook for the Mental Health Practitioner*, 3rd ed. New York: Springer.

Yalom, I. D. 1980. *Existential Psychotherapy*. New York: Basic Books.

Ying, Y., and Akutsu, P. D. 1997. Psychological adjustment of South-East Asian refugees: the contribution of sense of coherence. *Journal of Community Psychology* 25:125–39.

Zimmerman, M., McGlinchey, J. B., Chelminski, I., and Young, D. 2006. Diagnosing major depressive disorder: V. Applying the DSM-IV exclusion criteria in clinical practice. *Journal of Nervous and Mental Disease* 194:530–33.

CHAPTER 8

Demoralization and Hope in Clinical Psychiatry and Psychotherapy

So she sat on, with closed eyes, and half believed herself in Wonderland, though she knew she had but to open them again and all would change to dull reality.
—*Alice's Adventures in Wonderland*

James L. Griffith, M.D., and
Anjali DSouza, M.D.

The influence of positive emotional states upon physical disease has been noted since antiquity and forms the basis of all forms of psychological healing.
—*PERSUASION AND HEALING*, 1991, P. 124

The second edition of *Persuasion and Healing* (Frank 1973) defended the radical assertion that people seek psychotherapy largely because they feel demoralized, not because they have a mental illness. "Demoralization" referred to the distress felt by people aware of their failure to meet their own or others' expectations, while seeing themselves as powerless to change the situation or themselves (see chapters 6 and 7 in this volume). In linking demoralization to the common features of psychotherapy described in the first edition (1961), Frank fostered a quiet revolution. Teaching therapists how to inspire hope, mastery, trust, and expectation for change, rather than specialized techniques of particular schools, became the core of training.

Recognizing demoralization rather than mental illness as the main grounds for psychotherapy also widens the scope of who should be offered such care. Demoralization is a common form of "normal suffering" for people who have chronic medical illnesses, victims of disasters, unemployed workers, or immigrants in an unfamiliar culture. All may benefit from systematic efforts to restore hope and mastery in the face of overwhelming circumstances.

In the decades since *Persuasion and Healing* first appeared, substantial progress has been made in clinical theory and psychotherapeutic technique. The third edition (Frank and Frank 1991) suggested that psychotherapists might develop their skills by cultivating qualities identified in the study of rhetoric. Rhetorical principles suggest that therapists could build on the *ethos* attached to their cultural and personal status to enlist a patient's trust. As a form of rhetoric, psychotherapy arouses moderate levels of emotion through culturally resonant language, imagery, or prescribed acts. Such rhetorical methods empower therapists to offer patients convincing hope that they may counter feelings of helplessness by changing either themselves or their circumstances.

Hope and Demoralization in Clinical Practice

Though the principles of effective therapy are simple, their application requires skill and sophistication. Hope is most needed but hardest to find when one is caught in the depths of despair. A patient undergoing renal dialysis, who alarmed his physicians by his refusal to adhere to a renal diet, commented: "At age fifty-one, you don't change the way you eat. The foods I like are the ones I like. You want to enjoy life somewhere . . . Not able to eat food I like, I'd be like the living dead." His nihilistic defiance voiced his loss of expectations that anything was to be gained by accommodating to his illness. Where does one begin in helping such a man to recover hope? Merely exhorting a struggling person to feel hope when life's conditions appear bleak is futile. The normal human response to exhortation is often paradoxical; commonly, demoralized people feel even more isolated and helpless when others say: "Look on the bright side!" or "Things can't be as bad as they seem!"

In the place of cheerleading, psychotherapists learn to target processes that enable hope or overcome obstacles that constrain it. These clinical strategies focus on the interplay of desire, agency, planning, and action. Can one feel desire for a better future? Can one act in a manner that makes a difference? Can paths be envisioned from the present toward a better future? Can some action be initiated along one of those paths? Answers to the challenge of demoralization differ depending on what a particular theory identifies as the factors that typically undermine hope, what capabilities a patient can bring to the task of hope-building, and what beliefs and expectations are conveyed by the surrounding social and cultural environment.

Hope as Expectation of Success

John de Figueiredo and Jerome Frank argued that demoralization does not inevitably follow when stressful life events pile up (de Figueiredo and Frank 1982; de Figueiredo 1993). At its heart, demoralization is a moral judgment, a self-evaluation that one is incompetent and cannot meet expectations. Even though circumstances may be objectively harsh, an individual's assumptive world mediates his or her level of morale. A demoralized person believes—as reflected in thoughts, feelings, and actions—that problems will endure and that his or her efforts cannot change them.

Jerome Groopman's inspiring accounts (2004) of patients fighting against the odds illustrate the power of hope. He offers the example of Dr. George Griffin, a Harvard Medical School professor of pathology diagnosed with anaplastic adenocarcinoma of the stomach, a particularly malignant cancer with no good treatment. His colleagues and students shook their heads when Dr. Griffin refused palliative care and chose instead a maximally aggressive course of chemotherapy and surgery. He suffered enormously from drug side effects and surgical complications. Inexplicably, however, the cancer disappeared, and Dr. Griffin was cured. Dr. Griffin's defiance of death, his courage to go against his doctors' recommendations, demonstrates the power of optimism and refusal to remain in a posture of helplessness.

Jerome and Julia Frank (1991) noted that psychotherapy helps patients recognize, then accept, that their own beliefs and attitudes contribute to their suffering. Acknowledging that one's assumptions help create one's difficulties can, paradoxically, be uplifting. Such awareness suggests possibilities for changing the beliefs and attitudes that are problematic. Addressing cognitive distortions helps a catastrophizing patient see that he or she is interpreting life circumstances as having more limited possibilities than actually exist. The cognitive elements of psychotherapy that persuade patients to see the world more accurately and realistically can sometimes mobilize hope. Fostering self-efficacy can raise hope to a level that motivates action, including action that changes the demoralizing circumstances.

Less strictly rational approaches may be equally powerful. Religions extend hope beyond the limits of earthly existence. Life may feel fundamentally unjust, with the powerful preying on the weak and the dispossessed forgotten. Yet religion can promise that the inexorable workings of the law of karma, the coming of an eschatological perfect age, or an eternal afterlife with God will make everything all right in the end. Such promises usually include prescriptions for present action meant to strengthen faith, actions that may have immediate beneficial effects.

Clinical thinking about hope as expectation of successful achievement provides the foundation for positive psychology as a new movement in psychotherapy. Martin Seligman (1998) studied extensively the adaptive power of a personality style tending toward optimistic interpretations of events. Albert Bandura (1997) emphasized the importance of self-efficacy, a person's perception of his or her capacity to carry out actions that might successfully attain goals. J. P. Hewitt (1998) focused on self-esteem as the personal judgment of one's worthiness based on capabilities for achieving goals.

Hope as the Product of Agency Thinking and Pathways Thinking

Over the past two decades, C. R. Snyder and colleagues at the University of Kansas have conducted extensive empirical studies detailing how expectations work to support hope (Lopez et al. 2000; Michael, Taylor, and Cheapens 2000; Rodriguez-Hanley and Snyder 2000; Snyder 2000a, 2000b; Snyder and Taylor 2000). These studies describe hope as the product of both *agency thinking* and *pathways thinking*. Agency thinking involves the perceptions and beliefs about one's capabilities for acting effectively. Pathways thinking connotes the perceptions, strategizing, and planning routes needed to reach goals. Hope is thus the sum of perceived capabilities ("I can do it") and strategizing and planning ("I know a way to do it") to reach a goal.

Building on these studies, Snyder and his associates have designed and tested a range of methods for strengthening hope in psychotherapy (Snyder, McDermott, et al. 1997; Snyder 2000a, 2000b). Lopez and colleagues (2000) propose "hope therapy" as a specific approach organized by these ideas. Hope therapy offers techniques for guiding patients to formulate goals more clearly, produce many possible pathways for attaining these goals, recruit the energy to make a strong effort, and reframe obstacles as surmountable challenges. Evaluating candidates for therapy involves a systematic search for sources of hope in the patient's life story. The process also fosters hope through the therapist's modeling. Therapists who express high levels of optimism do best in engendering hope in their patients.

As an example, Lopez et al. (2000) described Kurt, a twenty-eight-year-old man self-referred for depression. In his first session, Kurt stated: "I am directionless and can't seem to meet people." The therapist elicited from Kurt narratives from his childhood years about friendships he had been able to establish. The therapist conducted a systematic inquiry about how he had made these friendships and maintained them, noting also that Kurt had been able to relocate to a new town for work, support himself, work toward a college degree, and initiate therapy. These conversations directed Kurt toward agency thinking by implying that he was capable of acting competently and effectively in pursuit of his goals. The therapist also worked with Kurt to imagine the steps needed to become an interesting conversationalist. Kurt began focusing on a work routine in which he began the day by chatting with colleagues over coffee. He initiated a daily discipline of reviewing the newspaper, identifying interesting topics, and initiating conversations. These efforts directed Kurt toward pathways thinking, helping him strategize and plan routes toward his goal.

Limitations of Hope as Expectation of Success

Clinical approaches to hope-building that rely solely on expectations of success have limitations. Many individuals are caught in circumstances that are starkly overwhelming and lacking in conceivable solutions. Patients who have genetic diseases such as Huntington disease or Duchenne muscular dystrophy, for example, face a relentless progression of illness, suffering, disability, and death, with no hope for a cure. Diseases such as schizophrenia bring stigma and social isolation. The high suicide rate in schizophrenia is due less to hallucinations or delusions than to the profound demoralization that comes during moments of lucidity, when a patient grasps realistically how much schizophrenia has taken from his or her life (Shea 2002). For such "non-neurotic" demoralization, a cognitive psychotherapy designed to foster a more realistic appraisal of one's circumstances may, paradoxically, worsen morale.

Hope as expectation for achieving goals also veers into fantasy when a person invests in imaginative assumptions not grounded in reality. In *Man's Search for Meaning*, Victor Frankl described how certain prisoners at Auschwitz clung to magical hopes that they would be freed by the end of the year, then succumbed to despair when the date came and passed with no deliverance: "The death rate in the week between Christmas, 1944, and New Year's, 1945, increased in camp beyond all previous experience. In his [the camp doctor's] opinion, the explanation for this increase did not lie in the harder working conditions or the deterioration of our food supplies or a change of weather or new epidemics. It was simply that the majority of the prisoners had lived in the naive hope that they would be home again by Christmas. As the time drew near and there was no encouraging news, the prisoners lost courage and disappointment overcame them" (Frankl 1984, p. 84). Valiant attempts to force a hope of expectations run the danger of collapsing and exacerbating demoralization when expectations are not fulfilled.

Hope as a Practice

Sometimes a person lives with hope even in the absence of any expectable good outcome from any available path of action. Consider the diary of Etty Hillesum (1984, p. 130), a German citizen writing as she awaited transport to her death in Auschwitz: "I wish I could live for a long time so that one day I may know how to explain it, and if I am not granted that wish, well, then somebody else will perhaps do it, carry on from where my life has been cut short. And that is why I must try to live a good and faithful life to my last breath: so that those who come after me do not have to start all over again, need not face the same difficulties." Hillesum's story, though extreme, is not unique. People may act consistently in accordance with hope even when they recognize the odds are overwhelmingly against them.

Kaethe Weingarten (2007) reiterates the value of considering hope as a practice, rather than as a feeling or idea. She defines a *practice* as something done with intention, yet with a different focus from most goal-directed actions. A practice is a program of action undertaken, not for utilitarian reasons, but to shape one's being as a person and how one chooses to live in relation to others. The "wanting to have" of achievement-seeking is replaced by the "wanting to be" of a practice. Practices are often connected to social, religious, or ideological traditions whose values extend beyond individual motivation. For this reason, a demoralized person sometimes can engage in hope as a practice, despite feelings of entrapment and helplessness. Hope need not be tethered to expectations of success.

In practical terms, hope as a practice means identifying an important desire or commitment and taking deliberate steps toward it (Weingarten 2007). Whether the steps are large or small matters less than their direction. One becomes a hopeful person by adopting practices of hope, then claiming ownership of these practices as "who I am" as a person.

Individual and Relational Practices of Hope

Western culture classifies hopefulness as a facet of individual character (Weingarten 2007). This perspective leaves little for a helping professional to do, other than exhort or encourage the demoralized patient's efforts. A demoralized person usually suffers from apathy and a sense of incompetence at exactly those points where hope is most needed. Expecting dispirited individuals to be agents of their own hope can be both useless and cruel.

Weingarten (2007) and Ellen Pulleyblank Coffey (2007) propose fostering hope by relying on relational rather than individual qualities. From a relational perspective, agency thinking becomes: "Who understands my situation?" "Whom may I turn to?" "Whom can I count on to help?" From a relational perspective, pathways thinking becomes: "Who can help get this done?" "Who might have good ideas for how to solve it?"

In her study of the lives of resilient women, Pulleyblank Coffey (2007) describes how her subjects responded to conditions of extreme loss, trauma, and threat. Some were "keepers" who reached back to their family traditions for resources to cope with the here and now. Some were "seekers" who crossed social boundaries of age and culture to find what their present moment demanded. Others were "teachers" who moved past their personal tragedies by joining with others in advocacy, social action, and the pursuit of political justice. All based their coping in their relationships with others. Consider Eva, an ethnic Hungarian who found herself extruded by Serbian neighbors after multicultural Bosnia splintered in the 1980s. A new life in Germany faltered after rejection by her in-laws, divorce by her husband, and displacement from work by the influx of East Germans that followed reunification. She arrived in the United States without friends, family, or job, yet promptly set to work forming new relationships. At the time Pulleyblank Coffey interviewed her, she served as the center of energy for a community of Bosnian refugees, helping new families resettle, organizing church programs, leading a support group for women, sometimes acting as a paid professional and sometimes as a volunteer.

Eva's reflections on the struggles of her life were noteworthy for combining realistic cynicism with inspiring optimism and self-assurance (Pulleyblank Coffey 2007, p. 131): "I live alone, and instead of a family, I create a community that depends on me, and that I depend on. I am free to change this community when the situation requires me to do so. We live in a world that is fragmented, where families are fragmented, where change is often necessary. I know there is no guarantee I can count on the protection of others. Security does not come from holding on, it comes from knowing you can't count on protection, and therefore you take care of yourself as best you can, mostly by reaching out to others."

The relational perspective delineates how a clinician's role in fostering hope differs from a patient's role (Weingarten 2003, 2007). As witness to, rather than bearer of, suffering, the therapist has a responsibility to sustain awareness of the patient's suffering, to avoid retreating into indifference or neglect. Conscious commitment to awareness is important because demoralization is contagious. Clinicians often struggle with their own demoralization when feeling keenly a patient's despair. Resisting indifference—"zoning out," avoiding encounters with a patient, feeling contempt toward the patient's helplessness—is a crucial skill in helping a demoralized person to mobilize hope. A disciplined commitment to empathy, or compassionate witnessing, underlies all effective therapy, especially therapy for trauma.

As witnesses, individual clinicians have little power to change the circumstances that engender patients' demoralization (Weingarten 2003, 2007). Managing helplessness thus presents a second challenge in responding effectively to a demoralized patient. Clinicians may consciously choose to pursue agency on behalf of their patients, to counter their own feelings of helplessness. Sustained commitment to advocacy and activism is a valuable professional practice for clinicians who see their task as helping demoralized patients find hope. The activist clinician becomes a model and a resource for resilience.

Introducing Practices of Hope into Psychotherapy with People Who Are Medically Ill

Although many counseling roles involve sustaining and fostering morale, a focus on psychotherapy as a specific intervention to relieve demoralization particularly helps medical professionals who treat patients with serious, chronic illness (Frank and Frank 1991) (see also chapters 6, 7, and 9 in this volume). Efforts to teach medical patients practices of hope can take place within both formal psychotherapies and informal conversations, including those that occur on hospital medical services, on inpatient psychiatric units, and during outpatient visits for medications.

As a practice, hope requires an active verb, to do hope, rather than its usual partners—to have hope, to find hope, or to feel hope. In psychotherapy, hope can be mobilized by imagining vividly a desired future, then formulating doable steps toward this goal. As Snyder (2000a, 2000b) pointed out, "doable" connotes engaging in agency thinking; "steps" means engaging in pathways thinking. Weingarten (2003, 2007) noted that this clinical work occurs through mobilizing resources in two domains: the patient's inner experiential world and the patient's outer relational world, including the clinician-patient relationship. Typically, current therapies give priority to action, recognizing that hope will follow upon actions of hope, rather than the other way around.

Such a strategy poses problems for psychotherapists. Talk about desire, future, and action is counterintuitive for nearly any demoralized person. Most people who come for psychotherapy do so only when they feel that they have failed and that life has become intolerable. So aware of what they hate or fear, the question of what they desire seems irrelevant, even cruel.

Compassionate witnessing bridges this impasse. A path to dialogue about desire and future nearly always travels first through a full hearing of the patient's story of pain. Listening, understanding, and witnessing this narrative often quiets the pain sufficiently to begin a different conversation about the future. As Weingarten (2003, p. 232) states: "It has been my experience that compassionate witnessing first invites a telling of the story that allows people to express the states of vulnerability. This story is often one that has been silenced, blocked, denied, or forbidden. As difficult as it is to put this story into words—and as painful as it is to feel the states of vulnerability—it is also the beginning of an antidote to the violence that inspired it." Compassionate witnessing does not terminate suffering, but it does open space in which the patient can speak not only about suffering but also about resilience.

Characteristically, narratives about loss, trauma, and violence position the patient within the story as a victim trapped in overwhelming circumstances. Patients' real lives are always more complicated. Such narratives leave out the patients' strengths, competencies, past accomplishments, and problem-solving that may have been partly effective. They may omit supportive contributions from friends and family members. A clinician who listens helps uncover unacknowledged strengths and competencies. Catching glimpses of hope within stories of loss, trauma, and violence is vital.

CASE EXAMPLE

Mr. Lee was a middle-aged man hospitalized by his internist for chronic pain after reconstructive joint surgery. He had developed fatigue so severe he could not walk the length of the hall. His team requested psychiatric consultation for treatment of depression. However, his Hamilton Depression Scale score proved to be in the normal range. The consultant concluded that he was demoralized, without hope that his physical disabilities and suffering could ever improve. After hearing Mr. Lee's account of violent injury, a seemingly miraculous rescue, and rehabilitation to a productive work life despite physical disabilities, the consultant responded:

Consultant: "It sounds like the pain after surgery was a bad surprise."

Mr. Lee: "It was frustrating. I was surprised. I had done everything I was supposed to do."

Consultant: "You did everything you were supposed to do . . . It must feel unfair."

Mr. Lee: "I don't think the surgeon knows what to do next. He is off the map . . . I wonder whether the pain will ever get better."

Consultant: "From what I've heard about your life, you've not been a person lacking confidence or easily afraid. And you don't have a depression according to our evaluation."

Mr. Lee: "Sounds right."

Consultant: "What stands out to me is your saying you don't know what to expect next . . . and that you don't know who or what you can count on—your body, your surgeon, even a fair God."

Mr. Lee: (nods)

Consultant: "It is unsettling not to be able to count on your body and confusing not to know what to expect. You have become discouraged and frustrated, and I think that has made your fatigue and pain worse."

Patient and therapist agreed on a plan of slowly progressive aerobic exercise, a switch of antidepressants that might improve analgesia, and outpatient psychotherapy to take stock of where Mr. Lee was in his life now and what his next steps would be.

When Mr. Lee arrived at his first outpatient psychotherapy session, he commented to the consultant: "Within seconds of your walking out of my room, my mood did a 180 degree turn. I felt I knew what was wrong and that it could be fixed." As Mr. Lee told about his life in more detail, it became clearer that he had become demoralized when he concluded that his body was unreliable and no one was available to help. His frustration built until he said to himself, with apathy and resignation: "Why bother? Every time I try, I get knocked down."

Clinical thinking and interview methods introduced during recent decades by Michael White, David Epston, and other narrative therapists provide guidance for sensitive and nuanced interviews that encompass both compassionate witnessing of patients' suffering and the eliciting of strengths, competencies, and sources of resilience (Epston 1989; White 1989, 2007; Epston and White 1992; Freedman and Combs 1995). Likewise, the methods of Solution-Focused Therapy discern strengths and competencies that have been omitted, ignored, or silenced in usual narratives of suffering (de Shazer 1985; O'Hanlon and Wiener-Davis 1989; Walter and Peller 2000). Existential questions are particularly important for the compassionate witnessing of the whole of a person's life—both vulnerability and resilience (Griffith and Gaby 2005). They provide a ground on which doable actions can be built.

Existential Questions to Locate Practices of Hope

Existential questions inquire about adversity, such as illness, pain, and disability, and about patients' responses. Therapeutically, existential questions serve a dual role. First, they help the patient articulate his or her experience of suffering, thereby facilitating both therapist's and patient's compassion. Second, they identify personal practices that the patient has used to manage the suffering. Once identified, these practices can be incorporated explicitly into the psychotherapy as personal practices of hope (Griffith and Gaby 2005).

An existential posture describes the patient's stance toward adversity, how the patient readies himself or herself to respond. The existential postures in the left column of table 8.1 describe common ways in which illness, pain, and disability adversely affect people. Collectively, these existential postures make up features of demoralization as a human condition. They are listed here as existential postures of vulnerability. The existential postures in the right column of table 8.1 describe how people respond to adversity when they cope effectively. Resilience is the capacity to endure hardship or to emerge from adversity stronger than before. These are the existential postures of resilience. Table 8.1 emphasizes that a person facing a life crisis simultaneously feels the impact and mobilizes a response, either to embrace or to retreat from adversity. This list of existential postures is not exhaustive, nor would these necessarily be the most important ones for a particular individual's life. They do illustrate common themes that clinicians encounter with their patients.

Hope versus Despair

Hope requires identifying a desired future and taking steps to build it. Its opposite, *despair*, represents resignation and the relinquishing of desire. Illness

Table 8.1.   Existential Postures of
Resilience and Vulnerability

Despair	Hope
Confusion	Coherence
Isolation	Communion
Helplessness	Agency
Indifference	Commitment
Resentment	Gratitude
Meaninglessness	Purpose
Cowardice	Courage

often makes a good future difficult to imagine. For patients who have medical or psychiatric disorders, despair often poses a greater threat to survival than the disease itself. Certain questions can open conversations that mobilize hope:

1. When did you last feel hopeful? What was that like?
2. Which people in your life most help you to stay hopeful?
3. When times are hard, what keeps hope alive?
4. Who have you known in your life who would not be surprised to see you staying hopeful amid adversity? What did this person know about you that other people may not have known?

Coherence versus Confusion

Coherence is the capacity to make sense of experience. Its opposite is *confusion*, the sense that the world is chaotic or capricious. Confusion in clinical settings arises from many different sources. Cognitive impairments from dementia or encephalopathy produce confusion resulting from changes in the brain. Similarly, the ravages of schizophrenia and dissociative disorders create confusion for psychiatric patients. Confusion can have social origins due to absent or inaccurate information or conflicting information from different health care professionals (Frank 1946). Questions that can facilitate a sense of coherence include:

5. Do you have some idea what information you would need to have in order to feel less confused?
6. Tell me about times in the past when you were able to sort through the confusion and make sense of things.
7. When you feel confused and uncertain, how do you go about making sense of your experience?
8. Who most helps you untangle situations that become confusing?

Communion versus Isolation

Communion is the felt presence of a trustworthy person. Its opposite, *isolation*, is an acceptance of its impossibility. Medical or psychiatric illness heightens awareness of who is or is not available as a supportive presence. Communion differs from "family," "friends," or "social support." One may feel deeply lonely when surrounded by people. Certain questions identify relationships that involve communion:

9. When did you last feel the close presence of someone who cares for you?
10. Who knows what you are going through? To whom do you turn when you need help? With whom do you feel most comforted when you are hurting?
11. As you go through this illness, how do you stay connected to people who matter in your life?
12. Toward whom do you most freely feel love?
13. In whose presence do you feel peace and comfort within your body?

Agency versus Helplessness

Agency is acting in the expectation that one's initiative can make a meaningful difference. *Helplessness* is giving up the expectation that one's actions will have some effect. Medical and psychiatric illnesses erode a person's sense of agency. "I had my second heart attack . . . The medical bills were coming in . . . and I couldn't work. It all piled up." Yet reflective questions may help a person mobilize a sense of agency, as in Norman Cousins's maxim (1990) that "there is never a time when nothing can be done":

14. When was a time that you knew you were managing your life well, despite this illness?
15. Who helps you to stay strong against this illness?
16. How have you managed to keep this illness from taking total control of your life?

Commitment versus Indifference

Commitment describes embracing one's life mission, taking ownership for one's roles and actions and their consequences. In religious contexts, this kind of commitment has been termed a "calling" or "vocation." Commitment implies awareness not only that one's actions have consequences for other people but also that certain jobs will not get done, or will not get done well enough, unless one steps forward. The opposite of commitment is *indifference*, a disregard, disavowal, or abdication of such accountability. Some questions that can open a discussion of commitment include:

17. When did you become aware of how your choices affected the other people in your life?
18. Who helped you realize how your actions were affecting other people in your life?
19. How have you sustained an awareness of how your choices and actions make a difference for others?
20. What keeps you from walking off and leaving people to their problems?
21. How does your life matter? How does it make a difference that you are alive on the face of the earth?

Gratitude versus Resentment

Gratitude is an appreciation of desired elements that have occurred throughout the events and happenings in one's life. Its opposite, *resentment*, arises from rejection of one's life until specific unrealized desires are granted. Some questions to help elicit gratitude are:

22. When have you felt moments of gratitude?
23. Who are the people you particularly appreciate for what they have added to your life?
24. For what things do you feel thankful, despite the sufferings of your illness?
25. How do you stay able to feel appreciation for good things when so much has been difficult with this illness?

In response to different themes of a person's story, existential questions ask how adversity has affected the patient as a person and how he or she responded. "For many this is a hard illness. What gets you through your worst days? What keeps you from giving up? Who understands what you are going through? Whom can you count on? What matters most about the days to come?" Because of their universality, existential questions normalize a patient's struggle. They ask about challenges that all humans face, regardless of power or rank—the agony of illness, loss, isolation, or death. Patients respond to these questions with first-person narratives of courage, endurance, and accomplishment. The patient usually comes across as an honorable person doing the best he or she can, given the circumstances. Not surprisingly, existential questions naturally open conversations about a person's spiritual or religious life when that has played an important role in coping.

Using Spiritual Practices to Build Hope

Conceptualizing hope as a practice opens possibilities for incorporating spiritual practices into psychotherapy (Griffith and Griffith 2002) (see also chapters 14 and 15). For hundreds and thousands of years, religious leaders and followers of various religious traditions have honed spiritual practices of many sorts. Some spiritual practices can be adopted as practical techniques of hope, whether or not a patient fully embraces the religious identity and belief system that originally gave birth to the practices.

Mindfulness practices from the Buddhist tradition exemplify spiritual practices that can serve as a resource for hope (Kornfield 2007). Mindfulness, also called *vipassana* or insight, refers to the capacity for awareness of moment-to-moment changes in experience within an attitude of curiosity, acceptance, and suspended judgment (Fleischman 1999). Mindfulness alters a patient's relationship to his or her personal experience, rather than changing its content directly (Safran 2003). For a demoralized patient, mindfulness practices can transform a sense of entrapment or subjective incompetence in ways that heighten hope and diminish demoralization.

CASE EXAMPLE

Mr. Atkins was a forty-three-year-old man hospitalized for complications of AIDS that included Kaposi sarcoma, chronic infections, and severe pain. Concerned that he was depressed, his primary medical team requested a psychiatric consultation. The psychiatric consultant concluded that he did not meet criteria for a primary mood disorder. Rather, he was demoralized, feeling hopeless and helpless in the face of his worsening illness:

Mr. Atkins: "Why wouldn't I feel like crap? This disease has taken everything from me. It has left me with nothing but pain."

Consultant: "I can imagine how that feels like you have no control."

Mr. Atkins: "Yeah, well that's true, but the worst part is that I have no choice and I am consumed with rage about it."

Consultant: "The disease taking things—your losing control and feeling passive but consumed with rage—it almost sounds like the two of you are in a fight."

Mr. Atkins: "We sure are, every single day."

Consultant: "I can imagine how unfair this all must feel, and how terrified you must feel to never know what's coming next. But, because of this—I wonder how much energy in your life is lost to being angry *against* your disease?"

Mr. Atkins: "Well, it never leaves my mind, night and day, so its fair to say almost all of it."

Consultant: "So where does that leave your time, energy, and attention for the life that remains?"

Mr. Atkins: (starts crying)

After listening compassionately for some time, the consultant wondered with Mr. Atkins how it might be different if he could somehow find space in his experience for both the disease and himself. He said that he would be willing to try anything, as he was exhausted from his fury and wanted to enjoy things again. The consultant suggested he try the Tonglen meditation, which is derived from the Tibetan Buddhist tradition (Chodron 1997, 2007). The meditation is premised on the idea that one may coexist with suffering. *Tonglen* literally means "receiving or acceptance" and "sending or letting go."

Consultant: "You have so much pain and sadness within you, and you are exhausted because you are fighting so hard against it. I want you to take some deep breaths, and as you do just imagine that you are breathing in all of that negativity."

Mr. Atkins: "I respect your expertise, but that just seems like I'm taking in more bad stuff."

Consultant: "It does sound somewhat self-defeating but when you do it try having some openness and compassion to what you breathe in. Then focus on breathing out goodness."

Mr. Atkins: (begins to engage in this exercise with the consultant)

The consultant worked with Mr. Atkins to open his heart to his suffering, to feel it fully, and in so doing to allow space for other experiences and emotions. His suffering would then be more readily understood as a part of existence, as opposed to existence itself.

During his first attempts, Mr. Atkins experienced only grief, and he wept profusely. After a few days, he no longer wept but meditated quietly. Three weeks after beginning this daily practice, he was discharged from the hospital with little evidence of his prior demoralization.

Mr. Atkins: (half chuckling) "I think I made friends with it."

Consultant: "With what?"

Mr. Atkins: "My suffering."

Consultant: "And where has that left you?"

Mr. Atkins: (still chuckling) "I feel that I can finally enjoy my real friends now. It's strange. Somehow I don't feel as defeated. It's like I am me and my disease . . . and not just my disease . . . But I'm scared. Will this last?"

Consultant: "I truly hope so, and with continued practice I believe it will."

The consultant gave Mr. Atkins some information on sources for mindfulness teaching and practice in the community. Subsequently, Mr. Atkins began volunteering with people who had AIDS. He commented: "My time in the hospital made me realize how horrible things were for me, not in a 'woe is me' way but in a 'concern for others' way. I want to do something to help others."

A mindfulness practice can help a patient move from passivity to action—to develop self-knowledge, experience compassion for self and others, reclaim control over experience. Experience can be viewed through eyes of curiosity and marvel rather than judgments about success or failure. These processes may culminate in an attitude of acceptance that permits continuous realization of hope.

Conclusion

Hope has long been recognized as a potent antidote for demoralization and a critical element in successful psychotherapy. Hope as a mere feeling that reflects life's circumstances offers few options for aiding a demoralized patient already in despair. However, hope regarded as an expectation for achievement often opens avenues for helping a patient either to sustain an expectation for success or to revise expectations to make them more realistic. Hope has been found to be the product of agency thinking and pathways thinking. Psychotherapists can strategize with patients how best to strengthen a sense of personal agency and how to generate realistic routes to achieve feasible goals.

Hope is anchored in both individual and relational resources. A psycho-therapist can work with a demoralized patient to regain a sense of both personal agency ("There is something I can do that matters") and relational agency ("There is someone I can turn to for help"). Likewise, a psychotherapist can bolster personal pathways thinking ("There are steps I can take to solve this problem") and relational pathways thinking ("These are people who can help me take steps to solve this problem").

Viewed as an expectation for successful achievement, hope has its limitations. Some demoralized patients have lost all conviction of the possibility of attaining goals. Others live in circumstances bereft of possibilities for taking effective actions or devising solutions to problems. Viewing hope as a practice circumvents these limitations. Hope as a practice makes the goal one's stance or posture toward the problem. Success involves sustaining a desired identity or quality of relatedness with others. A psychotherapist can help a demoralized patient adopt practices of hope by clarifying the person's important commitments or desired future and encouraging deliberate steps toward those ends. The stories of loss, trauma, and humiliation that patients first tell in therapy provide clues about what a desired future might be. Existential questions can help patients develop personal practices of hope that psychotherapy can build on. Spiritual practices drawn from religious traditions may enrich or complement psychotherapy as resources for hope.

REFERENCES

Bandura, A. 1997. *Self Efficacy: The Exercise of Control.* New York: W. H. Freeman.
Chodron, P. 1997. *When Things Fall Apart.* Boston: Shambala Classics.
———. 2007. Tonglen meditation: changing pain into compassion. www.beliefnet.com.
Cousins, N. 1990. *Head First: The Biology of Hope and the Healing of the Human Spirit.* New York: Penguin.
de Figueiredo, J. M. 1993. Depression and demoralization: phenomenological differences and research perspectives. *Comprehensive Psychiatry* 34:308–11.
de Figueiredo, J. M., and Frank, J. D. 1982. Subjective incompetence, the clinical hallmark of demoralization. *Comprehensive Psychiatry* 23:353–63.
de Shazer, S. 1985. *Keys to Solution in Brief Therapy.* New York: W. W. Norton.
Epston, D. 1989. *Collected Papers.* Adelaide, South Australia: Dulwich Centre Publications.
Epston, D., and White, M. (eds.). 1992. *Experience, Contradiction, Narrative, and Imagination.* Adelaide, South Australia: Dulwich Centre Publications.
Fleischman, P. R. 1999. *Karma and Chaos: New and Collected Essays on Vipassana Meditation.* Onalaska, WA: Pariyatti.

Frank, J. D. 1946. Emotional reactions of American soldiers to an unfamiliar disease. *American Journal of Psychiatry* 102:631–40.

———. 1961. *Persuasion and Healing: A Comparative Study of Psychotherapy.* Baltimore: Johns Hopkins University Press.

———. 1973. *Persuasion and Healing: A Comparative Study of Psychotherapy,* rev. ed. Baltimore: Johns Hopkins University Press.

Frank, J. D., and Frank, J. B. 1991. *Persuasion and Healing: A Comparative Study of Psychotherapy,* 3rd ed. Baltimore: Johns Hopkins University Press

Frankl, V. 1984. *Man's Search for Meaning,* 3rd ed. New York: Touchstone Books.

Freedman, J., and Combs, G. 1995. *Narrative Therapy: The Social Construction of Preferred Realities.* New York: W. W. Norton.

Griffith, J. L., and Gaby, L. 2005. Brief psychotherapy at the bedside: countering demoralization from medical illness. *Psychosomatics* 46:109–16.

Griffith, J. L., and Griffith, M. E. 2002. *Engaging the Sacred in Psychotherapy: How to Talk with People about their Spiritual Lives.* New York: Guilford Press.

Groopman, J. 2004. *The Anatomy of Hope: How People Prevail in the Face of Illness.* New York: Random House.

Hewitt, J. P. 1998. *The Myth of Self-Esteem: Finding Happiness and Solving Problems in America.* New York: St. Martin's Press.

Hillesum, E. 1984. *An Interrupted Life: The Diaries of Etty Hillesum 1941–43.* Trans. A. J. Pomerans. New York: Pantheon.

Kornfield, J. 2007. Doing the Buddha's practice. *Shambala Sun,* July, pp. 38–45.

Lopez, S. J., Floyd, R. K., Ulven, J. C., and Snyder, C. R. 2000. Hope therapy: helping clients build a house of hope. In C. R. Snyder (ed.), *Handbook of Hope: Theory, Measures, and Applications* (pp. 123–50). New York: Academic Press.

Michael, S. T., Taylor, J. D., and Cheapens, J. 2000. Hope theory as applied to brief treatments: problem-solving and solution-focused therapies. In C. R. Snyder (ed.), *Handbook of Hope: Theory, Measures, and Applications* (pp. 151–66). New York: Academic Press.

O'Hanlon, W., and Wiener-Davis, M. 1989. *In Search of Solutions: Creating a Context for Change.* New York: W. W. Norton.

Pulleyblank Coffey, E. 2007. *Blowing on Embers.* Tamarac FL: Llumina Press.

Rodriguez-Hanley, A., and Snyder, C. R. 2000. The demise of hope: on losing positive thinking. In C. R. Snyder (ed.), *Handbook of Hope: Theory, Measures, and Applications* (pp. 39–54). New York: Academic Press.

Safran, J. D., ed. 2003. *Psychoanalysis and Buddhism: An Unfolding Dialogue.* Boston: Wisdom Publications.

Seligman, M. 1998. *Learned Optimism.* New York: Simon and Schuster.

Shea, S. 2002. *The Practical Art of Suicide Assessment.* New York: John Wiley.

Snyder, C. R. 2000a. Genesis: the birth and growth of hope. In C. R. Snyder (ed.), *Handbook of Hope: Theory, Measures, and Applications* (pp. 25–38). New York: Academic Press.

———. 2000b. Hypothesis: there is hope. In C. R. Snyder (ed.), *Handbook of Hope: Theory, Measures, and Applications* (pp. 3–21). New York: Academic Press.

Snyder, C. R., McDermott, D., Cook, J., and Rapoff, M. 1997. *Hope for the Journey: Helping Children through Good Times and Bad.* Boulder, CO: Westview / Harper Collins.

Snyder, C. R., and Taylor, J. D. 2000. Hope as a common factor across psychotherapy approaches: a lesson from Dodo's Verdict. In C. R. Snyder (ed.), *Handbook of Hope: Theory, Measures, and Applications* (pp. 89–108). New York: Academic Press.

Walter, J. L., and Peller, J. E. 2000. *Recreating Brief Therapy: Preferences and Possibilities.* New York: W. W. Norton.

Weingarten, K. 2003. *Common Shock: Witnessing Violence Every Day—How We Are Harmed, How We Can Heal.* New York: Dutton Press.

———. 2007. Hope in a time of global despair. In C. Flaskas, I. McCarthy, and J. Sheehan (eds.), *Hope and Despair in Narrative and Family Therapy* (pp. 13–23). New York: Routledge.

White, M. 1989. *Selected Papers.* Adelaide, South Australia: Dulwich Centre Publications.

———. 2007. *Maps of Narrative Practice.* New York: W. W. Norton.

CHAPTER 9

Psychotherapeutic Communication in Medical Settings

Arthur M. Freeman III, M.D.

"Take care!" cried Alice. "You're holding it all crooked!" And she caught at the brooch; but it was too late: the pin had slipped, and the Queen had pricked her finger.

"That accounts for the bleeding, you see," she said to Alice with a smile. "Now you understand the way things happen here."

—*Through the Looking Glass*

... hopelessness can retard recovery or even hasten death, while the mobilization of hope plays an important part in many forms of healing in both nonindustrialized societies and our own. —*PERSUASION AND HEALING*, 1991, P. 132

The conceptual blueprint for psychotherapy outlined in *Persuasion and Healing* has particular relevance for those who provide psychotherapy in medical settings (Frank and Frank 1991). This chapter explores how Jerome and Julia Frank's emphasis on the power of therapists' conceptual orientation, the commonalities of all psychotherapies, and the role of demoralization as a final, clinical pathway applies to the care of hospitalized patients who are medically ill (see also chapters 4, 7, 8, and 15 in this volume). As Jerome Frank proposed, disciplines related to the persuasive arts—specifically, rhetoric—also contribute substantially to the relief of distress for patients of all kinds, including those who have serious medical conditions (Frank and Frank 1991). Beyond medical psychotherapy as a clinical and technical intervention, psychosomatic medicine in general and consultation-liaison psychiatry in particular would benefit from further application of Frank's ideas, as discussed at the conclusion of this chapter.

Justifying Therapy: Medical History as Apologia

Medical care typically begins with a patient's account of symptoms, which the examiner scrutinizes primarily for clues to an underlying disease process. This "history of the present illness" is, in Frank's terms, an "apologia." Patients' accounts provide an essential but imprecise guide to diagnosis, necessarily limited by the ambiguity of language. As the patient adapts to the clinical setting, the apologia may shift in response to the examiner's questions. For example, the patient who first describes a distressing, band-like pain in the head after an argument will be prompted to clarify whether the pain is better or worse in particular positions, associated with visual changes, and so on, until the examiner can decide between it most likely being a tension headache or a brain tumor.

While the medical questioner follows the logic of pathophysiology, many patients either lack a "coherent plot that explains why the experience occurred" or offer a story based on personal factors that have little specific medical relevance. A medical encounter that leaves patient and doctor in alignment involves closing the "hermeneutic circle" by the construction of a mutually satisfactory story, be it medical, personal, or both.

When some objective test explains the story, the physician, at least, feels gratified. When, as often happens, definitive resolution proves impossible, validation of the story becomes an ongoing process without a clear end point. If the physician and patient negotiate a common understanding—for example, "being upset makes your neck muscles tense, and that causes pain"—the story seems at least partly validated, though for the patient the meaning of the pain may have many other dimensions. Thus, even in medical encounters, truth resides in plausibility rather than in objectivity. Truth can be an interpretation that "is the most satisfying or makes the most sense" to the patient. Psychotherapy in any setting requires the mutual construction of a new clinical history (Frank and Frank 1991, pp. 24–39).

As implied in the simple example above, psychotherapy applies as well to medically ill patients as to those with belief-related, emotional or behavioral problems. Stress is a foundational concept for understanding psychotherapy in the context of medical care. Stress typically structures the plot of the stories that patients recount. Psychotherapy may play a useful role when patients either seek relief for physical symptoms related to stress or are unsuccessful in adapting to the stress of physical ailments.

Psychotherapy cannot treat organic illness directly, but it does restore patients' morale in the face of disease. The corresponding concept of stamina, or resilience, in the face of stress varies across patients, conditions, and treatment settings. At one extreme, most people require moderate stress to promote good health. Excessive, uncontrollable stress, by contrast, may make mild disease worse and serious disease fatal.

Stress, moreover, connotes more than the external challenges to patients' adaptation. As is well known, individual factors mediate how a person perceives and reacts to stress. Social support, in particular, buffers or exacerbates stress. The meaning of a stressor also influences help-seeking. Those who attribute their stress to bodily causes seek out general physicians. Those who believe their stress is psychological, though they may seek help from counselors, family members, mental health professionals, and/or psychotherapists, often first consult a general physician to assess their physical symptoms. Even today, a medical explanation or the care provided by a medical practitioner entails less stigma, and may be more face-saving, than other forms of care. It follows that the nonpsychiatric physician must be prepared to provide psychotherapeutic care. Too often, generalists lack a conceptual framework for such work.

In this context, the concept of the patient's "assumptive world" proves extremely useful for understanding the origin of distress (see chapter 1). All people evaluate their experience in light of assumptions rooted in culture and personal experience. In technical psychological terms, people's assumptions may be grouped into *schemata*. Such constellations of assumptions have cognitive, affective, and behavioral components. Different schools of psychotherapy focus primarily on emotions, cognition, or behavior. In the end, however, the effectiveness of any form of therapy relates to the extent to which its techniques influence or fully articulate the interactive components of the experience of being ill (Frank and Frank 1991, pp. 39–44).

In general, to develop a sense of self-efficacy, patients must learn what they can manage or withstand. Therapy engenders hope and motivation to continue in their efforts to master the demands of their circumstances. Though this seems simple, as the Franks put it: "unconscious assumptive systems may profoundly influence behavior, yet they are especially resistant to change" (p. 26). To mobilize hope, clinicians of all medical fields must take the time to determine and characterize the assumptive systems of their patients. Understanding how assumptions develop and are sustained suggests strategies for promoting therapeutic change. Humans are motivated to seek "consensual validation," to harmonize their personal assumptive worlds with those of people who are important to them. Indeed, at times, the distress leading a person to enter therapy reflects less an internal conflict and more a feeling of alienation, the result of not finding the validation the person seeks. Such alienation may result in the painful state of "identity diffusion." Offering a therapeutic relationship to a patient, even a brief encounter that draws out a coherent apologia, is intrinsically validating and may directly counteract this distressing state.

One of Jerome Frank's richest contributions to understanding the experience of physical and mental illness was his recognition of the role of demoralization. Demoralization results from a person's failure to meet expectations of the self or others, leading to powerlessness and inability to cope. By definition, demoralization entails hopelessness, helplessness, and isolation. It accounts for much help-seeking in both general medical populations and other groups. Studies of college students, for example, have found high levels of demoralization in students entering therapy. People seek help not just because of the specific symptoms of their condition but also because they are no longer able to cope with their symptoms (Frank and Frank 1991, pp. 274–83).

Shared Components of Psychotherapies for People Who Are Medically Ill

A positive therapeutic interaction, a healing setting, a conceptual scheme, and a series of procedures or "rituals" are important elements of a psychotherapy oriented to alleviate demoralization. Whether the patient seeks help from a primary care or family physician or is referred to a mental health professional, these are the indispensable elements of a solid "therapeutic alliance." Patients work best with a therapist whose role matches their expectations and in whom they perceive genuine concern for them and their ailments. Beyond such concern, patients respond to the perception that the therapist is a healer sanctioned by society on the basis of a particular expertise that he or she possesses and that will benefit them. Expertise has particular salience and may function in isolation. At times, self-help books and therapeutic manuals serve as effective substitutes for the presence of the therapist. In the medical arena, books dedicated to chronic medical conditions (hypertension, arthritis, diabetes) foster hope on the basis of their conceptual schemes, new information, and instructions on how to put their recommendations into practice in a systematic fashion (Frank and Frank 1991, pp. 44–61).

Psychotherapy in Medical Settings

Disease is by definition the manifestation of disordered bodily function. Illness may be better understood as an imbalance between a patient's intrinsic and/or environmental stress and his or her coping capacity. In addition to biological vulnerabilities, negative meanings, which people attribute to events such as experiencing a medical illness, determine maladaptive responses—a prelude to demoralization (Frank and Frank 1991, pp. 65–70).

Secular therapies take place in a hospital or clinic rather than in a sacred place, but the hospital has a distinctive, almost religious, aura of science (Frank 1975). Physicians are the new priests, and medical procedures serve ritual as well as actual, physical purposes. The last chapter of *Persuasion and Healing* describes the setting of psychiatric hospitals, and much of what is outlined there applies equally to general hospital settings (Frank and Frank 1991, pp. 280–83). The reputation of the hospital may increase the therapist's prestige and mobilize patients' expectations of help. Patients in psychiatric and general medical settings adhere to rules of dress and activity, as do the participants in many healing rituals. Helping personnel operate in hierarchies in which each person, from the physician at the helm to the nurses, social workers, and physician assistants who supposedly act on the doctor's instructions, derives therapeutic authority from his or her assigned status.

At the same time, both types of setting have depersonalizing qualities that may undermine patients' resilience. In a general hospital unit or service, consultation-liaison psychiatrists make conscious efforts to combat the negative institutional tone and enhance the positive environmental features. Frequently, this involves forming an ongoing liaison with staff to teach them to respond to the psychosocial as well as physical or organic needs of patients. Liaison activity adapts the essential idea of milieu therapy, historically developed in psychiatric hospitals, by trying to shape the hospital environment in the service of minimizing its disempowering features and enhancing those that may be of benefit. An important aspect of any therapeutic milieu is its separation from daily life, which implies or explicitly guarantees that patients can be candid with their doctors and be secure in the confidentiality of their interactions.

Psychotherapy for people who are medically ill thus becomes an exercise focusing on the essential unity and integration of the human being.

Physicians should recognize that the offer of medical help, in itself, may have psychotherapeutic properties, by increasing the expectancy of help, providing new learning, and arousing the patient emotionally. Interactions around medical care create and strengthen the doctor-patient relationship and may facilitate the patient's hope and sense of mastery. Obtaining consent from a patient requires the doctor to elicit and respond to the patient's fears and concerns. Sharing therapeutic "rituals" or procedures increases the emotional and cognitive ties between therapist and patient. In the medical setting, the impact of a procedure may be even more dramatic, as the patient may see immediate or rapid evidence of improvement or recovery. Rituals sustain a bond as patients disclose their distress and yet continue to feel accepted. Like myths, rituals of this kind build morale and relieve symptoms while arousing hope.

As described by the Franks, elements in psychiatric settings, particularly role induction, experiential learning, and emotional arousal, also enhance medical psychotherapy. Role induction (see chapter 1 in this volume), or preparation for psychotherapy, helps patients engage in treatment; simple explanations justifying therapy and explaining to patients how to participate fit easily into brief bedside or medical clinic visits. Experiential learning makes patients aware of how they are perceived, in contrast to how they experience themselves. Explanations of illness and monitoring of treatment response, both common medical interventions, foster such learning by highlighting positive changes in the patient's condition. Any caregiver may extrapolate from medical to psychological matters to increase the patient's self-awareness: "I see you are able to move around now without so much pain." "Your symptoms seem much better controlled when you take the medicine regularly." Emotional arousal may assist people who are medically ill to acquire the energy and stamina required for change. It allows them to depend on the physician-therapist for symptom relief. Physicians, whether they want to be or not, are teachers, role models, and providers of new information.

The interventions of the consultation-liaison psychiatrist and/or of the psychotherapeutically astute nonpsychiatrist are intended to relieve demoralization rather than foster personality change. The conceptual scheme shared by therapist and patient can play a major role in the patient's sense of self-efficacy.

The scheme "names" sometimes ineffable experiences. New insights and learning about how to cope with illness-generated anxiety show patients that they can tolerate and survive emotional stress. Giving patients and their hard work credit for improvements and providing opportunities for them to practice what they have learned from participating in medical care greatly enhance morale.

Psychotherapy and People Who Are Medically Ill: Specific Features

Diseases and radical treatments may permanently change patients' bodies. "Body image," or a somatic sense of self, develops early and is experienced both symbolically and perceptually. The context in which an injury occurs can powerfully shape the meaning of a changed body image. Accidental injuries, self-inflicted wounds, or injuries resulting from torture will have quite different meanings. Hair loss from cancer chemotherapy can be as threatening to patients as the underlying illness. Favazza and Conterio (1988) demonstrated how self-mutilation may have different meaning based on different motivations for this behavior: alterations in body image, extreme anxiety, delusional thinking, and the pursuit of individual or religious goals.

In some cases, demoralization can contribute to the progression of chronic illness. The Franks observed that hope optimally counters demoralization in a variety of medical contexts (see chapters 7 and 8). In the field of cardiac disorders, for instance, patients' psychological states affect the rate of complaints and complications following myocardial infarction. Studies show that cardiac surgery outcomes can be affected by psychological states (Freeman, Foulks, et al. 1988; Freeman, Sokol, et al. 1988).

Healing blends scientific medicine with less quantifiable aspects of patients' behavior and patient-physician interactions. Patients seek out self-help organizations, hypnosis, culturally derived approaches such as acupuncture or Ayurvedic medicine, and therapies loosely called complementary, alternative, or integrative medicine, in addition to reliance on physicians. As the Franks (1991) pointed out, the appropriate strategies for successful psychotherapy for medically ill people involve instilling hope, by changing the meaning of the illness or injury, and fostering mastery. Science, combined with psychotherapy and expectant trust, may enhance overall clinical success (Frank 1974, 1986; Blumenfield 2006).

What Kind of Psychotherapy?

In the past, psychoanalysis and psychodynamic psychotherapy provided the foundations for psychosomatic medicine and consultation-liaison psychiatry. Today's clinicians believe that these forms of therapy are not feasible or cost-effective for most patients (see chapter 10). Nonetheless, some residency training programs still emphasize psychodynamic principles, even if the techniques are not widely used. These programs may combine general supportive measures and role induction for future psychodynamic or other therapies (Turner, Mancl, and Aaron 2006).

Cognitive behavioral therapy (CBT) has achieved widespread acceptance in the treatment of people who are medically ill, including those with a history of chronic pain (Turner, Mancl, and Aaron 2006). It has a stronger research base than psychodynamic therapy and more quantifiable end points. For medical patients who are demoralized, dysthymic, or depressed, CBT may be more efficient, if not more effective, than older methods. Much of the effectiveness of CBT lies in the reliance on "rhetorical devices which persuade patients to change maladaptive attitudes" (Frank and Frank 1991, p. 240). Such is also the purpose of relevant manuals available to psychotherapists.

People who are medically ill, such as those with multiple sclerosis, rheumatoid arthritis, cancer, or other chronic medical illnesses or injuries, may benefit from group therapy. Individuals who share a specific illness or condition can receive psychoeducation from the group. Alcoholics Anonymous exemplifies the benefits of a group approach. Its official text is the members' "Bible," and religious principles are often invoked. The group powerfully supports the individual, and sponsors are available between group meetings. Help also accrues to the sponsors as altruism bolsters self-esteem (see chapter 13). Alcoholics Anonymous and other self-help groups clarify issues for their members. They help patients as much by providing coherent belief systems as by offering concrete help and opportunities for belonging.

Family therapy for people who are medically ill may uncover attitudes or patterns of interaction ("family dynamics") that contribute to or precipitate exacerbations of illnesses, particularly stress-responsive conditions such as asthma and ulcerative colitis (Turner, Mancl, and Aaron 2006). The decision to call the specialist or make a referral to a psychotherapist must be made after careful deliberations among the patient, family members, primary physician, and consultation-liaison psychiatrist. The objectives of therapy should be clearly specified and, if possible, the patient's expectations should be modified by the description of a timetable and steps of the recovery process.

Therapists for People Who Are Medically Ill

Early studies showed that "active personal participation" characterized therapists successful in treating patients with schizophrenia. Later work has confirmed that effective therapists demonstrate empathy, warmth, and genuineness. Beyond these general findings, precise definitions of therapists' healing power have eluded description. It may be, as Frank suggested, that healing power is similar to musical ability: most people have some of this quality, some are especially talented, and a few are tone deaf.

Several forms of professional training besides psychiatry teach the ability to establish a good therapeutic relationship. Human warmth, common sense, some sensitivity, and a desire to help are foremost in the ability to help those who are demoralized, regardless of whether the therapist is a psychiatrist, psychologist, nurse, social worker, or a nonpsychiatric physician or other medical practitioner. Therapists of any background who foster patients' expectations of help and self-confidence can be successful. At the same time, specific training may enhance the therapists' ability to foster improvement in patients. Increasingly, primary care and family medicine training programs offer some formal didactics in the principles and techniques of psychotherapy. Though this training is quite limited, mastery of a particular method may not be important. To a large extent, at least in medical settings where psychotherapy is not the main focus, patients themselves determine how closely a therapist may adhere to a particular technique. In many cases, patients seem to respond more to the personal qualities of the therapist than to any particular intervention.

Physicians have always used the placebo response, the inspiring of expectant trust, as part of their therapeutic armamentarium (see chapter 1). Jerome Frank wrote about how time-bound we are as humans; our attitudes toward the future have a great impact on how we are currently. Favorable expectations may generate positive feeling and promote healing. Hope is perceived as the possibility of achieving a goal. Symbolic power defines the value of the placebo. Strong support for this latter statement comes from an early study of placebo surgery in which both mammary artery ligation and incision without ligation provided relief of angina and shortness of breath and increased exercise tolerance, in spite of the lack of measurable cardiac improvement (Beecher 1961).

Psychotherapy and Medication

Psychotherapy has physical effects, just as medications have psychological effects. Frank anticipated this long before basic scientists even considered that psychotherapeutic interventions might affect brain structure or the expression of genes. Such insight requires a nonreductionist view of humans as constituting a "psychobiological unit" (see chapters 3 and 4).

Scientific medicine can be combined with the healing principles discussed above, especially in the use of psychoactive substances. In a holistic sense, medication can exert its effect directly on the brain or indirectly through its symbolic connotations. The Franks (1991) discussed how psychotherapy may interact with medications, noting that medications may have negative meaning for some patients, but more often enhance therapeutic optimism in both patients and therapists.

At times, such enhancement may be a direct rather than symbolic effect. Patients who have chronic pain, for example, may become dependent on opiates even after their pain no longer responds, in part due to the mood-enhancing qualities of these drugs. Other psychotropic drugs may play a role in the care of people who are medically ill. Their ability to stabilize mood, relieve anxiety and depression, or improve memory exemplifies another facet of the psychobiological treatment of psychiatric and medical disorders.

Challenges for Psychosomatic Medicine and Consultation-Liaison Psychiatry

In the years since publication of the third edition of *Persuasion and Healing*, consultation-liaison psychiatry has not fulfilled the Franks' vision. One of the major shortcomings of the field is the inadequate availability of bedside psychotherapeutic strategies. Simply put, for various reasons, particularly time constraints and minimal reimbursement, not enough psychotherapy is being offered. For example, at the 2006 meeting of the Academy of Psychosomatic Medicine, one course in psychoanalysis took place before the meeting, but nothing was offered during the event on more relevant forms of psychotherapy for people who are medically ill. Given that a preponderance of patients seen by consultation-liaison services have demonstrated demoralization, some form of affective disorder, or significant mood changes, it is disappointing that nonpsychiatric physicians and other health care providers still have such limited access to psychotherapy training.

Furthermore, psychiatric diagnosis in the medical setting often lacks precision and specificity (see chapters 6 and 7). Perhaps in consequence, only a few rigorous psychopharmacological studies have been undertaken for people who are medically ill, the exceptions being in stroke, cardiology, and endocrinology. The studies that do exist are often too small to provide significant, clinically relevant data (Ilchef 2006). They lack the power to explore the psychological impact of the use of medication, an area that goes beyond the field of placebo studies. The lack of new knowledge in the applications of psychopharmacology and the infrequent use of psychotherapy make studies combining the two areas almost nonexistent. With such scarcity of data, psychosomatic medicine is unable to provide excellent, evidence-based guidelines. Even today, "evidence" in this field is mostly anecdotal, and guidelines reflect only expert opinion or consensus.

The methods of biological psychiatry have been underused in psychosomatic medicine. If basic biological and clinical psychopharmacological studies were combined with the Franks' psychotherapeutic insights, consultation-liaison psychiatry and psychosomatic medicine would be far stronger. Development of a conceptual position would be a beginning for the field. The American Psychiatric Association's *Textbook of Psychosomatic Medicine* lacks a chapter on this topic (Levenson 2006). Emphasizing the mechanisms that link trust, hope, and symbolization to basic biological processes could lead to important translational research, which, in turn, could be followed by clinical research enhancing a fully comprehensive treatment for people who are medically ill.

Conclusion

The contributions of *Persuasion and Healing* and the brief examination of current knowledge presented in this chapter reflect basic notions of healing and medicine, focused on the psychiatric care of people who have medical illness. Unfortunately, current consultation-liaison psychiatry fails to make full use of the principles presented. Today's consultations often entail a brief assessment, rapid introduction of psychotropic medication, and deferred psychotherapy. The psychobiological care of people who have medical illness is clearly incomplete, as the field is largely based on anecdotes or "expert opinion." Practitioners urgently need a stronger framework for understanding these essential aspects of medical healing. Clearly, there is a pressing need for expanded research in relevant basic, conceptual, and clinical areas that could result in evidence-based psychosomatic medicine.

REFERENCES

Academy of Psychosomatic Medicine. 2006. Annual Meeting Preliminary Program, pp. 3–13.

Beecher, H. K. 1961. Surgery as placebo: a quantitative study of bias. *JAMA: Journal of the Amercian Medical Association* 176:1102–7.

Blumenfield, M. 2006. The place of psychodynamic psychiatry in consultation-liaison psychiatry with special emphasis on counter-transference. *Journal of the American Academy of Psychoanalysis and Dynamic Psychiatry* 34:83–92.

Favazza, A. R., and Conterio, K. 1988. A plight of chronic self-mutilators. *Community Mental Health Journal* 24:22–30.

Frank, J. D. 1974. Therapeutic components of psychotherapy: a 25–year progress report of research. *Journal of Nervous and Mental Disease* 159:325–42.

———. 1975. The faith that heals. *Johns Hopkins Medical Journal* 137:127–31.

———. 1986. Psychotherapy: the transformation of meanings (discussion paper). *Journal of the Royal Society of Medicine* 79:341–46.

Frank, J. D., and Frank, J. B. 1991. *Persuasion and Healing: A Comparative Study of Psychotherapy*, 3rd ed. Baltimore: Johns Hopkins University Press.

Freeman, A. M., Foulks, D. G., Sokol, R. S., and Fahs, J. J. 1988. Cardiac transplantation: clinical correlates of psychiatric outcomes. *Psychosomatics* 29:47–54.

Freeman, A. M., Sokol, R. S., Foulks, D. G., McVay, R. F., McGiffin, A. F., and Fahs, J. J. 1988. Psychiatric characteristics of patients undergoing cardiac transplantation. *Psychiatric Medicine* 6:8–23.

Ilchef, R. 2006. Diamonds in a coalface: new research in consultation-liaison psychiatry. *Current Opinion in Psychiatry* 19:175–79.

Levenson, J. L. 2005. *Textbook of Psychosomatic Medicine*. Washington, DC: American Psychiatric Publishing.

Turner, J. A., Mancl, L., and Aaron, L. A. 2006. Short- and long-term efficacy of brief cognitive behavioral therapy for patients with chronic temporal mandibular disorder pain: a randomized controlled clinical trial. *Pain* 121:181–94.

CHAPTER 10

Psychodynamic Psychotherapy

From Psychoanalytic Arrogance to Evidence-Based Modesty

Lloyd A. Wells, M.D., Ph.D., and Julia B. Frank, M.D.

"Tut, tut, child!" said the Duchess . . . And she squeezed herself up closer to Alice's side as she spoke . . .
"'Be what you would seem to be'—or if you'd like it put more simply—'Never imagine yourself not to be otherwise than what it might appear to others that what you were or might have been was not otherwise than what you had been would have appeared to them to be otherwise.'"
—*Alice's Adventures in Wonderland*

Conceptualizations and accompanying procedures based on psychoanalysis have mushroomed . . . Founders of allegedly new therapeutic methods continue to emerge . . . These claims range from reasonably modest assertions to extravagant boasts of having at last discovered the royal road to mental health for everyone. —*PERSUASION AND HEALING*, 1991, PP. 186–87

Cognitive behavioral therapies dominate the evidence-based literature on psychotherapy, yet the majority of therapists still ascribe to methods loosely termed "psychodynamic." A brief review of recent history helps account for both the apparent eclipse and the hardiness of such therapy. Though psychoanalysis offers a clear starting point for such a review, the field has not been static either in its models of mind and distress or in its methods of treatment. Psychodynamics, loosely defined as the interplay between memory, past social experience, stimuli and motivational pressures outside awareness, and conscious meaning (Yeomans, Clarkin, and Levy 2005), still provides a blueprint for treatment in the era of neuroscience, descriptive diagnosis, and societal support based on outcome research.

Ideally, one would want to define psychodynamic psychotherapy more precisely before attempting to evaluate it. Persistent ambiguity of definition contributes both to the durability of this approach to psychotherapy and to the problems of validation (Abbass et al. 2009). Shedler (2010) offers a useful list of qualities of psychodynamic therapies (table 10.1).

Table 10.1.   Qualities of Psychodynamic Psychotherapy

Focus on affect
Exploration of avoidance of distress
Identification of recurring themes
Discussion of past experience as shaper of the present
Focus on relationships
Attention to therapeutic relationship
Acceptance and exploration of fantasy, dreams, desires, and fears

Source: Adapted from Shedler 2010.

Different authors emphasize different aspects of the theory and practice of psychodynamic psychotherapy in trying to account for both benefits and failures. Studies designed to demonstrate that any one element—for example, interpretation of transference (Gabbard 2006)—accounts for therapeutic effect have produced mixed or negative findings. Studies of cognitive therapy face similar problems (see chapters 1, 11, and 12). Patients apparently respond to something more general than any particular theory implies. As Frank and many others have found, the quality of the therapeutic alliance largely accounts for the effects of any therapy. When the therapist's theory fosters interchanges in which patients feel understood, accepted, and encouraged, it continues to have therapeutic power. Psychodynamic therapies and their underlying theories, as modified over the past half-century, focus on the relationship between patient and provider, capitalizing on this essential element of effectiveness.

In the past, length of treatment distinguished psychodynamic therapies from more structured ones. Today, time-specified or time-limited forms are common (Abbass et al. 2009). Beyond time limits, modern psychodynamic therapies include shaping patients' expectations, setting goals, and monitoring progress (Gabbard 2006). Even with these modifications, psychodynamic therapies are less prescriptive than cognitive behavioral ones. This is neither a strength nor a weakness. Some patients clearly prefer a more receptive therapeutic posture to a more directive one; some don't.

To be effective, a theory must be credible to the therapist and plausible to the patient. Being an offshoot of psychoanalysis both helps and hinders psychodynamic psychotherapy in this regard. Much of psychoanalysis is tied to a specific period of history and a small, fractious group of theorists. Between the 1930s and the 1970s, American psychoanalysts seriously oversold themselves as scientists and healers, provoking a significant backlash among professionals and the public (Shorter 1997). At the same time, psychoanalysis has retained considerable prestige and many are familiar with its teachings. Psychoanalytic institutes and societies have kept the movement alive and continue to attract trainees.

To thrive, however, psychodynamic psychotherapy, as the child of an aging parent, must prove itself in modern terms. A small but increasing number of well-designed outcome studies provide evidence that such therapy may be beneficial. While these studies cannot validate underlying theories, they do show that psychodynamic psychotherapies may foster clinically significant changes. Moreover, the benefits of such therapy continue beyond the end of the formal relationship (Levy and Ablon 2010). In the treatment of depressed mood and related dysfunctions, for example, the effect size (measurement of improvement, relative to no treatment) for extended but still time-limited psychodynamic psychotherapy is at least as good as that for cognitive behavioral therapy (CBT), and better than the effect size for antidepressant medication (Shedler 2010).

The real appeal of psychodynamic therapy may lie, not in the outcome data, which remain modest, but in the human fascination with narrative. A relatively unstructured treatment focused on the patient (as opposed to the patient's symptoms) may slowly modify the stories that patients tell themselves about who they are and why they behave as they do. Psychotherapy provides a way to alter the life narrative, a quality that Jerome Frank emphasized and others—notably Paul McHugh and Phillip Slavney (1998), writing about the life story perspective (see chapter 2), and Michael White and David Epston (1990)—have developed under the heading of "narrative therapy." Strict cognitive therapy focuses on identifying patterns of distorted thinking, essentially trying to correct the grammar of the story. Psychodynamic psychotherapy may bend the arc of the plot. In the effort to isolate the effective elements of particular therapies, controlled research tends to magnify the differences among them. As actually practiced, the outcomes of many approaches and techniques overlap.

Perhaps most important, in the age of neuroscience, psychodynamic approaches seem broad enough to capture essential elements of human thought and behavior that more symptom-focused methods have tended to overlook. Modern technological tools, especially functional neuroimaging, have made it possible to investigate some of the patterns of behavior and thought described within psychoanalysis (see chapter 3). Developmental studies in primates show that very early experiences may create patterns of social interaction that shape behavior in adult animals (Suomi 1997). Studies that combine behavior with imaging also show that responses to present experience activate brain areas that subserve memory and nonconscious reaction patterns. This supports the obvious insight that memory and subcortical processes strongly shape thought and behavior in all animals, including humans. Cognitive behavioral therapies typically focus on the "here and now" and on the near future. This is a valid and useful therapeutic posture, but humans live, act, and react to the "there and then" in ways that generations of therapists have studied and used to help their patients gain self-awareness, self-control, and other nebulous but important adaptive qualities.

In this chapter we examine the historical background of psychoanalysis in American psychiatric training and the forces that challenged its legitimacy. The essay then looks toward the future of psychoanalytically derived (psychodynamic) psychotherapy, in terms of contemporary efforts to revise its theories, role in training, and contributions to clinical practice.

The Evolution of Psychodynamic Psychotherapy in the United States

In the decades before the first edition of *Persuasion and Healing* (Frank 1961), psychoanalysis held American psychiatry in a stranglehold (Shorter 1997). Beyond the prominence of the psychoanalytic institutes, many professors of psychiatry adhered to psychoanalysis, though its mission, methods of validation, and modes of training fit poorly with existing science or medical education. Universities, including Johns Hopkins, extended the influence of competing theories, especially behaviorism, but could not dislodge psychoanalytic dominance over psychiatry as an intellectual discipline and psychotherapy as a clinical activity.

Opening a new window of investigation, *Persuasion and Healing* broadened both the scientific and the cultural study of psychotherapy, shining light into a darkening room (see chapters 2 and 5 in this volume). Jerome Frank showed that psychoanalysis represented but a small subfield of psychotherapy, a transcultural phenomenon much older and more diverse than others recognized. His work encouraged expanding the scope of psychotherapy to include the care of medically ill people and those who suffered adversity outside the "neuroses" recognized by psychoanalysis. In addition, Frank and colleagues pioneered research into the broad assessment of psychotherapy outcome (see chapters 1, 11, and 12). These elements of Frank's work contributed to a seismic shift in the place of psychoanalysis in American medicine and psychiatry.

In the decades after World War II, Frank's empirical and phenomenological approach to psychotherapy was an anomaly. Accidents of history had derailed the development of psychiatry and psychotherapy in the United States. Though European psychiatrists were advancing phenomenological approaches to major psychiatric disorders from the late nineteenth century onward, their American counterparts were mainly pathologists who studied psychiatric disorders based on autopsies of patients in state insane asylums. The theory of moral treatment, a behavioral approach grounded in religious and political theory rather than science, initially guided whatever psychotherapy such institutions provided.

Asylum care deteriorated drastically in the late nineteenth century, at a time when neurology was evolving as both a scientific field and, to a lesser extent, a source of treatment for "nervous distress." Partly in consequence, the interaction between psychiatry and neurology was profoundly contentious. Criticism of American psychiatry by leading neurologists such as S. Weir Mitchell (1894) challenged early twentieth-century American psychiatry to reestablish itself on a more scientific footing, outside institutions. In the process of modernizing itself, the profession essentially abandoned the moral treatment model. Psychiatrists began searching for ways to apply scientific principles to problems more treatable than the intractable psychoses, neurosyphilis, and dementia that affected most patients in the asylum.

Freud's visit to Clark University, in Worcester, Massachusetts, in 1909, and his subsequent conversations with the eminent neurologist James Jackson Putnam diverted much of this activity into peculiar channels. His influence encouraged psychiatrists to view psychopathology through the distorting lens of unprovable theories about sexual conflict and unconscious motivation (Hale 1995). Interest in studying behavior became the purview of academic psychologists, many of whom did not provide any type of treatment. The large influx of European psychoanalysts displaced by World War II strengthened the intellectual dominance of psychoanalysis in the United States as a method of classifying and treating mental distress.

Psychoanalysis did not maintain its hegemony for long. By the mid twentieth century, political forces internal to the profession seriously compromised its influence. In 1941, for example, the New York Psychoanalytic Society decredentialed Karen Horney, on the grounds that she was "disturbing the students"

(Eckhardt 2006). She and several colleagues resigned, writing: "For the past few years it has become . . . apparent that the scientific integrity of the New York Psychoanalytic Society has steadily deteriorated. Reverence for dogma has replaced free enquiry; academic freedom has been abrogated; students have been intimidated; scientific sessions have deteriorated into political machinations" (quoted in Eckhardt 2006, p. 7). Some of the authors of this letter founded a new institute, but within two years another split occurred, when Eric Fromm's privileges were revoked. Harry Stack Sullivan's Washington Institute promoted more free inquiry, but other psychoanalysts treated him as a renegade, limiting his impact on the field.

Robert Knight wrote in 1953 that "the spectacle of a national association of physicians and scientists feuding with each other over training standards and practices . . . calling each other orthodox or deviant . . . is not an attractive one to say the least. Such terms belong to religious or fanatical political movements and not to science and medicine . . . Perhaps we are still standing too much in the shadow of that giant Sigmund Freud to permit ourselves to view psychoanalysis as a science of mind rather than a doctrine of its founder." Sandor Rado was even more pessimistic: "A professional organization cannot help becoming in due course of time a police organization, unfortunately" (Eckhardt 2006, p. 10).

These public controversies exposed the inherent weaknesses of psychoanalysis as a discipline. Beyond its theoretical limitations, the intensity and expense of a "classic psychoanalysis" compromised clinical application of psychoanalytic ideas. Not all patients could withstand (or pay for) four or five sessions per week. In consequence, a derivative, psychodynamic psychotherapy, became a popular alternative and persists today, especially in psychotherapy training programs.

Psychodynamic psychotherapy may be conducted with patients on the couch, though most often patients and therapists sit face to face. Although many have proposed modifications to limit its focus (e.g., Lester Luborsky's Core Conflictual Relationship Theme; see Luborsky and Crits-Christoph 1998), most such therapy still involves identification by the therapist of a patient's unconscious conflicts, as revealed in the free flow of the patient's words or in the ways the patient responds to or perceives the therapist and others, based on earlier relationships ("transference" or "object relations") (table 10.1). Such therapy typically involves an initial psychodynamic formulation that links the patient's current problems to early experiences (Perry, Cooper, and Michels

1987). Therapists base their interventions on such organizing principles as resistance, ego mechanisms of defense, transference, and countertransference (Gunderson and Gabbard 1999).

Some psychodynamic practitioners, infatuated with complexity, have been known to refer to psychodynamic practice as a "definitive" therapy, in condescending contrast to methods they consider "superficial," especially CBT. The evidence for the efficacy of psychodynamic psychotherapy is strong (Shedler 2010), but few data support claims for its superiority over other methods. While many studies explore psychodynamic processes, outcome research in this field is plagued by many difficulties. The typical length of psychodynamic psychotherapy poses particular problems. During treatment that may stretch over several years, patients get married, have children, fall ill, suffer losses, change jobs, and generally face life's vicissitudes and joys. Attributing change to the treatment is difficult in the face of so many coinciding life events. Freud established the "rule of abstinence" to overcome this obstacle: he forbade analysands to make major life changes while in his care. However, Freud's analyses were relatively brief—well under a year—in contrast to the length of psychoanalysis and psychoanalytic psychotherapy from the 1950s onward. The evidence base for both brief psychodynamic therapy and longer, open-ended treatments is improving (see below), but still lags far behind studies of other modalities of treatment.

Early Empirical Studies of Psychoanalytic Psychotherapy

Like most influential academic psychiatrists of the 1950s and 1960s, Frank had some psychoanalytic training. However, he, too, had run afoul of unchecked orthodoxy and institutional politics, prompting him to question some of the received truths of the profession. Recognizing the dilemma posed by the impact of life events on the outcome of therapy, his early research addressed the simple question of how long and intense treatment needed to be to benefit the patient. Comparing intensive and far less intensive treatments led him to the following conclusion:

> Duration of treatment also may be more closely related to the therapist's conception of how long treatment should take than to the patient's condition. Practitioners of long-term therapy find that their patients take a long time to respond; those who believe that they can produce good results in a few weeks report that

their patients respond promptly. There is no evidence that a larger proportion of patients in long-term treatment improve or that improvement resulting from long-term treatment is more enduring than that produced by briefer treatment. However, psychotherapy has tended to become increasingly prolonged in settings where there are no external obstacles to its continuance. (Frank 1961, pp. 14–15)

Frank's claim that the duration or intensity of therapy did not account for more than a small percentage of its results represented a huge renunciation of psychoanalytic articles of faith.

Frank was not alone in sticking a pin into many of psychoanalysis's inflated claims. Percival Bailey offered a brilliant attack on its pretensions:

There is no proof that the system is true. It is an intellectually closed world, but the argument that it is internally consistent is no proof . . . and it is, moreover, demonstrably false. Another proof sometimes adduced is its triumph over opposition. This is the proof that theologians sometimes use to prove the truth of Christianity . . . Oberndorf remarks on the profuse number of new books, based upon psychoanalytic thinking, which appear weekly. Of the making of books there is no end: Swedenborgian and Rosicrucian books are still written . . . Another proof of which one hears is its therapeutic efficacy. This is the weakest proof of all. Freud remarked toward the end of his life that psychoanalysis would be remembered as a psychology of the unconscious and not as a method of treatment. Brill said that psychoanalysis has a very limited therapeutic applicability. Horney wrote, "My desire to make a critical revision of psychoanalytic theories had its origin in a dissatisfaction with its therapeutic results." (Bailey 1956, pp. 396–97)

In an important comment, Bailey predicted Frank's work, initially quoting Wortis: "It would also appear, as one looks over the data on . . . the effectiveness of various therapeutic procedures, that approximately one-third get well with treatment and one-third may be influenced to a greater or lesser degree by treatment." He continues: "This checks with Oberndorf's statement that 30% of his patients have previously been analyzed without success. And Dr. Denker reported that 72% of psychoneurotics recover within two years with no other assistance than that of a general practitioner of medicine. Esquirol reported identical results 120 years ago. There seems little doubt that the results of psychotherapy are independent of ideology" (Bailey 1956, p. 397).

Bailey's critique was an effective polemic that widened the rift between psychoanalysts and "biological psychiatrists" but did not add greatly to an understanding of what therapy is and how it works. Being more balanced critics, Frank and those who followed his lead paradoxically helped to rehabilitate some of the elements of psychodynamic therapy that had been overlooked in the contentious theoretical debates of mid-century. They restored a focus on the power of the relationship between therapist and patient, the importance of a theory that explains distress and offers hope, and the value of patients' reevaluating present assumptions (or cognitive schemata) in relation to a personal past. Frank did not disprove tenets of psychoanalytic theory that linked improvement to resolving unconscious conflict or challenging defenses or analyzing transference, but he did show that these were neither necessary nor sufficient for positive therapeutic outcomes.

Contemporary Revisions of Psychoanalysis

Psychoanalytic theory has not been static. Contemporary psychotherapy research encompasses many approaches that reflect diverse traditions of studying conscious beliefs, cognitive processing, interactions between people, situational factors, and cultural qualities, in addition to problems rooted in the past experience of individuals. Clinical practice draws on all these perspectives, some of which—object relations, for example—have long and valued intellectual pedigrees, though few have been developed or tested, much less validated, by systematic research.(Kohlenberg and Tsai 1991). Whether such validation is a goal worth pursuing remains an open question.

A review of this kind should not neglect an evaluation of how effective the methods described have been in helping the patients attending an individual therapist's practice. This kind of personal survey, although obviously limited by its subjective nature, complements the more "scientific" studies of psychotherapy outcome, which themselves are hampered by major methodological problems.

The problems of moving beyond justification of psychoanalysis by personal experience are legion. The field lacks replicable data (Colby and Stoller 1988). Though American psychoanalytic institutes originally offered training only to physicians, psychoanalysis never fit well into medicine, discouraging research. The picture is improving, but slowly. Broad principles, such as the impact of early experience, can be correlated with neurobiological findings (see chapter

3). The application of psychoanalytically derived ideas makes sense of many complex phenomena such as the patterns of small group interaction (see chapter 13). Nevertheless, most mentalist psychoanalytic constructs, however intriguing, cannot be tested. Outside a few academic centers, psychoanalysts lack training in neuroscience or experimental psychology and, instead, try to develop and support their insights by revising and synthesizing the work of prior theorists or offering analyses of historical figures and artists. Psychoanalytic work has also moved into the fields of philosophy and literature (Mills 2004).

These activities still have cultural relevance. Although writing almost two decades ago, Levenson (1994) provides commentary on the continuing relevance of psychoanalysis in the present: "What we all held in common was that the analyst, like the artist, had a mandate to represent but also to stand outside of his/her society." He points out that psychoanalysis arose in part as social criticism of the mores of the Victorian era. Well into the 1950s, its advocates accepted that societal factors contributed to the etiology of most neuroses. In the late twentieth century, many analysts became fascinated with various forms of mass hysteria, including a proliferation of patients claiming multiple personality and victimization in satanic ritual abuses. Levenson calls for a return to careful scrutiny of culture in the practice of psychoanalysis, a salutary suggestion.

While often fascinating, historical case studies, philosophical musing, and cultural commentary differ from the literature of clinical psychiatry. Stephens (1990), for example, published a paper on the nonexistence of God. However interesting this and other papers of its ilk may be, it is hard to imagine a similar literature in cardiology.

A more encouraging development has been some analysts' willingness to question their work and revise its precepts, in distinct contrast to the period in which Frank was writing. As one of many examples, Walter Bonime's great paper "The Therapeutic Relationship" (1983) rejects the classical concept of transference, on which much of the analytic enterprise hangs. Many other analysts now deal with questionable analytic concepts, in intellectually acceptable ways (Corradi 2006). While institutes continue to function outside the realm of academic criticism, more diversity of thought is generally tolerated, including renewed interest in ideas generated by those once expelled from the movement.

Psychoanalysts, faced with the critique of their profession as archaic and unscientific, are also attempting to forge links with the neural sciences, creating new resources such as the *Journal of Neuropsychoanalysis*. The fit between these fields is as intriguing, and sometimes as awkward, as the name of the journal. Whitehead (2005), for example, discusses "downward causation" as an organizing principle in psychoanalysis and neural sciences, with the highest level being, essentially, "mind" and the lowest level being "molecule." He contrasts this perspective with the position taken by Solms and Turnbull (2002) in *The Brain and the Inner World*. These authors argue for the philosophical position of dual-aspect monism and assert that Freud was, unwittingly, an advocate and practitioner of such perspective.

Though the movement to reground psychoanalysis in neuroscience is commendable, significant difficulties plague the efforts to develop clear evidence for its therapeutic effects. An attempt at meta-analysis (Friedman et al. 2005), reviewing the outcome of therapy provided by fifty-one experienced psychoanalysts for 551 patients, yielded interesting information about the demographics of such treatment in the United States. However, the main outcome measure—therapists' rating of Global Assessment of Functioning (GAF) compared with remembered rating at the beginning of treatment—falls far short of any current standard of psychotherapy research.

Another approach many contemporary analysts use to demonstrate relevance to modern psychiatry is to assert that psychodynamic principles have value exclusive of psychoanalytic treatment. Jay Lefer (2006), for example, argues cogently for their role in consultation-liaison psychiatry. Psychodynamic principles are certainly relevant and sometimes very useful in this regard. Focusing on patients' emotional distress, exploring how early experience may influence their behavior in medical settings (while not ignoring the qualities of the setting itself), and exploring the possible symbolic meaning of their disease or symptoms circumvents the pitfalls of the usually troubled relationships such patients have with medical professionals, especially in the hospital (see chapters 7–9). Contemporary group psychotherapies also draw heavily on psychoanalytic concepts (see chapter 13).

Old methods die hard. Analysts writing for their own journals continue to generalize from single cases, often with hyperbolic images. Marilyn Charles (2006), for example, published "Silent Scream: The Cost of Crucifixion—Working with a Patient with an Eating Disorder." This article typifies many in the psychoanalytic and psychodynamic literature. Do such metaphors belong in an allegedly scientific paper? Charles claims that patients who have eating disorders "have experienced extreme deprivation" in early relationships and that they are "individuals who communicate proto-symbolically." The experience of one of us (LAW) in treating such patients is not compatible with her assertions: my patients do not describe extreme early deprivation. They communicate in many different ways, most of them not proto-symbolic. Articles of the kind published by Charles—essentially case reports—generalize to an almost ridiculous extent and would not be publishable in any other branch of medicine.

From Psychoanalysis to Psychodynamic Psychiatry

Much debate persists about the differences between psychoanalysis and psychodynamic psychotherapies, well summarized by Paul Chodoff. Table 10.2 broadly compares the two therapies, based on the work of advocates for retaining elements of psychoanalysis within contemporary psychotherapy. Chodoff views psychoanalysis and psychodynamic psychotherapy as merging:

> I do not see a sharp demarcation with DP (dynamic psychotherapy) on one side and PA (psychoanalysis) on the other . . . This view is rejected by those unreconstructed analysts who still accept Freud's dictum that only treatments that rely on the analysis of the transference deserve the name of psychoanalysis . . . However, analysts for whom the therapeutic alliance rather than resolution of the transference is the main focus of treatment take a more nuanced view of the differences between analysis and DP. They are more likely to range themselves on one side of a distinction between therapies that rely on the relationship between therapist and patient on the one hand and cognitive-behavioral treatments on the other. (Chodoff 2006)

Chodoff goes on to propose that the key attributes of psychodynamic psychotherapy are emotional support, hope, listening, insight, and guidance (see also table 10.1). This view differs markedly from that which prevailed when the first edition of *Persuasion and Healing* was published. Its links with the principles that *Persuasion and Healing* brought to the field are obvious.

In any case, psychodynamic psychotherapy, though not a precise analog to open-ended psychoanalysis, has proven to be more amenable to rigorous evaluation. Leichsenring and Rabung (2008) published a meta-analysis of outcome in 1,053 patients treated with long-term psychodynamic psychotherapy between 1960 and 2008. They were able to demonstrate that such treatment has a sus-

Table 10.2.   Comparison of Psychoanalysis with Psychodynamic Psychotherapy

	Psychoanalysis	Psychodynamic Psychotherapy
Technique	Patient lying down, facing away from therapist	Therapist and patient sitting face to face
	Strict therapist neutrality	Therapist encouragement
	Implicit support	Overt support
	Strict free association including dreams and fantasy	Guided free association
	Four or five hours/week	One or two hours/week
	Open-ended	Open-ended or time-limited
Theory	"Neurosis" results from conflict between basic drives and social demands; developmental arrest	Symptoms or adaptive failures result from interplay of conscious and unconscious mental processes
	Past determines present	Past influences present
	Treatment based on interpretation of intrapsychic conflict and transference/countertransference	Treatment based on transference/countertransference
	Focuses on nonrational thought, including irrational/immature thought ("defenses")	Incorporates both rational ("cognitive") and nonrational thought ("defenses")
	Resistance seen as internal conflict between conscious and unconscious	Resistance seen as rupture in relationship
	Modifies patterns of thought and reaction; changes life story	Modifies patterns of thought and reaction; changes life story

tained, measurable effect on people with chronic or complex disorders. However, even the application of rigorous meta-analytic methods could not compensate for the difficulty of small, heterogeneous patient samples and the problems of valid placebo psychotherapy (Glass 2008). Two other meta-analyses support the efficacy of time-limited psychodynamic psychotherapy (Abbass et al. 2009; Levy and Ablon 2010), while acknowledging ongoing problems of defining and standardizing treatments.

One of the implied advantages of a psychodynamic approach has been that it is less likely to be harmful than more prescriptive methods. This is an unjustified and potentially dangerous assumption. Psychotherapeutic outcomes are not universally benign. Some people are clearly harmed by psychotherapy of many forms, including psychodynamic ones. Harm may reflect destructive views openly embraced by groups within the profession (e.g., the fairly recent epidemic of false memories of many kinds of abuse), incompetence on the part of an individual therapist, a poor patient-therapist fit, including a lack of capacity to handle transference and countertransference phenomena, and idiosyncratic bad results (Crown 1983). In an ideal world, psychotherapy training in any modality would include teaching therapists to elicit and document informed consent at the outset of any course of treatment, even if the goals and expected outcome are uncertain. Frank's research into the value of a role induction interview (see chapter 1) hinted at such developments, though his purpose was more to increase benefit than to avoid harm. Being better grounded in research, CBT is more likely to incorporate an initial discussion of risks and benefits than is typical psychodynamic psychotherapy.

Education of Psychotherapists

Ongoing concerns about ethics and the difficulties inherent in training in psychoanalysis are described in a book by Reeder (2004). Beyond the problems of training within institutes, changes in the insurance environment, as well as advances in understanding of the biology of some psychiatric disorders, have led to a major shift in psychiatry residents' knowledge of psychotherapy. Even while studies are emerging that strongly support the efficacy of short-term psychodynamic psychotherapies (Leichsenring et al. 2009; Shedler 2010), academic psychiatry places much less emphasis on psychodynamic theory and practice than was the case in the past (Plakun 2006) (see chapter 2).

In the face of these opposing forces, the current status of training in psychoanalysis and psychoanalytic psychotherapy remains uncertain. Managed care has, unfortunately, minimized the role of psychiatrists in providing psychotherapy of any kind. More important, most major academic departments of psychiatry are currently heavily engaged in neurobiological research and medical models of treatment. Psychodynamic theory and therapy are not generally a priority, and many training programs lack faculty qualified to teach in this area. Eric Plakun (2006) proposes a "Y" model for residents' psychotherapy competencies. He views short-term, supportive, and medication-inclusive therapies as the stem, which then branches into the arms of the Y as CBT and psychodynamic psychotherapy. While cogent, it is hard to see how this model will salvage the role of psychodynamic education in training programs and harder still to see how the model of specialized training in one of the handful of psychoanalytic hospitals could restore the place of psychodynamic psychotherapy as an area of core competence for all psychiatrists.

Myron Glucksman (2006) examines the same phenomenon—increased dominance of biological psychiatry and decreased time for psychodynamic psychiatry in training programs. He is concerned that residents now view psychoanalysis as "an archaic, time-consuming, costly treatment" and that "if this trend continues, there is a realistic possibility that medical psychoanalysts as well as psychodynamically oriented psychiatrists will . . . perhaps vanish altogether" (p. 219). Glucksman's suggested remedy is to provide more integrated psychodynamic and psychoanalytic training during residency, with these viewed as subspecialty tracks eligible for training credit, including credit for actual, psychoanalytic training. However, residents who view psychoanalysis as "an archaic, time-consuming, costly treatment" are unlikely to sign up for such tracks.

Clarice Kestenbaum (2006) offers her own views on the future of training in dynamic psychotherapy. She describes her own training in the early 1960s:

> Psychoanalysis in the 1960's was the jewel in the crown of psychiatric training . . . Most of my colleagues were either in analysis or training to become psychoanalysts themselves. Ninety percent of my supervisors were psychoanalysts, and I did not need to be convinced to apply to an institute for training . . . We had dozens of fascinating cases to discuss with half a dozen supervisors and attending physicians . . . There were few forms to complete and no structured instruments. Our notes read like novels—full of speculation, fantasy, hyperbole, and sometimes a thoughtful analytic dynamic formulation to make sense of the confounding signs, symptoms and historical events. Because there were no formal standards, each supervisor provided his own model, or paradigm, based on his own bias . . . A supervisor, after a Clinical Case Rounds Presentation, might say, "He has the feel of schizophrenia," and we took his word for it . . . One day I decided to conduct an experiment and presented the same case (a suicidal 19–year-old man) to five different supervisors and received five different points of view. (Kestenbaum 2006, p. 31)

Kestenbaum details her long career as a psychiatric educator and notes that many residents applying to her child and adolescent psychiatry training program have experience in psychopharmacology, CBT, interpersonal psychotherapy, and group therapies, but no real experience of psychodynamic psychotherapy. She cites cases in which being psychodynamically informed can help treatment. Hers is a thoughtful report about a real problem, but it ends problematically with the assertion that we *know* that dynamic endeavors with children can change them, citing Fonagy and Target (1996), who provided only a retrospective study. While Kestenbaum claims that Mullen and colleagues' test (2004) of psychodynamic competence is helpful, my (LAW's) examination of versions of this test finds it replete with ambiguity.

The problem remains: how can there be "correct" answers in a field without an evidence base? Such concern confounds Kestenbaum's statement (2006, p. 40) that "without a thorough knowledge of the psychodynamic base upon which all psychological treatments are built, a psychiatrist cannot become a true 'physician of the mind, the brain, and the soul.'" Psychiatrists of the twenty-first century, including those who do psychotherapy, will need to continue to be physicians of brain and mind (a perplexing metaphysical construct), as the two become one. (McHugh 2006) Many educators (including ourselves) are suspicious of attempting to make them "physicians of the soul," a concept that far more intelligent people have been unable to define.

Much more limited reforms may do better in preserving the best of the psychodynamic tradition for residents in psychiatry (see also chapters 2, 7, 8, 13, and 15). Douglas Ingram (2006), for example, wrote a delightful paper, "Teaching Psychodynamic Therapy to Hardworking Psychiatry Residents," in which he describes his approach to making complex psychodynamic concepts accessible to today's trainees. He does not refer trainees to the psychoanalytic institute, does not introduce an all-encompassing but as yet unrealizable embrace of a union between neural sciences and psychoanalytic theory, and does not stand at the wall with last-ditch defenders of the true faith. Rather, Ingram holds a few seminars with residents in which he asks such questions as:

> You have been treating a dysthymic 250–pound woman once weekly, and she announces that she has lost fifteen pounds on a new diet—what might you say, if anything?

> In dynamic psychotherapy, why don't we use the question, "Why . . ."?

> What shall we do while waiting for the other residents to arrive—if they arrive? . . . Any thoughts? Well, let me ask you: What is waiting? Is it an affect, an idea—what is it? Why do we say, "A watched pot never boils!"? (Ingram 2006)

Such intuitive teaching does not aim to teach the complete fabric of psychodynamic theory and therapy, but instead demonstrates the utility of aspects of this approach in residents' personal experience and day-to-day clinical prac-tice. Such an approach helps preserve many beneficial aspects of psychody-namic theory and practice—because some of them are indeed pragmatic and helpful—and will interest residents in studying aspects of the theory.

Lacy and Hughes (2006), nonanalysts sympathetic to psychodynamic theo-ries, also tackle the issue of education in psychodynamic theory. Their thought-ful and thought-provoking article echoes Pulver's belief (2003) that psychody-namics and neural sciences need a common language. These authors rely on neuroanatomy, neurochemistry, and neural networks as organizing principles. They describe a course that teaches residents the basic concepts of neurobiol-ogy, psychopharmacology, and clinical neuropsychiatry, with each part of the course having "psychodynamic correlates." These are included for such topics as anatomy, functional neural processing, executive functioning, language, and memory. These correlates are ingenious, and many of them succeed—certain dynamic concepts can now be located in the brain and understood within a neural or general biological framework (see chapters 3 and 4).

Lacy and Hughes hope to rescue psychoanalytic teaching from an approach that employs archaic language and is dogmatically defensive, unrelated to medi-cine or neuroscience, and taught in a historic rather than data-driven fashion. They promote an approach expressed in common scientific language, driven by data, and open to new findings, clearly related to medicine and psychiatry and consistent with neuroscience. The specific course described has many strengths but does not fully realize this hoped-for synthesis. Over time, how-ever, such model building is likely to extend psychodynamic theory and bring aspects of it back into the medical mainstream.

Other offerings in the current literature do not pose new models but rather explicate old ones (Davidson 2006). Such contributions, of which Goin's article (2006) is a fine example, praise neurobiological research and speak of nascent efforts to link psychoanalysis and psychodynamic psychiatry to it. Many arti-cles refer to Eric Kandel's research (1998) showing that psychotherapy may induce changes in the brain. Such efforts, while salutary, pair hard neurosci-ence data with psychodynamic speculation and supposition in ways that often seem forced. Because all psychotherapy changes the brain, any claims that findings like Kandel's specifically validate psychodynamic psychotherapy are as yet inherently tautological. In sum, as one examines recent contributions to the literature on teaching psychoanalysis and psychodynamic psychotherapy, one finds apologia, false hope for a rapid unification of psychoanalysis and neural science, and intriguing new proposals plagued by inherent philosophical and scientific problems.

A Personal View

During thirty-five years of practicing psychiatry, my (LAW's) views of psychotherapy have changed, as has the role of psychotherapy in the larger field of psychiatry. As an undergraduate, I learned about many approaches to and types of psychotherapy. Even then, the field included evidence-based therapies, especially behavioral therapy of various kinds. As a resident in psychiatry, however, it soon became apparent that when mentors talked about psychotherapy, they were referring to psychoanalytically informed, psychodynamic psychotherapy. The training culture patronized other approaches, including supportive psychotherapy. Although the department chair was a pragmatic consultation-liaison psychiatrist and the department included a growing number of faculty interested in psychotropic medication, the analysts on the faculty were clearly viewed as "better" than their nonanalytic colleagues, especially in the eyes of the residents.

And some of them were very good. A Sullivanian analyst taught me a great deal about observing myself and the other in dyadic interactions in the here and now; another analyst taught me to focus on and reconstruct an hour from beginning to end without notes; and a child analyst taught me how to take aspects of theory and apply them pragmatically in brief psychotherapy with children. These skills have been invaluable to me throughout my career. I worry that such skills will be less available to future psychiatrists and patients.

Other psychoanalytic faculty, however, sexualized everything. Many were extremely judgmental and critical of each other, but instead of saying that a given colleague was a jerk, they would express concern that the colleague's "analysis had been incomplete." In retrospect, this created heavy burdens for the residents, who feared that disloyalty or skepticism would indicate that they, too, had failed in analytic terms. I know that the first group of psychoanalytic faculty helped many patients, personally and through the residents. It is hard for me to imagine that the second group could make similar claims.

Reflecting on my personal experience leads me to further questions about current and future research. Take, for example, the question of the dyadic nature of individual psychotherapy of any sort. If I refer someone for pacemaker implantation, any trained and experienced interventional cardiologist could do the work. If I refer a patient for one of the evidence-based therapies that is entirely manual-based, the same conclusion should theoretically apply. But if I refer a patient for sophisticated and personalized CBT or psychodynamic psychotherapy, a great deal depends not just on the training of the therapist but also on the *person* of the therapist. It is a matter not just of "cognitive behavioral therapy" or "psychodynamic psychotherapy" but of psychotherapy with Ms. X. or Mr. Y. and therapist Z.

The effect of therapist-patient matching is but one of the problems of studying the effectiveness of treatment. As noted earlier, insurmountable obstacles compromise the study of open-ended treatment that may last many years and encompass many life events. Improvement or deterioration, however measured, is not attributable merely to the patient and the treatment: it is the patient, the treatment, graduation, marriage, career changes and advancements or demotions, losses—all of the phenomena of human life. Efficacy studies usually measure behavioral change. If Mr. Smith seeks behavioral therapy to correct his fear of heights, it is relatively easy to determine, some weeks later, whether he can look down three thousand feet from the rim of the Grand Canyon with pleasure or terror. If Ms. Jones seeks psychodynamic psychotherapy with the concern that she is not living up to her potential, assessing efficacy is much more difficult because the criteria, however important to the patient, become much more subjective. Qualitative research methods may provide other sources of validation in future studies, but these are not as evolved as current methods based on quantification and statistical analysis.

Beyond the difficulty of demonstrating that psychodynamic psychotherapy rests on a solid foundation of research, those who would like to encourage enthusiasm for psychodynamically informed therapy often defeat themselves by urging trainees to use this approach with patients who are poor candidates for the evidence-based treatments that target discrete dysfunctions and demand patients' commitment. As one resident described his psychodynamic psychotherapy patients, these are "the patients nobody wants." Patients assigned to relatively unstructured treatment are often those with severe symptoms or multiple comorbidities. Such patients typically arrive late, miss appointments, or occasionally come for sessions while moderately intoxicated. A vicious cycle occurs: unmotivated patients disillusion novice therapists, who further devalue the psychodynamic perspectives they are supposed to apply. Such skepticism then compromises therapists' effectiveness and patients' responsiveness.

Over the years, I have seen many unseemly psychotherapies come and go. Nonpsychodynamic primal scream therapy is a thing of the past. Masterson's dynamic therapy for "borderline" teenagers—a specific therapy for a syndrome that does not exist—has few contemporary adherents. Group therapies persist—they were among the first therapies to have good efficacy studies, and some of these studies would be relevant to efficacy studies of psychodynamic psychotherapies. It is the growth of evidence-based psychiatry, in spite of its problems, that is gradually driving out treatments of little worth—a salutary development.

Nevertheless, despite the difficulties of demonstrating its value, psychodynamic psychotherapy, in my opinion, can be helpful in defined situations, with thoughtfully selected patients. Three cases from my own practice illustrate the point.

CASE EXAMPLE 1

Dr. S. was a young physician. She came for help about a career decision—should she stay in medicine or train in molecular biology? She loved basic science, which was her passion and avocation. She had pursued medicine to please her father, who had frequently told her: "There's no money in molecular biology." The patient had a hard time asserting her own wishes. She had had a series of bad relationships with men and had no female friends. Over the course of a five-year treatment, she opted to train in molecular biology and was able to deal with untangling a thorny matrix of ambivalent feelings about both parents and about her other relationships. Dr. S. left the treatment with good feelings about herself. She occasionally sends me a Christmas card. She is pleased with her work in academic molecular biology, content in her marriage, and delighted by her two children. She continues to view her treatment as "the hardest and most important work I've ever done."

Admittedly, Dr. S. could have resolved her career choice in many other forms of psychotherapy or, for that matter, without any psychotherapy at all. Nevertheless, the therapy helped her ground her choice in the overall context of her life and relationships, a perspective of great value to her.

CASE EXAMPLE 2

Ms. T. was an older adolescent who had severe bulimia nervosa and self-cutting. When I became the attending physician on the short-term hospital unit where she was hospitalized, I learned that she was about to be sent to a state hospital because of her many "borderline" features. She demonstrated many behavioral sequelae of sexual abuse and readily acknowledged a long-term, nonconsensual sexual relationship with her much older brother. Instead of going to the state hospital, the patient engaged in psychodynamic psychotherapy. She took the work seriously. After many months without symptom relief, she started to improve. Ms. T. was symptom-free after two years but continued in therapy for another year.

Several years later, she remains symptom-free, happily married, and working professionally while raising two well-attached young children. She commented to me recently that she recalls the therapy as immensely hard and demanding work and that the very ability to do it had helped her realize that she was capable of hard work and not a worthless person. It had given her hope.

Unlike Dr. S., this patient would not have "done well" without significant intervention. While several of her specific problems could have been addressed by other therapies, psychodynamic psychotherapy was a good match for the totality of her problems and strengths.

CASE EXAMPLE 3

A twenty-eight-year-old married woman, Mrs. W., sought treatment because "I am devastated." She had been doing well in life, in her work, marriage, and family. She, her husband, and children had spent a weekend day with her mother, who had been very critical of her. Her husband had said nothing on her behalf, which had angered her. After arriving home, she and her husband argued, and became angry with each other. He told her that they were not going to resolve the issue that evening and that he was going to bed. This infuriated the patient, who said, "Drop dead!" as her husband headed for bed.

When Mrs. W. went to bed a couple of hours later, she found her husband dead. An autopsy revealed that he had died of a cerebrovascular event. Over the next few days, the patient felt overwhelming guilt and responsibility, as well as a terrible foreboding of retribution.

I treated this patient with psychodynamically informed, brief supportive psychotherapy in which she dealt with rage, guilt, love, and all the ambivalence that demarcates every intimate relationship. One can argue that grief is self-limited, but this was an unusual grief reaction. I am not aware of other treatments that could have addressed this situation so specifically and helpfully, in such a brief time.

Conclusion

This chapter has been roundly critical of psychoanalysis and psychodynamic psychotherapy, yet asserts that valuable insights and methods may be found within that troubled legacy. As a formal treatment modality, orthodox psychoanalysis may not survive much longer. Yet psychoanalytically informed psychodynamic therapy could have a bright future, even within medicine, if its practitioners would more carefully consider to whom they offer the treatment and what such treatment does or does not accomplish (Levitt, Butler, and Hill 2006).

The complexity and flexibility of contemporary psychodynamic theories aligns well with the complexity of emerging understanding of brain organization (see chapter 3). The field needs, and is beginning to have, methodologically sound outcome studies, rather than "Do your patients get better?" questionnaires filled out by its advocates.

The ineluctable point is that paradigms have shifted. Psychiatry will never again be a culture in which psychoanalysis rests at the very top of the hierarchy. Psychodynamic psychotherapy must instead find its place as one perspective and treatment among many. New ways to inspire trainees' interest and commitment, especially by encouraging them to work with patients likely to benefit, are needed, as are new methods of research capable of capturing the real complexities of distress, treatment, and outcome in human psychological experience.

REFERENCES

Abbass, A. A., Hancock, J. T., Henderson, J., and Kisely S. R. 2009. Short-term psychodynamic psychotherapies for common mental disorders. *Cochrane Database of Systematic Reviews* 1. Most recent substantive revision August 20, 2006. Accession number 075320-100000000-03657.

Bailey, P. 1956. The academic lecture: the great psychiatric revolution. *American Journal of Psychiatry* 113:387–406.

Bonime, W. 1983. The therapeutic relationship. *Academy Forum, American Academy of Psychoanalysis* 27(4):3–4.

Charles, M. 2006. Silent scream: the cost of crucifixion—working with a patient with an eating disorder. *Journal of the American Academy of Psychoanalysis and Dynamic Psychiatry* 34:261–85.

Chodoff, P. 2006. Dynamic psychotherapy: a 50–year perspective. *Journal of the American Academy of Psychoanalysis and Dynamic Psychiatry* 34:19–27.

Colby, K. M., and Stoller, R. J. 1988. *Cognitive Science and Psychoanalysis*. Hillsdale, NJ: Lawrence Erlbaum Associates.

Corradi, R. B. 2006. A conceptual model of transference and its psychotherapeutic application. *Journal of the American Academy of Psychoanalysis and Dynamic Psychiatry* 34:415–39.

Crown, S. 1983. Contraindications and dangers of psychotherapy. *British Journal of Psychiatry* 143:436–41.

Davidson, L. 2006. Supervision and mentorship: the use of the real in teaching. *Journal of the American Academy of Psychoanalysis and Dynamic Psychiatry* 34:189–95.

Eckhardt, M. H. 2006. Celebrating the 50th anniversary of the American Academy of Psychoanalysis and Dynamic Psychiatry. *Journal of the American Academy of Psychoanalysis and Dynamic Psychiatry* 34:5–12.

Fonagy, P., and Target, M. 1996. Predictors of outcome in child psychoanalysis: a retrospective study of 763 cases at the Anna Freud Center. *Journal of the American Psychoanalytic Association* 44:27–77.

Frank, J. D. 1961. *Persuasion and Healing: A Comparative Study of Psychotherapy*. Baltimore: Johns Hopkins University Press.

Friedman, R. C., Garrison, W. B., Bucci, W., and Gorman, B. S. 2005. Factors affecting change in private psychotherapy patients of senior psychoanalysts: an effectiveness study. *Journal of the American Academy of Psychoanalysis and Dynamic Psychiatry* 33:583–610.

Gabbard, G. O. 2006. When is transference work useful in psychotherapy? *American Journal of Psychiatry* 163:1667–69.

Gabbard, G. O., Gunderson, J. G., and Fonagy, P. 2002. The place of psychoanalytic treatments within psychiatry. *Archives of General Psychiatry* 59:505–10.

Glass, R. 2008. Psychodynamic psychotherapy and research evidence: Bambi survives Godzilla? *JAMA: Journal of the American Medical Association* 300:1587–89.

Glucksman, M. L. 2006. Psychoanalytic and psychodynamic education in the 21st century. *Journal of the American Academy of Psychoanalysis and Dynamic Psychiatry* 34:215–22.

Goin, M. K. 2006. Teaching psychodynamic psychotherapy in the 21st century. *Journal of the American Academy of Psychoanalysis and Dynamic Psychiatry* 34:117–26.

Gunderson, J. G., and Gabbard, G. O. 1999. Making the case for psychoanalytic therapies in the current psychiatric environment. *Journal of the American Psychoanalytic Association* 47:679–704.

Hale, N. G. 1995. *Freud and the Americans: The Beginnings of Psychoanalysis in the United States, 1876–1917*. New York: Oxford University Press.

Ingram, D. H. 2006. Teaching psychodynamic therapy to hardworking psychiatric residents. *Journal of the American Academy of Psychoanalysis and Dynamic Psychiatry* 34:173–88.

Kandel, E. R. 1998. A new intellectual framework for psychiatry. *American Journal of Psychiatry* 155:457–69.

Kestenbaum, C. J. 2006. Reminiscences of a training director and the future of training programs. *Journal of the American Academy of Psychoanalysis and Dynamic Psychiatry* 34:29–41.

Knight, R. P. 1953. Present status of organized psychoanalysis in the United States. *Journal of the American Psychoanalytic Association* 1:197–221.

Kohlenberg, R. J., and Tsai, M. 1991. *Functional Analytic Psychotherapy: Creating Intense and Curative Therapeutic Relationships.* New York: Plenum Press.

Lacy, T. J., and Hughes, J. D. 2006. A systems approach to behavioral neurobiology: integrating psychodynamics and neuroscience in a psychiatric curriculum. *Journal of the American Academy of Psychoanalysis and Dynamic Psychiatry* 34:43–74.

Lefer, J. 2006. The psychoanalyst at the medical bedside. *Journal of the American Academy of Psychoanalysis and Dynamic Psychiatry* 34:75–81.

Leichsenring, F., and Rabung, S. 2008. Effectiveness of long-term psychodynamic psychotherapy: a meta-analysis. *JAMA: Journal of the American Medical Association* 300:1551–65.

Leichsenring, F., Salzer, S., Jaeger, U., Kächele, H., Kreische, R., Leweke, F., et al. 2009. Short-term psychodynamic psychotherapy and cognitive behavioral therapy in generalized anxiety disorder: a randomized, controlled trial. *American Journal of Psychiatry* 166:875–81.

Levenson, E. A. 1994. A short visit with Jeremiah. *Academy Forum, American Academy of Psychoanalysis* 38:11–13.

Levitt, H., Butler, M., and Hill, T. 2006. What clients find helpful in psychotherapy: developing principles for facilitating moment-to-moment change. *Journal of Counseling Psychology* 33:314–24.

Levy, R. A., and Ablon, J. S. 2010. Talk therapy: off the couch and into the lab—researchers gather evidence that talk therapy works, and keeps on working. *Scientific American*, February 23. www.scientificamerican.com/article.cfm?id=talk-ther.

Luborsky, L., and Crits-Christoph, P. 1998. *Understanding Transference: The Core Conflictual Relationship Theme Method*, 2nd ed. Washington, DC: American Psychological Association.

McHugh, P. R. 2006. *The Mind Has Mountains: Reflections on Psychiatry and Society.* Baltimore: Johns Hopkins University Press.

McHugh, P. R., and Slavney, P. R. 1998. *The Perspectives of Psychiatry*, 2nd ed. Baltimore: Johns Hopkins University Press.

Mills, J. A. 2004. *Rereading Freud: Psychoanalysis through Philosophy.* Albany: State University of New York.

Mitchell, S. W. 1894. Address before the fiftieth annual meeting of the American Medico-Psychological Association. *Journal of Nervous and Mental Disease* 30:413–37.

Mullen, L. S., Rieder, R. O., Glick, R. A., Luber, B., and Rosen, P. J. 2004. Testing psychodynamic psychotherapy skills among psychiatric residents: the Psychotherapy Competence Test. *American Journal of Psychiatry* 161:1658–64.

Perry, S., Cooper, A. M., and Michels, R. 1987. The psychodynamic formulation: its purpose, structure and clinical application. *American Journal of Psychiatry* 144:543–50.

Plakun, E. M. 2006. Finding psychodynamic psychiatry's lost generation. *Journal of the American Academy of Psychoanalysis and Dynamic Psychiatry* 34:135–50.

Pulver, S. E. 2003. On the astonishing clinical irrelevance of neurosciences. *Journal of the American Psychoanalytic Association* 51:755–72.

Reeder, J. 2004. *Hate and Love in Psychoanalytic Institutions: The Dilemma of a Profession.* New York: Other Press.

Shedler, J. 2010. The efficacy of psychodynamic psychotherapy. *American Psychologist* 65:98–109.

Shorter, E. 1997. *The History of Psychiatry: From the Era of the Asylum to the Age of Prozac*. New York: John Wiley.

Solms, M., and O. Turnbull. 2002. *The Brain and the Inner World*. New York: Other Press.

Stephens, E. M. 1990. Green monkeys, strong feelings and God. *Academy Forum, American Academy of Psychoanalysis* 34:1, 15.

Suomi, S. J. 1997. Early determinants of behaviour: evidence from primate studies. *British Medical Bulletin* 53:170–184.

White, M., and Epston, D. 1990. *Narrative Means to Therapeutic Ends*. New York: W. W. Norton.

Whitehead, C. C. 2005. Toward a "new" paradigm of therapeutic action: neuro-psychoanalysis and downward causation. *Journal of the American Academy of Psychoanalysis and Dynamic Psychiatry* 33:637–56.

Yeomans, F. E., Clarkin, J. F., and Levy, K. N. 2005. Psychodynamic psychotherapies. In J. M. Oldham, A. E. Skodol, and D. S. Bender (eds.), *The American Psychiatric Publishing Textbook of Personality Disorders* (pp. 275–289). Washington, DC: American Psychiatric Publishing.

CHAPTER 11

Curtsey while you're thinking
what to say, it saves time.
—*Through the Looking Glass*

Behavioral and Condition-Specific Approaches to Psychotherapy

Diane McNally Forsyth, R.N., Ph.D., and Virginia Nash, D.N.P., R.N., C.N.S.

There are many opportunities ... for aiding patients to become aware of their difficulties in living, and for developing participant skills that are needed for solving problems that will recur in the future.   —HILDEGARD E. PEPLAU, 1952, P. 258

Specific psychotherapies are those that aim to relieve symptoms, complexes of symptoms, dysfunctional behaviors, or disorders, as well as general distress. Such therapies typically engage patients directly, without seeking to understand their nonconscious or cryptic symbolic lives. These treatments involve measuring symptoms systematically and often quantitatively and instructing patients to take steps toward recovery. In *Persuasion and Healing*, Jerome Frank, borrowing from the former Hopkins Psychiatry chairman, John Whitehorn, termed these therapies "directive" approaches, in contrast to the "evocative" therapies now loosely grouped as "psychodynamic," "narrative," or "holistic." In Frank's view, even these broad distinctions were somewhat arbitrary, as directive therapies produce nonspecific improvements, and evocative therapies sometimes relieve specific symptoms. The unique aspect of the directive approaches, which developed in the twentieth century under the influence of academic psychology, is that most were designed, from the outset, to be testable.

In contemporary terminology, Frank's directive therapies fall mostly into the domain of cognitive behavioral therapies. Not surprisingly, many, though not all, are now supported by multiple randomized studies using replicable diagnostic and outcome criteria. They consequently occupy a prominent place in the era of evidence-based medicine. Beyond proving their efficacy, the creators of these approaches have refined and revised them in light of the studies that test the therapies and their components.

Today, many therapies are subclassified according to the conditions they aim to relieve. In this chapter, after a brief conceptual overview, we discuss behavioral therapies in general and cognitive behavioral therapy (CBT) approaches in particular. We also review the applications of these techniques and of some newer methods or technical variants (such as dialectical behavioral therapy [DBT], or behavioral activation therapy [BAT]), as well as essential aspects of the research that supports their use in several clinical conditions.

What Are Behavioral and Condition-Specific Approaches in Psychotherapy?

One of the essential general principles in the practice of behavioral therapy is that therapist and patient together plan interventions that the patient carries out. Later, both evaluate the effects of these steps and revise the plan as needed. Similar steps occur in research: therapies are tested and modified in light of their impact on target symptoms or behaviors.

Since the time of Pavlov (Goodwin 1999), behavioral therapies have benefited from their scientific links with experimental animal models whose components can be rigorously tested. In the 1960s and 1970s, behavioral therapy research emphasized the application of general principles such as systematic desensitization (Foa and Rothbaum 1998). More contemporary therapies have targeted specific symptoms, using both general and closely focused techniques. Both therapists and patients have access to well worked out, often manualized therapeutic protocols aimed at encouraging specific skills, such as enhancing assertiveness, overcoming phobias, fears, and panic, and increasing positive social behaviors (Kanfer and Goldstein 1991).

Strictly behavioral therapies typically relieve discrete, measurable symptoms, such as phobic avoidance. Though patients must be persuaded to engage in the treatment, improvement is attributed to the effects of behavioral interventions that do not depend on the human capacity for language and can be analogized to the results of animal research. Cognitive therapy has a broader focus: it engages patients in reflection about their conscious thought processes, along with behavioral practice and advice. Cognitive behavioral therapy, furthermore, has evolved beyond an early, strict focus on present experience and thought. Contemporary variants include limited investigation into the historical roots of the patient's thinking patterns and discussion of less rational or more symbolic elements of his or her experience, particularly imagery and strong emotion, as determinants of behavior (Beck 2005, p. 324). In contrast to traditional psychodynamic approaches, both behavioral and cognitive behavioral therapies assume that patients' symptoms are the problems in need of resolution, rather than a manifestation of underlying unconscious motives or conflicts. As Jerome Frank and Julia Frank emphasized in the 1991 edition of *Persuasion and Healing,* though the term *cognitive behavioral therapy* implies specificity, such treatment brings about improvement by modifying meaning in a broader sense. Turnbull (1996, p. 11) describes CBT as an "approach to helping people cope more effectively with problems by equipping them with a framework of thinking and behaving, which enables them to lead more fulfilling lives. The essential components . . . are based on a belief that the world is experienced differently by each person." Therefore, the individual will develop his or her own unique sets of beliefs, which, in turn, "will influence how events are interpreted and, ultimately, how the person will act."

Research supports CBT as a proven treatment for mild to moderate depression (Ebmeier, Donaghey, and Steele 2006) and other conditions (Brewin 2006). It clearly benefits patients seeking treatment for anxiety and those recovering from physical problems (Turnbull and Marshall 1996). The application of CBT to personality disorders, relational dysfunctions, and other complex or nebulous problems is an evolving field of study.

Most forms of CBT trace their roots back to Albert Ellis's rational emotive therapy. Ellis emphasized the relevance of cognition and evaluative beliefs in the development of maladaptive behavior. CBT examines and manipulates cognitive and behavioral symptoms, with the assumption that a change in either of these areas leads to adaptive changes in the other (Freeman and Diefenbeck 2005). Cognitive behavioral therapists use a variety of techniques, such as daily logs of behaviors and cognitions, imagery exercises, and role playing (Salovey and Singer 1991), self-help, education, and the pointing out of changes and improvement throughout the course of therapy (Stevens 1996).

The use of "homework" or assignments given to patients between sessions (Kazantzis and Ronan 2006) is a central, significantly motivating element of

CBT. In research studies, patients' completion of such homework is strongly associated with enhanced treatment outcomes. As with behavioral prescriptions, cognitive behavioral therapists break their cognitive interventions into multiple, concrete steps (Feldman 2007). Initially, the patient is instructed to monitor negative thoughts (e.g., "I always fail") and to identify how such thinking patterns generate unpleasant feelings and maladaptive behaviors. Patients who believe that they always fail may feel sad and incompetent and may deploy prominent avoidance behaviors at work and in their social contacts. When these thoughts have been made explicit, the therapist (or manual) instructs patients to evaluate the accuracy of their beliefs, to test them empirically, and eventually to replace them with more adaptive or balanced thoughts ("There are many things that I do well in my life") chosen from a well-elaborated list of alternatives. In addition to identifying and modifying negative thoughts, patients are guided to uncover and challenge their underlying assumptions and to practice new, more adaptive behaviors.

The particular intervention called "behavioral activation" falls within the domain of CBT (Feldman 2007), particularly in the treatment of depression. This type of intervention involves targeting inertia and increasing contacts with and involvement in experiences that are rewarding. Activation might include implementing problem-solving strategies, setting small goals, and considering pros and cons in making a decision. Initially, the patient may be asked to monitor activity levels, then gradually schedule pleasant events, and, finally, work on progressively more challenging goals.

Despite the demonstrated efficacy of CBT, uncertainty surrounds how and for whom it works. Some authors speculate that cognition and biochemical functioning are interwoven and that CBT may be one avenue of interrupting the psychobiological cycle of depression (Free and Oei 1989; Beckham 1990). Oei and Free (1995) hypothesize that the changes occur through: (1) separate processes; (2) a linear process, with change in one function followed by change in another; or (3) a circular process, with a reciprocal interaction between biological and psychological processes. Beckham (1990) postulates a homeostasis model: depression disrupts homeostasis, whereas psychotherapy restores it by altering well-identified deficient or disruptive elements within the patient's functional system and effecting a gradual, expanded change in others. Brewin (2006) conceptualizes cognitive changes within memory representations, some negative and some positive, with circumstances dictating which are retrieved.

He postulates that therapy produces "new" memories that can be retrieved when depressive symptoms recur. Despite the recognized need for more theoretical understanding of its effects, clinical evidence shows that CBT and related therapies induce robust positive changes in patients.

Complexity of Measuring Behavioral and Cognitive Therapies: Assessing and Applying Research Findings

Reading the evidence-based literature on CBT and other types of therapy poses many problems. These include the particular brand or exact nature of the therapy under study and the research therapists' fidelity in implementing the approach. Ablon and Jones (2002, p. 776) note that much research does less to validate the processes of the therapy than it does to support the measured outcome: "When a participant in a controlled clinical trial improves after undergoing psychotherapy, it is assumed that the improvement was caused by the specific interventions that were prescribed by a manual and monitored for adherence. However, this assumption relies heavily on the clinician's ability to apply certain techniques without using others, and adhere to a particular treatment approach." When these authors compared the processes of interpersonal therapy (IPT) and CBT, for example, they found the approaches to be strikingly similar. Often, the names given to various therapies depend more on the theoretical language used than on genuinely discriminating elements. Similar observations led Frank to explain therapeutic effects in terms of the "common factors," features or "ingredients" of all psychotherapies (see chapter 1 in this volume). Current research into the effectiveness of CBT supports this point of view, even while pursuing evidence for the impact of particular elements upon specific symptoms or disorders.

Smaller studies tend to focus on the impact of particular interventions, while larger meta-analyses, the core of the evidence-based research literature, help clinicians apply research findings across a spectrum of settings and disorders. Meta-analytic studies broaden the populations to which findings may be applied, but problems remain in translating research into clinical practice. Many therapies involve twelve to twenty sessions, by design a big advantage over open-ended treatments, but still an investment that may require more commitment, or insurance support, than many patients can mobilize. Research studies control for the impact of comorbid conditions, but comorbidity is the rule in clinical settings. Some studies do try to ascertain the minimum amount of treatment that may be needed to achieve a desired outcome, while others isolate target symptoms that may occur in the context of many conditions. Studies that simultaneously address effectiveness, minimum elements, and the real limits or extent of applicability are almost impossible to conduct.

Parker and Fletcher (2007) challenge the clinical evidence for both CBT and interpersonal psychotherapy (IPT) in the treatment of depressive symptoms, highlighting serious methodological flaws in the multisite clinical trial that supported their effectiveness. In all psychotherapy studies, the selection of comparison groups is particularly problematic. Waiting-list controls may be inappropriate, and comparator therapies may lack the *bona fides* or credibility of the method to be tested. Credibility is an underappreciated variable. As Frank and many others have noted, a plausible or convincing rationale that links the principles of the proposed treatment to the relief of patients' distress is an essential component of all psychotherapies (see chapter 12). Parker and Fletcher (2007) suggest that, rather than operating on the simplistic medical analogy that a particular treatment is specific for a particular disorder regardless of the patient's expectations or belief, further research should consider what types of treatment, under what set of circumstances, are most effective for specific individuals with a specific problem. Another important question, they assert, is to determine who is best suited to carry out the therapies.

A more fundamental criticism of research in this field is that the underlying paradigm derives from logical positivism. In many studies, especially those included in meta-analyses, only objective and verifiable outcomes are valued. Such studies cannot and do not measure what improvement means to the patient (Kutney 2006). Further, conclusive results or definitions of outcomes are often equivocal (Carroll 2006; Weersing and Brent 2006). While finding a solid evidentiary base for psychotherapy remains a worthy goal, the dangers of uncritical acceptance, unreasonable rejection, or blind gullibility loom as large as when *Persuasion and Healing* first pointed them out to earlier generations.

Despite the need for a principled skepticism, current evidence strongly supports cognitive therapy or CBT for a variety of psychiatric disorders. We present here some important recent findings about the outcomes of CBT, primarily in adults, with some additional attention to children and adolescents (see also chapter 12). Following the current organization of the field, we classify therapies first by the specific symptoms or conditions they are designed to relieve.

Controlled Clinical Trials with Depressive Symptoms

Even compared with the "pharmacological revolution" and its results in the past four or five decades, CBT produces remarkable improvements for patients with depression (Kwon and Oei 2003). In a study testing a cognitive therapy model, Oei, Bullbeck, and Campbell (2006) found that the relationship between negative thinking and other symptoms of depression was bidirectional: a reduction in negative thinking reduced depression, and a reduction in depression reduced negative thinking.

Several groups of authors have completed meta-analyses on the subject. Wampold et al. (2002), reviewing twenty-two studies, found that the benefits of cognitive therapy were about equal to the benefits of bona fide non-cognitive therapy and behavioral treatments, but superior to non–bona fide treatments for depression. These authors note the limitations of many of the reviewed studies, such as questionable definitions of bona fide and non–bona fide therapies. They found one "flawed" study, but the overall results were the same when they deleted it from their analysis. To establish effect sizes for CBT, Butler et al. (2006) completed a review of sixteen meta-analyses and found that cognitive therapy was "highly effective" for adults and adolescents with unipolar depression, generalized anxiety disorder, panic disorder, social phobia, posttraumatic stress disorder (PTSD), and childhood depressive and anxiety disorders. They report that the grand mean effect size for these disorders, when compared with no-treatment, waiting-list, or placebo controls, was 0.95 (SD = 0.08). They note that CBT shows promise for a variety of other clinical problems. Finally, Cuijpers, van Straten, and Warmerdam (2007) completed a meta-analytic study to explore the effects of the behavioral intervention of activity scheduling for adult patients with depression (N = 16 studies with 780 subjects). They note that when patients monitor the connection between their mood and daily activities, they tend to increase pleasant activities, in consequence experiencing fewer depressive symptoms. When the researchers compared the effects of activity scheduling with controls, the mean effect size was 0.87 (95% CI = 0.60–1.15), indicating that activity scheduling is effective. As limitations for this analysis, the authors note the small number of studies reviewed, some of them having, in turn, small sample sizes; also, the quality of the studies reviewed was not optimal, and comparison groups may have differed.

Free, Oei, and Appleton (1998) examined the change in subjects' automatic thoughts during twelve weeks of CBT. Seventeen subjects were considered improved, and eighteen unimproved, based on Beck Depression Inventory (BDI) scores. The researchers note that the Automatic Thought Questionnaire (ATQ) measured changes in negative thinking over time, changes that were maintained on a constant and continuous basis. ATQ scores of patients in the "improved" group changed from a mean of 96.29 at pretest to 52.35 at posttest, whereas mean scores in the "not improved" group were 81.44 at pretest and 61.83 at posttest.

In another study, Oei and Sullivan (1999) explored changes in cognitions following a twelve-week group CBT program with recovered (N = 35) and nonrecovered (N = 32) patients with mood disorder. Using the ATQ (negative scale), these authors found that recovered participants exhibited significantly lower levels of negative cognitions by the end of the program. They concluded that remediation of negative cognition with group CBT was consistent with other studies of recovery from depression. The findings also confirmed that the outcome of group CBT was comparable to that of individual therapy.

Chen et al. (2006) evaluated the impact of group CBT on depression and self-esteem in clinically depressed outpatients in Taiwan. The experimental group subjects (N = 26) received at least twelve weeks of CBT group therapy, led by a clinical nurse specialist with experience in CBT and group therapy. The comparison group subjects (N = 25) began group CBT after the experimental group had completed therapy. Pre- and post-CBT measures included the BDI and the Rosenberg Self-Esteem Scale. The researchers found that group members who received CBT were significantly better after treatment, with the mean BDI score decreasing from 40.15 to 9.42, and the mean Rosenberg Self-Esteem Scale score increasing from 13.65 to 37.46. These findings are consistent with those from similar studies conducted in Western countries.

In short, many studies have shown the utility of CBT in reducing negative thinking, with coincidental reduction of depressive symptoms. Furthermore, these studies show that CBT may be effective in both individual and group applications.

Cognitive Behavioral Therapy for Anxiety Disorders

Recent decades have seen the development of specific CBT protocols for generalized anxiety disorder (Dugas et al. 2003; Norton and Hope 2005). Effective behavioral-based therapies are also available for panic disorder, PTSD, and obsessive-compulsive disorder (OCD). Although exclusively behavioral approaches, such as exposure, have been used extensively, researchers are increasingly incorporating cognitive interventions into individual, group, and marital therapies focused on anxiety symptoms and related behaviors.

Generalized Anxiety Disorder

Norton and Hope's randomized study (2005) supported the positive effects of a broad spectrum of CBT protocols, involving twelve weekly (2.5–hour) treatments, on anxiety symptoms. The sample size was small, with nine subjects completing the treatment, compared with ten subjects who continued on a waiting list. The treatment was conducted in two phases: phase 1 focused on alleviating present fears, and phase 2 consisted of ways to check on underlying perceptions of uncontrollability, unpredictability, and threat. Both phases involved the application of CBT principles. After treatment, six of the nine subjects in the treatment group no longer met criteria for anxiety disorder, while none of the waiting-list controls remitted spontaneously. The researchers found that those in the treatment group "evidenced a significant decrease in self-reported fear to personally relevant stimuli, whereas no significant change was observed among the wait list and control condition participants" (Norton and Hope 2005, p. 91). They suggest that such cost-effective, time-efficient treatment may both relieve current symptoms of anxiety and shift underlying anxiety-generating assumptions.

Research also supports the effectiveness of group CBT for generalized anxiety disorder, a method that may be more cost-effective than one-to-one therapy. In one well-designed study (Dugas et al. 2003), fifty-two patients with generalized anxiety disorder were randomized either to a waiting list or to fourteen weekly (2–hour) CBT group sessions. The study measured changes in the subjects' uncertainty, worry, and intolerance of stress. The researchers found significantly decreased scores in all areas tested and concluded that group and individual CBT for generalized anxiety disorder may have comparable effects. However, they noted a 10.4 percent dropout rate for their groups, a potential disadvantage for widespread application of group CBT.

Panic Symptoms / Panic Disorder

Cognitive behavioral therapy includes strategies to ameliorate symptoms of panic (Curran, Machin, and Gournay 2006). These include providing education about the biological aspects of anxiety and panic, graded exposures to panic-producing situations or to symptoms of panic and anxiety, and behavioral experiments conducted by the patients themselves. Persons with panic disorder express the common fear that their physical symptoms portend catastrophe or death. Therapists implementing CBT first provide clear and realistic explanations of how patients come to make such erroneous assumptions. Next, they ask the patients to talk about previous experiences with panic and anxiety, and note that none of these episodes had the feared consequences. Focusing closely on the patients' experience builds rapport, which allows the therapist to introduce behavioral experiments, prompting the patient to undertake activities to induce the feared symptoms. These may include simple physical maneuvers such as spinning to induce dizziness, voluntarily breathing fast, or running in place to raise heart rate. Patients also learn to consciously control their breathing and relax their muscles, further demonstration that they can control their experience to some extent. In successful treatment, patients realize that symptoms, while difficult, are not life threatening and need not be viewed as signs of impending death. They stop anticipating the symptoms and no longer avoid situations where they might occur—resuming normal life with a sense of self-efficacy that drugs alone cannot induce.

Untreated panic disorder seriously diminishes the sufferer's quality of life. Heldt et al. (2006) explored improvements in quality of life for a group of such patients, using brief group CBT. Thirty-two patients attended twelve group CBT sessions; the results showed significant improvement in all domains of quality of life, along with decreases in general and anticipatory anxiety and reduced agoraphobic avoidance. This study suffered from the lack of a control group. However, Dannon et al. (2004) compared the effectiveness of group CBT to pharmacotherapy with paroxetine in the treatment of panic disorder. They found that both treatments reduced anxiety symptoms, decreased the frequency of panic attacks, and increased general well-being, clearly demonstrating that CBT was comparable to treatment with psychotropic agents.

Kenardy et al. (2003) report on a novel approach comparing several methods of CBT for the treatment of panic disorder. They randomly assigned 186 patients to one of four conditions: the standard treatment of twelve sessions of therapist-delivered CBT, six sessions of therapist-delivered CBT, computer-augmented CBT, and a waiting-list control. Attrition left 93 patients for the analysis of follow-up data nine months later. The researchers found that all treatments were more effective than being on a waiting list, across all measures. Brief (six sessions) CBT augmented with a computer did not differ significantly from standard (twelve sessions) CBT treatment. Reducing the length of effective treatment has implications for reducing the cost of care overall and relative to other treatments, such as nonspecific psychotherapy or medication. The high attrition rate in this study, however, casts doubt on the widespread applicability of the research findings.

Posttraumatic Stress Disorder

Cognitive behavioral therapy has also demonstrated effectiveness for PTSD. Friedman (2006, p. 586) notes that all practice guidelines for PTSD published to date consider some form of CBT as "the treatment of choice." Cognitive therapists view the symptoms of PTSD as examples of conditioned fear, manifested as automatic negative thoughts. The corresponding therapeutic approach is to encourage cognitive restructuring, teaching the patient to recognize and challenge the thoughts coupled with memories of the trauma. Foa (2006) advocates the use of CBT, either alone or in combination with other behavioral techniques, including prolonged exposure or anxiety management, for patients with chronic PTSD. Spira et al. (2006, p. 46) note that, in this context, exposure is intended to decouple the patient's thoughts from the "fear response to internal and external cues that would otherwise cause symptom intensification." Several types of exposure therapy exist, including asking the patient to describe the traumatizing event while simultaneously using relaxation techniques. A technical variation involves graded exposures, gradually increasing the intensity of the exposure through imaginary or in vivo stimulation to induce arousal, while teaching the patient to tolerate each gradient of exposure.

Sijbrandij et al. (2007) evaluated the efficacy of brief CBT with patients experiencing symptoms of PTSD resulting from various *recent* traumatic events. Many barriers impede the conducting of rigorous research with newly traumatized populations. This study is noteworthy because of the large sample size (N = 79 in treatment, N = 64 in control), the attempt to maintain fidelity to the treatments, and the use of a control group. The brief, early CBT program significantly reduced patients' specific PTSD symptoms, anxiety, and depression at one week postintervention. However, at four months, scores for the brief CBT group and the control group no longer differed significantly. The authors conclude that a brief CBT intervention is feasible in the immediate aftermath of trauma. Though treatment did not definitively improve outcome in the long term, early relief of symptoms is valuable, and the treatment requires limited time from the health care system and from the patients.

The need for effective, inexpensive treatments for PTSD has grown since the September 11, 2001, attacks and subsequent wars in Iraq and Afghanistan. According to Kaplan (2006), 6.4 percent of soldiers evacuated from Iraq and 7.2 percent from Afghanistan developed persistent psychiatric disorders. More recent estimates suggest an even higher prevalence of emotional/mental casualties; many of these soldiers have been diagnosed with PTSD (Manderscheid 2007). This sudden surge in the need for treatment has stimulated a new form of graded assisted exposure therapy using the technology of virtual reality (Spira et al. 2006). By definition, people with PTSD avoid stimuli that remind them of their trauma. Virtual reality uses computer graphics to recreate the visual environment of the traumatic events experienced and described from the point of view of the patient. The patient controls the experience, using a joystick or computer mouse to navigate through the computer-generated visual field. As with all exposure therapies, the virtual reality environments are meant to trigger emotional responses. In this context, such arousal also provides access to traumatic memories, which the patient may then be able to place in appropriate context. Using techniques supplied by the therapist, the patient learns to encounter triggering stimuli without responding symptomatically, achieving "mastery over cognitive, affective, and physiologic arousal" (Spira et al. 2006, p. 47).

The use of virtual reality may apply particularly to traumatized soldiers, building on their expectation of personalized treatment, their familiarity with technology, and their secular, individualized understanding of trauma. It shows great promise for other traumatic conditions in groups with similar experiences, such as survivors of motor vehicle accidents, rape, or fires, in Western countries. However, one cannot directly extrapolate these studies to the treatment of PTSD after natural disasters in different parts of the world, as in survivors of catastrophes such as the Southeast Asian tsunami of 2004, Hurricane Katrina in Louisiana in 2005, or the spate of earthquakes devastating Haiti, Chile, Pakistan, and Indonesia in 2009–10. Culturally syntonic treatments relying on shared rituals of mourning, family intervention, and activities related to community building are likely to play a more prominent role than purely evidence-based CBT for these and similar groups.

Obsessive-Compulsive Disorder

According to Abramowitz (1997), exposure with response prevention (ERP) is the psychotherapy of choice for OCD, but he has also shown that cognitive approaches are "at least as effective as exposure procedures" (p. 44). This similarity may reflect the significant overlap between ERP and cognitive approaches. ERP involves exposure to symptom triggers under conditions that may lead the patient to challenge dysfunctional beliefs; cognitive approaches may challenge these same beliefs through cognitive restructuring.

Cordioli at al. (2003) compared patients receiving a twelve-week group CBT with a control (waiting-list) group of patients and found that the group CBT reduced OCD symptoms and improved quality of life. In a follow-up study to evaluate the efficacy of group CBT compared with sertraline for OCD symptoms, Sousa et al. (2006) found that both were effective in reducing symptoms and improving participants' quality of life over a twelve-week period. They also found that patients receiving the group CBT displayed a greater reduction in the intensity of compulsions, a decreased percentage of OCD symptoms, and a higher rate of full remission than those who received only sertraline.

Considerations for Evidence-Based Practice

Antony and Rowa (2005) highlight several issues related to evidence-based treatment of anxiety. Critical evaluation of such data requires attention to what measures are used, how they are used, and how well they correlate with fear or anxiety ratings on well-standardized instruments. These authors ponder whether "we should be developing assessment strategies for the most important dimensions that are thought to be relevant across disorders, regardless of what the most appropriate diagnostic label or labels may be" (p. 257). They note that the current disorder-based approach to classifying anxiety and its treatment does little to guide the choice of therapeutic technique. A particular method may not be relevant for a given patient, even if that person "meets criteria" for a given study diagnosis. Conversely, some strategies may be neglected for a patient who is not diagnosed with the problem for which the interventions were designed. This disjunction between methods and targets of treatment compromises efforts to broaden the evidence base for psychotherapy. Antony and Rowa recommend supplementing or replacing DSM diagnoses with other criteria, including such patient-specific assessment data as idiographic diaries, monitoring forms, and behavioral tests. Such assessment strategies allow for a closer view of changes in patients' symptoms and social functioning. They advocate, for example, using tools such as the Anxiety Sensitivity Index or the Body Sensations Questionnaire in clinical settings to measure interoceptive cues that trigger anxiety and fear. They further advocate the clinical use of behavioral diaries cataloging avoidance patterns. Using such measures would permit a more reliable assessment of treatment outcomes in the world of clinical practice and would make it easier to identify the patients that research suggests may benefit from a particular treatment.

In summary, anxiety disorders can be chronic but manageable illnesses. Research finds "CBT to be the nonpharmacologic treatment of choice for anxiety disorder symptoms across diagnoses" (Schweitzer and Miller 2005, p. 85).

Behavioral Interventions for Other Specific Conditions

Some evidence supports behavioral interventions, usually CBT, for symptoms of borderline personality disorder, schizophrenia, and other disorders. However, the measures used and the specific symptoms described vary widely, making definitive conclusions elusive.

Borderline Personality Disorder

Borderline personality disorder (BPD) seriously burdens the health care system, with admissions to psychiatric hospitals and rates of suicide more than fifty times higher than in the general population (Brazier et al. 2006). It also occurs comorbidly with a variety of other conditions, particularly substance abuse, chronic pain, or mood disorders. Leichsenring and Leibing (2003) did a meta-analysis comparing the effectiveness of psychodynamic therapy and CBT in the treatment of BPD. Although they found evidence supporting the effectiveness of both modalities, they noted that a major limitation of their analysis was the small number of credible studies to review. They analyzed fourteen studies of psychodynamic therapy and eleven of CBT, conducted between 1974 and 2001. The authors further noted that the effect sizes could not be directly compared between the two types of therapy, because the groups studied did not use comparable experimental methods: some were randomized controlled trials, some used a comparison method, and others were naturalistic observational studies. Leichsenring and Leibing concluded that, while the two approaches seem to be effective, further research is needed to evaluate specific forms of psychotherapy for specific types of personality dysfunctions.

Specific therapies are becoming more common for patients diagnosed with BPD. A prominent example is DBT, which aims to foster behavioral control, stability, and connection with the care provider. Brazier et al. (2006) extensively reviewed evidence-based therapies for BPD. Their findings, based on nine randomized controlled trials and one non–randomized controlled trial, were inconclusive. They note that: (1) some evidence supports the claim that DBT is more effective than "treatment as usual" for chronically parasuicidal and drug-dependent women with BPD; (2) DBT-oriented therapy is more effective than client-centered therapy; (3) partial hospitalization showed superior improvement compared with treatment as usual; (4) manual-assisted CBT is no more effective than treatment as usual; and (5) interpersonal group therapy is no more effective than individual mentalization-based partial hospitalization. The same authors compared the costs of various treatments. They found mixed results with DBT, concluding that, despite some potential savings, the findings did not demonstrate that DBT is more cost-effective than other methods for treating patients with BPD.

Schizophrenia

The United Kingdom's National Institute for Clinical Excellence guidelines recommend that CBT be offered to all individuals with a diagnosis of schizophrenia who experience persistent positive symptoms. Bradshaw and Mairs (2006) reviewed five studies using group CBT with such patients. Although all the reviewed studies had methodological flaws, the authors concluded that group CBT was more effective than treatment as usual in reducing levels of anxiety. Reductions in auditory hallucinations were inconsistent. Other studies report similar difficulty in reducing or maintaining reduced hallucinations with behavioral interventions (Buccheri et al. 2004).

Wykes et al.'s study (2005) on the impact of group CBT on auditory hallucinations produced similarly mixed results. The authors found that treatment improved the patients' social behavior, probably because of the group interactions. Although they did not find significant differences in total symptom scores between the group CBT and control groups, group CBT provided participants with an opportunity to practice their social skills while "testing out abnormal beliefs that had previously reduced their social contact" (p. 208). Wykes and colleagues concluded that CBT, used in a group setting, induces some positive changes for persons with schizophrenia.

Bechdolf et al. (2004) compared group CBT with group psychoeducation for patients with schizophrenia. They found that those who received CBT were readmitted to a hospital less frequently during the six-month follow-up period. However, both approaches, CBT and psychoeducation, "led to significant clinical improvement at the end of treatment, and at 6–month follow-up" (p. 25). These authors explain the difference between the two treatments by suggesting that group CBT interventions change complex behavior patterns that can influence treatment adherence and vulnerability to relapse, along with other factors that lead to rehospitalization. Psychoeducation, on the other hand, may have less impact because of its focus on knowledge and illness concepts rather than on behavior.

Finally, older patients with chronic schizophrenia may benefit from psychotherapeutic intervention. Granholm et al. (2005) report on a randomized clinical trial of older persons with schizophrenia or schizoaffective disorder. Patients who received treatment as usual plus cognitive behavioral skills training performed social functioning activities significantly more frequently than patients in the treatment-as-usual group. The authors note that participants in the cognitive behavioral skills training group had excellent group attendance, homework completion, and participation; this research clearly showed that the patients were able to learn the content of the intervention.

Overall, studies of the efficacy of cognitive behavioral interventions in serious and costly disorders such as borderline personality disorder and schizophrenia suggest that core symptoms may not be amenable to such approaches but that the demoralization, isolation, and distress that attend any chronic illness respond to therapeutic attention. As with the treatment of depression and anxiety, therapies of this nature reduce confusion, focus on what patients can do to cope with their conditions, provide opportunities for rewarding experiences, and may mitigate disorders that the treatments do not necessarily "cure."

Behaviorally Focused Interventions for Children and Adolescents

Well-designed research evaluating behaviorally focused interventions for children and adolescents is rare, though strides are being made in this area. Weersing and Brent (2006, p. 953) note that despite recent controversy, CBT for depression in young people "seems to be a promising intervention and a rational treatment choice." Methods that teach therapeutic principles to parents or teachers may also be of benefit (see chapter 12).

Barkley (2004) reports that behavioral therapies are generally ineffective for attention-deficit/hyperactivity disorder (ADHD). Moreover, the results of research studies often transfer poorly to naturalistic settings. He found that early, small studies showed promising results for CBT or cognitive therapy alone, but identified few, if any, significant treatment-specific effects. At the same time, Barkley suggests that parent training for children with ADHD can help reduce parent-child conflicts. Training parents involves elements of cognitive treatments, such as problem solving, communication, and cognitive restructuring.

Involving parents shows even clearer benefits in the treatment of anxiety disorders in children. A small study of thirty anxious children between the ages of eight and eighteen compared thirteen families in a treatment group and seventeen families in a waiting-list group (Bögels and Siqueland 2006). Research therapists taught CBT skills to both parents and children. The authors found reduced child and parental anxiety, reduced dysfunctional beliefs in both children and parents, and improved parental rearing and family functioning in the treated group. Furthermore, fathers, but not mothers, improved on self-reported fear. Bögels and Siqueland note that fathers had reported elevated fear at baseline while mothers had not. They conclude that family-based CBT offers a good alternative to CBT with individual children.

Group CBT was also tested against sertraline in a randomized clinical trial for treatment of OCD in children and adolescents (N = 40) aged nine to seventeen years. Treatment stretched over a nine-month period (Asbar et al. 2005). Twelve weeks of treatment led to improvement in both groups, but relapse occurred at a significantly lower rate in the group CBT subsample. The authors note that more than 50 percent of subjects who received sertraline in the first twelve weeks required its reintroduction during the follow-up period, so they were not included in the final analysis. The report's conclusions state that group CBT "may enhance adherence to treatment through providing modeling, peer support, and opportunities to share and exchange information about their symptomatology and their exposure interventions during sessions" (p. 1134). When parents were included in the treatment, clinical outcomes seemed to improve as well.

Cognitive behavioral therapy is "the most studied nonpharmacologic intervention for the treatment of depression in youth" (Weersing and Brent 2006, p. 939), with high effect sizes identified in meta-analyses conducted in the 1990s. Weersing and Brent state that new findings cast doubt on these strong outcomes. However, in re-reviewing twenty-two trials of CBT for depression in children and adolescents, they conclude that CBT is effective for mild to moderate cases of depression. Clinicians not constrained by research protocols should, of course, consider adding medication to CBT—a combination that, incidentally, proves more effective than either treatment alone.

Two helpful reviews of treatment interventions confirm Weersing and Brent's observations. Scott, Mughelli, and Deas (2005) provide an overview of controlled studies of anxiety disorders in children and adolescents. These studies compared CBT, family-based interventions, and pharmacotherapy. Results suggested benefits from CBT, as well as from pharmacotherapy, in treating anxiety disorders. However, small sample sizes and other methodological issues will require additional research to be resolved. A second review (O'Kearney, Anstey, and von Sanden 2006) examined the efficacy of behavioral therapy and CBT versus pharmacotherapy for pediatric OCD. Based on their findings, these authors consider behavioral and cognitive behavioral therapies as "promising" treatments that lead to better outcomes when combined with medication, compared with medication alone.

Given recent controversies over the dangers of psychotropic medication in the pediatric and adolescent population, studies suggesting the utility of cognitive behavioral approaches, especially when applied by family members, should stimulate researchers and clinicians to find ways to make such therapies more widely available to young patients.

Other Uses of Behavioral and Specific Therapies

Behavioral approaches have also been applied in marital therapy. Shadish and Baldwin (2005) performed a meta-analysis (N = 30 randomized studies) on the effects of behavioral marital therapy (BMT). Comparing this therapy with no-treatment controls, they found better outcomes for the BMT group. Dunn and Schwebel (1995) found that BMT, cognitive BMT, and insight-oriented marital therapy were all equally effective in helping couples change behaviors. All also improved couples' general assessment of their relationships. However, cognitive BMT was the only one of these approaches that induced significant changes in relationship-related cognitions in the posttherapy period.

Finally, implementing behavioral therapy via the internet is an emerging field of study. Spek et al. (2006) completed a meta-analysis of twelve randomized controlled trials comparing internet-based CBT for symptoms of depression and anxiety. They found that this unique treatment option had stronger results for anxiety than for depressive symptoms. Addition of therapist support to a computer-based treatment fostered even greater improvement. Advan-

tages and related benefits from this approach, particularly anonymity and flexibility, are duly emphasized. However, the authors note many limitations in
their analysis, including the small number of studies reviewed (N = 12) and
similarly small numbers of subjects within each study. Kenardy et al. (2003)
have developed computer-augmented CBT for panic disorder. The advantages
of such treatment are obvious, not so much in terms of outcome as in possible
cost effectiveness and potential for wide application. The internet makes such
help available internationally or for those who are unable to report to therapy
in person. Kenardy and colleagues note that "the use of computers as an innovative adjunctive therapy tool received some support and merits further
investigation" (p. 1074).

Conclusion

Clearly, systematic research supports the effectiveness of behavioral approaches
in a variety of disorders and clinical settings. Applications of behavioral therapies or cognitive behavioral therapy extend beyond the treatment of anxiety
and depression to borderline personality disorder, schizophrenia, and family
conflicts. These therapies have proven beneficial for persons in individual,
family, group, marital, and computer-based applications. They benefit individuals across a variety of age groups. Emphasizing that CBT is one of the most
extensively researched forms of psychotherapy, Butler et al. (2006) cite more
than 325 published outcome studies on cognitive behavioral interventions.

Moving from research to clinical care requires consideration of factors that
may confound the research findings. Outside a research setting, many uncontrolled factors influence the choice of any specific or behavioral technique.
Environmental, work, or family conditions and their meaning vary widely,
even within groups of patients who are homogeneous for the specific condition
described in the research. Because the patient must ultimately execute the
treatment plan, it is vital that the program makes sense to him or her. This, in
turn, requires a therapist to understand the patient's world and adapt to it, even
if this step moves the therapist away from the test protocol. Cultural factors,
including belief in science, religious practices, or mistrust of professional authority, may influence the expression of symptoms, affect measures of outcome, and diffuse or intensify the impact of treatment interventions (Antony
and Rowa 2005). Enhanced measurements and more well-controlled studies
into general and condition-specific cognitive and cognitive-behavioral treat-

ments will lead to ever more useful guidelines, but the application of research findings in the world of clinical practice will always involve uncertainty, variation, and unpredictable outcomes. It is here, as happens with all psychotherapeutic approaches, that messages such as Frank's emphasis on the role of hope, the value of remoralization, and the strengths of a solid therapist-patient relationship will exercise their solidly ecumenical impact.

REFERENCES

Ablon, J. S., and Jones, E. E. 2002. Validity of controlled clinical trials of psychotherapy: findings from the NIMH Treatment of Depression Collaborative Research Program. *American Journal of Psychiatry* 159:775–83.

Abramowitz, J. 1997. Effectiveness of psychological and pharmacological treatments for obsessive compulsive disorder: a quantitative review. *Journal of Consulting and Clinical Psychology* 65:44–52.

Antony, M. M., and Rowa, K. 2005. Evidence-based assessment of anxiety disorders in adults. *Psychological Assessment* 17:256–66.

Asbar, R. R., Castillo, R., Ito, L. M., LaTorre, M. R., Moreira, M. N., and Lotufo-Neto, F. 2005. Group cognitive-behavioral therapy versus sertraline for the treatment of children and adolescents with obsessive-compulsive disorder. *Journal of the American Academy of Child and Adolescent Psychiatry* 44:1128–36.

Barkley, R. A. 2004. Adolescents with attention-deficit/hyperactivity disorder: an overview of empirically based treatments. *Journal of Psychiatric Practice* 10:39–56.

Bechdolf, A., Knost, B., Kuntermann, C., Schiller, S., Klosterkötter, J., Hambrecht, M., and Pukrop, R. 2004. A randomized comparison of group cognitive-behavioural therapy and group psychoeducation in patients with schizophrenia. *Acta Psychiatrica Scandinavica* 110:21–28.

Beck, J. S. (ed.). 2005. *Cognitive Therapy for Challenging Problems: What to Do When the Basics Don't Work*. New York: Guilford Press.

Beckham, E. E. 1990. Psychotherapy of depression at the crossroads: directions for the 1990's. *Clinical Psychology Review* 10:207–28.

Bögels, S. M., and Siqueland, L. 2006. Family cognitive behavioral therapy for children and adolescents with clinical anxiety disorder. *Journal of the American Academy of Child and Adolescent Psychiatry* 45:134–41.

Bradshaw, L. R., and Mairs, H. 2006. Group cognitive behavioural therapy for schizophrenia: a systematic review of the literature. *Journal of Psychiatric and Mental Health Nursing* 13:673–81.

Brazier, J., Tumur, I., Holmes, M., Ferriter, M., Parry, G., Dent-Brown, K., and Paisley, S. 2006. Psychological therapies including dialectical behavior therapy for borderline personality disorder: a systematic review and preliminary economic evaluation. *Health Technology Assessment* 10(35):1–136.

Brewin, C. R. 2006. Understanding cognitive behaviour therapy: a retrieval competition account. *Behaviour and Research Therapy* 44:765–84.

Buccheri, R., Trygstad, L., Dowling, G., Hopkins, R., White, K., Griffin, J. J., et al. 2004.

Long-term effects of teaching behavioral strategies for managing persistent auditory hallucinations in schizophrenia. *Journal of Psychosocial Nursing* 42:18–27.

Butler, A. C., Chapman, J. E., Forman, E. M., and Beck, A. T. 2006. The empirical status of cognitive-behavioral therapy: a review of meta-analyses. *Clinical Psychology Review* 26:17–31.

Carroll, B. J. 2006. Recent developments and controversies in depression (letter to the editor). *Lancet*, April 15, pp. 1235–36.

Chen, T., Lu, R., Chang, A., Chu, D., and Chou, K. 2006. The evaluation of cognitive-behavioral group therapy on patient depression and self esteem. *Archives of Psychiatric Nursing* 20:3–11.

Cordioli, A. V., Heldt, E., Bochi, D. B., Margis, R., de Sousa, M., Tonello, J. F., et al. 2003. Cognitive-behavioral group therapy in obsessive-compulsive disorder: a randomized clinical trial. *Psychotherapy and Psychosomatics* 72:211–16.

Cuijpers, P., van Straten, A., and Warmerdam, L. 2007. Behavioral activation treatments of depression: a meta-analysis. *Clinical Psychology Review* 27:318–26.

Curran, J., Machin, C., and Gournay, K. 2006. Cognitive behavioural therapy for patients with anxiety and depression. *Nursing Standard* 21(7):44–52.

Dannon, P. N., Gon-Usishkin, M., Gelbert, A., Lowengrub, K., and Grunhaus, L. 2004. Cognitive behavioral group therapy in panic disorder patients: the efficacy of CBGT versus drug treatment. *Annals of Clinical Psychiatry* 16:41–46.

Dugas, M. J., Freeston, M. H., Ladouceur, R., Leger, E., Langlois, F., Provencher, M. D., and Boisvert, J. 2003. Group cognitive-behavioral therapy for generalized anxiety disorder: treatment outcome and long-term follow-up. *Journal of Counseling and Clinical Psychology* 71:821–25.

Dunn, R., and Schwebel, A. 1995. Meta-analytic review of marital therapy outcome research. *Journal of Family Psychology* 9:58–68.

Ebmeier, K. P., Donaghey, C., and Steele, J. D. 2006. Recent developments and current controversies in depression. *Lancet* 367:153–67.

Feldman, G. 2007. Cognitive and behavioral therapies for depression: overview, new directions, and practical recommendations for dissemination. *Psychiatric Clinics of North America* 30:39–50.

Foa, E. B. 2006. Psychosocial therapy for posttraumatic stress disorder. *Journal of Clinical Psychiatry* 67(suppl. 2):40–45.

Foa, E., and Rothbaum, B. 1998. *Treating the Trauma of Rape: Cognitive-Behavioral Therapy for PTSD.* New York: Guilford Press.

Frank, J. D., and Frank, J. B. 1991. *Persuasion and Healing: A Comparative Study of Psychotherapy.* Baltimore: Johns Hopkins University Press.

Free, M., and Oei, R. 1989. Biological and psychological processes in the treatment and maintenance of depression. *Clinical Psychology Review* 9:653–88.

Free, M. L., Oei, T. P. S., and Appleton, C. 1998. Biological and psychological processes in recovery from depression during cognitive therapy. *Journal of Behavior Therapy and Experimental Psychiatry* 29:213–26.

Freeman, A., and Diefenbeck, C. 2005. Depression. In S. Freeman and A. Freeman (eds.), *Cognitive Behavior Therapy in Nursing Practice* (pp. 51–84). New York: Springer.

Friedman, M. 2006. Posttraumatic stress disorder among military returnees from Afghanistan and Iraq. *American Journal of Psychiatry* 163:586–93.

Goodwin, C. 1999. *A History of Modern Psychology.* New York: John Wiley.

Granholm, E., McQuaid, J. R., McClure, F. S., Auslander, L. A., Perivoliotis, D., Pedrelli, P., et al. 2005. A randomized, controlled trail of cognitive behavioral social skills training for middle-aged and older outpatients with chronic schizophrenia (online). *American Journal of Psychiatry* 162:520–30.

Heldt, A., Blaya, C., Osolan, L., Kipper, L., Teruchkin, B., Otto, M. W., et al. 2006. Quality of life and treatment outcome in panic disorder: cognitive behavior group therapy effects in patients refractory to medication treatment. *Psychotherapy and Psychosomatics* 75:183–86.

Kanfer, F. H., and Goldstein, A. P. 1991. Introduction. In F. H. Kanfer and A. P. Goldstein (eds.), *Helping People Change: A Textbook of Methods*, 4th ed. (pp. 1–19). Boston: Allyn and Bacon.

Kaplan, A. 2006. Hidden combat wounds: extensive, deadly, costly (online). *Psychiatric Times* 15(1):1–3.

Kazantzis, N., and Ronan, K. R. 2006. Can between-session (homework) activities be considered a common factor in psychotherapy? *Journal of Psychotherapy Integration* 16:115–27.

Kenardy, J. A., Johnston, D. W., Thomson, A., Dow, M. G. T., Newman, M. G., and Taylor, C. B. 2003. A comparison of delivery methods of cognitive-behavioral therapy for panic disorder: an international multicenter trial. *Journal of Consulting and Clinical Psychology* 71:1068–75.

Kutney, A. M. 2006. An examination of psychiatric-mental health outcomes from the perspectives of logical positivism and phenomenology. *Journal of the American Psychiatric Nurses Association* 12:22–27.

Kwon, S., and Oei, T. P. S. 2003. Cognitive change processes in a group cognitive behavior therapy of depression. *Journal of Behavior Therapy and Experimental Psychiatry* 34:73–85.

Leichsenring, F., and Leibing, E. D. 2003. The effectiveness of psychodynamic therapy and cognitive behavior therapy in the treatment of personality disorders: a meta-analysis (online). *American Journal of Psychiatry* 160:1223–32.

Manderscheid, R. 2007. Helping veterans return: community, family, and job. *Archives of Psychiatric Nursing* 21:122–24.

Norton, P. J., and Hope, D. A. 2005. Preliminary evaluation of a broad-spectrum cognitive-behavioral group therapy for anxiety. *Journal of Behavior Therapy and Experimental Psychiatry* 36:79–97.

Oei, T. P. S., Bullbeck, K., and Campbell, J. M. 2006. Cognitive change process during group cognitive behaviour therapy for depression. *Journal of Affective Disorders* 92:231–41.

Oei, T. P. S., and Free, M. 1995. Does cognitive behavior therapy validate cognitive models of mood disorders? A review of empirical evidence. *International Journal of Psychology* 30:145–79.

Oei, T. P. S., and Sullivan, L. M. 1999. Cognitive changes following recovery from depression in a group cognitive-behaviour therapy program. *Australian and New Zealand Journal of Psychiatry* 33:407–15.

O'Kearney, R. T., Anstey, K. J., and von Sanden, C. 2006. Behavioural and cognitive behavioural therapy for obsessive compulsive disorder in children and adolescents. *Cochrane Database Systematic Reviews* 4:CD004856.

Parker, G., and Fletcher, K. 2007. Treating depression with the evidence-based psychotherapies: a critique of the evidence. *Acta Psychiatrica Scandinavica* 115:352–59.

Peplau, H. 1952. *Interpersonal Relations in Nursing: A Conceptual Frame of Reference for Psychodynamic Nursing.* New York: G. P. Putman.

Salovey, P., and Singer, J. A. 1991. Cognitive behavior modification. In F. H. Kanfer and A. P. Goldstein (eds.), *Helping People Change: A Textbook of Methods,* 4th ed. (pp. 361–95). Boston: Allyn and Bacon.

Schweitzer, P., and Miller, C. 2005. Anxiety-spectrum disorders. In M. Freeman and A. Freeman (eds.), *Cognitive Behavior Therapy in Nursing Practice* (pp. 85–112). New York: Springer.

Scott, R. W., Mughelli, K., and Deas, D. 2005. An overview of controlled studies of anxiety disorders treatment in children and adolescents. *Journal of the National Medical Association* 97:13–24.

Shadish, W. R., and Baldwin, S. A. 2005. Effects of behavioral marital therapy: a meta-analysis of randomized controlled trials. *Journal of Counseling and Clinical Psychology* 73:6–14.

Sijbrandij, M., Olff, M., Reitsma, J. B., Carlier, I. V. E., de Vries, M. H., and Gersons, B. P. R. 2007. Treatment of acute posttraumatic stress disorder with brief cognitive behavioral therapy: a randomized controlled trial. *American Journal of Psychiatry* 164:82–90.

Sousa, M. B., Isolan, L. R., Oliveira, R. R., Manfro, G. G., and Cordioli, A. V. 2006. A randomized clinical trial of cognitive-behavioral group therapy and sertraline in the treatment of obsessive-compulsive disorder. *Journal of Clinical Psychiatry* 67: 1133–39.

Spek, V., Cuijpers, P., Nyklicek, I., Riper, H., Keyzer, J., and Pop, V. 2006. Internet-based cognitive behaviour therapy for symptoms of depression and anxiety: a meta-analysis. *Psychological Medicine* 37:319–28.

Spira, J., Pyne, J., Wiederhold, B., Wiederhold, M., Graap, K., and Riaao, A. 2006. Virtual reality and other experiential therapies for combat-related posttraumatic stress disorder. *Primary Psychiatry* 13(3):43–49.

Stevens, A. 1996. A framework for intervention. In J. Turnbull and S. Marshall (eds.), *Cognitive Behavior Therapy: An Introduction to Theory and Practice* (pp. 91–120). Philadelphia: Baillière Tindall.

Turnbull, J. 1996. The context of therapy. In J. Turnbull and S. Marshall (eds.), *Cognitive Behavior Therapy: An Introduction to Theory and Practice* (pp. 11–28). Philadelphia: Baillière Tindall.

Turnbull, J., and Marshall, S. 1996. Introduction: the aims of this book and how to use it. In J. Turnbull and S. Marshall (eds.), *Cognitive Behavior Therapy: An Introduction to Theory and Practice* (pp. 1–10). Philadelphia: Baillière Tindall.

Wampold, B. E., Minami, T., Baskin, T. W., and Tierney, S. C. 2002. A meta-(re)analysis of the effects of cognitive therapy versus "other therapies" for depression. *Journal of Affective Disorders* 68:159–65.

Weersing, V. R., and Brent, D. A. 2006. Cognitive behavioral therapy for depression in youth. *Child and Adolescent Psychiatric Clinics of North America* 15:939–57.

Wykes, T., Hayward, P., Thomas, N., Green, N., Surguladze, S., Fannon, D., and Landau, S. 2005. What are the effects of group cognitive behaviour therapy for voices? A randomised control trial. *Schizophrenia Research* 77:201–10.

CHAPTER 12

Weighing Evidence for Common and Specific Factors in Psychotherapy with Children

Natoshia Raishevich Cunningham, Ph.D.,
Thomas Ollendick, Ph.D., and
Peter S. Jensen, M.D.

"Now you talk like a reasonable child," said Humpty Dumpty, looking very much pleased. "I meant by 'impenetrability' that we've had enough of that subject, and it would be just as well if you'd mention what you mean to do next, as I suppose you don't mean to stop here all the rest of your life."
—*Through the Looking Glass*

Because they focus on the conquest of specific symptoms, cognitive and behavioral therapies may be more effective than evocative ones in heightening the sense of mastery and in generally increasing self-confidence. They teach patients to confront situations and inner feelings they have previously avoided, thereby opening up new opportunities for learning and growth. These therapies seem effective in treating depression, and for such specific symptoms as panic attacks, compulsions and phobias.

—*PERSUASION AND HEALING*, 1991, P. 240

S ince publication of the first edition of *Persuasion and Healing* (1961), our understanding of the necessary ingredients of effective psychotherapy has grown substantially. In the main, the book's key insights about the centrality of empathic, healing relationships, informed by keen appreciation and respect for patients' cultural contexts, have withstood rigorous scrutiny. Arguably, these concepts apply even more strongly to child psychotherapies, in which effectiveness depends both on the therapist's relationships with the child *and* the parents and on the therapist's understanding of the cultural context of the child's family.

Though child and adolescent psychotherapy research has lagged behind studies in adults, the literature pertaining to the treatment of children's mental disorders has grown exponentially in recent years (Wang et al. 2003). This surge of publications has been a mixed blessing. In many ways, the field resembles the entrepreneurial decades of the 1960s and 1970s, when adult therapies ranging from abreaction to Zen far outran careful research meant to develop or evaluate them. More than 90 percent of the more than 550 "psychotherapies" claimed as useful to treat childhood disorders have not been studied empirically (Kazdin 2000). The field of child psychotherapy cries out for rigorous studies of the efficacy and effectiveness of both common and novel treatments.

About ten years before *Persuasion and Healing*, Eysenck (1952) asserted that psychotherapeutic practices were no more effective than the passage of time, a claim that Frank and others repeatedly refuted, citing evidence from numerous well-designed studies in adults. Nevertheless, early reviews of the child psychotherapy literature (Levitt 1957, 1963) supported Eysenck's assertion and led many clinicians and researchers to question the efficacy of psychotherapy for both adults and children. Even in more recent years, Bickman and colleagues noted that a large, expensive attempt to provide optimal mental health services for children and adolescents was of no more benefit than usual care provided to a control group, combined with the passage of time—the so-called clock-setting cure (Bickman et al. 1995; Bickman, Noser, and Summerfelt 1999; Lambert and Bickman 2004).

Notably, the early discouraging reviews stimulated valuable further studies of developmental psychopathology, diagnostic nomenclature, and assessment and treatment of children and adolescents. Researchers now typically focus on the ingredients of effective care, not just how it is organized or whether it is empathic and "family friendly." Current research in child psychotherapy seeks to determine the conditions under which certain treatments are effective, moving past the older question of *whether* therapy is effective. This has led to an exponential increase in studies of treatment process and outcome, using more rigorous experimental designs (Durlak et al. 1995; Kazdin 2000). Four major meta-analyses examining the effects of child psychotherapy (Casey and Berman 1985; Weisz, Weiss, Alicke, and Klotz 1987; Weisz, Weiss, Han, et al. 1995) counter the findings of Lambert and Bickman, offering good evidence that certain forms of child psychotherapy are beneficial for children and their families. Specifically, the current research suggests that *some* of the psychotherapies for children may be superior to waiting-list and attention-placebo conditions, although exceptions abound (Jensen et al. 2005).

Merely demonstrating the efficacy of therapy in general or of one particular method against placebo leaves many questions unanswered. *Persuasion and Healing* was prescient in highlighting the difficult next step: differentiating among therapies and demonstrating that specific approaches might be best for particular conditions. Every edition of the book evaluated new claims of those who touted the superiority of their brand of treatment for adults. In the end, the book adopted the agnostic position that, with the exception of exposure for anxiety, such assertions were unproven.

Meta-analyses published in the decades since the third edition of *Persuasion and Healing* (Frank and Frank 1991) provide new evidence that some forms of psychotherapy work to correct certain behavioral, emotional, and social problems in children of particular ages, under specified conditions. This step necessarily precedes that of demonstrating that any particular therapy outperforms any other active therapy. "Comparative effectiveness" research, much sought by policymakers, remains an unattainable goal for the field, with the possible exception of the few studies that compare psychotherapy with medication.

This chapter briefly reviews the current state of research in child and adolescent psychotherapy (see also chapters 1 and 11). Specifically, we attempt to document the movement toward evidence-based practices, defined here as evidence derived from randomized controlled trials (RCTs) (Ollendick and King 2004). In RCTs, patient-subjects are randomly assigned to treatment or to some control condition, such as a waiting-list, attention-placebo condition or an alternative form of treatment.

After defining empirically supported treatments and examining their current status, we focus on certain trends emerging from a systematic search of the literature. In particular, we emphasize recent investigations that compile reports on types and targets of treatment. Next, we illustrate and discuss current issues associated with evidence-based treatments and their development. Beyond discussing differential effects of various treatments, we examine the use of treatment manuals, relationship variables, and the challenge of aligning clinical practice with rigorously tested, evidence-based approaches.

Defining the Domain of Empirically Supported Treatments

In 1995, the Task Force on Promotion and Dissemination of Psychological Procedures of the Society of Clinical Psychology (American Psychological Association's Division 12) published its report on empirically supported psychological treatments. The task force reviewed only reports that described specific treatments, client characteristics that predicted treatment outcome, and the therapeutic mechanisms thought to be associated with behavioral changes.

The task force proposed three categories of evidence for treatment efficacy: (1) *well-established treatments*, (2) *probably efficacious treatments*, and (3) *experimental treatments*. Treatments could be placed initially in one category then moved to another, depending on the empirical support available for that treatment over time. The report labeled as *well-established* both specific psychotherapeutic approaches that had proven superior to placebo and commonly accepted psychosocial treatments, including education and support. In classifying a treatment as well-established, the task force imposed the further requirement that two independent investigatory teams must have provided evidence supporting its effects. They reserved the term *probably efficacious* for interventions shown by at least one research group to be superior only to a waiting-list or no-treatment control condition. The parameters for either category required the standardization of the intervention through adherence to treatment manuals in the study design. Reports also had to specify subjects' demographic characteristics. In its review, the task force considered only studies using "good" designs, either valid comparisons between groups or appropriately controlled single-case designs. "Good" designs allow the conclusion that any benefits observed are effects of treatment, not merely attributable to chance or such confounding factors as passage of time, the effects of psychological assessment, or the heterogeneity of participants in the various treatment conditions (Chambless and Hollon 1998; for a fuller discussion of research design issues, see Kazdin 1998; Kendall, Flannery-Schroeder, and Ford 1999).

The task force reiterated that the strongest evidence of efficacy comes from randomized controlled trials—group designs in which participants are assigned randomly to the treatment of interest or to one or more comparison conditions. The report also called for the development of additional treatments and for better designed studies of existing ones.

Empirically Supported Child Psychotherapies

The 1995 report of the Task Force on Promotion and Dissemination of Psychological Procedures identified eighteen well-established treatments and seven probably efficacious treatments. Of these twenty-five efficacious treatments, they found adequate controlled research supporting only *three* well-established treatments for children (behavior modification for developmentally disabled individuals, behavior modification for enuresis and encopresis, and parent training programs for children with oppositional behavior) and *one* probably efficacious treatment for children (habit reversal and control techniques for children with tics and related disorders). Though the numbers are sobering, the report noted that the list of empirically supported treatments was *representative* of efficacious treatments, rather than *exhaustive*.

Given the need to identify additional psychosocial treatments effective with children, concurrent task forces were set up by the Society of Clinical Psychology and the Society of Clinical Child and Adolescent Psychology (Division 53 of the American Psychological Association). Subsequently, these groups reviewed empirically supported treatments for children with autism, anxiety disorders, attention-deficit/hyperactivity disorder (ADHD), depression, and oppositional and conduct problem disorders. Like the earlier report, these reviews were not meant to generate an exhaustive list of treatments that could be considered empirically supported. Rather, they sought to identify effective treatments for a limited number of disorders seen frequently in clinical settings serving children and adolescents (Lonigan, Elbert, and Johnson 1998).

Additionally, Chambless and Ollendick (2001) reviewed the work of other scholars instrumental in cataloging empirically supported treatments for children. For example, edited books by Roth and Fonagy (*What Works for Whom?*; 1996) and Nathan and Gorman (*A Guide to Treatments That Work*; 1995) identified some previously overlooked treatments while also evaluating many of those discussed by the Society of Clinical Psychology and the Society of Clinical Child and Adolescent Psychology. In rating treatments, various groups have applied criteria similar to those used by Division 12, although some relatively minor differences are evident (for details, see Chambless and Ollendick 2001). In many instances, two or more of these groups identified the same treatments as effective.

Overall, these reviews affirmed the existence of well-established and/or probably efficacious treatments for a few serious and costly child and adolescent problems such as the already mentioned behavior modification for developmentally disabled individuals and parent training programs for children with oppositional behavior. At the same time, these reviews could not identify well-established treatments for such common problems as autism, childhood depression, or childhood anxiety. The groups classified several interventions for these childhood disorders as probably efficacious, but rigorous evidence supporting these treatments has remained relatively modest until the present time.

Since the publication of these reviews, evidence has been accumulating about the effectiveness of defined psychosocial interventions for eating disorders in children and adolescents (Keel and Haedt 2008). These disorders are manifestly both behavioral and psychological, and despite their severity (anorexia nervosa entails a shocking mortality rate of around 10%), they do respond to a variety of psychotherapeutic approaches, particularly those that normalize eating behavior before addressing other areas of distress. Several small but well-designed trials document the efficacy of family-based therapy for adolescents and children with anorexia nervosa, and for either family-based therapy or individually focused therapy for adolescents with bulimia. Further evidence from the results of several multisite studies from Stanford University and the University of Chicago should become available within the next few years (Lock and Fitzpatrick 2009).

Building upon the work of task forces and scholarly reviews, the scientific community as a whole has adopted methods and standards for meta-analyses, the compilation and critical comparison of data from multiple studies. Meta-analyses provide the firmest foundation for evidence-based practice. By comparing findings in large numbers of subjects and emphasizing adequate study design and outcome, meta-analyses facilitate the translation of disparate research findings into coherent approaches that practitioners can adopt with confidence. Often, however, the rigorous designs required for inclusion in meta-analyses must be adapted when therapists attempt to implement treatment in clinical settings—where patients may not meet the full criteria applied to research subjects, therapists have less access to or interest in standardized training, quantitative measurement is not emphasized, and nonquantifiable qualities of the treatment may be of crucial importance. This chapter adds new data to the task force reports, offering a systematic review of information from abstracts of research articles on psychotherapy with children and adolescents. In particular, we discuss information that reflects changes in diagnostic categories and examine the treatment modalities most frequently studied in investigations of outcome.

An Overview of Trends in Child Psychotherapy Studies

We conducted a systematic literature review using Medline and PsychInfo databases to examine the general frequency of RCTs and broad trends in the literature, from the point at which this type of empirical studies first began to emerge. Specifically, we searched both by terms describing the symptoms and disorders most commonly addressed in RCTs and by the type of treatment modalities used to treat these symptoms. We limited our review to English-language reports of RCTs of psychotherapies for children and adolescents. Overall, and as expected, our literature search found an exponential increase over the past thirty years in the number of RCTs in the general field of psychotherapy with children, with particular increases in the rigorous testing of treatments for childhood anxiety.

In an attempt to capture the breadth of this literature, we created comprehensive search terms to operationalize *youth* and *psychotherapy* (table 12.1). The term *youth* yielded the greatest number of studies, followed by the term *psychotherapy*. Merging these search terms yielded more than sixty thousand studies; limiting these investigations specifically to RCTs left about two thousand studies. We reviewed the abstracts of these studies, finding 423 citations of RCTs of psychotherapy in youth. By way of caution, we note the possibility of limitations imposed by creation of *youth* and *psychotherapy* terms, in that a finite number of phrases were used to create each of these broader terms. Though we aimed to be comprehensive, our search strategy may have missed some appropriate citations.

From the 423 citations, we coded each abstract for the symptom type or disorder targeted in the study and the authors' description of the therapy modality. Because a given treatment may have targeted more than a single disorder or symptom type, secondary and tertiary terms were also coded. Likewise, a given study may have compared two different forms of therapy or may have employed a combination of therapeutic modalities. We coded additional or combined modalities, but for each study we selected a primary disorder or symptom and a primary therapeutic modality. The coauthors recoded a small sample of the abstracts to ensure reliability of the coding process.

Table 12.2 indicates, in descending order, the most common forms of therapy studied against controls in RCTs. The most common therapy types investigated include: cognitive behavioral therapy (CBT), broadly defined behavioral therapy (BT), parent management training / parent-child interaction therapy, family therapy, and cognitive therapy. One-third of the studies tested CBT, while one-fifth dealt with BT. It should be noted that reviewing only abstracts made it impossible to parse out all the variations of CBT and BT used across these investigations.

Table 12.1. Child Psychotherapy Literature Studies: Key for Search Criteria

Term and Adjustments	Phrases Used to Create Search Term	Number of Citations
Youth	child *or* adolescent *or* infant *or* toddler *or* teen *or* preschool *or* youth *or* latency	2,649,953
Therapy	psychotherapy *or* behavior therapy *or* aversive therapy *or* biofeedback (psychology) *or* cognitive therapy *or* desensitization, psychologic or relaxation techniques *or* psychoanalytic therapy *or* free association *or* transactional analysis *or* psychotherapeutic processes *or* psychotherapy, brief/ *or* psychotherapy, multiple/ *or* psychotherapy, rational-emotive *or* reality therapy *or* socio-environmental therapy *or* psychother *or* psychologic therap *or* cognitive therap *or* behavior therap *or* group therap *or* family therap *or* individual therap *or* behavior intervene	244,668
Youth therapy	youth term and therapy term	61,304
Limit to randomized controlled trial (RCT)	limit to RCTs	2,325
Remove duplicates	remove duplicates	2,198
Limit to English	limit to English	2,110
Appropriate for analysis		423

Our review reflects the bias of the literature toward therapies with observable techniques and behavioral outcomes that can be rigorously measured. For example, interpersonal therapy, an empirically supported but more subjectively focused treatment for child and adolescent depression, was used in less than 1 percent of the studies we investigated. As shown in table 12.2, bibliotherapy, humanistic therapy, attachment-based therapy, and hypnosis, among other approaches with long traditions and sound rationales, are also poorly represented in the domain of rigorous controlled trials. Future research should focus on developing ways to apply the methods of RCTs and systematic reviews (including meta-analytic reviews) to additional psychotherapeutic approaches in the treatment of childhood disorders.

The most common treatment foci are listed in table 12.3. These ranged from externalizing symptoms (about 20%), to depression/suicide, anxiety, ADHD,

Table 12.2.   Types of Therapy Studied in Randomized Controlled/Clinical Trials

Therapy Type	Percent	Number
Cognitive behavioral	34.68	146
Behavioral	22.57	95
Parent management training/ parent-child interaction	8.31	35
Family	7.13	30
Cognitive	6.65	28
Therapy (not otherwise specified)	5.70	24
Skills	3.09	13
Multisystemic	2.85	12
Psychoeducation	2.14	9
Neurofeedback	1.90	8
Psychodynamic	1.19	5
Art	0.95	4
Interpersonal	0.71	3
Bibliotherapy	0.48	2
Ecology-based	0.48	2
Humanistic	0.48	2
Attachment-based	0.24	1
Hypnosis	0.24	1
Peer competency	0.23	1

aggression, and finally posttraumatic stress disorder (about 7%). The externalizing symptoms category encompassed treatments specifically geared to treat ADHD and oppositional and conduct problems. However, given the nature of our abstract-level review, we were unable to further refine the specifics of the symptomatology covered by the inclusion and exclusion criteria in these studies.

Table 12.3 also reveals a paucity of randomized controlled studies that specifically examine autism-spectrum disorders, psychosis, and other childhood disorders. One very recent meta-analysis of family therapy for eating disorders (Fisher, Hetrick, and Rushford 2010) did find evidence for the value of family-based approaches for anorexia nervosa, though it emphasized the difficulty of valid meta-analysis, given the range of family approaches, inadequate measuring of adherence to treatment protocols, and the necessarily small number of subjects in family therapy studies. Future child psychotherapy research should promote methodologically sound trials that target these important, under-researched areas.

We note several limitations of our overview. First, our search was limited to Medline and PsychInfo search engines and the authors' knowledge of RCTs in children's mental health research. Perhaps more importantly, our search was primarily an abstract-level review, a necessary restriction given the large number of studies that met initial search criteria. Nonetheless, the results of our review show clear trends, in terms of the increasing frequency of the randomized control design in children's psychotherapy outcome studies over the past three decades. While our results highlight a laudable movement toward stricter methodological design, future reviews might specifically focus on types of control groups (e.g., waiting list, treatment as usual) employed in the RCTs. Some controls do not address the legitimate concern that any therapeutic relationship and/or attention to the patient's symptoms may have a stronger impact than specific therapeutic procedures (Jensen et al. 2005). However, our review could not identify trends toward greater use of attention control groups, because most studies did not describe the nature of the control condition. We were also unable to confirm the integrity of the treatments we reviewed. The abstracts often did not report whether the research treatment was administered according to a manual, rigorously adhered to by the treating therapists. A comprehensive review rather than an abstract-level review would provide such information. Similarly, additional information pertaining to treatment focus (e.g., family

Table 12.3. Treatment Focus Types

Focus	Percent	Number
Externalizing	19.66	82
Depression/suicide	17.03	71
Anxiety	17.03	71
Attention-deficit/hyperactivity disorder	14.87	62
Aggression	7.67	32
Posttraumatic stress disorder	7.43	31
Internalizing	4.32	18
Obsessive compulsive disorder	3.12	13
Resilience	2.40	1
Eating disorder	1.92	8
Social phobia	1.92	8
Conduct disorder	1.44	6
Autism	1.20	5
Oppositional defiant disorder	0.72	3
Tourette syndrome	0.48	2
Stress	0.24	1
Asperger syndrome	0.24	1
General mental health	0.24	1
Psychosis	0.24	1

therapy versus individual child therapy) and treatment design (manualization and adherence) would be beneficial. Exploration of moderators such as age and gender and of mediators such as therapeutic alliance and the cultural fit between therapists' and patients' mental models would also be of interest.

Trends in Child Psychotherapy and the Future of Child Psychotherapy Research

To identify and foster implementation of empirically supported treatments, the field must confront several major issues identified early on by Ollendick (1999): differential effectiveness, the advantages and drawbacks of expecting therapists to adhere to manualized protocols, the need for a continuing focus on the contribution of nonspecific or common factors to therapeutic outcome, and the challenges of translating the findings of rigorous, university-based research into real-life settings.

Findings of differential effectiveness confound, or appear to confound, the time-hallowed notion that no psychosocial treatment is superior to another. The insights of *Persuasion and Healing* that much of the effectiveness of psychotherapy depends on common factors (see chapter 1 in this volume) support this position, effectively challenging the competitive claims of both psychoanalysts and cognitive behavioral therapists that their methods are superior. However, once one assumes that all reasonably designed therapies include the common factors, much as all medical elixirs share similar solvents, the search for differential effectiveness takes on new meaning. Our review here identifies limited but important proof of differences in treatment effects in certain areas.

We are also in a position to address lingering concerns that the use of treatment manuals might lead to mechanical, inflexible interventions, which in turn could stifle creativity and innovation in therapy. Most therapy researchers discount this possibility, but are there certain therapists or supervisory training conditions for which such concerns might prove valid?

Our interest in the rigorous study of differential effectiveness and the use of manualized protocols has, paradoxically, led us to recognize that more work also remains to be done in characterizing "nonspecific" therapeutic variables, such as the therapeutic relationship, that may influence or determine the outcome of therapy. What kind of training is needed to maximize this relationship, and can it, in fact, be instilled by training? Further work in these areas will ultimately have to answer the question of whether treatments shown to have measurable effects in RCTs, administered by researchers in university settings, adhering to treatment manuals, can be translated or transported into general clinical practice settings.

Differential Effectiveness of Psychosocial Treatments

The differentiation between well-established or probably efficacious and other treatments, as described above, offers some proof of differential effectiveness. Overall, behavioral therapies (BT) and CBT procedures seem to have better treatment outcomes than other interventions (Weisz, Weiss, Alicke, and Klotz 1987; Weisz, Weiss, Han, et al. 1995; Weisz, Huey, and Weersing 1998; Ollendick, King, and Chorpita 2006). However, the evaluating committees were able to apply the assessment of "well-established" to only two psychosocial treatments for specific phobias in children (participant modeling, reinforced practice), two treatments for ADHD (behavioral parent training, operant classroom management), and two treatments for oppositional and conduct problems (Webster-Stratton's videotape modeling parent training, Patterson's social learning parent training program). Even within the universe of well-established therapies, the evidence of superiority for specified approaches remains relatively modest.

Interventions other than behavioral or cognitive behavioral ones have not been extensively examined in RCTs. For example, for autism, phobias, anxiety, ADHD, oppositional behaviors, and conduct problems, we were unable to identify any RCTs for psychotherapeutic approaches outside cognitive behavioral interventions. Even with depression, only one method outside the cognitive behavioral realm, interpersonal psychotherapy, has rigorously demonstrated its effectiveness. In our view, additional efficacy studies are needed for most of the remaining 550 psychotherapies, as well as for many behavioral and cognitive behavioral ones. We simply do not have sufficient evidence at this time to assess the efficacy of most of the psychosocial treatments advocated for many child behavior problems. In the first decade of the twenty-first century, claims to differential efficacy have been mostly claims to differential degrees of proof of efficacy. Such distinctions are still helpful in guiding the choice of therapeutic method and for justifying societal and professional support for particular treatments. Future RCTs should provide evidence for the efficacy of more treatments for more child and adolescent problems, but until the evidence base grows, we will continue to rely on treatment-as-usual procedures in clinical practices—hardly a happy state of affairs.

Studies of treatment as usual seem to support the position that the effects of psychotherapy cannot be distinguished from the passage of time and intercurrent events in the child's life. A meta-analysis by Weisz, Huey, and Weersing (1998), for example, found that after a course of therapy, the treated children were no better off than those left untreated. Similarly, Bickman and colleagues reported that a comprehensive mental health services program for children was no more effective than a treatment-as-usual condition (Bickman et al. 1995; Bickman 1996). Weiss et al. (1999) found that a school-based treatment-as-usual condition was no more effective than a control condition (academic tutoring). Yet the demand remains high for professional help to improve the lives of psychologically or behaviorally disturbed children and adolescents and their families. Large studies that do not find proof of efficacy should not discredit the field, but should spur efforts to identify and then disseminate effective treatments to clinical settings, closing the gap between empirically supported treatments and clinical practice.

Manualization of Psychosocial Treatments

Professional task forces, as noted above, require that for a treatment to be classified as well-established, the technique to be evaluated must be clearly specified in a manual (Chambless 1996). This step is necessary to control for variation in administering the therapy. A treatment manual defines and standardizes the treatment approach and allows measurement of the treating professionals' adherence to a protocol. Manualization also clarifies the type or variant of therapy under study. For example, CBT comes in many forms. A study that concludes that CBT is effective is largely meaningless in the absence of details about the specifics of the therapy. In addition, studies based on protocols translated into manuals may permit further analyses of what specific components of the therapy contribute to the findings.

Not everyone approves of the use of manuals in clinical psychotherapy or psychotherapy research. Some authors view manuals as "cookie cutters" (Strupp and Anderson 1997), expressing concern that their use conceals the possible therapeutic benefits of a therapist improvising in response to the unique qualities of working with a particular patient. Critics also express concern that manualized treatments may not be generalizable to real-life clinical settings in which the effectiveness of the treatment has not yet been demonstrated. While well-controlled research designs require consistency in the measured variable to reach valid conclusions, clinical practice inevitably demands flexibility, improvisation, and adaptation to circumstances. A clinician who tries to apply a research finding by adopting a manualized approach may feel compelled to abandon either the text or the patient.

Others express a more positive view of the use of treatment manuals, particularly as an element of sound scientific methodology (e.g., Ollendick 1995, 1999; Wilson 1996a, 1996b; Chambless and Hollon 1998; Craighead and Craighead 1998; Heimberg 1998; Kendall 1998; King and Ollendick 1998; Strosahl 1998). Beyond their value in allowing valid replication studies and identification of specific elements that affect outcome, manuals may facilitate the dissemination of research-supported treatments into clinical settings.

What is the current status of this movement toward manualization in the treatment of children? Kendall and colleagues identified six (mis)perceptions that plague manual-based treatments (Kendall 1998; Kendall et al. 1998) How flexible are these treatments? Do they replace clinical judgment? Do manuals detract from the creative process of therapy? Does a treatment manual reify therapy in a fixed and stagnant fashion, and thereby stifle improvement and change? Are manual-based treatments effective with patients who have multiple diagnoses or clinical problems? Are manuals primarily designed for use in research programs, with little application in clinics providing service? Some preliminary work addresses several of these issues. Kendall and Chu (2000) examined treatment flexibility in the use of a manual. They defined flexibility as a measurement of the therapist's adaptive stance to the *specific* situation at hand while adhering *generally* to the instructions and suggestions in the manual. The results revealed that therapists reported being flexible in their implementation of the treatment plan (both in general and with specific strategies). Thus flexibility, however defined, is compatible with careful and systematic inquiry.

Individualization of Therapy

Matching certain characteristics or profiles of the individuals being treated to specific elements or components of previously established effective treatments permits the individualization of manualized treatment. Acierno et al. (1994) label this step "prescriptive matching." Such matching assumes that an idiographic approach to treatment is more effective in producing positive outcomes than a nomothetic approach. (*Nomothetic* implies that all patients who receive the same diagnosis or demonstrate similar problematic behaviors are fundamentally identical; an *idiographic* position assumes that such naming conceals important fundamental differences between individuals; see Kiesler 1966).

Although RCTs involving prescriptive matching have not yet been conducted in children and adolescents, Eisen and Silverman (1993, 1998) provide preliminary support for the value of prescriptive matching in the treatment of anxious children in a multiple-baseline design. They examined the efficacy of cognitive therapy, relaxation training, and a combination of the two with four overanxious children, six to fifteen years of age, using a multiple-baseline design across subjects. The children received both relaxation training and cognitive therapy (counterbalanced), followed by an intervention combining elements of both treatments. Results indicated that the children with primary symptoms of worry responded more favorably to cognitive therapy, whereas children with primary symptoms of somatic complaints responded best to relaxation treatment. Similar findings were obtained in a second study with four overly anxious children between the ages of eight and twelve years (Eisen and Silverman 1998). The interventions that prescribed cognitive therapy for cognitive symptoms and relaxation therapy for somatic symptoms produced the greatest changes and resulted in enhanced treatment effectiveness. Together, these admittedly small, but intensive, studies provide preliminary support for individualizing treatment and exploring flexibility, while still using empirically supported treatment manuals. The MacArthur Foundation is funding further studies to test these questions in the context of an RCT (Chorpita, Daleiden, and Weisz 2005).

Relationship Variables

Few studies of child psychotherapies have systematically examined the impact of the common factors, especially the impact of the therapeutic relationship, first outlined in *Persuasion and Healing*. A meta-analysis by Shirk and Karver (2003) examined the relationship between therapeutic relationship variables and treatment outcomes in twenty-three child psychotherapy studies. These investigations used a variety of alliance/therapeutic relationship scales and outcome measures, with very little overlap among studies. Overall, they found moderate associations between relationship factors and treatment outcomes.

The lack of any standard measure of relationship variables or outcome measures used across the investigations limits the strength of these findings. Nonetheless, these preliminary results are of interest because the reviewers found that the effect of therapeutic relationship variables on treatment outcome was consistent across the children's ages and the types of therapy under study. Moreover, the association between therapeutic relationship variables and treatment outcome was moderated by the type of patient problem, time and source of relationship measurement, type and source of outcome, and shared (versus cross) measurement of relationship variables and outcome variables. Children with "externalizing" behaviors or symptoms (agitation, anxiety, restlessness, aggressiveness) demonstrated a stronger association between therapeutic relationship and treatment outcome than "internalizing" children. The review also noted that relationship variables measured later in treatment were more aligned with outcome than those measured early on, suggesting a bidirectional relationship. That is, a strong relationship enhances treatment, and success in treatment may strengthen a relationship. The associations between relationship and outcome were stronger for therapists' reports than for child-patients' reports. Finally, shared source associations (e.g., correlations between therapists' reports of therapeutic relationships and their reports of patients' outcomes) had a stronger association than cross-source associations (e.g., correlations between therapists' reports of therapeutic relationships and patients' reports of patients' outcomes).

Buttressing their earlier findings, in a more recent meta-analysis Karver and colleagues (2006) examined the association between therapeutic relationship variables and treatment outcome in forty-nine youth treatment studies. Correlations between the relationship variables and treatment process variables (e.g., treatment attendance, therapeutic alliance, treatment engagement) were moderate to high. Additionally, the best predictors of treatment outcomes included, but were not limited to, counselor's interpersonal skills, therapist's direct influence skills, and parents' and child's participation.

These findings suggest a clear and measurable association between therapeutic relationship factors and the process/outcome of treatment. To adequately build on Frank's seminal insights and these recent findings, it is imperative to develop valid, reliable, and standardized means of measuring therapeutic relationship across studies. Such measures are needed to study both the direct and the moderating effects of relationship variables on treatment process/outcome. Careful measurement may also clarify *which* therapeutic relationship variables are most important in treatment. With such information, future research may encourage interventions that improve the therapeutic relationship and thus positively influence treatment outcomes (Ollendick and Shirk 2010).

Real-World Implementation (Transportability) of Treatments

The current research literature distinguishes between *efficacy* studies and *effectiveness* studies (Hoagwood et al. 1995; Hibbs 1998; Ollendick 1999). Efficacy studies demonstrate that the benefits obtained from a given treatment administered in a fairly standard way (with a treatment manual) are due to the treatment, not to chance factors. Typically, these studies are conducted in laboratory or university settings under tightly controlled conditions. Most consist of RCTs, provide clear specification of sample characteristics, and use rigorous experimental designs. Effectiveness studies measure the utility of a given psychotherapy treatment in a real-world setting. Controversies abound as to whether "laboratory-based" treatments, which generate the strongest evidence of efficacy, lose impact when transported to real-world clinical practice. For example, skeptics argue that the exclusionary criteria applied to participants in RCTs make their subjects poor examples of real-life clients. Others note the significant differences between laboratory settings and real-world clinical practice settings. These distinctions raise the ever-present concern about the need to build a bridge between science and practice, as the gap remains wide between efficacy and effectiveness studies.

Largely unstudied additional issues further complicate the problem of transporting evidence-based care to clinical practice. These include consideration of the training of therapists, supervision of therapists, homogeneous versus heterogeneous samples, development of manuals, adherence to manuals, competence in executing manual-based treatments, and acceptability of manual-based treatments to clinicians and clients (Weisz, Huey, and Weersing 1998). Weisz and colleagues (1998) identified a set of characteristics that frequently (but not always) distinguishes efficacy from effectiveness in child psychotherapy outcome research. Efficacy research is conducted with relatively homogeneous groups of children who exhibit less severe forms of psychopathology and have single-focus problems. These studies are conducted in research laboratories or school settings, with clinical researchers who are carefully trained and supervised and have light client loads. Such studies typically use behavioral or CBT treatments.

The subject populations in effectiveness research, by contrast, are often heterogeneous groups of children referred for treatment because of complex and diverse clinical problems. Treatment is delivered in a clinic, school, or hospital setting by therapists who have heavy caseloads and limited training, and who may not be carefully supervised or monitored. Finally, treatment in clinical settings rarely follows a treatment manual and often uses nonbehavioral methods.

Clearly, many of these issues require further study. The distinctions described between laboratory and real-world practices are broad generalizations that may or may not be true for various studies conducted in laboratory *or* clinical settings. They serve to accentuate differences in types of studies rather than defining areas of rapprochement. Demarcations between efficacy and effectiveness studies should be considered a general guideline, lest they inadvertently create a chasm, rather than a bridge, between laboratory study and clinical application (for an extended discussion of this issue, see Ollendick et al. 2008).

Conclusion

We have broadly reviewed the state of research in child psychotherapy through a systematic literature review and identified salient issues associated with empirically supported treatments. Findings indicate that some treatments are, in fact, more effective than others, that manualization need not be a stumbling block to providing effective psychotherapies in both research and clinical settings, that relationship variables must be studied and accounted for as an essential component of therapeutic healing, and that the transportability of treatments from the laboratory setting to the practice setting is viable but still in the developmental stage.

Our overview of empirically supported psychosocial treatments for children reveals the extent of what remains unstudied and unknown. To date, few psychosocial treatments are *well-established* in either research or clinical settings. Further systematic reviews of the literature may uncover different trends than those we have highlighted here. The role of manuals, the nature of control groups, and potential mediators and moderators of therapy across child psychotherapy outcome studies are not fully understood at this time. Still, the ever developing movement toward providing evidence-based treatments in real-world settings may allow us to bridge the gap between laboratory and clinic studies, for the purpose of developing comprehensive, clinically sensitive, and truly healing practices (see Chorpita et al. 2002; Ollendick and Shirk 2010).

REFERENCES

Acierno, R., Hersen, M., Van Hasselt, V. B., and Ammerman, R. T. 1994. Remedying the Achilles heel of behavior research and therapy: prescriptive matching of intervention and psychopathology. *Journal of Behavior Therapy and Experimental Psychiatry* 25:179–88.
Bickman, L. 1996. A continuum of care: more is not always better. *American Psychologist* 51:689–701.
Bickman, L., Guthrie, P. R., Foster, E. M., Lambert, E. W., Summerfelt, W. T., Breda, C. S.,

and Heflinger, C. A. 1995. *Evaluating Managed Mental Health Services: The Fort Bragg Experiment*. New York: Plenum Press.

Bickman, L., Noser, K., and Summerfelt, W. T. 1999. Long-term effects of a system of care on children and adolescents. *Journal of Behavioral Health Services Research* 126:185–202.

Casey, R. J., and Berman, J. S. 1985. The outcome of psychotherapy with children. *Psychological Bulletin* 98:388–400.

Chambless, D. L. 1996. In defense of dissemination of empirically supported psychological interventions. *Clinical Psychology: Science and Practice* 3:230–35.

Chambless, D. L., and Hollon, S. D. 1998. Defining empirically supported therapies. *Journal of Consulting and Clinical Psychology* 66:7–18.

Chambless, D. L., and Ollendick, T. H. 2001. Empirically supported psychological interventions: controversies and evidence. *Annual Review of Psychology* 52:685–716.

Chorpita, B. F., Daleiden, E. L., and Weisz, J. R. 2005. Identifying and selecting the common elements of evidence based interventions: a distillation and matching model. *Mental Health Services Research* 7:5–20.

Chorpita, B. F., Yim, L. M., Donkervoet, J. C., Arensdorf, A., Amundsen, M. J., McGee, C., et al. 2002. Toward large-scale implementation of empirically supported treatments for children: a review and observations by the Hawaii Empirical Basis to Services Task Force. *Clinical Psychology: Science and Practice* 9:165–90.

Craighead, W. E., and Craighead, L. W. 1998. Manual-based treatments: suggestions for improving their clinical utility and acceptability. *Clinical Psychology: Science and Practice* 5:403–7.

Durlak, J. A., Wells, A. M., Cotton, J. K., and Johnson, S. 1995. Analysis of selected methodological issues in child psychotherapy research. *Journal of Clinical Child Psychology* 24:141–48.

Eisen, A. R., and Silverman, W. K. 1993. Should I relax or change my thoughts? A preliminary examination of cognitive therapy, relaxation training, and their combination with overanxious children. *Journal of Cognitive Psychotherapy* 7:265–79.

———. 1998. Prescriptive treatment for generalized anxiety disorder in children. *Behavior Therapy* 29:105–21.

Eysenck, H. J. 1952. The effects of psychotherapy: an evaluation. *Journal of Consulting Psychology* 16:319–24.

Fisher, C. A., Hetrick, S. E., and Rushford, N. 2010. Family therapy for anorexia nervosa. *Cochrane Database of Systematic Reviews* 4:CD004780.

Frank, J. D. 1961. *Persuasion and Healing: A Comparative Study of Psychotherapy*. Baltimore: Johns Hopkins University Press.

Frank, J. D., and Frank, J. B. 1991. *Persuasion and Healing: A Comparative Study of Psychotherapy*, 3rd ed. Baltimore: Johns Hopkins University Press.

Heimberg, R. G. 1998. Manual-based treatment: an essential ingredient of clinical practice in the 21st century. *Clinical Psychology: Science and Practice* 5:387–90.

Hibbs, E. D. 1998. Improving methodologies for the treatment of child and adolescent disorders: introduction. *Journal of Abnormal Child Psychology* 26:1–6.

Hoagwood, K., Hibbs, E., Brent, D., and Jensen, P. 1995. Introduction to the special section: efficacy and effectiveness in studies of child and adolescent psychotherapy. *Journal of Consulting and Clinical Psychology* 63:683–87.

Jensen, P. S., Weersing, R., Hoagwood, K. E., and Goldman E. 2005. What is the evidence for evidence-based treatments? A hard look at our soft underbelly. *Mental Health Services Research* 7:53–74.

Karver, M. S., Handelsman, J. B., Fields, S., and Bickman, L. 2006. Meta-analysis of therapeutic relationship variables in youth and family therapy: the evidence for different relationship variables in the child and adolescent treatment outcome literature. *Clinical Psychology Review* 26:50–65.

Kazdin, A. E. 1998. *Research Design in Clinical Psychology*, 3rd ed. Boston: Allyn and Bacon.

———. 2000. Developing a research agenda for child and adolescent psychotherapy. *Archives of General Psychiatry* 57:829–36.

Kazdin, A. E., Bass, D., Ayers, W. A., and Rodgers, A. 1990. Empirical and clinical focus of child and adolescent psychotherapy research. *Journal of Consulting and Clinical Psychology* 58:729–40.

Keel, P. K., and Haedt, P. 2008. Evidence based psychosocial treatments for eating problems and eating disorders. *Journal of Clinical Child and Adolescent Psychology* 37:39–61.

Kendall, P. C. 1998. Directing misperceptions: researching the issues facing manual-based treatments. *Clinical Psychology: Science and Practice* 5:396–99.

Kendall, P. C., and Chu, B. C. 2000. Retrospective self-reports of therapist flexibility in a manual-based treatment for youths with anxiety disorders. *Journal of Clinical Child Psychology* 29:209–20.

Kendall, P. C., Chu, B., Gifford, A., Hayes, C., and Nauta, M. 1998. Breathing life into a manual: flexibility and creativity with manual-based treatments. *Cognitive and Behavioral Practice* 5:177–98.

Kendall, P. C., Flannery-Schroeder, E., and Ford, J. D. 1999. Therapy outcome research methods. In P. C. Kendall, J. N. Butcher, and G. N. Holmbeck (eds.), *Handbook of Research Methods in Clinical Psychology*, 2nd ed. (pp. 330–63). New York: John Wiley.

Kiesler, D. J. 1966. Some myths of psychotherapy research and the search for a paradigm. *Psychological Bulletin* 65:110–36.

King, N. J., and Ollendick, T. H. 1998. Empirically validated treatments in clinical psychology. *Australian Psychologist* 33:89–95.

Lambert, W., and Bickman, L. 2004. Child and adolescent psychiatry—the "clock-setting" cure: how children's symptoms might improve after ineffective treatment. *Psychiatric Services* 55:381–82.

Levitt, E. E. 1957. The results of psychotherapy with children: an evaluation. *Journal of Consulting and Clinical Psychology* 21:189–96.

———. 1963. Psychotherapy with children: a further evaluation. *Behaviour Research and Therapy* 60:326–29.

Lock, J., and Fitzpatrick, K. K. 2009 Advances in psychotherapy for children and adolescents with eating disorders. *American Journal of Psychotherapy* 63:287–303.

Lonigan, C. J., Elbert, J. C., and Johnson, S. B. 1998. Empirically supported psychosocial interventions for children: an overview. *Journal of Clinical Child Psychology* 27:138–45.

Nathan, P. E., and Gorman, J. M. (eds.). 1998. *A Guide to Treatments That Work*. New York: Oxford University Press.

Ollendick, T. H. 1995. AABT and empirically validated treatments. *Behavior Therapist* 18:81–82.

———. 1999. Empirically supported treatments: promises and pitfalls. *Clinical Psychologist* 52:1–3.

Ollendick, T. H., and King, N. J. 2004. Empirically supported treatments for children and adolescents: advances toward evidence-based practice. In P. M. Barrett and T. H. Ollendick (eds.), *Handbook of Interventions That Work with Children and Adolescents: Prevention and Treatment* (pp. 1–26). Chichester, UK: John Wiley.

Ollendick, T. H., King, N. J., and Chorpita, B. 2006. Empirically supported treatments for children and adolescents. In P. C. Kendall (ed.), *Child and Adolescent Therapy*, 3rd ed. (pp. 492–520). New York: Guilford Press.

Ollendick, T. H., Jarrett, M. A., Grills-Taquechel, A. E., Hovey, L. D., and Wolff, J. 2008. Comorbidity as a predictor and moderator of treatment outcome in youth with anxiety, affective, AD/HD, and oppositional/conduct disorders. *Clinical Psychology Review* 28:1447–71.

Ollendick, T. H., and Shirk, S. R. 2010. Clinical interventions with children and adolescents: current status, future directions. In D. H. Barlow (ed.), *Oxford Handbook of Clinical Psychology*. Oxford: Oxford University Press.

Roth, A., and Fonagy, P. 1996. *What Works for Whom? A Critical Review of Psychotherapy*. New York: Guilford Press.

Shirk, S. R. and Karver, M. S. 2003. Prediction of treatment outcome from relationship variables in child and adolescent therapy: a meta-analytic review. *Journal of Consulting and Clinical Psychology* 71:452–64.

Strosahl, K. 1998. The dissemination of manual-based psychotherapies in managed care: promises, problems, and prospects. *Clinical Psychology: Science and Practice* 5:382–86.

Strupp, H. H., and Anderson, T. 1997. On the limitations of therapy manuals. *Clinical Psychology: Science and Practice* 4:76–82.

Task Force on Promotion and Dissemination of Psychological Procedures. 1995. Training in and dissemination of empirically validated treatments: report and recommendations. *Clinical Psychologist* 48:3–23.

Wang, P. S., Tohen, M., Bromet, E., and Angst, J. 2003. Psychiatric epidemiology. In A. Tasman, J. Kay, and J. A. Lieberman (eds.), *Psychiatry*, 2nd ed., vol. 1 (pp. 211–33). New York: John Wiley.

Weiss, B., Catron, T., Harris, V., and Phung, T. M. 1999. The effectiveness of traditional child psychotherapy. *Journal of Consulting and Clinical Psychology* 67:82–94.

Weisz, J. R., Huey, S. J., and Weersing, V. R. 1998. Psychotherapy outcome research with children and adolescents: the state of the art. In T. H. Ollendick and R. J. Prinz (eds.), *Advances in Clinical Child Psychology*, vol. 20 (pp. 49–91). New York: Plenum.

Weisz, J. R., Weiss, B., Alicke, M. D., and Klotz, M. L. 1987. Effectiveness of psychotherapy with children and adolescents: a meta-analysis for clinicians. *Journal of Consulting and Clinical Psychology* 55:542–49.

Weisz, J. R., Weiss, B., Han, S. S., Granger, D. G., and Morton, T. 1995. Effects of psychotherapy with children and adolescents revisited: a meta-analysis of treatment outcome studies. *Psychological Bulletin* 117:450–68.

Wilson, G. T. 1996a. Empirically validated treatments: reality and resistance. *Clinical Psychology: Science and Practice* 3:241–44.

———. 1996b. Manual-based treatments: the clinical application of research findings. *Behaviour Research and Therapy* 34:295–314.

CHAPTER 13

Contemporary Realities of Group Psychotherapy

J. Scott Rutan, Ph.D., and
Joseph J. Shay, Ph.D.

"No room! No room!" they
cried out when they saw
Alice coming. "There's plenty
of room!" said Alice
indignantly, and she sat
down in a large arm-chair at
one end of the table.
—*Alice's Adventures in*
Wonderland

Small groups provide the illusion, if not the substance, of safety.
They may prove to be the most promising means of counteracting certain damaging features of contemporary life,
especially alienation from the past and from one's fellow
humans. —*PERSUASION AND HEALING*, 1991, P. 244

All editions of *Persuasion and Healing: A Comparative Study of Psycho-*
therapy (Frank 1961, 1973; Frank and Frank 1991) thoroughly explore the
principles of group psychotherapy. Early experience as an army psychiatrist
inspired Jerome Frank to join Florence Powdermaker in pioneering group psychotherapy for distressed soldiers. Their collaboration inspired Frank's later
forays into psychotherapy research (Powdermaker and Frank 1953). In the
1950s and 1960s, Wilfred Bion, Helen Durkin, Martin Grotjahn, Max Rosen-
baum, Clifford Sager, Hyman Spotnitz, and many others (including Fritz Redl
and Saul Scheidlinger, working with children) joined Powdermaker and Frank
in promoting groups as a vehicle for delivering effective therapy, guided by a
variety of theories.

Frank practiced and taught group psychotherapy throughout his career.
This activity contributed heavily to his development of the theory that psychotherapy, in general, works primarily through relieving demoralization. Morale
is, after all, a property of groups as well as individuals. Frank's text emphasized
that building on the processes of small group interactions could restore and

sustain morale. *Persuasion and Healing* applied this insight to both formal group psychotherapy and the effects of groups organized around particular rationales, including cults and self-help groups.

A History of Group Therapy

The origins of group therapy may be traced to the work of Joseph Pratt (Rutan, Stone, and Shay 2007), an internist in Boston, taking care of patients with tuberculosis in the years before World War I. In 1919, soon after Pratt, Edward Lazell, at St. Elizabeth's Hospital in Washington, DC, thought to group together patients who had schizophrenia for treatment. Trigant Burrow and Alfred Adler treated patients in groups as early as 1920 and 1921. Julius Metzel pioneered group work with alcoholic patients in 1927, and Rudolf Dreikurs began offering private practice therapy groups in 1930. American values and conditions of practice strongly influenced the development of group and other types of therapy, a process due in part to the influence of the many psychotherapy practitioners and innovators forced to emigrate to the United States because of the adverse conditions in Europe in the 1930s.

Jerome Frank's own enthusiasm for groups reflected the influence of Kurt Lewin, one of his primary role models (Meinecke 1987, p. 226; Wampold and Weinberger 2010). Frank delayed entering graduate school to study with Lewin in Germany in 1930. Lewin taught him to consider the individual as a unit interacting in an environment. Frank's experience in Germany also exposed him to the power of mob psychology and large group processes. His early research as a psychologist measured the impact of social pressure on individual behavior.

Plato, in *The Republic*, noted that necessity is the mother of invention. The necessity of providing services for large numbers of damaged soldiers and veterans in the 1940s led to experiments with various models of group therapy. In the 1940s, theories underlying group therapy clashed with Freudian psychoanalysis, then the dominant force in the field of mental health. Freud had some theoretical interest in group processes, but psychoanalysis as a therapy focused on individuals. On principle and by convention, psychoanalysis required the therapist to be a "blank screen" onto which the individual patient was to project conflicted emotions and beliefs. A classically trained analyst strove to remain opaque to facilitate transference. The multiple-person field of group therapy, many felt, would impede the formation of transference. Thus, while many analysts were intrigued by the potential of group therapy, those who tried to apply classic theory to patients in groups found it not always a comfortable fit.

For some therapists (Wolf and Schwartz 1962), groups represented primarily an opportunity to psychoanalyze individuals in a group setting. Most group practitioners, however, recognized the need to modify classic theory. For example, in Europe, the "group-as-a-whole" method, promoted by Wilfred Bion (1961), gained many adherents. Bion, an analysand of Melanie Klein, was particularly impressed with the power of regression in bringing about change. He hypothesized that groups offer unique opportunities to induce and allow regression. Borrowing from classic German Gestalt psychology (Kohler 1969), practitioners of the group-as-a-whole method held that altering the *ground* (the group) would inevitably bring change to the *figure* (the individual members).

A decorated tank commander in World War I, Bion was plagued with post-traumatic symptoms throughout his life. Personal experience, including exposure to combat, the death of his beloved mother just before the war, and the death of his wife in childbirth in 1943 (Kosseff 2001, p. 244), presumably contributed to his deep interest in treating "shell-shocked" soldiers. Historians debate how much he used groups in his treatment of these patients. It *is* known that Bion used groups to select and train officers. Above all, he used groups to study themselves, coining the term "study groups."

Present-day group theorists consider Bion's exclusive focus on group processes, to the exclusion of any individual dynamics, a valuable educational process rather than a therapeutic modality. His early efforts illuminated the powerful forces at work in all groups. Now nearly all branches of group therapy incorporate a recognition of the group-level processes he identified.

Henrietta T. Glatzer (1953) and Helen E. Durkin (1964) were early, influential proponents of integrating the work of group-as-a-whole theorists with that of the individuals-in-a-group theorists. Glatzer and Durkin each pointed out that no less than individual interactions, group processes elicit transferences. Like classic psychoanalysts, they recognized the importance of templates provided by early experiences, noting that groups typically stimulate emotions and behaviors characteristic of sibling rivalry. They also noted the development of subgroups as a common element of group interactions.

Enter *Persuasion and Healing*: Group Therapy as a Unique Modality

In contrast to other practitioners of the mid twentieth century, Frank focused his attention, not on the *micro* elements of psychotherapy, but on the *macro*. His imprint on both individual and group therapy was profound.

Before joining the military, Frank, both a psychologist and a psychiatrist, was a resident at Johns Hopkins under Adolf Meyer. Together, Lewin and Meyer guided Frank along the path of understanding psychiatric disorders through a social lens. After the war, Meyer's successor, John Whitehorn, another psychiatric iconoclast, recruited Frank back to Hopkins to head a training program in group and individual psychotherapy. As shown by his work with Powdermaker (Powdermaker and Frank 1953), Frank saw the immense value of treatment in groups early on. When *Classics in Group Psychotherapy* was published in 1992, the editor asked Frank to write the foreword. In this piece, he begins: "Humans are social creatures" (Frank 1992, p. v), and articulates his belief that "throughout history and in every culture sufferers have sought relief through group rituals led by healers."

At the time of its publication in 1961, when models of therapy were proliferating at an alarming rate, *Persuasion and Healing* developed the thesis that, however disparate in theory, most types of therapy—indeed, even therapeutic efforts in vastly different cultures—are equally effective. The text then explored the elements these therapeutic endeavors shared. As Downing (2004, p. 132) states, "Jerome Frank's *common factors* approach attempts to bypass the idiosyncratic contents and methods associated with particular theories of Western psychotherapy by focusing on factors that are associated with mental healing across history, culture, and similar institutional forms (e.g., faith healing or religious conversion). Frank noted that therapists' socially sanctioned status awakens clients' faith and hope. He concluded that theoretical rationales—which can be likened to 'myths'—are useful, not because they are 'true', but because they function to convey new meanings to a demoralized sufferer" (see chapter 5).

This notion of demoralization—and the attendant benefits of restoring morale—moved to center stage in later editions of *Persuasion and Healing*. Demoralization, Frank (1974) said, "results from *persistent failure to cope* with internally or externally induced stresses that the person and those close to him expect him to handle. Its characteristic features . . . are feelings of impotence, isolation, and despair. The person's self-esteem is damaged, and he feels rejected by others because of his failure to meet their expectations. Insofar as the meaning and significance of life derives from the individual's ties with persons whose values he shares, alienation may contribute to a sense of the meaninglessness of life ... The most frequent symptoms of patients in psychotherapy—anxiety and depression—are direct expressions of demoralization" (p. 271, emphasis added) (see also chapters 6 and 8 in this volume).

To combat demoralization, Frank proposed that across cultures, all effective interventions share four elements: a relationship, a healing setting, and a rationale to explain the cause of the demoralization, linked to particular healing rituals that guide the sufferer along this path (Frank and Frank 1991). These elements are as common in groups as in dyadic relationships. As Jorgensen (2004, p. 533) says, "According to Frank's theory of the active agents in therapy, it is not particularly important which of the many well-established and coherent clinical theories the therapist chooses, so long as he has chosen one of them and is able to use it as a solid base for structuring and focusing his clinical work."

Whatever theory guides the treatment, the therapist or healer must establish a genuine connection with the sufferer. First and foremost, all forms of therapy include a *relationship* between therapist and patient (Frank and Frank 1991). This notion now so deeply saturates the air that therapists breathe that it seems obvious, even clichéd. But it was not obvious until Frank articulated it so clearly.

Persuasion and Healing was the first significant attempt by any clinician or theorist to examine the DNA, if you will, of group therapy across diverse schools. Adding to the immense influence of his work, Frank also took on a student who came to dominate the field—Irvin Yalom. Yalom (personal communication, 2007) recalls that "for the first year of my residency, I watched Jerry Frank's group through a tiny one way mirror, one of the very first examples of an experienced therapist allowing students to observe his ongoing psychotherapy with patients. I also learned the importance of epistemology from Frank, that is, how we know what we know, and was introduced to the fledgling field of psychotherapy research."

In his classic work *The Theory and Practice of Group Psychotherapy*, which first appeared in 1970, Yalom took up several of Frank's views—most notably, affirming that patients suffer from demoralization. Yalom argued that patients can best be helped by methods that foster hope, activating the expectation that relief of suffering is possible. Group methods accomplish this by providing a sense of belonging, as participants learn that they share universal problems. Groups also offer a context for altruistic acts that may counter demoralization. Frank (1961, p. 76) had earlier emphasized techniques that had the "ability to arouse the patient's hope, bolster his self-esteem, stir him emotionally and strengthen his ties with a supportive group." Yalom (2005, p. 4) echoed these insights in his own work: "The instillation and maintenance of hope is crucial in any psychotherapy. Not only is hope required to keep the client in therapy so that other therapeutic factors may take effect, but faith in a treatment mode can in itself be therapeutically effective. Consider also the massive data documenting the efficacy of faith healing and placebo treatment—therapies mediated entirely through hope and conviction. A positive outcome in therapy is more likely when the client and the therapist have similar expectations of the treatment."

Though group therapy achieved respectability after World War II, individual therapy remained the gold standard for the field at mid-century. In countering this trend, *Persuasion and Healing* highlighted the numerous advantages of group therapy over individual treatment. Compared with individual therapy, groups provide a "greater nearness to everyday life" (Frank 1961, p. 189). Group therapy, as well, offers "encouragement to speak freely and honestly and the de-emphasis on outside success or achievement for gaining status." These attributes may powerfully "lead the patient to change his assumptive world and behavior even after repeated discussion of the same material with the psychiatrist privately [has had] no effect" (p. 178).

This concept of the *assumptive world*, repeatedly discussed in *Persuasion and Healing*, requires elucidation (see chapter 1 in this volume). The goal of psychotherapy, Frank said, was "to help a person feel and function better by enabling him to make appropriate modifications in his assumptive world" (Frank 1961, p. 30)—the patient's beliefs and understandings about how things work and what interactions mean. Frank's focus on the contextual lens through which we all filter experience prefigured later developments now known as "constructivist" models, theories that explicate the working models that guide human perception and interaction (Lewis 1986; Janoff-Bulman 1989; Bruner 1990; Neimeyer and Mahoney 1995; Koltko-Rivera 2004). Group therapy, with its focus on the exploration of social perceptions and experience among individuals, each with unique perceptions and experiences, has proven to be a potent medium for the examination—and modification—of a person's assumptive world.

Moreover, for people demoralized by the feeling that they must wrestle with their problems alone, therapy groups "diminish the members' sense of isolation, heighten their hopes, and increase their self-esteem by means differing in some respects from those of individual therapies" (Frank 1961, p. 182). Just belonging to a group is "a major means of maintaining one's sense of self-identification and self-esteem" (p. 171). A complementary equation evolves, balancing belonging, holding environment, and enhancing power and (constructive) conflict as sources of the healing power of group therapy.

Belonging

Belonging implies much more than simply being *a member of* a club or group. One can be *in* a group and have no feeling of *belonging to* it. Indeed, some of the most painful experiences of isolation and rejection occur in the midst of others. A sense of belonging appears in Maslow's hierarchy of human needs (1943). He placed it right in the middle, above safety and physiological needs (health, food, and sleep) and below psychological needs for esteem and self-actualization.

Belonging to groups offers members relationships that can be destructive, healing, and/or self-enhancing. Winnicott (1960) noted this potential in coining the term the *holding environment*. Bion (1961) proposed a similar concept for groups, saying they provide a venue of "containment." Beyond infancy, the "holding environment" of the family and then of other groups offers more—a place within which individuals *belong*. Those who have been members of a team, an orchestra, a choir, or other such groups know the potential power of belonging. Belonging to a group, then, reawakens the sense of relationship instilled by a person's earliest experiences. Simple group membership may not in itself be healing, but if an individual *feels* that he or she belongs, the experience engenders feelings of safety and being cherished that enhance self-confidence and self-worth.

Yalom's list of twelve "therapeutic factors" in group psychotherapy includes "group cohesiveness," which Yalom (2005, p. 53) defines as "the group therapy analogue to relationship in individual therapy." In the group setting, "belonging" extends beyond the relationship to an individual therapist. In Yalom's research, patients reported that group cohesiveness included the following:

- "Belonging to and being accepted by a group."
- "Continued close contact with other people."

- "Revealing embarrassing things about myself and still being accepted by the group."
- "Feeling no longer alone."
- "Belonging to a group of people who understood and accepted me."

The healing power of the sense of belonging finds further support in research noting a much higher morbidity rate among elderly people when they are isolated (Glass, Mendes de Leon, and Berkman 1999).

A Holding Group

Groups draw a boundary of support within which individual members feel protected. Winnicott (1960), who started out as a pediatrician, arrived at this insight by analogizing therapeutic relationships to the mother securely holding her distressed infant. He considered this experience essential to psychological survival, as implied in his often quoted observation that "there is no such thing as a baby." A baby can exist only in relation to a mother. Present-day group therapists generally adopt the following principles to maximize the opportunities for groups to be "holding environments":

- Present a clear set of group *agreements*.
- Provide clear *boundaries* (Scharff and Scharff 1987), which are critical to establishing a successful holding environment.
- Focus on *attachment* rather than *detachment*.
- Understand behaviors, however obnoxious and off-putting, as defenses against expected pain.
- Be alert to potential subgrouping, scapegoating, and narcissistic injury. Be sure to interpret these before a sense of belonging is damaged.

Enhancing Power, Promoting Conflict

In contrast to individual therapy, group treatment may enhance a member's feeling of personal power by fostering his or her ability to influence others. The influence of a particular member may, in turn, instill hope, as members watch others improve. The process encourages members to develop faith in one another's capabilities and in their own. As Frank (1961, pp. 182–83) noted, groups also provide unique opportunities for altruistic acts that further build self-esteem.

Group therapy allows—even promotes—interpersonal tension. Frank was one of the first to emphasize that "the structure and code of therapy groups greatly enhance opportunities for learning from antagonisms and conflicts" (p. 187). Frank also described the many benefits of group therapy in institutional settings. Within the context of a general program of containment and treatment, groups may stimulate apathetic patients, control overanxious or excitable ones, reduce isolation, correct misperceptions of others, and improve communication abilities (pp. 201–3). Yalom (personal communication) commented about Frank that "I remember his placing much emphasis on correcting misperceptions of others, and improving communication abilities in his groups that I observed."

Contemporary Group Therapy

The relation of patient to therapist is crucial in every type of psychotherapy. Groups inevitably foster multiple relationships through promoting interactions between members and leaders and among the members themselves. Modern group therapists emphasize in-group interactions. They pay particular attention to the type of "interpersonal force field" that individuals bring with them.

CASE EXAMPLE

Adam entered a group to deal with his depression and his lack of career success, but almost immediately he began bitterly complaining about his wife, whom he portrayed as a critical, ungrateful, utterly unsupportive "princess." His story was compelling and he received great sympathy, especially from the women in the group.

Within six months, however, the women in the group were furious with Adam and often indicated that they wished he had never joined the group. One evening, in desperation, Adam said: "You women are just like my wife! I can't stay here any longer!" There was a moment of stunned silence as everyone considered that comment, and finally the leader said: "So now we can explore how you managed to train these women, all of whom were your staunchest supporters, to become critical and angry in only six months."

The women began to point out that Adam steadfastly dismissed all their suggestions, leaving them feeling insignificant and powerless. The more they cared, the harder they tried, and still he would not follow any of their suggestions or be curious about any of their confrontations. Adam, to his credit, became self-reflective and wondered whether he did the same with his wife, and indeed whether that behavior might explain his conflicts at work. He further associated to his highly intrusive mother and recalled that she had lost a two-year-old son to pneumonia just before his birth. "You know, it makes sense that she was overprotective and worried about my every move."

Some weeks later, the group therapist was surprised to receive a letter from Adam's wife. She requested that he read the letter to the group, and he did. In it she thanked the group for "bringing my husband back to me."

As this example demonstrates, groups provide a laboratory where patients simultaneously *have* their problems and *talk* about them.

Enhancing Strengths, Building Skills, Encouraging Courage

It is inspiring to observe the interactions by which patients gain the emotional strength to combat their problems, practice new skills, and find the courage to take relational risks—all in the group therapy room itself! Consider the simple example of one group member trying to help another, an experience unavailable in the context of individual therapy. As Frank's text (1961, p. 183) emphasized, altruism is itself a healing factor: "Perhaps the most potent way in which therapy groups strengthen members' self-esteem is by giving them an incentive and an opportunity to help each other. Altruism combats morbid self-centeredness, enhances the individual's feelings of kinship with others, and strengthens his sense of personal worth and power." Yalom (2005, p. 13) endorses this view: "Many psychiatric patients beginning therapy are demoralized and possess a deep sense of having nothing of value to offer others . . . Group therapy is unique in being the only therapy that offers clients the opportunity to be of benefit to others."

Learning to conduct groups may benefit the therapist as well as the group members. The leader's role is, by definition, one valued by others, and moderating group interactions may enhance the therapist's ability to tolerate anxiety and withstand conflict. Frank himself acknowledged this possibility. In his remarkably candid way, he spoke of his personal struggles, revealing a profound self-awareness. He once described his adolescent self as "flatfooted, puny, unathletic" (Kanigel 1983, p. 36). In another interview, he said this of himself: "As for troublesome characteristics, there's my tendency to be anxious. Also, I can't stand hostility in people. I'm an expert at avoiding it, and, I believe, this has kept me from being an effective leader . . . because the leader has to incur hostility and has to make decisions that will disappoint somebody. It's very, very difficult for me to do that. I want to make everybody happy all the time" (Meinecke 1987, p. 227).

Knowing this desire to make everyone happy was an impossible goal, Frank learned to accept anxiety and some degree of conflict as positive elements in individual and group therapy. His recognition that group members will typically step up to protect the leader or another member who feels embattled influenced his groundbreaking ideas about the centrality of relationships in fostering change. The arc of this approach led, as noted above, to Yalom's theoretical innovations and prefigured the development of the relational movement in the field of psychotherapy generally. Current psychodynamic theory encompasses many of Frank's ideas without losing contact with more classic psychodynamic thinking about the nature of psychopathology and the nature of change.

Interpersonal Problems, Interpersonal Solutions

In this era of pressure to shorten treatments, use only evidence-based methods, and understand psychological distress from a biological perspective, it is important to remember that the literal translation of *psychopathology* is "suffering of the soul." Further, it seems self-evident that most patients come with problems that can be viewed as interpersonal. While intrapsychic, biological, sociological, and other sources of suffering certainly exist, patients experience their discomfort primarily in terms of their satisfaction or dissatisfaction with their relationships.

Therapy groups address interpersonal problems directly, exposing the interpersonal styles of the members, with their assets and liabilities. As Siegfried Foulkes (1961) said, groups are "halls of mirrors." Members have the opportunity to receive feedback on how their interpersonal styles are perceived by and influence others.

Contemporary psychodynamic theory incorporates this interpersonal emphasis (see chapter 10). Gabbard and Westen (2003, pp. 823–24) characterize three main current trends and controversies in today's dynamic theory: "(1) the waning of the 'interpretation versus relationship' debate, and the acknowledgement of multiple modes of therapeutic action; (2) the shift of emphasis away from . . . reconstruction to the here-and-now interactions between analyst and patients; and (3) the importance of negotiating the therapeutic climate."

Contemporary leaders in group psychotherapy place similar emphasis on the centrality of patients' experiences with others in the here and now, citing three related perspectives: (1) object relations theory, (2) self psychology, and (3) intersubjective and relational theories.

Object Relations Theory

Classic psychodynamic theory implied a fundamental commitment to a biological understanding of psychological distress. Freud's focus on biological instincts and his referring to the goal of psychoanalysis as "cure" reflect this stance.

Those who followed Freud emphasized that individual development involves much more than biological maturation. Klein (1946) was among the first to suggest that humans are fundamentally driven, not by the need to satiate hunger or to procreate, but rather to relate to one another. She continued to reference biology, as she saw the "drive" to connect to an "object" (another human being) as innate.

Klein's subtle reframing of a basic tenet of human development has many consequences. Models of both human development and techniques designed to correct or heal developmental processes gone awry postulate a genetic predisposition to be in relationship, or at least to *seek* relationship, as the primary organizing principle of human behavior. Freud and Klein built their theories on radically different fundamental assumptions about what both termed *object relations*. Winnicott (1965) and Fairbairn (1952), among others, magnified these differences as they moved away from drive theory, while championing the position that human life includes a basic need to be in sustained relationship to others.

Though essential for survival and growth, humans' relational needs are often thwarted or unmet, because individuals act in self-defeating ways familiar to all clinicians. Some individuals fail to develop the ability to engage others in nurturing relationships. Others, even those with a panoply of skills, sabotage themselves repeatedly in the service of competing psychological needs, such as the need to protect oneself against anticipated aggression, annihilation, or loss. Such concerns may induce a reluctance to pursue intimacy, as closeness may prefigure loss. Object relations theory attributes difficulties in establishing and maintaining fulfilling relationships to the governing effects of self-representation and object representation, inner structures appropriate to past conditions but no longer fitting guides to the present. Such patterns may guide thought and behavior without the person being aware of their lack of fit. Group therapy provides a marvelous context in which to observe how members negotiate and titrate relationships, with both their assets and their liabilities on display. This modality also provides multiple opportunities for participants to reassess assumptions about relationships and their own role in developing or avoiding them.

As people interact with one another in group therapy, the nature of their internal self- and object representations inevitably comes to light in words and actions. Group therapists describe this process as *projective identification*, first named by Klein (1946) and taken up by the field prominently from the 1970s onward (e.g., Grinberg 1973; Ogden 1982; Horwitz 1983; Morrison 1986; Malcus 1995).

Ahead of his time in this area as well, Frank was among the first to describe projective identification in group therapy. While Frank did not use the term, which had not yet gained the core importance it carries today, one of his clinical examples provides a clear illustration of it. He was leading a group in which two Jews were consistently feuding, one flaunting his Jewishness and the other concealing it. After some time, "each finally realized that he was combating in the other an attitude he repressed in himself. The militant Jew finally understood that he was disturbed by the many disadvantages of being Jewish, and the man who hid his background confessed that he secretly nurtured a certain pride in it" (Yalom 2005, p. 365). Frank called this a *reverberating double-mirror reaction.*

Proponents of group treatment now regularly recognize this type of interaction, when group members scapegoat an individual for beliefs, behaviors, or attitudes that the other members reject or disavow in themselves. The concept of projective identification is central to understanding scapegoating (Klein 1946; Fairbairn 1952; Guntrip 1969; Ogden 1982; Weber 2005). "Projective identification is both an act of communication and a defensive maneuver in which an individual projects onto others his or her traits or self- or object-representations, and their associated affects, that are often unacceptable to oneself—sometimes even if they are positive qualities with which the person is uncomfortable" (Rutan, Stone, and Shay 2007, pp. 251–52). Gabbard (2005, p. 35) describes it in this way: "Both an intrapsychic defense mechanism and an interpersonal communication, this phenomenon involves behaving in such a way that subtle interpersonal pressure is placed on another person to take on characteristics of an aspect of the self or an internal object that is projected into that person. The person who is the target of the projection then begins to behave, think and feel in keeping with what has been projected." Simultaneously, the individual retains a connection with the other through identification—although whether it is the projector or the recipient of the projection (i.e., the group) that is doing the identifying is fluid and ambiguous in the current literature (Shay 2001).

Theory further implies that in projective identification, the projector no longer has complete access to the feelings as his or her own, as illustrated in Frank's example of feuding between the two Jews in his group. Both a splitting of good ("I am proud to be a Jew") and bad ("I am ashamed to be a Jew") self-representations and a blurring of ego boundaries are consistent with the developmental level or the regressive state of the person projecting.

The projection is not random. Rather, it is directed to a willing recipient, an individual—or group—that in some substantial way demonstrates a willingness to accept the unacceptable qualities. The projector, in attempting to "change" the other, also maintains contact with the hated and dreaded—or loved—parts of the self, which require continued projection. This ongoing involvement with the other is an essential clue to the process of projective identification (Guntrip 1969), as is a polarization of attributes within a dyad or a group. Thus, projective identification refers to a two-party (or more) phenomenon that involves both projection by one party and acceptance of the projected traits by the other, and therefore represents both intrapsychic and interpersonal processes. Here are two simple ways to express this: (1) an intrapsychic tension becomes an interpersonal interaction; (2) you can hate your cake and eat it too. Recognizing the confusion surrounding this concept, Shay (2001) tried to clarify it by renaming it *projective recruitment*, thereby emphasizing that one can recruit another to play out an aspect of one's internal drama, but the other must be "recruitable" for the process to unfold (Rutan, Stone, and Shay 2007)

To underscore the centrality of this concept for contemporary group therapists, we offer this clinical example:

> In the process of working through a therapist's departure from the group at the end of training, the members expressed considerable sorrow but not anger. Jane, who had rarely been outspoken in the group, began one session by mentioning that she had felt annoyed by the therapist's attempt to be funny last session. As she spoke, Jane's tone got angrier, and several group members challenged her perception and defended the therapist, who remained silent. But these members encouraged her to explain more thoroughly what else she might be angry at the

therapist for, since they assumed it must run deeper than poor humor. Jane began to back down, but the members pressed her for more while reiterating they didn't share her reaction to the therapist. In this instance, Jane could have served as a potential scapegoat for the group and been chastised as the "angry one" had not the therapist understood—and then commented upon—the projective identification process. The therapist said, "While Jane alone is speaking about her anger at me, she may be voicing the feelings of many of you. It may be difficult to believe that feelings of sorrow about my leaving can exist side by side with feelings of anger at me and perhaps also fear that the group may not survive." (Rutan, Stone, and Shay 2007, pp. 252–53)

Group therapists are aware that scapegoats often are not simple victims, but play an active role in their fates. As Jane's behavior in the case example illustrates, a member may "volunteer" to be recruited for the role by engaging in behaviors that provoke the group's wrath, thereby setting in motion familiar patterns. Not uncommonly, such patterns reenact earlier family interactions. As Sandler (1976) observed, patients adopt particular roles that elicit particular responses from the other(s), thereby completing a life script that the patient expects to occur.

Self Psychology

Contemporary group therapy relies on another strand of psychodynamic thought, developed by Heinz Kohut (1971, 1977, 1984). Kohut's work with narcissistic patients culminated in his generalized theory of self, or *self psychology*. Kohut offered a *deficit* theory rather than a *conflict* theory, expressing his conviction that the root of psychopathology is an immature or ill-formed "self." For Kohut, too little attention had been paid to the patient's experience of himself or herself. As Socor (1997, p. 113) said, "an explanation was sought that was capable of addressing the indisputable psychological awareness of one's own being."

Interactions with significant others lie at the root of the sense of self (Mead 1934). At different points, a person may view another as a separate being or may experience the other as part of the self, under the control of the self, and providing functions for the self. In these situations, self psychology speaks of the other not as a separate object but as a "selfobject."

Kohut (1977) identifies needs for three types of selfobject experiences. *Idealizing* selfobjects are regarded positively. They contribute to the self's feelings of enthusiasm, mature values, and ideals. *Mirror* selfobject experiences allow individuals to see themselves in others and can mature into confident self-assertiveness and ambition. If such self-assertion is frustrated, anger or (narcissistic) rage may result. Finally, *alterego* (twinship) selfobjects are fundamental to experiencing a feeling of belonging. Kohut (1984, p. 194) defines the alterego selfobject need as "the need to experience essential alikeness" and suggests that these types of selfobject experience are fundamental to learning skills (how to ride a bike or how to cook, and so on).

According to self psychologists, psychopathology involves maladaptive attempts to restore inner equilibrium to the sense of self, a failure of the self to mature. Empathy is the therapist's primary tool for facilitating growth. The therapist's sustained empathic efforts provide corrective emotional experiences that promote the maturation of the self. In addition, for self psychologists, change occurs when patients experience, identify, and repair narcissistic injury. Group therapy provides an excellent laboratory for both selfobject experiences and narcissistic injuries to occur, with multiple opportunities for group members to experience new selfobject and reparative interactions that foster maturation of their sense of self.

Influential self psychologists interested in group therapy speak of the "group self" (Kohut 1976). Kohut wrote that "we posit the existence of a certain psychological configuration with regard to the group—let us call it the 'group self'—which is analogous to the self of the individual" (pp. 420–21). All group therapists know that group members typically refer to the group experience as "group," not as "the group." A member will commonly say that "I'll be late to group next week" or "group was painful for me this morning," which reflects the unconscious experience of the group as something in which one is embedded, rather than something apart from the self. One doesn't say that "knee was painful for me this morning," but rather "my knee was painful for me this morning," because the knee seems separate from, not part of, the self.

Intersubjective and Relational Theory

Early psychodynamic theory focused exclusively on the inner world of the patient and consequently defined the role of the therapist as a neutral expert *analyzing* the patient. Object relations theory and self psychology redefined the therapist as a more equal and active participant in the therapeutic relationship, a person open to being influenced by the patient and the group.

Intersubjective and relational theories take the further step of examining how each side of a relationship affects the other. *Intersubjective theory* underlines the mutual influence effect in all relationships, including the relationship between patient and therapist or group and therapist (Goldberg 1998). *Relational theory* highlights the impossibility of the therapist removing himself or herself from group transactions, in fact stressing the benefits of *not* removing oneself (Mitchell 1988; Aron 1991). The patient or group has a story to tell, and the therapist has his or her own story. As Schafer (1983, p. 187) says, "In interpreting or retelling the analysand's narrative performances, the analyst follows certain storylines of personal [psychological] development, conflictual situations, and subjective experience that are distinguishing features of his or her analytic theory and approach." The technique that flows from this theoretical foundation focuses therapeutic interaction on the here and now (recognizing but not emphasizing the influence of the past). As Benjamin (2005, p. 449) puts it, in a mature relational experience, "two people influence each other, but that interaction creates a space for both subjects' separate but recognizable centers of feeling and initiative."

In both the intersubjective and relational models, the therapist is free to judiciously disclose personal reactions and even personal experiences, behaviors discouraged in earlier dynamic models. For Freud, the analyst was like the expert surgeon dissecting the object before him. Given the Victorian *zeitgeist*, delving into the sexual and aggressive concerns of predominantly female patients was explosive. The earliest analysts were understandably cautious about entering too personally into relationships with analysands. Indeed, Freud's own insecurities led him to place his patients on a couch, facing away from him; at least in theory, this configuration reduces the likelihood of therapists' self-disclosure. When Freud's protégé Sandor Ferenczi allowed a patient to analyze *him* in a "mutual analysis," Freud was stunned, ultimately severing his relationship with him (Ferenczi 1988).

Contemporary clinicians who espouse the relational perspective, however, assert that the opacity of the therapist is a myth. They argue that even the most conservative analysts or therapists reveal a great deal about themselves merely by the way they select particular comments of the patient for exploration (Renik 1996). Currently, no one believes it is possible or desirable to practice what Leo Stone (1961) once referred to as the "cadaver model" of the therapist.

While group therapists agree that patients do not come to the group to hear about the therapist's life, they debate how much patients might profit from hearing. The interpersonal matrix of a therapy group invites more self-disclosure from the therapist than does individual psychotherapy. While many therapists, most notably West and Livesley (1986), have argued against therapists' self-disclosure in group therapy, many others take an opposing view (Rachmann 1990; Cohen and Schermer 2001). Yalom, an interpersonal group therapist, advocates an intermediate position. "We use our transparency and self-disclosure to maintain a therapeutic position with our clients that balances us in a position midway between the client's transference and its therapeutic disconfirmation. Your disclosure about the client's impact on you is a particularly effective intervention because it deepens understanding for the mutual impact between therapist and group member" (Yalom 2005, p. 214).

Conclusion

Few, if any, treatment modalities test a therapist's abilities or challenge a therapist's emotions in the way that group therapy does. It is difficult to form a group and nerve-wracking to lead one. Rutan, Stone, and Shay (2007) suggest that group therapy commonly threatens the clinician's sense of competence and leaves the therapist feeling "unknowledgeable, unskilled, or unhinged." Yet group therapists characteristically extol the benefits of group therapy, despite its challenges. Jerome Frank, himself, was supremely optimistic about what group therapy had to offer. In 1969 Frank wrote: "I don't believe that the increased understanding of processes involved in the dyadic relationship will greatly affect practice in the future. If significant breakthroughs in therapy are to come, I believe they will be through methods that mobilize group forces to involve the whole person" (p. 122). In 1992 he added: "the powerful therapeutic properties of group methods, coupled with their relative economy, will eventually lead them to become treatments of choice for most persons suffering from psychologically-caused distress and disability" (p. vii).

We close with the words of a patient in group therapy, a woman whose experience illustrates the principles of group healing explicated by Frank and those who followed him. Embedded in her narrative one can see the centrality of the healing relationship (here, with the group), the impact of the healing setting, internalization of the rationale of group treatment, and acceptance of the rituals of open and honest expression of feeling. She also notes the awareness of altruism as a healing force, as well as the benefit of emotional arousal, with such forces leading to a genuine change in her assumptive world.

My experience in group therapy has contributed to my emotional strength and shown me how my ability to be present for others, even when I have had pending issues of my own, is rewarding and edifying. The group is a sacred thing to me, a place where people come together and experience their deepest selves. We are there for one another by sharing thoughts and reactions, sometimes just by sharing in a moment of sadness. We challenge each other to ever-ascending levels of honesty. The group experience is a liberating one for many reasons, one of which is the relative equality that group members enjoy within the bounds of a session. No one member has more right to time than another; no one member has the right to steer the session. We learn to assert ourselves in one of the only atmospheres that exist that are artificially free of pre-defined power structures, a rare luxury, to be sure.

I have learned a great deal about dealing with conflict from my experiences in group therapy. It has confirmed my notion that I am averse to conflict and will sometimes avoid it, given the freedom to do so. But I have learned that conflict arises naturally when people are being honest with one another; it is the price we pay to really know one another. So I have learned to accept conflict, though I still treat it with utmost care. I tend to try to take away any emotional sting my expression of conflict might hold, so that even if the idea is hostile, it is couched in neutral terms. And I try to own any part of the conflictual idea that belongs to my reading of a situation, and that may not reside in the situation itself. In this way I respect the perceptions and emotions of the person with whom I am experiencing conflict. If he or she is able to similarly engage, we have a strong potential not only to avoid breaking down into hostility but to positively change our relationship by learning about one another.

If only all of our patients could profit as much from our efforts.

REFERENCES

Aron, L. 1991. The patient's experience of the analyst's subjectivity. *Psychoanalytic Dialogues* 1:29–51.
Benjamin, J. 2005. Creating an intersubjective reality. *Psychoanalytic Dialogues* 15:447–57.
Bion, W. R 1961. *Experiences in Groups.* New York: Routledge.
Bruner, J. 1990. *Acts of Meaning.* Cambridge, MA: Harvard University Press.
Cohen, B. D., and Schermer, V. L. 2001. Therapist self-disclosure in group psychotherapy from an intersubjective and self psychological standpoint. *Group* 25:41–57.

Downing, J. N. 2004. Psychotherapy practice in a pluralistic world: philosophical and moral dilemmas. *Journal of Psychotherapy Integration* 14:123–48.

Durkin, H. 1964. *The Group in Depth.* New York: International Universities Press.

Fairbairn, W. R. D. 1952. *An Object-Relations Theory of the Personality.* London: Tavistock.

Ferenczi, S. 1988. *The Clinical Diary of Sandor Ferenczi.* Ed. J. Dupont; trans. M. Balint and N. Z. Jackson. Cambridge, MA: Harvard University Press. First published 1932.

Foulkes, S. H. 1961. Group process and the individual in the therapeutic group. *British Journal of Medical Psychology* 34:23–31.

Frank, J. D. 1961. *Persuasion and Healing: A Comparative Study of Psychotherapy.* Baltimore: Johns Hopkins University Press.

———. 1969. Common features account for effectiveness. *International Journal of Psychiatry* 7:122–26.

———. 1973. *Persuasion and Healing: A Comparative Study of Psychotherapy,* rev. ed. Baltimore: Johns Hopkins University Press.

———. 1974. Psychotherapy: the restoration of morale. *American Journal of Psychiatry* 131:271–74.

———. 1992. Foreword. In R. C. MacKenzie (ed.), *Classics in Group Psychotherapy* (pp. v–vii). New York: Guilford Press.

Frank, J. D., and Frank, J. B. 1991. *Persuasion and Healing: A Comparative Study of Psychotherapy,* 3rd ed. Baltimore: Johns Hopkins University Press.

Gabbard, G. O. 2005. *Psychodynamic Psychiatry in Clinical Practice,* 4th ed. Washington, DC: American Psychiatric Press.

Gabbard, G. O., and Westen, D. 2003. Rethinking therapeutic action. *International Journal of Psychoanalysis* 84:823–41.

Glass, T. A., Mendes de Leon, C., and Berkman, L. F. 1999. Population based study of social and productive activities as predictors of survival among elderly Americans. *British Medical Journal* 310:478–83.

Glatzer, H. T. 1953. Handling transference and resistance in group psychotherapy. *Psychoanalytic Review* 40:36–43.

Goldberg, A. 1998. Self psychology since Kohut. *Psychoanalytic Quarterly* 67:240–55.

Grinberg, L. 1973. Projective identification and projective counter-identification in the dynamics of groups. In L. Wolberg and E. Schwartz (eds.), *Group Therapy* (pp. 145–53). New York: Intercontinental Medical Book Corp.

Guntrip, H. 1969. *Schizoid Phenomena, Object-Relations, and the Self.* New York: International Universities Press.

Horwitz, L. 1983. Projective identification in dyads and groups. *International Journal of Group Psychotherapy* 33:259–79.

Janoff-Bulman, R. 1989. Assumptive worlds and the stress of traumatic events: applications of the schema construct. *Social Cognition* 7:113–36.

Jorgensen, C. R. 2004. Active ingredients in individual psychotherapy: searching for common factors. *Psychoanalytic Psychology* 21:516–40.

Kanigel, R. 1983. The story of a quiet radical. *Johns Hopkins Magazine,* June, pp. 34–39.

Klein, M. 1946. Notes on some schizoid mechanisms. *International Journal of Psychoanalysis* 27:99–110.

Kohler, W. 1969. *The Task of Gestalt Psychology.* Princeton, NJ: Princeton University Press.

Kohut, H. 1971. *The Analysis of the Self.* New York: International Universities Press.

———. 1976. Creativeness, charisma, group psychology. In P. Ornstein (ed.), *The Search for the Self*. New York: International Universities Press.

———. 1977. *The Restoration of the Self*. New York: International Universities Press.

———. 1984. *How Does Analysis Cure?* Chicago: University of Chicago Press.

Koltko-Rivera, M. E. 2004. The psychology of worldviews. *Review of General Psychology* 8:3–58.

Kosseff, J. F. 2001. Wilfred Bion: the questing man. *Group* 25:243–51.

Lewis, D. 1986. *On the Plurality of Worlds*. Malden, MA: Blackwell.

Malcus, L. 1995. Indirect scapegoating via projective identification and the mother group. *International Journal of Group Psychotherapy* 45:55-71.

Maslow, A. 1943. A theory of human motivation. *Psychological Review* 50:370–96.

Mead, G. H. 1934. *Mind, Self, and Society*. Chicago: University of Chicago Press.

Meinecke, C. 1987. Jerome Frank: persuader and exemplar. *Journal of Counseling and Development* 65:226–32.

Mitchell, S. A. 1988. *Relational Concepts in Psychoanalysis: An Integration*. Cambridge, MA: Harvard University Press.

Morrison, A. P. 1986. On projective identification in couples' groups. *International Journal of Group Psychotherapy* 36:55-73.

Neimeyer, R. A., and Mahoney, M. J. 1995. *Constructivism in Psychotherapy*. Washington, DC: American Psychological Association.

Ogden, T. H. 1982. *Projective Identification and Psychotherapeutic Technique*. Northvale, NJ: Jason Aronson.

Powdermaker, F. B., and Frank, J. D. 1953. *Group Psychotherapy*. Cambridge, MA: Harvard University Press.

Rachmann, A. W. 1990. Judicious self-disclosure in group analysis. *Group* 14:132–44.

Renik, O. 1996. The ideal of the anonymous analyst and the problem of self-disclosure. *Psychoanalytic Quarterly* 65:681–82.

Rutan, J. S., Stone, W. N., and Shay, J. 2007. *Psychodynamic Group Psychotherapy*, 4th ed. New York: Guilford Press.

Sandler, J. 1976. Countertransference and role responsiveness. *International Review of Psychoanalysis* 3:43–47.

Schafer, R. 1983. *The Analytic Attitude*. New York: Basic Books.

Scharff, D., and Scharff, J. 1987. *Object Relations Family Therapy*. Northvale, NJ: Jason Aronson.

Shay, J. 2001. My problem with projective identification. *Northeastern Society for Group Psychotherapy Newsletter* 23:1–2.

Socor, B. J. 1997. *Conceiving the Self: Presence and Absence in Psychoanalytic Theory*. Madison, CT: International Universities Press.

Stone, L. 1961. *The Psychoanalytic Situation*. New York: International Universities Press.

Wampold, B. E., and Weinberger, J. 2010. Jerome D. Frank: psychotherapy researcher and humanitarian. In L. G. Castonguay, J. C. Muran, L. Angus, J. A. Hayes, N. Ladany, and T. Anderson (eds.), *Bringing Psychotherapy Research to Life: Understanding Change through the Work of Leading Clinical Researchers—Legacies from the Society for Psychotherapy Research*. Washington, DC: American Psychology Association.

Weber, R. 2005. Unraveling projective identification and enactment. In L. Motherwell and J. Shay (eds.), *Complex Dilemmas in Group Therapy: Pathways to Resolution* (pp. 75–86). New York: Brunner-Routledge.

West, M., and Livesley, W. J. 1986. Therapist transparency and the frame for group psychotherapy. *International Journal of Psychotherapy* 36:5–19.

Winnicott, D. 1960. The theory of the parent-child relationship. *International Journal of Psychoanalysis* 41:585–95.

———.1965. *The Maturational Process and the Facilitating Environment.* New York: International Universities Press.

Wolf, A., and Schwartz, E. K. 1962. *Psychoanalysis in Groups.* New York: Grune and Stratton.

Yalom, I. D. 1970. *The Theory and Practice of Group Psychotherapy.* New York: Basic Books.

———. 2005. *The Theory and Practice of Group Psychotherapy,* 5th ed. With M. Leszcz. New York: Basic Books.

CHAPTER 14

Cultural Dynamics in Psychotherapy and Cultural Psychotherapies

Ingredients, Processes, and Outcomes

Renato D. Alarcón, M.D., M.P.H.,
Julia B. Frank, M.D., and
Mark Williams, M.D.

How funny it'll seem to come out among the people that walk with their heads downward! The Antipathies, I think, . . . but I shall have to ask them what the name of the country is, you know. Please, Ma'am, is this New Zealand or Australia? . . . And what an ignorant little girl she'll think me for asking! No, it'll never do to ask: perhaps I shall see it written up somewhere.
—*Alice's Adventures in Wonderland*

. . . the psychotherapist, as a socially sanctioned expert and healer and a symbolic member of the patient's reference groups, may be able to mobilize forces that are sufficiently powerful to combat demoralization and produce beneficial changes in the patient's assumptive world, thereby improving the patient's adaptation and bringing about a concomitant reduction in symptoms.

—*PERSUASION AND HEALING*, 1991, P. 51

Jerome Frank's definition of psychotherapy captures its essential sociocultural nature: "a healing relationship . . . [in which] the healer tries to bring about relief of symptoms . . . typically accompanied by changes in emotional state, attitudes, and behavior . . . The healing influence is exercised primarily by words, acts and rituals in which sufferer, healer, and sometimes a group participate jointly" (Frank and Frank 1991, p. 2). It follows that the practice of psychotherapy requires both training and expertise and a solid cultural competence. Cultural competence is the individual clinician's demonstration of respect for and interest in the cultural factors that shape a given patient's context and behavior (Tseng 2004; Lu 2006). While exercising the ability to translate and integrate cultural information into a comprehensive therapeutic approach, clinicians must remain aware of their own perspectives or biases. At the same time, the cultural norms of the society in which the psychotherapeutic encounter takes place dictate the roles of therapist and patient. The therapist's methods and skills, the nature of the transactions, and even the outcomes of treatment reflect expectations nurtured by culture. Thus, culture itself becomes a therapeutic tool, a different lens through which to evaluate human transactions.

Culture and psychotherapy mutually or reciprocally influence one another. Some psychotherapeutic schools have, on occasion, changed the cultural climate of their time; the best example is the "liberating" effect of psychoanalysis on the rigid Victorian codes of late nineteenth-century Europe. Psychoanalysis provided seemingly rational and logical ("scientific," as Freud claimed) explanations for mysterious or profoundly troubling inner feelings or emotions and the behaviors that expressed them (Assoun 1981). Freud and his followers precipitated a dramatic shift in the surrounding culture, placing the effort to understand human subjective life in scientific terms, on an equal footing with religion and moral philosophy.

Against culture as a conceptual frame, as outlined in a chapter 5, patient and therapist interact in ways that express culturally derived knowledge, beliefs, and the very notion of who they are and what made them the way they are. Participation in therapy exposes these qualities to scrutiny by another person, as each expresses views and emotions in an effort to understand the other. This dynamic, then, follows two converging routes: one that defines the patient and his or her problems and the therapist's perceptions and skills (we call them "cultural endowments"), and another that delineates the psychotherapeutic encounter and its outcomes as a thoroughly cultural occurrence. In this chapter we explore the influence of culture on the participants in the psychotherapeutic encounter and discuss how culture structures the encounter and its outcome in light of the thoughts and perspectives expressed by Jerome Frank in *Persuasion and Healing*.

Cultural Endowments of Patient and Therapist

The cultural qualities of therapists and patients range from the "assumptive world" of each protagonist to the manifestations of the "culture-bound syndromes" (Paniagua 2000; Baer et al. 2003). These syndromes, and the corresponding notion of culture-bound psychotherapy, create a loose network linking culture, symptoms, and the dynamics of psychotherapeutic transactions. The threads of this network, the active influence of meaning and identity as individual ingredients and of stigma as a more group-based and group-oriented occurrence, at once broaden and constrain the interaction of patient and therapist.

Assumptive World

Jerome Frank enriched the conceptual catalogue of psychiatry in elaborating Cantril's "assumptive world," a topic discussed in chapters 1, 6, and 7 of this volume. Based on another strong cultural notion, that of "meaning," in every human transaction, each person's assumptive world represents an effort to "make sense [of] . . . even the most nonsensical behavior." The result of each person's evaluation of "internal and external stimuli, in the light of assumptions about what is dangerous, safe, important, unimportant, good or bad," the assumptive world organizes beliefs "into sets of highly structured, complex, interacting values, expectations and images of self and others that are closely related to emotional states and feelings." In turn, enduring assumptions "become organized into attitudes with cognitive, affective and behavioral components" (Frank and Frank 1991, p. 25).

The development of the assumptive world reflects, at times subtly, at times explicitly, the determining force of culture. It starts "as soon as the infant enters into transactions with the environment." Such experiences "coalesce into generalizations whose validity depends on three factors: the representativeness of the sample on which they are based, the accuracy of the information it provides, and *the social world to which the infant belongs*" (p. 27, emphasis added).

This process cogently articulates cultural determinants of motivation, perceptual and cognitive processing, and behavioral expression of these factors. Frank advances a biocultural connection between these processes when affirming that "like all fundamental needs, the need to attribute meaning to events probably has a neurophysiological base" (p. 54). (See also chapters 3 and 4.) Furthermore, Frank applies Sullivan's concept (1953) of "consensual validation" as a useful tool in the "harmonization" of different assumptive worlds, an interpersonal process that is also eminently cultural. Thus, the dynamic value of the assumptive world in any psychotherapeutic transaction is compelling and unequivocal: it is the (partly cultural) baggage that patient and therapist will carry and use along their psychotherapeutic journey.

Meaning

Meaning ranks high among the cultural variables and is one of the key concepts in cultural psychiatry. While certainly not a pathological concept, meaning may have a powerful pathogenic impact on human behavior if distorted by perceptions, demoralization, existential crises, or symptoms. Meaning is the attribution of significance to facts, actions and reactions, emotions, and behaviors. As such, its cultural bases are self-evident: the way we perceive things, the views we elaborate about events and their effects, are influenced definitively by how we were raised, how we learned to interact in society, and our assumptions about our own and others' roles. As a deeply rooted cultural concept, at the core of our assumptive worlds, meaning entails patterns of thinking transmitted through generations. Again, if such schooling followed rigid cultural codes or was defective or distorted, or if it deviated from the usual cultural rules of the individual's milieu, the results may reach clinical proportions. Conversely, if the rules of a culture are themselves destructive, as in an environment saturated with violence, culturally syntonic assumptions that would be pathological in another context may not necessarily denote illness. The cultural meaning of an act, feeling, or belief determines whether or not it expresses pathology. Those who kill in fits of rage or for gain are criminals; soldiers who kill in battle are fulfilling their duty. Psychotherapy, in Frank's language, aims at "*the transformation of [distorted] meanings*" (Frank and Frank 1991, p. 59, emphasis added). To be successful, this transformation must occur in a cultural context that supports it.

Frank says clearly, in many passages of his book, that therapy may be effective for reasons other than its scientific rationale. What any psychotherapy does is restore into the patient's self-perception workable meanings sanctioned by his or her cultural codes. Realignment with meanings derived from culture is one of the most "persuasive" mechanisms of every psychotherapeutic process. Frank cites several possible explanations, other than a specific therapeutic rationale, for why some patients improve: justifying to themselves the effort involved in completing the treatment, working harder as the end of the process gets closer, attempting to satisfy the therapist, and getting ready for the immediate future. In the "microculture" of psychotherapy, such processes embody the patient's need to reconcile the meaning of events and behaviors with dominant or acceptable cultural perceptions. Working hard, pleasing authority, and looking ahead are, to some extent, culturally specific rather than universal principles or values.

Frank incorporates other cultural "ingredients" into the concept of meaning in psychotherapy. "In Western culture," he writes, "statements gain credibility by being couched in the language of science" (Frank and Frank 1991, p. 58): the therapist's interpretations or explanations of the patient's problems become credible when draped in the mantle of objective rationality. The therapist's conviction about the validity of the treatment rationale enables the patient "to construct a more optimistic apologia," that is, to change the meaning of his or her own interpretation of events. This gentle confrontation of the patient's adult self with the distortions he or she may have unconsciously carried over from earlier periods enhances a sense of mastery. Frank makes clear that "it is important not to confuse the cause of a symptom with its current meaning, since the current meaning can often be changed, regardless of the symptom's cause" (p. 207). If the symptom, on the other hand, is a "miscarried communication," and each communication (cultural feature) has an assigned meaning (another cultural feature), the definition of "insight" can very well be, again, the reestablishment of culturally supported meanings in the life of the patient. In essence, the therapist guides patients to adopt meanings appropriate to their milieu. A scientific pedigree for the therapy implies that the theory involved has been systematically tested in others who resemble the patient in some important way. To link therapy with systematic investigation is inherently an act of shared meaning, an expression of the power of culture, as well as a particular "Western" method of supporting a healer's authority (see chapter 4).

Identity

Identity has many definitions, including those offered by philosophy, psychology, and social science. For philosophers, the "identity of a person" results from inquiring how our successive perceptions of that person coalesce in a "causal" context (Baier 1979; Hume 1988). Kant (1933) asserted that the *self* could be known only in its relation with the world, while William James (1891, 1912) postulated that personal identity entails "a sense of being always the same." Descartes (1954) emphasized the "incorporality" of identity, and Heidegger (1927) linked identity with a "potential of self-actualization." Parfit (1971) insisted that the fundamental nature of identity resides in its "psychological continuity." Glover (1988) explained identity as a quality based on the "social construction of an inner world," enhanced by emotionally charged features such as "the need of recognition."

Philosophical anthropologists, including Buber (1948), propose that identity originates from notions such as species, soul and life nurtured by peoples and communities, types and characters, and vital stages. Social scientists (Dahrendorf 1959) have explored the dimensions and ingredients of identity:

language and ethnicity, history and geography, organized around the central notion of culture. In the individual psychological sphere, Erik Erikson (1964) emphasized intrapsychic processes, parental influences, environmental factors, and ethical principles. Identity, in short, is an interpretation of the *self*, a manner of self-definition and self-knowledge, the culmination of our potentials as unique individuals in the world (Baumeister 1986).

Within this intellectual tradition, then, identity results from a convergence of multiple factors acting on an individual's life and contributing to his or her affirmation of selfhood in the face of the surrounding world. Identity reflects the individual's cultural environment, that is to say, history, language, education, beliefs, and societal laws, combined with biology, ethnicity, geography, and temperament. It is almost tautological to say that identity is essential for a human being to find his or her place in familial, community, and world interactions. In reciprocal fashion, collective experiences contribute heavily to individual identity. The psychological implications of identity are many, and so are the psychopathological consequences of its fracture or loss.

In a lucid socioanthropological way, Frank depicts Americans, for instance, as "taught to be aggressive, yet at the same time affable and considerate. Violence is simultaneously glorified in the mass media, and condemned in personal relationships or in the encounters of daily life." To add to the complexity of identity formation, "children in our society may be exposed less to clearly conflicting values than to amorphous and constantly changing ones." Frank goes on to reflect on the many factors, all deeply rooted in American culture, that constitute a constant threat to the integrity of the American identity: the confusion thus engendered is compounded by "the shifting modes and morals of the larger society." He concludes: "Such a society hampers the formation of a solid sense of identity in its members" (Frank and Frank 1991, p. 30).

This is the "identity diffusion" that Frank appropriately attributes to Erikson (1968). Many authors agree on this construct when defining "loss of identity" in relation to some essential aspects of clinical psychiatric entities: the emptiness, the confusion, or the painful transformation of self-concept that patients describe as alienation, the "loss of a sense of purpose" (Solle 1975). Alienation, the denial of identity, entails not only the cognitive distortions or the perceptual chaos of the psychotic but also the helplessness and worthlessness of the depressed, the loss of an existential compass in the anxious, and the total fragmentation and isolation of the demented. Thus, for potentially modifiable conditions, it is pertinent to consider psychotherapy as a systematic attempt to restore an individual's identity, to re-place him or her in the context of cultural and existential adequacy. Always challenging and provocative, Frank even suggests that the idiosyncratic symbolic processes (crucial to the establishment of identity) of some cultures can have a major impact on physical conditions. He concludes that life history and personality, the core of identity, may profoundly affect the course of chronic illness.

Stigma

From time immemorial, mental illness has carried the "dead weight" of stigmatization (Institute of Medicine 2005; Caldwell-Harris and Aycicegi 2006; Littlewood, Jadhav, and Ryder 2007). The impact and nature of stigma waxes and wanes over time and across cultures. The expression of social exclusion, finger-pointing, humiliation, and concomitant neglect may be somewhat subtler or less outrageous in contemporary times than in the past, when the phenomena now called mental illness might have led to allegations of witchcraft or divine influence. Nevertheless, stigma persists and is arguably the most pervasive cultural dynamic aspect of the way society defines mental illness, profoundly affecting both those who suffer from it and those who hope to take care of them (Balsa and McGuire 2003).

Persuasion and Healing added a new dimension to the consideration of stigma: the notion of "shifting boundaries" as part of the task of distinguishing between accepted and outcast groups in American society. These unnamed, tacit and draconian, yet fluid rules create "an inexhaustible pool of those considered deviant because of illness, oddity, different beliefs, or unacceptable behaviors." Frank, however, keeping in mind the goals and purposes of psychotherapy, particularly the strength of group modalities, offered the idea that groups effectively counter this dynamic by providing their participants "with a coherent system of values . . . [that] relieve alienation and despair" (Frank and Frank 1991, p. 244). In the past several decades, former mental patients have joined together in an effort to achieve this type of synthesis and self-respect. In parallel fashion, their relatives, acquaintances, and other people of good will have been somewhat successful in reducing stigma through the creation and work of lay organizations at local, national, and even international levels, such as the National Alliance on Mental Illness, the National Mental Health Association, and the World Federation for Mental Health.

Stigma is closely related to alienation or the negation of a genuine identity. It originates from ignorance, which in turn nurtures fear. Defensiveness becomes a strategy in the name of an ill-conceived protectiveness, and later leads to aggressiveness, even violence, as a way to keep the stigmatized away. Protectiveness, defensiveness, and aggressiveness flourish in the face of the "shallow and shifting sociability" that attends the weakening of the traditional stable family constellations, long-lasting friendships, and predictable group interactions that are the bedrock of emotional security. The prevailing *ethos* of a pluralistic society with multiple religious, legal, and educational systems may paradoxically foster a narrow or rigid view of normality, or an ambiguous/confusing definition of it. In this context, it becomes easier to "identify" those who are "different." From society's absorption of all those ingredients to the establishment of a sort of institutionalized stigma, the distance is indeed minimal. This is the fate of "deviants," as psychotic patients, homosexuals, the poor, and the underprivileged are called by some sectors of the general public or by followers of a crude sociological perspective.

In a society of shifting identities, efforts to eradicate stigma may paradoxically strengthen it. The anti-psychiatry movement (Hubbard 1950; Szasz 1974), initially an effort to protect mentally ill people from mistreatment, discarded the cultural safeguards of careful scholarship by extending its critique beyond the ambiguity of psychiatric diagnoses or the social labeling of mental illness. In a peculiar twist, this initially principled, philosophically based opposition to psychiatry became the foundation of a movement, Scientology, that adopted the American cultural form of a religious sect. Scientology took ownership of the views of other critics (especially Thomas Szasz, who, sadly, did not object to this maneuvering) to call psychiatry "the industry of death." While purporting to condemn an assumed mismanagement of human beings, the anti-psychiatry movement unwittingly exacerbates the stigma and the isolation of the mentally ill with barrages of insults and barriers of denial, especially in diverting social resources, such as adequate insurance coverage, from the care of psychiatric patients. In his essay "Psychiatry, the Healthy Invalid," Frank provided a culturally resonant answer to these critics:

> Pessimists both within and outside the profession . . . [enumerate] various signs of illness. High on the list appears to be a widespread public disenchantment with psychiatry. It has become abundantly clear, for example, that psychiatrists do not have the answers to race relations, truancy, criminality and war . . . Another criticism is that psychiatrists, in the guise of diagnosing and treating the mentally ill, are actually agents of social control, imprisoning deviants in mental

hospitals by labeling them "ill" and then punishing them with electroconvulsive treatment, seclusion, and the like under the label of therapy . . . [But] although psychiatry is indeed experiencing distressing symptoms, they are not dangerous. Rather, most are analogous to the growing pains that accompany maturation . . . Psychiatry, rather than being on the verge of death, is about to enter a period of vigorous health . . . We are shedding some of our infantile omnipotence and our dependence on father figures like Sigmund Freud and Uncle Sam. (Frank 1977, pp. 1354–55)

"Culture-Bound Syndromes"

First identified by Yap (1951) more than five decades ago, culture-bound syndromes (CBSs) constitute one of the most debated and controversial issues in clinical psychiatry (Guarnaccia and Rogler 1999; Tseng 2001; Draguns and Tanaka-Matsumi 2003). The most widely accepted definition describes them as symptomatic conglomerates with peculiar clinical characteristics, different from the usual diagnostic categories, and closely related to unique cultural factors in the patient's milieu. The early literature on CBSs emphasized the exotic nature of these conditions and named them in the original languages in which they were first described (Prince and Tcheng-Laroche 1987). The culturally accepted etiologies of these categories were religious or spiritual, entailing notions of "soul loss, possession by an evil spirit, the magical insertion of a harmful body by a sorcerer" (Frank and Frank 1991, p. 3), sin, punishment, divine warnings, and the like. They also involved attributions of destructive social or interpersonal processes, including "machinations of offended or malicious ancestral ghosts," envy, anger, shame, conflict. Some expressed "existential" themes: issues of fate, position in the world, vulnerability due to transgressions, or loneliness.

Reflecting the anthropology of the times, books, articles, essays, and therapeutic manuals described and offered interventions for conditions such as *koro, amok, Taijin Kyofusho, susto,* "evil eye," *Hwa-Byung, Dhat, Latah,* or *ataque de nervios* (Malhotra and Wig 1975; Carr 1978; Kimura 1982; Kenny 1983; Guarnaccia, Angel, and Guorobey 1989; Chowdhury 1996; Roberts, Han, and Weed 2006). These CBSs were identified and described in societies of Asia, Africa, Australia, or Latin America, adding to their mystery and exoticism. Social scientists and culturally oriented clinicians reached a tacit agreement about the pathoplastic role of culture in the delineation and expression of symptoms and signs of CBSs, with authors strongly maintaining that conventional nosologies could not appropriately describe them. Those who described these conditions provided elaborate explanations about causality, treatment norms, and procedures that reflected the perspectives of the cultural groups in which they originated. Treatment involved rituals that included prayers, exorcism ceremonies, dances, fasting, and use of herbs and, in some cases, hallucinogenic plants and infusions (Tsai, Butcher, and Munoz 2001; Tseng 2001; Sánchez-Beltrán and Avelar-Gutierrez 2009; Villaseñor and Reyes Rivas 2009).

Modern anthropological perspectives stress that cultural influence is universal and ordinary, not some exotic process typical only of non-Western societies. For this reason, the term "cultural syndromes" better reflects the role of culture in the delineation of clinical conditions seen in all regions of the world. By illuminating the universal, common features of many healing activities, including psychotherapy, *Persuasion and Healing* contributed to this intellectual evolution. Though recognizing the essentially cultural nature of the explanatory models of a number of clinical pictures in different societies, Frank avoided using the CBS concept, even when describing the illnesses treated successfully in shamanistic rituals or other forms of faith healing, including Christian ones found in the West. He adopted a truly biopsychosociocultural approach, suggesting that theoreticians of psychiatry or abnormal psychology had much to learn from the many nonindustrial societies that "regard illness as a misfortune involving the entire person, including disturbed relationships with the spiritual realm, and with other members of the community." He added: "In particular, non-Western societies may not distinguish sharply between mental and bodily illness, or between natural and supernatural causes of illness" (Frank and Frank 1991, p. 89). He devoted convincing paragraphs to the notion of "taboo death," the demise of individuals following states of panic triggered by having been "cursed or . . . [having] inadvertently broken a taboo" within their cultural milieu (p. 90). Frank had no qualms about relating psychotherapy to the activities of shamans or native healers in the alleviation and even prevention of these culturally determined clinical events.

The assertion that CBSs are not unique to faraway, exotic lands and that it is better to speak of "cultural syndromes" has added substance to the debate on the nosological status of these conditions. Western, industrialized societies include entities of similar pathogenesis and strong cultural implications. Anorexia nervosa and related eating disorders most clearly exemplify Western cultural syndromes. While self-starvation and gluttony have been identified in many cultures throughout history (Brumberg 1989), the meaning that patients and others attribute to disordered eating has varied dramatically over time. Earlier anorectic women struggled to attain holiness or moral purity. Today's starving girls are often motivated by the desire to conform to a culturally sanctioned image of the ideal female body, born out of media-induced descriptions, the show-business industry, and iconic celebrities—a truly cultural etiopathogenic chain (Gordon 1990). Culturally determined aspects of the physical environment, especially the abundance of "hyperselected" foods of different kinds, also contribute to contemporary eating disorders. Although the biological effects of starvation are identical in a devout, aspiring saint or a restricting dieter, effective treatment for either one must address the cultural elements, as expressed in the meaning that the patient and others attribute to her behavior. A culturally informed approach to contemporary anorexia nervosa involves, or should involve, the arbiters of mass media, exercise consultants, beauticians, dietitians, and nutritionists as well as medical personnel and scientifically trained therapists. Enlisting such agents to foster change would be completely consistent with Frank's view that treatment may depend on, but not recognize, many cultural interpreters. Such figures are the Western equivalent of native healers and their entourage.

The classificatory schemes of the American Psychiatric Association's *Diagnostic and Statistical Manual of Mental Disorders* and the World Health Organization 's *International Classification of Diseases and Health Related Problems* reflect a second theme in the current debate about the appropriate status of CBSs. The debate is two-sided, and not free of political implications: universalists or "lumpers" criticize the "uniqueness" of CBSs and advocate their inclusion in existing diagnostic groups (e.g., *ataque de nervios* as an anxiety disorder, *koro* as a delusional disorder, *amok* as a depersonalization/dissociative disorder) (Tseng 2009). "Splitters," the defenders of a primarily cultural etiopathogenesis, warn that incorporating CBSs into the existing categories would do a disservice to many groups of patients throughout the world, a new form of "benign neglect"—stigmatization by exclusion—of everything cultural in clinical psychiatry. These positions reflect both the essential ambiguity of descriptive diagnosis and the interests of different constituencies jockeying for the power and resources associated with being acknowledged as experts and healers. The only acceptable position for a clinician-researcher in the tradition of *Persuasion and Healing* would be to advocate further research, with well-delineated comparative studies of the diagnostic identification and processing of the disorders, as well as of distinctive management strategies, including, but not limited to, psychotherapy. CBSs are a fertile field of reflection and research, events that incorporate defining cultural characteristics into the clinical setting of psychotherapeutic encounters.

Cultural Ingredients and Their Dynamic Impact on the Psychotherapeutic Encounter

Psychotherapy practitioners with scientific aspirations seek to ground their work on universal principles that transcend the particularity of cultural context. Such neutrality may occasionally be possible in medicine, since the human body is essentially the same everywhere, but psychotherapy almost inevitably reflects the cultural context in which it is practiced and the cultural endowments of its protagonists. Many cultural variables affect treatment relationships and treatment outcomes. Three considered most influential are social ranking, expressed emotions, and the nature of the placebo response. These and other variables imply dynamic interaction between the sufferer, the healing agent, and the healing relationship itself (figure 14.1).

Socioeconomic Status of Therapist and Patient

Social ranking is a cultural variable, changing and even volatile at times, but always an essential component of any society's life. In the West this is captured primarily in the variable of socioeconomic status (SES), a composite of income and education (Hollingshead and Redlich 1958). Other societies also assign status based on wealth, but may give equal weight to age, social role, gender, or group identification. Furthermore, hierarchical differences between social groups occur and have occurred in the most egalitarian cultures or civilizations. In industrialized societies, a large volume of research has documented the impact of patients' SES on the pathogenesis, degree of severity, actual illness experience, and even outcomes of different medical and emotional conditions (Chandra and Skinner 2003; Horwitz 2004; Yung et al. 2005). Recently, the interactions between SES and health have become a prominent research topic under the rubric of "health care disparities." Many studies show that those who are relatively poor have earlier onset, more severe course, and more negative outcomes (including earlier death) for many conditions (Alegría, Bijl, et al. 2000; Wagstaff and van Doorslaer 2000; Alegría, Canino, et al. 2002; Stone 2004). These disparities reflect both the subtle effects of relative disadvantage and the more concrete ones of educational level, pathogenic occupational con-

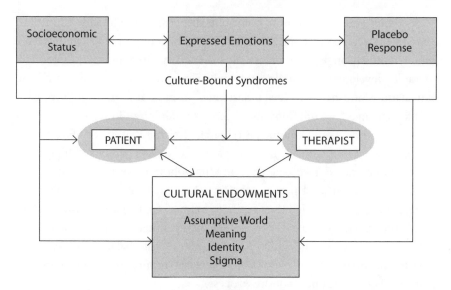

Figure 14.1. Cultural Dynamics in the Psychotherapeutic Encounter.

ditions, availability and accessibility of care services, and timing of professional interventions. Disparities exert a particularly strong influence on psychotherapy, in which issues of interpersonal relationships and resulting support or neglect play an important role.

Studies of the effect of therapists' SES complement early work on the role of patients' status. The therapist's status influences his or her conscious or unconscious perception of the patient, while the patient's status may affect his or her willingness to consider the therapist as an authority figure (Skultans 2004). Deep in the patient's cultural baggage, issues of self-esteem and level of openness emerge as decisive ingredients of the quality of relationships between equals or, perhaps even more intensely, between those of different social rank. No less than early family experiences, SES may thus be a decisive element of the "transference/countertransference" context, not necessarily discussed during the clinical encounter. The therapist's social position, embodied in what Frank termed *ethos* (Frank and Frank 1991, p. 66), may influence the patient's feeling of confidence in the therapist even more strongly than the knowledge the therapist may have of the patient's condition. On the therapist's side, the most frequent, often unrecognized, negative reflection of his or her self-perception with regard to the patient may be a paternalistic, even condescending attitude (Koch and Turgut 2004).

As Frank and other authors point out, disparities in ethnicity, education, and SES between patient and therapist create a host of problems. Studies have centered mostly on psychodynamically oriented therapies in which "interview therapies developed for middle- and upper-class patients often fail to meet the expectations and needs of lower-class ones" (Frank and Frank 1991, p. 156). Frank challenged assumptions about the unsuitability of lower-class patients for such treatment, and conducted research showing that lower-SES patients *who do remain in treatment* "respond at least as well as patients of higher socioeconomic status" (see chapter 1 in this volume). He hypothesized that "strong motivation" and perhaps the fact that "for some, the therapist may represent a group to which they aspire to belong" (p. 157) are decisive factors in this unexpected responsiveness. Other therapeutic ingredients, such as the therapist's willingness and ability to listen, may counterbalance the tacit negative implications of socioeconomic differences. Training philosophies are certainly decisive components of this process.

Expressed Emotions

Another feature of the family microculture, "expressed emotions" became a well-known clinical and research topic in the early 1980s (Falloon, Boyd, and McGill 1984). This research found that a composite measure of family members' level of hostility toward, criticism of, and over-involvement with a relative diagnosed with schizophrenia predicted the frequency and severity of psychotic relapses. Therapy that reduced expressed emotion, moreover, reduced relapse rates. Illnesses exacerbated by high expressed emotion now extend beyond schizophrenic psychoses to refractory depression and chronic medical disorders, conditions for which psychotherapy was previously considered ineffective (Falloon 1992; Wearden et al. 2000; Hooley 2007).

Debates ensued as to whether such expressiveness "could exist independent of the patient's behavior . . . [or whether] this negative emotional climate may be the family's understandable reaction to a disruptive or withdrawn person" (Frank and Frank 1991, p. 271). Later research concluded that relapses might reflect both the expression of excessive negative emotions and the absence of positive, supportive emotions.

For our purposes, this variable exemplifies a cultural factor in need of appropriate consideration within the psychotherapeutic process. Frank asserted that the role of expressed emotions supported his contention that mental illness, at least the dimension of mental illness amenable to psychotherapy, is often a manifestation of demoralization. He postulated that the observed "critical over-involvement reflects the family's demoralization at being trapped in a situation over which they feel they have lost control" (p. 271). Individual and family therapies designed to ameliorate confusion, despair, and isolation address these dynamics, making them critical elements of treatment for many severe, chronic illnesses, medical or psychiatric.

The powerful impact of expressed emotions confirms the importance of language and, more broadly, communication, two well-established cultural variables (see chapter 5). By definition, pathogenic expression connotes the anger and disappointment felt by a family or group toward a member who is not meeting their expectations for responsible, culturally determined, age-appropriate behavior. In the research on schizophrenia, it further involves denying the patient the legitimacy of the sick role and attributing disturbing manifestations of psychiatric disorder to willfulness of some kind. The social or family groups expressing these feelings are transmitting a shared culture—a set of expectations, demands, and constraints—rather than buffering its impact on the person who is compromised by illness.

Universal commonalities in the expression of basic emotions should not distract therapists and mental health professionals from the unique, cultural features of the process. Rather than changing the patient, a therapist who represents a valued element of the culture (e.g., the scientific basis of a therapist's explanations or the moral strictures of a religious leader) may reshape the expectations and beliefs of the family or group, relieving the pressures that exacerbate illness in the most vulnerable member. In short, expressed emotions are not a simple, unidimensional issue; their cultural content is multifaceted, complex, and variously elaborated (Kymalainen and Weisman de Mamani 2008.) Treating them "in context," even if only to alleviate the depth and/or regulate the implications of overabundant or pathogenically limited expressiveness, is a worthwhile therapeutic objective.

Placebo Response

The placebo response, an essential expression of the common features of all psychotherapy (Frank and Frank 1991, chap. 7), varies widely across cultures. Taking an advertised pill may elicit a placebo response in a Western patient who watches television, but not in someone who doesn't; likewise, a healing ritual that may have great power in one society will have limited effect for someone who does not subscribe to the beliefs that inform it (Solomon 2001).

Placebos are not, then, simply pharmacological tools that act mysteriously on tissues or germs, but symbols that draw on the surrounding culture for concrete elements of their power.

Frank acknowledges the pharmacological aspects of the placebo response, but also remarks that it is due to much more than the mere satisfaction of the patient's expectations. He considered it misleading to attribute the placebo effect to the pill itself, since its therapeutic power depends on its "symbolic message." Similarly, he related part of the power of all psychotherapies to their symbolic or placebo effects. He defines the placebo elements of psychotherapy as "a procedure that conveys the therapist's attention, inspires the patient's hopes, and possesses other properties shared by all psychotherapies, but lacks the specific therapeutic components of the technique under investigation" (Frank and Frank 1991, p. 138). The cultural nature of a placebo response in psychotherapy can be demonstrated in several ways. First, personality features are decisive in the production of this response, and personality is, at least in part, the result of family and socioenvironmental factors (Alarcón, Foulks, and Vakkur 1998; Alarcón 2005). Second, early experience in the microculture of the family influences individuals' identification of symbols and assignment of meaning to them. Like responders to psychotherapy, those who respond to the symbolic elements of medicines, as embodied in placebos, "are better integrated socially, and are less mistrustful than non-responders," according to Frank's review of research in this area (Frank and Frank 1991, p. 144).

The overlap between placebo effects and psychotherapy confounds much contemporary research, which demands that treatments prove their effectiveness in comparison with, rather than in addition to, their placebo elements (see chapters 1, 4, 11, and 12). For clinical purposes, however, understanding the determinants and power of the placebo response may enhance therapeutic efficacy. Frank built on the understanding of placebos by highlighting role induction as an important step (see chapter 1). Originally a research technique, role induction has become a ritual aspect of much psychotherapy, especially for brief, focused approaches. In response to societal demands to formulate "treatment plans," therapists negotiate openly with their patients. This process involves explaining what to expect, what methods will be applied, and what the outcome may be. By fostering what Frank called "expectant trust," role induction techniques strengthen the placebo elements of psychotherapy rather than trying to factor them out. Such negotiation is essentially a cultural practice, reflecting the scientific training of many therapists, the reimbursement environment, and the expectation that patients and therapists should negotiate as equals, despite the power imbalance between them.

Patient-Therapist Relationship

These reflections prompt an examination of the patient-therapist relationship as the central, most powerful factor in the dynamics and the outcome of any psychotherapy. This dyad has received well-deserved attention from clinicians, researchers, patients and families, media, and the public at large. All the cultural elements examined so far converge on this relationship. The "chemistry" between the actors in the encounter is, in the last analysis, the result of either the collision or the harmonization of the actors' cultural endowments. To say that the complaints that bring patients to psychotherapy are only symptoms or manifestations of distress caused by some neurobiological malfunction (the "medical model" in its most reductionist form; see Guze 1992) would be dangerously simplistic. The patient brings his or her story, explanatory models full of culturally based views, beliefs, opinions, and expectations; the therapist brings knowledge, experience, skills, and predictions born out of the cultural sources of his or her own life, education, and training. Thus defined, culture, not necessarily science or technical expertise, may decisively determine the outcome of the therapeutic encounter. Cultural psychiatrists understand the importance of a rich set of what Frank calls "personal attributes of patients," including features such as the patient's "capacity and willingness to enter into close relationship with others," even at the risk of making "humiliating self-revelations" (Frank and Frank 1991, p. 168). A level of dependency (which can still be labeled "healthy") facilitates the acceptance of psychotherapy. All of this, along with features of patient's and therapist's assumptive worlds—particularly the patient's concrete or intuitive beliefs in the role and effectiveness of the therapist's interventions—crystallizes in hope for change, one of the most powerful determinants of a favorable outcome.

The theory and philosophy of the therapist's training, which necessarily reflect qualities and characteristics of the surrounding culture, provide the tools necessary to build and maintain a positive relationship. Training is a form of enculturation, as much for the psychoanalyst graduated after intense years of didactics and practice in more or less prestigious institutes as for the indigenous helpers, shamans, or *curanderos* educated by their elderly masters. Training allows "the development of a common body of shared experience, and the acquisition of a specialized vocabulary" (Frank and Frank 1991, p. 160), plus rituals and liturgy that provide cohesiveness to the group or school where the training takes place. Even in the presence of probable failures, the therapist's professional or ideological culture sustains the treatment by instilling faith, the belief that he or she is doing "the right thing." Always objective, however, Frank cautions us about "an overemphasis on training and theory . . . [that] can also be harmful to patients and therapists" (p. 162).

Beyond training, therapists' life experiences also often include personal suffering that they have faced and managed according to their own cultural patterns. This, Frank warns, "is not inevitably helpful." Empathy, warmth, and genuineness (concepts that can and should be cultivated within all theoretical perspectives) are necessary but not sufficient personal characteristics of the ideal therapist. Frank concludes that "the essence of some therapists' healing power may have eluded scientific definition" (p. 167). Such uncertainty may be the result of the cultural relativism inherent in those traditional characteristics of the ideal therapist: what is empathic, warm, or genuine in some cultures may be condescending, suffocating, or pretentious in others.

The psychotherapeutic dyad is a system whose properties are determined by the interactions between patient, therapist, and therapeutic procedures, "as well as by features of the broader context in which therapy transpires"— cultural background. This background and the germinal microculture of the dyadic relationship may together be the single most important factor in the success or failure of the treatment. Improvement is attained through "a convergence of certain values of therapist and patient"—cultural identification, sharing, or communion. To the "many contextual factors," both recognized and unrecognized, determining the outcome of therapeutic encounters, Frank adds another original feature with strong cultural implications: the power imbalance in the therapeutic encounter (pp. 174–75).

Few concepts have more cultural implications than that of "power." Variously defined throughout history, power has also been classified according to the areas in which it is exercised: political, religious, financial, social, and moral. Power is ubiquitous in its presence and impact. In the psychotherapeutic encounter, power resides primarily with the therapist. Frank, after recognizing that "the therapist's ascendancy has several sources," makes several culturally relevant points. First, he speaks of "the therapist's *ethos* as derived from a socially validated form of training." This includes the use of tools (e.g., rating scales or psychological tests) that invest the therapeutic procedure with apparent scientific objectivity. Such scientific sunlight warms the practice of therapists from many disciplines: "While psychiatric social workers and nonprofessional therapists lack specific symbols of professional competence, they partake of the prestige of the institutions or agencies in which they work" (p. 177). Furthermore, "the issue of power in psychotherapy is obfuscated by the currently popular use of terms borrowed from business and law, a trend undoubtedly influenced by the growing role of third-party payers who analogize psychotherapy to a contract for the provision of services" (pp. 179–80). Frank uses McHugh and Slavney's concept (1998) of "wounded humanity" to characterize this culturally induced, certainly negative, chain of events. It is clear that a therapist who understands the legitimate and cultural roots and boundaries of his or her power may be better able to control it; one who is less aware may have difficulty achieving authentic connection with a patient—a crucial element of therapeutic impact.

Culture and the Practice of Psychotherapy

The literature on applications of psychotherapy to patients across a cultural divide falls under the heading of "multicultural counseling" (Fuertes and Gretchen 2001; Bronstein and Quina 2003). Beyond the assertion that all types of psychotherapy are "cultural," the creation of this domain reflects the conditions of practice in a pluralistic society. Psychotherapy needs to be adaptable to the needs of subgroups within an ethnically and racially diverse population. Tseng and Streltzer (2001) and others (Constantine and Sue 2005; Lu 2006) have reviewed "adjustments" to a mainstream approach that a culturally competent therapist would want to consider, especially when treating patients from a background different from his or her own. Examples of such adaptations include fostering culturally relevant communication through language and media familiar to the patient and adopting definitions of health and maturity that take the patient's cultural judgments or perspectives into account. Though not always valued by the scientific community, such adaptation, or "contextual relativism" in Frank's terms, may greatly enhance clinical practice.

Different forms of therapy require different cultural adaptations. A therapist employing supportive techniques that address practical problems and strengthen existing elements of the patient's coping may have to recognize that issues that are acceptable foci for patients of one culture—for example, gender roles, age-related expectations, or problems of financial security—may be too distant or too intimate for discussion with patients of other backgrounds. The metaphors and symbols of traditional psychoanalytic therapy may inspire and motivate some heritors of the society that fostered it, but prove incomprehensible or offensive to others. Rather than raising "Oedipal" issues with someone unfamiliar with Greek mythology, for example, the culturally fluent analyst might relate a patient's difficulty with self-esteem or interactions with authority to a more culturally relevant story, be it a myth or a movie. Certain defenses, such as the rigid splitting of good and bad or the resort to fantasy to relieve stress, might be considered pathological in one culture but adaptive in another. How the analyst understands transference and countertransference issues might also change, depending on how the patient's culture shapes relations between subordinates and authority figures, as represented by the therapist.

Other approaches also require adaptation. Cognitive therapy tends to define as "dysfunctional" thoughts that may not be so labeled if and when the patient's cultural context is assessed. It may not be pathological, for example, for someone living in a society troubled by frequent, random violence to personalize general threats, focus on possible negative outcomes of future acts, or adopt a general mistrust of others' motives. In another context, such thoughts would be typical grounds for cognitive intervention. The rewards and punishments of behavioral therapy must be meaningful to be effective, and the meaning of any particular method of reinforcement will depend on the patient's background. Methods of marital and family therapy must take into account differences in role definition and interpersonal transactions in different sociocultural groups. For example, supporting independence or separation for family members might be extraordinarily helpful in one context and extraordinarily destructive in another (Kleinman 1980; Ware and Kleinman 1992). Finally, group therapy with a multicultural patient mix may be challenging due to differences among group members in social norms for communication and other types of relationship vis-à-vis the therapist and other mental health professionals.

In a broad review of these issues, Fuertes and Gretchen (2001) compare and critique nine theoretical formulations of multicultural counseling, using three dimensions for their comparison: comprehensiveness of the model, ease of operationalizing it for testing, and clinical utility. They give the highest ranking on all three dimensions to a cognitive behavioral model that "aspires to help clients develop a flexible, multicultural personality that adjusts to the environment" (p. 529). Fuertes and Gretchen's ranking is, paradoxically, subject to culturally based criticism. For example, although all therapies encourage mastery, explicitly directing clients to become active change agents, as is typical in cognitive behavioral therapy, may violate the gender- and age-related norms of patients from certain cultures. The high value placed on a therapy being operationalized for testing is also culturally questionable. Internally consistent, prescriptive approaches embodied in treatment manuals may alienate counselors and clients from diverse cultural groups. Those from stigmatized groups or minorities that are subject to discrimination may experience such directiveness as a devaluation of their own group's expertise or experience; therapists and patients from more privileged backgrounds may feel that such approaches do not foster the self-expression and creativity they value on cultural grounds.

Cultural Psychotherapies

The domain of "cultural psychotherapies" includes approaches tailored to the needs and characteristics of different cultural or ethnic groups. Increased migration and globalization (Okasha 2005) have fostered a proliferation of such therapies, but they remain relatively undocumented in the world literature. Many cultures have roles for healers/therapists who operate according to the precepts of their particular (primarily non-Western) health and health care belief systems. We briefly discuss two of the many non-Western psychotherapy systems (Marsella and Pedersen 1981): Morita therapy, of Japanese origin, and *Dichos* therapy, used exclusively among Hispanic/Latino populations.

Morita Therapy

Shoma Morita, a Japanese psychiatrist who had "fear of death" and "neurasthenia" but overcame them on his own, introduced this therapy in 1919 (Kitanishi and Mori 1995). He focused on patients who had a condition known as *shinkeishitsu*, characterized by features of "obsessional psychoneurosis": perfectionism, ambivalence, social withdrawal, and hypochondriacal preoccupations (Murase and Johnson 1974; Tseng 2004). Morita theorized that a patient who has a "hypochondriacal temperament" misconstrues his or her "natural" emotional response to some environmental condition as a threat to survival or adaptation and focuses excessive attention on the reaction itself. Exhibiting a defensive attitude, the patient struggles to get rid of this "natural reaction," considered to be a reflection of the conflict between an ideal and a real state of affairs. Morita asserted that because these reactions and processes of the mind and body are natural or instinctive, they are not something one can simply control through thoughts.

Morita based his treatment on the principles of Zen Buddhism, a not unusual connection between culture (religious attitude, in this case) and psychotherapy. His therapy operates through four "periods" or phases. The first consists of one week of near total bed rest and social isolation, to induce a "peaceful condition" in both mental and physical terms. In the second period (three to seven days), the patient engages in occupational therapy (still without social contacts) and records events in a diary, which the therapist reviews. The third period includes increasing physical work, reading of selected books, and increased contact with people; this phase aims to induce a state of natural physical tiredness accompanying simple but concrete accomplishments. In the fourth period, which lasts up to four weeks, the patient gradually resumes some previous occupational activities, returning to the hospital to attend group psychotherapy, listen to lectures, and meet individually with the Morita therapist. Successful treatment leaves the patient no longer obsessed with doubts or destructive self-consciousness and free of neurasthenic and/or psychophysiological symptoms.

Morita therapy institutions have published studies on effectiveness and treatment outcomes (Kitanishi and Mori 1995; He and Li 2008). These studies report recovery rates ranging between 77.6 and 93.3 percent for selected populations. Higher recovery rates occur for male patients between twenty and thirty years of age who voluntarily seek out Morita therapy for typical *shinkeishitsu* symptoms. From the cultural perspective, Morita therapy builds on prominent features of Japanese *ethos* (Frank's "assumptive world"), including regulated work, subjection to specific group rules (the treatment periods), obedience to authority figures (the therapist), and acceptance of weaknesses and guilt. These qualities, in turn, lead to a search for redemption, associated with monitored socialization and collective celebration of accomplishments.

Another Japanese approach, *Naikan* therapy, expresses a different but equally salient element of the culture: *amae*, or "the need to be cherished and held in special esteem by selected others" (Nukina et al. 2005). Murase and Johnson (1974) suggested that the cultural bases of both *Naikan* and Morita therapy contrast sharply with those of psychoanalysis and other Western approaches. They emphasize that contextual understanding is critically important, especially in the choice of patients who will benefit. Another distinctive cultural feature of Morita therapy is its emphasis on the social acceptance of anxiety (Kitanishi and Mori 1995). An interesting phenomenon, however, is the spread

of Morita therapy to the United States and other regions of the world, suggestive of a globalizing, intercultural pattern worthy of further study.

Dichos Therapy

In contrast to the Asian therapies, *Dichos* therapy is an approach that originated in the United States in response to the need for culturally relevant interventions for Hispanic/Latino immigrant patients who remain strongly identified with their language or culture of origin; these patients respond only
modestly to conventional therapeutic approaches (Aviera 1996). The therapy is
named for *dichos*, also known as *refranes*, which are sayings, idioms, or proverbs in the Spanish language, used by Hispanic/Latino peoples and communities across the globe to explain and understand, in a brief and metaphorical
way, a great variety of situations—their configuration, management, and outcomes. Frequently, *dichos* also contain ethical, supportive, or corrective messages prompting action.* These practical, didactic aphorisms play an important role in the teaching and handing down of cultural beliefs, attitudes, social
values, and mores. *Dichos* therapy is not a complete treatment approach but
rather a means to facilitate therapy by overcoming resistance and encouraging
acknowledgment of feelings (Aviera 1996). Used in a group setting, its success
depends on a correct interpretation of metaphorical content, leading to culturally relevant, vivid, and meaningful new understandings.

Among several reports on experiences with this modality, Aviera (1996) describes a *Dichos* group approach in a six-hundred-bed psychiatric hospital in
California. All group members were Hispanic/Latino, chronically ill patients
who had psychotic diagnoses. They came from lower socioeconomic groups
and had adapted poorly to life in the United States, as shown by a range of occupational and legal problems. *Dichos* therapy helped them focus their attention, express and explore emotion, and clarify their values. Other studies have
found *dichos* to be useful in assuaging depressive and anxious symptoms, as
well as in reducing behavioral problems in children, adolescents, and adults.

The use of *refranes* is embedded in the intergenerational transactions of
Hispanic/Latino families and communities. Sayings from other cultures or so-

---

* For instance, *No hay mal que por bien no venga* (good things always happen as a result of bad
things) invokes both resignation and resilience, but also hope and pragmatism. *Agua que no has de
beber, déjala correr* (water you are not going to drink, let it run) emphasizes prudence, discretion, and
convenience.

cieties may have a different structure, flavor, or emphasis. This can make it difficult to apply *Dichos* therapy in its original structure with patients of European, African, or Asian descent. Such uncertainty opens up the possibility of clinical research studies in non-Hispanic/Latino groups, using either *dichos* or sayings from the particular traditions of the patients involved. Some authors describe the value of broader storytelling or "narrative medicine" (Charon 2001), similar to the use of *dichos* but not relying on specific metaphors to prompt patients to share their stories. Adapting particular elements of a treatment while keeping the method intact can create links between similar approaches in a variety of cultural and ethnic groups (Zuñiga 1992; Calderón and Beltrán 2005).

A common denominator in this selected set of cultural psychotherapies is the cultural derivation of the therapist's "power." Jerome Frank says many times in *Persuasion and Healing* that the proponents of most established psychotherapies "seldom discuss the issue of a power imbalance between therapist and patient," adding that therapists "need not concern themselves with establishing their ascendancy in the therapeutic encounter; it is simply taken for granted" (Frank and Frank 1991, p. 176). Frank offered this observation about mainstream therapies, but it applies equally to culturally variant ones.

Cultural psychotherapies pay attention to inherently different views held by the individual, his or her role in society, and the use and relevance of power. Not even the "Western" psychotherapies prioritize the discussion of power issues as the procedure evolves. In both approaches—Western and non-Western—there seems to be an anticipated understanding of the implicit strength of what therapy symbolizes: an encounter of two human beings in a healing context, the sufferer and the healer, the one seeking care after reaching presumably intolerable anguish and pain, the other positioned to help, "knowing" what goes on and what needs to be done.

The goal of therapy should be to apply methods appropriately to the right persons and to the right problems. In this regard, Kirmayer (2007) insists that every form of psychotherapy "rests on particular cultural concepts of the person." The Japanese conceptions involve a "decentering" of the individual (*Naikan*) and an acceptance of suffering (Morita) that may or may not seem foreign to Western patients. The use of metaphors in any type of psychotherapy requires that the particular phrases have meaning for both the therapist and the patient. *Dichos* therapy aims at ensuring the use of such culturally relevant metaphors and results in improved outcomes.

Conclusion

The definition of psychotherapy embraced by *Persuasion and Healing* characterizes it as encompassing three elements: a "healing agent," a "sufferer," and a "healing relationship." Frank boldly acknowledged that this broad definition would include many methods of healing not commonly thought of as psychotherapy, such as religious conversions or even "brainwashing"—a view he explicated with references to studies from comparative anthropology. This definition would also include those forms of healing more commonly found in non-Western societies, such as shamanism, folk healers such as a *curanderos*, and specific therapies such as Morita therapy.

In Frank's view, what he called "modern psychotherapies" are rooted in three historical traditions of healing, that is to say, three cultural sources reflecting historical periods in human evolution: the religio-magical, the rhetorical, and the empirical or naturalistic. Cultural factors also influence the measurement of the success of therapy. Frank describes how a Western sense of self emphasizes the interaction between an individual and the world. A more productive person would be seen as a sign of psychotherapeutic success in the Western model, while an increased sense of self-awareness would exemplify recovery in an Eastern therapeutic model. Culture suffuses every aspect of the psychotherapeutic encounter and introduces a unique dynamic in each of its effective ingredients.

In a globalized and multicultural world, comparing and contrasting psychotherapeutic approaches will refine our understanding of and enhance our ability to build on the common principles embodied in different therapeutic traditions, without losing sight of their particular qualities. Cultural differences sometimes enhance and at other times obstruct the attainment of desired treatment outcomes. Multicultural counseling entails the adaptation of existing technologies to the cultural backgrounds and habits of diverse patients and problems. In settings where multiculturalism is the norm, therapists will need to adapt their approaches to each client, while still anchoring their practice in broadly applicable theoretical formulations that can be tested. In the tradition of *Persuasion and Healing*, current conditions require us, first, to broaden our view of psychotherapy to include a variety of healers, sufferers, and settings, and then to focus on their unique dynamics, values, processes, and outcomes.

REFERENCES

Alarcón, R. D. 2005. Cross-cultural issues. In J. M. Oldham, A. E. Skodol, and D. S. Bender (eds.), *Textbook of Personality Disorders* (pp. 561–78).Washington, DC: American Psychiatric Publishing.

Alarcón, R. D., Foulks, E. F., and Vakkur, M. 1998. *Personality Disorders and Culture: Clinical and Conceptual Interactions.* New York: John Wiley.

Alegría, M., Bijl, R. V., Lin, E., Waters, E. E., and Kessler, R.C. 2000. Income differences in persons seeking outpatient treatment for mental disorders. *Archives of General Psychiatry* 57:383–91.

Alegría, M., Canino, G., Ríos, R., Vera, M., Calderon, J., Rusch, D., and Ortega A. N. 2002. Inequalities in use of specialty mental health services among Latinos, African Americans, and non-Latino whites. *Psychiatric Services* 53:1547–55.

Assoun, P. L. 1981. *Introduction à l'epistemologie freudienne.* Paris: Payot.

Aviera, A. 1996. "Dichos" therapy group: a therapeutic use of Spanish language proverbs with hospitalized Spanish-speaking psychiatric patients. *Cultural Diversity and Mental Health* 2:73–87.

Baer, R. D., Weller, S. C., de Alba García, J. G., Glazer, M., Trotter, R., Pachter, L., and Klein, R. E. 2003. A cross-cultural approach to the study of the folk illness *nervios. Culture, Medicine, and Psychiatry* 27:315–37.

Baier, A. 1979. Hume on heaps and bundles. *American Philosophical Quarterly* 16: 285–95.

Balsa, A. I., and McGuire, T. G. 2003. Prejudice, clinical uncertainty and stereotyping as sources of health disparities. *Journal of Health Economics* 22:89–116.

Baumeister, R. F. 1986. *Identity: Cultural Change and the Struggle for Self.* New York: Oxford University Press.

Bronstein, P., and Quina, K. 2003. *Teaching Gender and Multicultural Awareness.* Washington, DC: American Psychological Association.

Brumberg, J. J. 1989. *Fasting Girls: The History of Anorexia Nervosa.* New York: First Vintage Books.

Buber, M. 1948. *Between Man and Man.* New York: Macmillan.

Calderón, J. L., and Beltrán, R. A. 2005. Rethinking language and literacy for ensuring culturally appropriate health communication. *Physicians and Patients* 3:1–4.

Caldwell-Harris, C. L., and Aycicegi, A. 2006. When personality and culture clash: the psychological distress of allocentrics in an individualist culture and idiocentrics in a collectivist culture. *Transcultural Psychiatry* 43:331–61.

Carr, J. E. 1978. Ethno-behaviorism and the culture-bound syndromes: the case of Amok. *Culture, Medicine, and Psychiatry* 2:269–93.

Chandra, A., and Skinner, J. 2003. *Geography and Racial Health Disparities.* Cambridge, MA: National Bureau of Economic Research.

Charon, R. 2001. Narrative medicine: a model for empathy, reflection, profession and trust. *JAMA: Journal of the American Medical Association* 286:1897–1902.

Chowdhury, A. N. 1996. The definition and classification of Koro. *Culture, Medicine, and Psychiatry* 20:41–65.

Constantine, M. C., and Sue, D. W. (eds.). 2005. *Strategies for Building Multicultural Competence in Mental Health and Educational Settings*. New York: John Wiley.

Dahrendorf, R. 1959. *Class and Class Conflict in Industrial Society*. Stanford, CA: Stanford University Press.

Descartes, R. 1954. *Philosophical Writings*. London: Auscombe and Geach.

Draguns, J. G., and Tanaka-Matsumi, L. 2003. Assessment of psychopathology across and within cultures: issues and findings. *Behavioral Research and Therapy* 41:755–76.

Erikson, E. H. 1964. *Childhood and Society*. New York: W. W. Norton.

———. 1968. *Identity, Youth, and Crisis*. New York: W. W. Norton.

Falloon, I. R. 1992. Psychotherapy of schizophrenia. *British Journal of Hospital Medicine* 48:164–70.

Falloon, I. R. H., Boyd, J. L., and McGill, C. W. 1984. *Family Care of Schizophrenia*. New York: Guilford Press.

Frank, J. D. 1977. Psychiatry, the healthy invalid. *American Journal of Psychiatry* 134:1349–55.

Frank, J. D., and Frank, J. B. 1991. *Persuasion and Healing: A Comparative Study of Psychotherapy*, 3rd ed. Baltimore: Johns Hopkins University Press.

Fuertes, J., and Gretchen, D. 2001. Emerging theories of multicultural counseling. In J. Ponterotto, J. M. Casas, L. A. Suzuki, and C. M. Alexander (eds.), *Handbook of Multicultural Counseling*, 2nd ed. (pp. 509–41). Montreal: Sage.

Glover, J. 1988. *The Philosophy and Psychology of Personal Identity*. London: Penguin Press.

Gordon, R. A. 1990. *Anorexia and Bulimia: Anatomy of a Social Epidemic*. Cambridge, UK: Basil Blackwell.

Guarnaccia, P. J., Angel, R., and Guorobey, J. L. 1989. The factor structure of the CES-D in the Hispanic Health and Nutrition Examination Survey: the influences of ethnicity, gender and language. *Social Science and Medicine* 29:85–94.

Guarnaccia, P., and Rogler, H. R. 1999. Research on culture-bound syndromes: new directions. *American Journal of Psychiatry* 156:1322–25.

Guze, S. B. 1992. *Why Psychiatry Is a Branch of Medicine*. New York: Oxford University Press.

He, Y., and Li, C. 2008. Morita therapy for schizophrenia. *Cochrane Database of Systematic Reviews* 2:CD06346.

Heidegger, M. 1927. *Sein und Zeit*. Tubingen: Niemeyer.

Hollingshead, A. B., and Redlich, F. C. 1958. *Social Class and Mental Illness*. New York: John Wiley.

Hooley, J. M. 2007. Expressed emotions and relapse of psychopathology. *Annual Review of Clinical Psychology* 3:329–52.

Horwitz, N. 2004. [The change in medical practice: psycho-social challenges for the profession] (in Spanish). *Revista Medica de Chile* 132:768–72.

Hubbard, L. R. 1950. *Dianetics, the Modern Science of Mental Health*. New York: Hermitage House.

Hume, D. 1988. *A Treatise of Human Nature*. Oxford: Oxford University Press.

Institute of Medicine. 2005. *Crossing the Quality Chasm: Adaptation for Mental Health and Addictive Disorders*. Washington, DC: Institute of Medicine.

James, W. 1891. *Principles of Psychology.* London: Macmillan.

———. 1912. *Does Consciousness Exist? Essays on Radical Empiricism.* London: Longman.

Kant, E. 1933. *Critique of Pure Reason.* London: Macmillan.

Kenny, M. G. 1983. Paradox lost: the Latah problem revisited. *Journal of Nervous and Mental Disease* 171:159–67.

Kimura, S. 1982. *Nihonjin no taijinkyofushio* [Japanese anthrophobia]. Tokyo: Keso Shobo.

Kirmayer, L. J. 2007. Psychotherapy and the cultural concept of the person. *Transcultural Psychiatry* 44:232–57.

Kitanishi, K., and Mori, A. 1995. Morita therapy: 1919 to 1995. *Psychiatry and Clinical Neurosciences* 49:245–54.

Kleinman, A. 1980. *Patients and Healers in the Context of Culture: An Exploration of the Borderland between Anthropology, Medicine, and Psychiatry.* Berkeley: University of California Press.

Koch, E., and Turgut, T. 2004. [The current problems and cross-cultural perspectives of patient-doctor relationship: an overview] (in Turkish). *Turk Psikiyatri Dergisi* 15:64–69.

Kymalainen, J. A., and Weisman de Mamani, A. G. 2008. Expressed emotions, communications deviance and culture in families of patients with schizophrenia: a review of the literature. *Cultural Diversity and Ethnic Minority Psychology* 14:85–91.

Littlewood, R., Jadhav, S., and Ryder, A. G. 2007. A cross-national study of the stigmatization of severe psychiatric illness: historical review, methodological considerations and development of the questionnaire. *Transcultural Psychiatry* 44:171–202.

Lu, F. 2006. DSM-IV outline for cultural formulation: bringing culture into the clinical encounter. *Focus* 4:9–10.

Malhotra, H. K., and Wig, N. N. 1975. Dhat syndrome: a culture-bound sex neurosis of the Orient. *Archives of Sexual Behavior* 4:519–28.

Marsella, A. J., and Pedersen, P. B. (eds.). 1981. *Cross-cultural Counseling and Psychotherapy.* New York: Pergamon Press.

McHugh, P. R., and Slavney, P. R. 1998. *The Perspectives of Psychiatry,* 2nd ed. Baltimore: Johns Hopkins University Press.

Murase, T., and Johnson, F. 1974. Naikan, Morita, and Western psychotherapy. *Archives of General Psychiatry* 31:121–28.

Nukina, S., Wang, H., Kamei, K., and Kawahara, R. 2005 [Intensive Naikan therapy for generalized anxiety disorder and panic disorder: clinical outcomes and background] (in Japanese). *Seishin Shinkeigaku Zasshi* 107:641–66.

Okasha, A. 2005. Globalization and mental health: a WPA perspective. *World Psychiatry* 4:1–2.

Paniagua, F. A. 2000. Culture-bound syndromes, cultural variations and psychopathology. In I. Cuellar and F. A. Paniagua (eds.), *Handbook of Multicultural Mental Health* (pp. 139–69). San Diego: Academic Press.

Parfit, D. 1971. Personal identity. *Philosophical Review* 80:3–27.

Prince, R., and Tcheng-Laroche, F. 1987. Culture-bound syndromes and international disease classifications. *Culture, Medicine, and Psychiatry* 11:3–19.

Roberts, M. E., Han, K., and Weed, N. C. 2006. Development of a scale to assess Hwa-Byung, a Korean culture-bound syndrome, using the Korean MMPI-2. *Transcultural Psychiatry* 43:383–400.

Sánchez-Beltrán, H. C., and Avelar-Gutierrez, J. 2009. Curanderismo urbano e indígena: procesos de curación física y mental. In S. J. Villaseñor (ed.), *Psiquiatría Naturaleza y Cultura: De lo singular a lo universal* (pp. 141–44). Guadalajara, Mexico: GLADET.

Skultans, V. 2004. Authority, dialogue and polyphony in psychiatric consultations: a Latvian case study. *Transcultural Psychiatry* 41:337–59.

Solle, D. 1975. *Suffering*. Philadelphia: Fortress Press.

Solomon, A. 2001. *The Noonday Demon: An Atlas of Depression*. New York: Scribner.

Stone, J. H. (ed.). 2004. *Culture and Disability*. Thousand Oaks, CA: Sage.

Sullivan, H. S. 1953. *The Interpersonal Theory of Psychiatry*. New York: W. W. Norton.

Szasz, T. S. 1974. *The Myth of Mental Illness*, rev. ed. New York: Harper and Row.

Tsai, J. L., Butcher, J. N., and Munoz, R. F. 2001. Culture, ethnicity and psychopathology. In H. E. Adams and P. B. Sutker (eds.), *Comprehensive Handbook of Psychopathology* (pp. 280–91). New York: Kluwer Academic / Plenum.

Tseng, W. S. 2001. Culture-related specific syndromes. In W. S. Tseng, *Handbook of Cultural Psychiatry* (pp. 211–63). San Diego: Academic Press.

———. 2004. Culture and psychotherapy. In W. Tseng and J. Streltzer (eds.), *Cultural Competence in Clinical Psychiatry: Core Competencies in Psychotherapy* (pp. 181–98). Washington, DC: American Psychiatric Publishing.

———. 2009. Susto and ataque de nervios: what kinds of culture-related specific syndromes are they? In S. J. Villaseñor (ed.), *Psiquiatría, Naturaleza y Cultura: De lo singular a lo universal* (pp. 63–71). Guadalajara, Mexico: GLADET.

Tseng, W. S., and Streltzer, J. (eds.). 2001. *Culture and Psychotherapy: A Guide to Clinical Practice*. Washington, DC: American Psychiatric Publishing.

Villaseñor, S. J., and Reyes Rivas, J. R. 2009. Tateposco: la magia de una tradición. In S. J. Villaseñor (ed.), *Psiquiatría, Naturaleza y Cultura: De lo singular a lo universal* (pp. 145–50). Guadalajara, Mexico: GLADET.

Wagstaff, A., and van Doorslaer, E. 2000. Income inequality and health: what does the literature tell us? *Annual Review of Public Health* 21:543–67.

Ware, N. C., and Kleinman, A. 1992. Culture and somatic experience: the social course of illness in neurasthenia and chronic fatigue syndrome. *Psychosomatic Medicine* 54:546–60.

Wearden, A. J., Tarrier, N., Barrowclough, C., Zastowny, T. R., and Rahill, A. A. 2000. A review of expressed emotions research in health care. *Clinical Psychology Review* 20:633–66.

Yap, P. M. 1951. Mental diseases peculiar to certain cultures: a survey of comparative psychiatry. *Journal of Mental Science* 97:313–27.

Yung, A., Gill, L., Sommerville, E., Dowling, B., Simon, K., and Pirkis, J. 2005. Public and private psychiatry: can they work together and is it worth the effort? *Australian and New Zealand Journal of Psychiatry* 39:767–73.

Zuñiga, M. E. 1992. Using metaphors in therapy: dichos and Latino clients. *Social Work* 37:55–60.

CHAPTER 15

Psychotherapy, Religion, and Spirituality

James L. Griffith, M.D.

"Well, it's no use *your* talking about waking him," said Tweedledum, "when you're only one of the things in his dream. You know very well you're not real."

"I *am* real!" said Alice, and began to cry . . .

"If I wasn't real," Alice said . . . "I shouldn't be able to cry."

—*Through the Looking Glass*

Successful instances of both psychotherapy and spiritual healing reduce psychologically caused suffering, increase self-esteem, and foster a sense of mastery in persons who seek their ministrations.

—*PERSUASION AND HEALING*, 1991, P. 85

Even today, mutual suspicion, ambivalence, and at times overt hostility characterize the relationship between theories supporting psychotherapy and those that underlie religious healing. Such tension is a legacy of the early modern period, when Freud's effort to explain human suffering in secular and scientific terms fostered the development of psychotherapy as a formal, medical intervention. In *Persuasion and Healing*, Jerome Frank (1961) shifted the debate by pointing out that religious healing remained one of the three major philosophical traditions, together with applied science and hermeneutics, on which modern psychotherapy rests. Frank's work helped clarify the place of psychotherapy in relation to other systems of healing.

Persuasion and Healing focused on cult and religious conversion experiences as forms of healing that could produce rapid and dramatic behavioral changes. Frank believed that, in learning from religious healers, psychotherapists could better understand their own effectiveness. He noted how religious healing techniques could mobilize hope, instill expectations of cure, bolster self-esteem, arouse emotions, and strengthen ties with a supportive community. Frank found parallels to each of these processes in the practices of psychotherapists.

Demoralization and Religious Healing

Jerome and Julia Frank (1991) reviewed evidence from a broad range of sources to argue that demoralization is the typical antecedent for the dramatic changes that ensue from religious conversion or cult membership. They postulated a similar role for demoralization in those who seek or benefit from psychotherapy. For example, J. P. Kildahl (1972, p. 57) found that "more than 85% of tongue-speakers had experienced a clearly defined anxiety crisis preceding their speaking in tongues." Such crises typically involved feelings of worthlessness and powerlessness. The glossolalic experience invariably resulted in increased feelings of confidence and security.

Religious leaders and groups may proselytize by exacerbating a targeted person's demoralization, before offering religious conversion as its solution. Sermons that begin by hammering on guilt and damnation of the soul typically end with offers of grace and salvation. In daily life, religion is more likely to be invoked in unusually difficult times than in response to mundane stressors. For example, Kenneth Pargament (1997) reviewed evidence that people are more likely to pray over catastrophes and health crises than over such minor stressors as problems in the workplace.

Clearly, religion, like psychotherapy, plays a major role in helping people manage demoralization. This observation raises further questions about its therapeutic effects. What mechanisms mediate the effect of religion as an antidote for demoralization? How can one partner religion and psychotherapy in rebuilding a patient's morale?

Psychotherapy and Spirituality

Comparing psychotherapy with religious healing through cults and religious conversions brings to light important differences. Unlike most psychotherapies, cults and religious conversions often rely on idiosyncratic and charismatic religious leaders who induce intense emotions and activate group processes that foster expectations for change. Further, religious activities dramatically change only a minority of those exposed to their methods, in contrast to psychotherapy, in which a majority of those who engage in treatment report behavioral changes (Lambert and Bergin 1994).

The past two decades in the United States have witnessed a rapprochement between psychotherapy and religion that permits comparisons with religious processes other than conversion experiences and involvement in cults. These practices are more akin to ordinary psychotherapy. Many psychotherapists distinguish between formal religions, toward which they remain skeptical, and personal spirituality, which they may embrace with enthusiasm. Clinical approaches for integrating psychotherapy and spirituality also have matured (Miller 1999; Griffith and Griffith 2002; Sperry and Shafranske 2005). These changes provide a fresh vantage point from which to inquire how religious healing can elucidate the processes of psychotherapy. To discuss spirituality, however, one needs to explain its relationship to the broader scope of religion.

Sociobiological Systems Express Religious Life

Religion describes a broad region of human life. Sociobiology and evolutionary psychology have provided tools for unraveling the complex psychological and social effects of religion. They demonstrate how religion is expressed through multiple sociobiological behavioral systems (Kirkpatrick 2005; Griffith 2010).

Sociobiological systems are compartmentalized behavioral systems that evolved according to the principle of inclusive fitness. These behaviors solve specific survival problems faced by early hominids, from two hundred thousand to two million years ago (Mithen 1996). These sociobiological systems persist and contribute to how humans organize groups and interpersonal relationships. As such, they both express and shape religious life. Sociobiological systems that are particularly salient in religious life are those for attachment, peer affiliation, kin recognition, social hierarchy, and social exchange (Griffith 2010).

Attachment

The attachment system evolved to ensure that mothers and their offspring would bond securely and in a protective manner. Within the brain, the attachment system is organized to guide motivational, emotional, and memory processes with respect to significant caregiving figures. Children and parents are motivated to seek each other when alarmed or insecure (Siegel 1999).

John Bowlby (1973) conceptualized attachment theory after World War II to better explain the different patterns of distress displayed by children when separated from their parents. According to Bowlby, the basic components of attachment are: (1) proximity, the child seeking nearness to a primary attachment figure; (2) secure base, the child playing and exploring with ease only when a primary attachment figure is felt to be close and available; and (3) safe haven, the child seeking a primary attachment figure when feeling threatened or insecure. Unlike the attachment systems of other mammals, processes based solely on physical proximity, human attachments are organized around the felt presence and responsivity of the caregiver (Bowlby 1973). In an attachment relationship, one's thoughts, feelings, and behaviors are guided, to a great extent, by the relationship with that person. An infant's early attachment to parents or other primary caregivers becomes internalized into an enduring attachment style that persists through life as a working model for how relationships ought to be managed. Problematic early attachments, for example, the absence of a sense of secure base, may produce an attachment style organized by felt insecurity, with impaired play, exploration, and social interactions (Siegel 1999).

For many religious people, God is one of their most important attachments. Psychologist Lee Kirkpatrick (2005, p. 52) noted that "the perceived availability and responsiveness of a supernatural attachment figure is a fundamental dynamic underlying Christianity and many other theistic religions. Whether that attachment figure is God, Jesus Christ, the Virgin Mary, or one of various saints, guardian angels, or other supernatural beings, the analogy is striking." In their studies of different kinds of prayer, Hood et al. (1996, p. 394) noted how some types of prayer seem preoccupied mainly with the responsivity of God, rather than the answering of any particular request for God's intervention through actions. Contemplative prayer is an attempt to approach and to relate deeply to one's God, while meditative prayer mainly reflects concerns about the quality of relationship with one's God.

Attachment styles provide a clinically useful paradigm for understanding the otherwise puzzling array of ways in which people relate to their personal gods. Thus, a person who has a *secure attachment style* feels that God is present and will respond if needed. Such felt conviction of God's responsiveness keeps anxiety at bay. By contrast, a religious person who has an *anxious attachment style* believes that God, however strong and capable, may not be reliably available. Such a person usually feels too weak or unworthy to merit God's attention. His or her religious life becomes preoccupied with entreating, placating, or otherwise worrying about God's availability. Sociobiologically speaking, these two psychological dispositions are attachment behaviors showing a low threshold for activation. A person who has an *avoidant attachment style* falls at the other end of the spectrum, activating attachment behaviors only under extreme conditions in the person-God relationship. Expressing a *dismissive avoidant style*, the person acts as though God were emotionally distant, either uninterested or incapable of assisting in times of need. The person expects little from God and relies only on the self. By contrast, someone who has a mixed *anxious/avoidant style* may feel that a relationship with God is too frightening to consider and thus cultivates self-reliance to avoid or avert God's involvement (Kirkpatrick 2005).

An individual's attachment style strongly influences the likelihood of a religious conversion. Most people who have dramatic religious conversions have anxious attachment styles, and a smaller number have avoidant attachment styles. People who have secure attachments to God tend to have religious lives that actively influence daily behavior, but with few religiously dramatic moments. While the suddenness and intensity of behavioral change through religious conversion can be striking, people with anxious attachment styles also are more prone to forsake their religious commitment at a later point (Kirkpatrick 2005).

A secure attachment to a personal God seems to act as a potent buffer against demoralization, but people who have insecure attachments to their God may be vulnerable to demoralization in the face of adversities.

Peer Affiliation

Like wolves and dogs and many primates, human beings appear to be hardwired to seek security as members of a pack or troop. Humans can use language, as well as the nonverbal gestures and social displays they share with other species, to signal togetherness. Religious beliefs, rituals, ceremonies, and other practices commonly provide an experience of belonging to a group. Cooperation within the group is facilitated by alliances and coalitions mediated through religious identification.

Drawing from his research on cult membership, Marc Galanter (1999) articulated a theory of religion based on group affiliation needs. Religious groups are typically characterized by social cohesion such that individual group members' circumstances are interlinked closely with those of other group members, and group members share important concerns. In cults, this social cohesion is intense, extending to common manners of dress, idiosyncratic language, and joint ownership of material possessions. Such mutuality fosters reciprocal altruism, with group members giving freely to one another, knowing that the same generosity will be experienced in return. Pargament (1997) detailed the many ways in which people provide mutual social support within religious congregations and fellowships.

A person who joins a cult commonly has been experiencing demoralization and social isolation prior to recruitment into the group. Galanter (1999) demonstrated a relationship between the lowering of initial anxiety and depression symptoms that a person experiences on joining a cult and the reciprocal elevation of social cohesion within the group, a phenomenon he termed the "relief effect." This finding is further supported by social identity theorists who have documented the importance of membership in national and ethnic groups to individuals' self-regard (Kirkpatrick 2005). Peer affiliation thus seems to restore or to protect morale in the face of adversity.

Kin Recognition

To survive, a social group must manage its boundaries with the outside world. Without a clear way to recognize who is and who is not a group member, the group ceases to exist. Religious groups seem to rely on kin recognition mechanisms that became components of human sociobiology eons ago. Neural circuits that underpin kin recognition may operate at the most fundamental level by discerning biological features shared among family members, such as facial features or olfactory cues (Daly and Wilson 2005). Religious groups may be able to tap into the power of these neural systems by evoking family metaphors and such descriptive language as "brother," "sister," and "father" when describing group members. Crippen and Machalek (1989) described religion as a "hypertrophied kin recognition process" (p. 74), in which "kin recognition mechanisms are 'usurped' to form communities of fictive kin" (p. 68). In turn, this process encourages "individuals to subordinate their apparent self-interest to the collectively-expressed interest of sovereign agencies" (p. 70). Kirkpatrick (2005, p. 249) noted that religious beliefs represent "a kind of cognitive error in which psychological mechanisms misidentify unrelated in-group members as kin, in much the same way that our taste-preference mechanisms can be fooled into enjoying soft drinks or potato chips flavored with artificial sweeteners and fat substitutes."

Shared religious language and practices can thus define an in-group, with in-group members receiving privileges and respect not afforded to outsiders. Fundamentalist religions typically depend on establishing and defending particular beliefs and practices that define an in-group, relegating those who are not observant to the out-group. Fundamentalism is thus a form of religion in which coalitional psychology takes precedence over religion's other psychological or social purposes (Kirkpatrick 2005). This may explain the perplexing observation that religious traditions founded on ethics of compassion, generosity, and love for others nevertheless can turn quickly to coercion, intimidation, and violence toward those who are not members of the elect. Those in the out-groups—pagans, heathens, infidels, or gentiles—are not recognized as full human beings (Griffith 2010). Despite the moral and ethical vulnerabilities, kin recognition and the protection of one's in-group status appear to be an effective counter to demoralization.

Social Hierarchy

Within a single generation after its founding, nearly every religion has proposed a social order that claims to have originated by divine decree. Groups often regard God, or other supernatural beings, as a powerful leader—the alpha male—of the religious group. Exegeses of sacred scriptures provide rules, commandments, and other prescribed behaviors to which group members must submit themselves to achieve status, prestige, honor, and respect within the community. The individual achieves closeness to God not through emotionally intimate interactions but through behavioral submission and obedience. Religious language often reflects a psychology of social hierarchy, as in references to the "Kingdom of God" or God as "Ruler of All."

Galanter (1999, p. 4) noted from his empirical research that strong group behavioral norms that influence members' conduct, coupled with imputation of divine power to cult leaders, distinguish cults from other religious groups. The power of religion in prescribing a social hierarchy, with its attendant roles and responsibilities, fosters obedience to directives from group leaders, particularly leaders perceived as divinely anointed, even when such obedience conflicts with a group member's personal moral impulses or moral reasoning. In religious cults, group members may demonstrate neglect, exploitation, or violence toward self or others out of a perceived need for obedience to the rule and order of God. Despite its vulnerability to abuse and exploitation, a religious social hierarchy and its roles of dominance and submission can be effective in protecting group members from demoralization.

Social Exchange and Reciprocal Altruism

Most religions articulate ethical rules and norms that prescribe correct social behavior. Moral precepts found in nearly every religion include reciprocal altruism, fair social exchange, and the detection and punishment of cheaters (Kirkpatrick 2005, p. 257). Michael Lerner (1980) noted that an extrapolation of social-contract thinking to the natural world may underlie a near universal belief in a just world. People everywhere tend to believe the world is a place where everyone gets his or her just deserts, where the good are rewarded and the wicked are punished. When bad things happen to good people, a common conclusion is that the suffering people must not have been good after all. As Pargament (1997, p. 227) noted, God is nearly always viewed as just: someone who may punish or destroy, but nearly always for a good reason.

Social exchange and reciprocal altruism can set the stage for exploitation, when an individual persists in roles or behaviors that are abusive or neglectful, in the expectation that present suffering will be requited later through cosmic justice (Griffith 2010). Such processes may also transmute into scapegoating, when those who suffer because they are unlucky shoulder the additional burden of being labeled moral transgressors. Despite these vulnerabilities, social exchange and reciprocal altruism remain forces that help sustain morale through setbacks and misfortunes.

Making Sociobiological Sense of Religion

Religion is perhaps so powerful because of the many sociobiological systems that it activates simultaneously (see chapters 3 and 4). These systems structure a person's interpersonal and social world. Religion activates not only attachment behaviors between an individual and his or her God but also social processes of peer affiliation, with attendant alliances and coalitions; kin recognition, with demarcation of an in-group separate from out-groups; social hierarchy, with dominance, submission, and status-seeking; and expectations for a just social exchange that includes reciprocal altruism. Religion so completely activates the full range of sociobiological systems that one might predict its spontaneous appearance, were it not already omnipresent in human life (Griffith 2010).

Balancing Spirituality and Religion

Between 800 BCE and 700 CE, visionary religious leaders emerged to transform religion from its archaic tribal orientation to a focus on the individual self-consciousness (Armstrong 1993; Barnes 2000, 2003). These religious leaders sought to discriminate institutionalized religious practices from an individual's personal religious experience, with the latter including beliefs, practices, and communal ways of living that alleviated personal suffering. Lao Tzu, a succession of Hebrew prophets, Jesus Christ, the Buddha, and Mohammed were major figures who formulated new religious beliefs and practices and reinterpreted older ones. Each of their attendant religious movements has survived to the present day to inspire individuals committed to personal tranquility and the ethics of compassion. These religious forms, motivated by ethical reflection rather than sociobiology, are commonly referred to as spiritualities. Such spiritualities were often reinstitutionalized and made concrete and formulaic by later generations of their followers. Yet each has remained viable by continuing to nurture the moral reasoning, self-reflection, and personal growth of individual adherents (Griffith 2010).

The spiritualities associated with Taoism, Judaism, Christianity, Buddhism, Islam, and other traditions share notable similarities (Griffith 2010):

- Facilitation of coherency, hope, purpose, gratitude, joy, and other existential states of resilience (Griffith and Griffith 2002; Griffith 2010).
- Advocacy for whole-person to whole-person relatedness with other individuals. This was characterized by Martin Buber as "I-Thou", rather than "I-It" relatedness (Buber 1958). Similarly, anthropologist Victor Turner (1969, 1982) characterized this relatedness as a social process of *communitas*. *Communitas* appears during the performance of rituals, when distinctions around social hierarchy and boundaries disappear and a powerful awareness of bonds that connect people takes hold (Turner 1974).
- Commitment to an ethic of compassion. Even the most inward-focused spiritualities nevertheless end in an ethic of compassion toward other human beings, often extending it to all living creatures (Armstrong 1993).
- A relationship with the sacred as liminal experience (Turner 1969). Liminality is a region of human experience located between subjective and objective realities and outside the purview of routinized daily life (Turner 1969, 1982). It is akin to D. W. Winnicott's psychoanalytic description (1975) of transi-

tional space. Liminal experience—found in art, play, and religion—is creative, fluid, and understandable only through evocative symbols.

- Priority given to the experience of the individual person rather the religious group.

Spirituality has traditionally existed in close relationship with the classical religions, enough so that religious practices can often be regarded as the methods and means to achieve spirituality (Griffith and Griffith 2002). In the postmodern era, however, reduction of suffering and promotion of individual health have become ends in themselves, often unmoored to ecclesiastical authority or religious doctrines. Postmodern spirituality is characterized by individuals seeking personal growth and fulfillment through spiritual practices, without any scaffolding of traditional religious beliefs and without ties to formal communities of worship.

The Dual Morality of Religion

The power of religion for activating sociobiological systems makes it a potent force for either healing or harm. This dual morality presents conundrums for theologians, ethicists, politicians, and every type of health care professional. A simple formula can largely resolve the perplexity: religion poses the greatest risk for doing harm to individuals when any sociobiological agenda takes primacy over the pursuit of spirituality. Sociobiological systems operate more for the survival of the group than for any particular individual. That is, sociobiological systems are teleological, imbued with purposes and ends for a social world—a mothering attachment, peer relationships, a social structure with roles, responsibilities, and leadership to ensure work gets done and enemies are kept at bay. Sociobiological systems produce a social context in which individuals survive for the sake of the group, not for personal happiness. This narrow focus on group survival often discounts suffering individuals, including both those within the religious group and those in out-groups. Spirituality, on the other hand, promotes the well-being of the individual, not group survival (Griffith 2010).

Healing Processes of Psychotherapy Akin to Those of Religion

The psychotherapeutic traditions that emerged in the twentieth century, excepting family therapy, focused on the person as an individual—interior experiences, the workings of the individual's mind, the individual's relatedness with others—to solve problems that bring the person to psychotherapy. An implicit aim of psychotherapy is to foster individuation, helping an individual develop an identity distinct from that of family or clan. The processes of psychotherapy are conducted in private dialogues with a professional psychotherapist, usually without participation by family or tribal representatives.

The sociobiological processes of religion, on the other hand, function to build a secure group that protects its members (Griffith 2010). Within a robust, thriving religious group, a person is made safe by a secure attachment to God or other supernatural beings, reciprocal altruism with peers within the group, and protection by the group against stresses and threats from the outside world. Religious healing uses adherence to doctrinal beliefs, personal or group prayers, ceremonies and rituals, spiritual practices such as meditation or dietary practices, and other prescribed communal activities to achieve these ends. To a great extent, the methods of religious healing and the methods of psychotherapy diverge.

Psychotherapy and religion may find common ground in strengthening personal spirituality. From a secular position, a psychotherapist may help a patient find within his or her religious tradition those beliefs, practices, and communal ways of living that best foster coherence, hope, communion, purpose, gratitude, and other existential states. A psychotherapist can also focus on the quality of relatedness with others, helping a patient become someone who speaks, listens, and reflects such that his or her relational world becomes that of a whole person relating to a whole person. A psychotherapist can also ask reflective questions that facilitate the creative ferment of a patient's encounters with the sacred. Finally, a psychotherapist can help a patient in identifying those religious beliefs and practices that stand in opposition to spirituality and in finding paths to resolution of this conflict (Griffith and Griffith 2002; Griffith 2010). Religion in its sociobiological expressions can exist with or without reference to spirituality (Griffith 2010). Psychotherapists can help patients to integrate the two.

CASE EXAMPLE

Miriam was a fifty-one-year-old woman who had been referred by her internist for probable fibromyalgia with multiple somatic symptoms, anxiety, and depression. These symptoms had become disabling since the recent death of her mother. Miriam had diffuse pains and muscle stiffness through much of her body. She was frightened by the difficulties her physicians were having in diagnosing her illness and lived in fear that she was developing systemic lupus erythematosus. Her anxiety left her agitated through the day and unable to sleep at night.

Miriam was a devout Protestant Christian. Her daily life centered around her church and its worship services, social life with friends, and volunteer programs of service to the community. Her psychotherapy was conducted in intervals, initially around exacerbations of her illness, for a total of fifty-five sessions (24 the first year, 13 the second year, 7 the third year, 10 the fourth year, 2 the fifth year). This five-year duration of contact made it possible to discern how psychotherapy, over time, addressed religious issues in ways that contributed toward more adaptive coping with her chronic illness.

Although one might expect that Miriam's strong religious faith would have protected her from demoralization when medically ill, this was far from the case. If anything, her religious life seemed to exacerbate her anxious and depressed emotional state.

At the start of psychotherapy, Miriam could clearly articulate her core religious beliefs. However, she acknowledged that she often did not feel the presence of God. She yearned for God's reassuring presence, but her fear of disease or death seemed to block it: "I want God to be a felt presence, but it doesn't happen now. I don't know how . . . Is God really there? If God isn't helping me, how do I know He is there?" She was prompted to examine how her religious metaphors and beliefs might influence her sense of insecurity. When asked what images and stories of her experience with God brought comfort, she responded: "I don't feel comforted at all when I think about God as a 'heavenly father.'"

Miriam's responses indicated an insecure, anxious attachment to God. Although her formal religious beliefs told her that God was an attentive, available, and responsive being, her emotional experience belied this conviction. In early conversations she described long-standing conflicts with her father, whom, she felt, had been intrusive and controlling when she was a child. It seemed that these struggles so contaminated her associations with the word *father* that imagining God as a father created emotional distance from God.

As her therapist, I asked whether she ever held other images of God. She paused, then recalled from the Bible the story of "the Good Shepherd who watches over his flock and knows each sheep by name." I asked her to imagine God as the Good Shepherd—to imagine the sheep in a fold, to feel the emotion of the image, and to let it fill her. She described a bodily sense of comfort when she entered into this story.

We then compared her experience of God as the Good Shepherd with other images of God presented in her religious tradition. In response to the metaphor of God as "a judge," her body became tense and vigilant. Her apprehension became most marked when she dwelled on the image of God from the story of the Elect from the Book of Revelation—the 144,000 souls supposedly chosen by God to go to heaven with everyone else dispatched to hell.

Of these metaphors, only the story of the Good Shepherd seemed to hold potential for bringing peace to her body amid the waiting and uncertainty. Recognizing this, she adopted as a spiritual practice the daily imaging of God as the Good Shepherd during her daily prayers. In time, she realized that this practice "evokes my mother's presence," constant in her concern and responsiveness. As Miriam practiced trusting God as she had once trusted her mother, she began sensing the warmth and vividness in God's presence that she had longed for.

Miriam's reenlivened relationship with God did not replace her formal religious practices. Always disciplined in her daily Bible study, she became even more consistent in setting aside a time each day to meditate on the Psalms and for personal prayer. She had previously played a vital role in organizing pastoral care within her congregation. She continued in this activity, with a shift of perspective. She found that she could focus her thoughts less on "Where is God?" and her preoccupations with illness. Instead, she could direct her thoughts toward "God has a greater plan" and "I am where I am supposed to be." Moreover, she was able for the first time to ask church members to pray for her. She had helped organize others' efforts to pray for those who were ill, troubled, or in need, but had never felt comfortable asking that she be the recipient of prayer.

Miriam's religious world provided the setting for her psychotherapy. Her psychotherapy addressed how her religious metaphors, narratives, beliefs, prayers, spiritual practices, rituals, and communal practices each mediated her roles, responsibilities, and relationships within her church (Griffith and Griffith 2002).

Allying Psychotherapy with Religious Healing

If religion and psychotherapy each own certain territories while sharing others, how can they join in ways that produce a synergy of healing efforts? Some religious clinicians conduct psychotherapy in a manner that merges professional and religious identities, describing themselves as "Christian therapists" or "Islamic therapists." More often, secular clinicians conduct psychotherapy that strives to be open to a patient's religious tradition but without publicly identifying themselves professionally with a particular religion.

Perhaps the most important assistance that a secular psychotherapist can provide to a religious patient is to conduct a careful inquiry that helps discern and strengthen personal spirituality and explores how the patient's religious life can more effectively realize this spirituality. Clarifying what constitutes a particular person's spirituality may involve asking direct, existential questions about his or her encounters with adversity. These questions need not have an explicit religious content (Griffith and Gaby 2005; Griffith 2010) (see also chapter 8). Some examples:

- What sustains you through hard times?
- What gives you hope when coping is most difficult?
- Who truly understands what you are experiencing?
- How do you find comfort in your suffering?
- How do you find some moments of joy despite being ill?
- For what are you most deeply grateful?
- How does your life matter?
- What is your best sense as to what your life is about and how your struggle fits in it?

Such conversations can explore a patient's struggle to answer these questions, either through the formal practice of religion or through epiphanies that emerge unexpectedly out of mundane moments of everyday life. They ask how one strives to sustain a personal sense of coherency, hope, purpose, communion, agency, gratitude, commitment, and other components of spirituality. As with Miriam, it then becomes evident where the patient's religious life succeeds or fails to enable this personal spirituality.

Using this formulation as a gauge, a psychotherapist can ask challenging questions about how a person's religious life does or does not serve these aims (Griffith 2010). For example:

- Does the patient's attachment style with his or her God promote security or insecurity?
- Do religious encounters with the sacred serve as a source of fear or creative inspiration?

- Are interactions within the religious group characterized by dialogue? That is, can a person—regardless of role or status—expect to be able to speak, to be heard and understood, and to have his or her perspective taken seriously by the group? How is the least powerful person treated?
- How are people in out-groups regarded? In practice, are they respected and valued as full human beings by members of the religious group?

Conclusion

A psychotherapist can inquire how well a patient's spirituality is sustained or confounded by the style of his or her attachment with God, peer affiliation within the religious group, relatedness with those in out-groups, and ethical practices grounded in expectations for social exchange. Refining these socio-biological dimensions of religious life to serve the aims of spirituality may invigorate the person's religious life. The aims of psychotherapy and personal spirituality can thus be brought into close alignment.

REFERENCES

Armstrong, K. 1993. *A History of God.* New York: Ballantine Books.
Barnes, M. H. B. 2000. *Stages of Thought: The Co-Evolution of Religious Thought and Science.* New York: Oxford University Press.
———. 2003. *In the Presence of Mystery: An Introduction to the Story of Human Religiousness.* Mystic, CT: Twenty-Third Publications.
Baumeister, R. F. 1991. *Meanings of Life.* New York: Guilford Press.
Bowlby, J. 1973. *Separation, Anxiety, and Anger.* Vol. 2 of *Attachment and Loss.* New York: Basic Books.
Buber, M. 1958. *I and Thou,* 2nd ed. New York: Macmillan.
Crippen, T., and Machalek, R. 1989. The evolutionary foundations of religious life. *International Review of Sociology* 3:61–84.
Daly, M., and Wilson, M. 2005. Parenting and kinship. In D. M. Buss (ed.), *The Handbook of Evolutionary Psychology* (pp. 443–46). New York: John Wiley.
Frank, J. D. 1961. *Persuasion and Healing: A Comparative Study of Psychotherapy.* Baltimore: Johns Hopkins University Press.
Frank, J. D., and Frank, J. B. 1991. *Persuasion and Healing: A Comparative Study of Psychotherapy,* 3rd ed. Baltimore: Johns Hopkins University Press.
Galanter, M. 1999. *Cults, Faith, Healing, and Coercion,* 2nd ed. New York: Oxford University Press.
Griffith, J. L. 2010. *Religion That Heals, Religion That Harms.* New York: Guilford Press.
Griffith, J. L., and Gaby, L. 2005. Brief psychotherapy at the bedside: countering demoralization from medical illness. *Psychosomatics* 46:109–16.

Griffith, J. L., and Griffith, M. E. 2002. *Encountering the Sacred in Psychotherapy: How to Talk with People about Their Spiritual Lives.* New York: Guilford Press.

Hood, R. W., Jr., Spilka, B., Hunsberger, B., and Gorsuch, R. 1996. *The Psychology of Religion: An Empirical Approach,* 2nd ed. New York: Guilford Press.

Kildahl, J. P. 1972. *The Psychology of Speaking in Tongues.* New York: Harper and Row.

Kirkpatrick, L. A. 2005. *Attachment, Evolution, and the Psychology of Religion.* New York: Guilford Press.

Lambert, M. J., and Bergin, A. E. 1994. The effectiveness of psychotherapy. In A. E. Bergin and S. L.Garfield (eds.), *Handbook of Psychotherapy and Behavior Change,* 4th ed. (pp. 143–89). New York: John Wiley.

Lerner, M. J. 1980. *Belief in a Just World.* New York: Plenum Press.

Miller, W. R. (ed.). 1999. *Integrating Spirituality into Treatment: Resources for Practitioners.* Washington, DC: American Psychological Association.

Mithen, S. 1996. *The Prehistory of the Mind: A Search for the Origins of Art, Religion, and Science.* London: Thames and Hudson.

Pargament, K. I. 1997. *The Psychology of Religion and Coping: Theory, Research, Practice.* New York: Guilford Press.

Siegel, D. J. 1999. *The Developing Mind.* New York: Guilford Press.

Sperry, L., and Shafranske, E. P. (eds.). 2005. *Spiritually Oriented Psychotherapy.* Washington, DC: American Psychological Association.

Turner, V. 1969. *The Ritual Process: Structure and Anti-Structure.* Ithaca, NY: Cornell University Press.

———. 1974. *Dramas, Fields, and Metaphors: Symbolic Action in Human Society.* Ithaca, NY: Cornell University Press.

———. 1982. *From Ritual to Theatre: The Human Seriousness of Play.* Baltimore: Johns Hopkins University Press.

Winnicott, D. W. 1975. Transitional objects and transitional phenomena. In *Through Paediatrics to Psycho-Analysis* (pp. 229–42). New York: Basic Books.

Contributors

Bernard D. Beitman, M.D., Professor and Chair, Department of Psychiatry, University of Missouri, Columbia, Missouri

David M. Clarke, M.D., Ph.D., Professor of Psychology, Psychiatry, and Psychological Medicine; Clinical Director, Primary Partnerships Southern Health, Monash University, Australia

Natoshia Raishevich Cunningham, Ph.D., Child Study Center, Department of Psychology, Virginia Polytechnic Institute and State University, Blacksburg, Virginia

John M. de Figueiredo, M.D., Sc.D., Associate Clinical Professor, Department of Psychiatry, University of Connecticut Medical Center, Hartford, Connecticut

Anjali DSouza, M.D., Assistant Clinical Professor, Department of Psychiatry and Behavioral Sciences, George Washington University, Washington, D.C.

Diane McNally Forsyth, R.N., Ph.D., Professor of Psychiatric Nursing, Winona State University, Winona, Minnesota

Arthur M. Freeman III, M.D., Professor Emeritus, Department of Psychiatry, University of Alabama School of Medicine, Birmingham, Alabama

James L. Griffith, M.D., Professor, Department of Psychiatry and Behavioral Sciences, George Washington University School of Medicine, Washington, D.C.

Peter S. Jensen, M.D., Professor, Department of Psychiatry and Psychology, Mayo Clinic College of Medicine

Paul R. McHugh, M.D., University Distinguished Service Professor, Department of Psychiatry and Behavioral Sciences, Johns Hopkins University School of Medicine, Baltimore, Maryland

Virginia Nash, D.N.P., R.N., C.N.S., Psychiatric Clinical Nurse Specialist, Pain Rehabilitation Center, Department of Psychiatry and Psychology, Mayo Clinic, Rochester, Minnesota

Thomas Ollendick, Ph.D., University Distinguished Professor and Director, Child Study Center, Department of Psychology, Virginia Polytechnic Institute and State University, Blacksburg, Virginia

J. Scott Rutan, Ph.D., Professor of Clinical Psychology, University of Pennsylvania School of Medicine, Philadelphia, Pennsylvania

Joseph J. Shay, Ph.D., CGP, FAGPA, Instructor, Department of Psychiatry, Harvard Medical School, Boston, Massachusetts

Glenn J. Treisman, M.D., Ph.D., Professor and Director of Education, Department of Psychiatry and Behavioral Sciences, Johns Hopkins University School of Medicine, Baltimore, Maryland

George I. Viamontes, M.D., Ph.D., Regional Medical Director, OptumHealth Behavioral Solutions, St. Louis, Missouri

Bruce E. Wampold, Ph.D., ADPP, Professor, Department of Psychiatry, University of Wisconsin, Madison, Wisconsin

Joel Weinberger, Ph.D., Professor, Department of Psychology, Derner Institute of Advanced Psychological Studies, Adelphi University, Garden City, New York

Lloyd A. Wells, M.D., Ph.D., Professor, Department of Psychiatry and Psychology; Vice-Chair of Education, Mayo Clinic College of Medicine, Rochester, Minnesota

Mark Williams, M.D., Assistant Professor, Department of Psychiatry and Psychology, Mayo Clinic College of Medicine, Rochester, Minnesota

Index

f indicates a figure; *t* indicates a table; *n* indicates a footnote; *v* indicates a vignette